Bordering on Chaos

Bordering on Chaos

Guerrillas, Stockbrokers,

Politicians, and Mexico's Road to

Prosperity

ANDRES OPPENHEIMER

LITTLE, BROWN AND COMPANY

Boston   New York   Toronto   London

First Edition

Library of Congress Cataloging-in-Publication Data

Oppenheimer, Andres
  Bordering on chaos : guerrillas, stockbrokers, politicians, and Mexico's road to prosperity / by Andres Oppenheimer.
    p.   cm.
  Includes bibliographical references and index.
  ISBN 0-316-65095-1
  1. Mexico—Politics and government — 1988–   2. Political corruption — Mexico — History — 20th century.   3. Business enterprises — Corrupt practices — Mexico — History — 20th century.   4. Mexico — Foreign economic relations — United States.   5. United States — Foreign economic relations — Mexico.   6. Business enterprises — United States — History — 20th century.   7. Guerrillas — Mexico — History — 20th century   I. Title.
F1236.068   1996
306.2¢0972 — dc20   95-45285

10 9 8 7 6 5 4

MV–NY

Published simultaneously in Canada by Little, Brown & Company (Canada) Limited

Printed in the United States of America

THIS BOOK IS FOR
Thomas Oppenheimer, his mother, Marina,
and his grandparents Evelyn, David,
and Alda.

Contents

Acknowledgments

Thanks to Doug Clifton and Saundra Keyes, the two top editors of the *Miami Herald*, who gave me the time to write this book; Tom Shroder, editor of the *Miami Herald*'s Sunday *Tropic* magazine, a resourceful editor who made excellent suggestions to liven up the manuscript; Mark Seibel, the *Miami Herald*'s International Edition editor, one of the smartest people I have met in the business; and computer whiz–librarian Liz Donovan. I am especially grateful to Mexican political scientist Jorge G. Castañeda, with whom I often disagree but whose intellect I greatly respect, for his insightful comments.

Three people without whom this book would not have been possible are Kris Dahl, my agent with ICM in New York; Little, Brown and Company vice president William D. Phillips; and Little, Brown and Company editor Roger Donald. Kris Dahl had the vision to back my idea of writing a book on Mexico in 1992, long before that country began making headlines. Phillips and Donald had the professional courage to believe in this project from the start, more than a year before Mexico exploded in the news.

There are dozens of journalists and academics in Mexico to whom I am deeply grateful for their time and advice. Among them are historian Héctor Aguilar Camin; *Reforma* managing editor Ramón Alberto Garza; *El Financiero* columnists Jorge Fernandez Menendez, Gustavo Lomelin, and Carlos Ramirez; *New York Times* Mexico correspondents Anthony De Palma and Tim Golden; *Newsweek* correspondent Tim

Padgett; *Le Monde* correspondent Bertrand de la Grange; *Frankfurter Rundschau* correspondent Rita Neubauer; *La Jornada* reporter José "Pepe" Ureña; *El Nacional* publisher Guillermo Ibarra; *El Universal* reporter Fidel Samaniego; Sonora-based author José Teran; historian Laura Delgado; NBC correspondent Hermes Muñoz; and Chiapas-born anthropologist Juan Castillo Cocom. My two research assistants, Guadalupe Lopez de Llergo Cornejo and Claudia Calvin Venero, are respected academics who were of precious help for their enterprise, sense of humor, and knowledge of Mexican society.

I also received great help from many government officials and politicians whose names I will not mention to save them from possible criticism for collaborating with this book. I would like to mention two, however, who despite not always agreeing with my impressions of Mexico were of enormous help: PRI activist Gerardo Cajiga, one of the youngest and most effective political operators I have seen anywhere, and Maria Elena Perez Jaén, who provided precious contacts. They are part of a new generation of Mexicans who place a greater value on efficiency than on rhetoric.

Finally, I would like to thank the dozens of Mexicans from all walks of life who took some time off their busy schedules to help me understand their country. Many will disagree with my conclusions. I only ask them to accept this book as an honest effort by a foreign reporter to make some sense of Mexico's tumultuous events of the mid-nineties and to help broaden what has traditionally been a very narrow debate on the nature of their country's politics.

Preface

No single country in the post–Cold War era affects the U.S. national
interest in more ways than Mexico. This may sound an overstatement
in light of the traditional U.S. foreign policy focus on the former Soviet
Union and Europe, but it is becoming increasingly evident in the late
nineties as Americans center their attention on day-to-day problems
that directly affect their lives. Whether it is illegal immigration, drugs,
the environment, the economy, or, increasingly, U.S. domestic politics,
Mexico is the country that influences life in America on the greatest
number of fronts.

The figures tell the story: A year after the signing of the North
American Free Trade Agreement (NAFTA), Mexico had by U.S. Commerce Department measures become one of America's three largest
trading partners, buying as many American goods as Germany, France,
Italy, China, and Russia together. At the same time, it was the port of
entry for 70 percent of the drugs coming into the United States and by
far the largest single source of illegal immigrants. Within the next two
decades, the estimated 18 million Mexican Americans living on U.S.

territory are projected to surpass black Americans as the largest U.S. minority and to become a formidable electoral bloc.

Until an explosion of violence thrust Mexico into the headlines in 1994, the country was far down the list of U.S. foreign policy priorities. The reason was simple: After more than six decades of continuous rule by the Institutional Revolutionary Party (PRI), it was considered one of the world's most stable nations — a place where nothing ever happened. But things changed dramatically on New Year's Day, 1994, when a Mayan-supported rebel army attacked several towns in the remote southern state of Chiapas and rattled Mexico's political system. Over the months that followed, key political figures — including the leading presidential candidate and a top official of the ruling party — were assassinated. Suddenly, Mexico was making big headlines everywhere. Was the world's oldest ruling party collapsing? Was the country headed for a second Mexican revolution?

I had begun my research for this book nearly two years before the January 1, 1994, Indian-supported Zapatista insurrection, prompted by Mexico's growing importance in the Americas. At the time, Mexico seemed the domain of academics and travel writers: There were few books written by journalists about Mexico's political and economic changes in the nineties. For nearly four years ending in late 1995 I traveled all over Mexico and interviewed more than six hundred people from all walks of life, including President Ernesto Zedillo Ponce de León, former president Carlos Salinas de Gortari, Zapatista rebel leader Subcommander Marcos, peasants, students, and housewives. The Zapatista rebellion and the political assassinations that followed caught me halfway through my research, allowing me to witness — and describe — an extraordinary period of Mexico's history.

This book is an attempt to tell the story of Mexico's dramatic events in the mid-nineties and to make some sense of them. I found it to be a monumental task, and not just because of the frantic pace at which things happened. Despite nearly two decades as a foreign correspondent in several Latin American nations, I found Mexico to be by far the most difficult country to cover: As Mexicans are the first to acknowledge, their country is a nation of masks, diversionary plots, and smoke screens. Things are seldom what they are supposed to be. Disinformation is a well-honed tradition dating back to the days of the colony. Today's headlines are tomorrow's objects of mockery, and vice versa. Documents or published accounts were good mostly as road maps: Often, people wrote one thing and privately conceded to me another.

Much of my work for this book involved penetrating the jungle of Mexican headlines, going back to the men and women behind them once public attention had shifted to the next crisis and trying to tell fiction from reality. Often, my research led me to conclusions that defied conventional wisdom or the way things were portrayed by international media, and that are bound not to be "politically correct" within U.S. and Mexican academic and political circles. I hope that even if criticized they will help widen the scope of discussion on Mexico: For too long, the debate has been based on sacrosanct assumptions — Mexico's nationalism and anti-Americanism, for instance — that deserve a closer look.

For the sake of clarity, I have included all sources and attributions in a special section at the end of the book. All the people quoted by name agreed to it. Only exceptionally, in cases involving senior officials who asked not to be identified, have I identified sources by their government jobs as "a top Mexican official" or "a senior U.S. diplomat."

Finally, a word on Mexico. Like many travelers, I couldn't help falling in love with the country. Mexico is a country of secrets — the ultimate challenge for a journalist. Its people are monuments to complexity, capable of simultaneous displays of sincere affection and deep-seated distrust. In their complexity lies their magic and their charm. I am deeply grateful to many of them who put aside apprehensions about nosy foreign correspondents and opened their hearts to me, some of them out of an honest desire to help make their country a more open society.

And a word of caution: Most of the events described in this book are open wounds that will take some time to heal. New versions of these events will surely come out in the near future. A more definitive story will have to be written taking current and future testimonies into account. If anything, this book can only begin to tell the story of Mexico's turbulent mid-nineties, benefiting from fresh memories and the cross-examination of participants at the scene of the events.

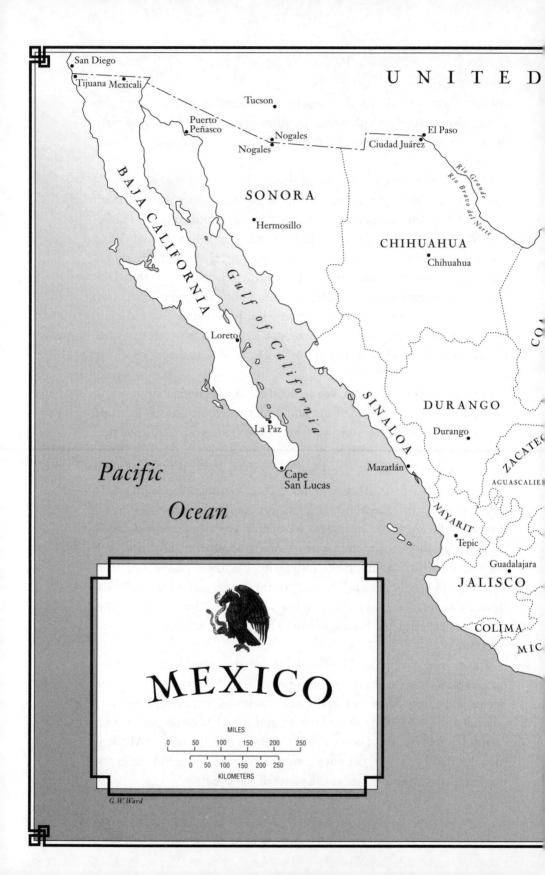

Austin

Houston

New Orleans

San Antonio

Laredo
Nuevo
Laredo

Brownsville

Monterrey

NUEVO LEÓN

Matamoros

TAMAULIPAS

N

LUIS POTOSÍ

Gulf of Mexico

Tampico

Cancún

JUATO

YUCATÁN

Cozumel I.

QUERÉTARO

VERACRUZ

HIDALGO

Campeche

QUINTANA
ROO

MEXICO

TLAXCALA

Veracruz

Bay
of
Campeche

CAMPECHE

Mexico City

Valley of Chalco

MORELOS

PUEBLA

TABASCO

BELIZE

UERRERO

Altamirano
Ocosingo

Lacandon jungle

Acapulco

OAXACA

Tuxtla
Gutiérrez

San Cristóbal
de las Casas

Guadalupe
Tepeyac

CHIAPAS

GUATEMALA

Gulf of
Tehuantepec

HONDURAS

EL SALVADOR

Bordering on Chaos

CHAPTER I

The Party Is Over

There was a jubilant atmosphere at the offices of Salomon Brothers on the thirty-sixth floor of New York's World Trade Center on Tuesday morning, December 20, 1994, as dark-suited traders of the securities firm got to work. The holiday spirit had already taken over the city: Salvation Army volunteers in red-and-white Santa Claus outfits were ringing their bells rhythmically on the sidewalks, the sounds of Christmas carols seemed to be coming from everywhere, and people in elevators and office corridors were greeting one another with once-a-year warmth. At their desks, the brokers were expecting the sweetest present — a fat Christmas bonus.

That day, members of Salomon Brothers' securities division were to attend an early morning briefing by John Purcell, the tall, youthful-looking fifty-four-year-old managing director of the firm's emerging markets research division. Topic: the international outlook for the coming year. The small audience followed Purcell's moderately upbeat speech with great attention: As in most Wall Street brokerage firms, Salomon Brothers' emerging markets department was an elite division, and its managers were company stars. Since American investors had rediscovered Mexico in the early nineties and made profits of up to 50 percent a year in that country's stock market, securities firms had made huge profits from a boom in U.S. investments in the fledgling economies of Latin America, Eastern Europe, and Southeast Asia.

Purcell had been a pioneer in the emerging markets success story: A

Ph.D. in political science from the University of California in Los Angeles who had given up teaching at age forty to try the excitement of Wall Street, he had been among the first to discover the potential of Mexico's stock market. In the late eighties — at a time when few Americans would consider investing a penny south of the Rio Grande — Purcell had published a report entitled "Mexico: A world class economy in the 1990's." Having lived in Mexico for a year in the staunchly nationalistic seventies, and fascinated by the bold free-market reforms that President Carlos Salinas de Gortari had begun to implement after his 1988 inauguration, Purcell had seen a golden future for Mexico. The subsequent phenomenal rise of Mexico's stock market had proved him right. By the early nineties, Salomon Brothers had placed more than $15 billion in Mexico, making juicy profits for its clients. In the process, Purcell's research department had grown from a one-person office — him — to a staff of twenty-five.

But at about 9:30 A.M. that morning, the world collapsed on Wall Street. Purcell had just concluded his speech and returned to his desk when there was a sudden commotion outside his office: A news bulletin flashing across the computer screens said that the Mexican government had just announced a devaluation of the currency. Everybody was stunned. Few on Wall Street had expected such a bombshell — at least not that soon. Just a few weeks earlier, in a November 22 report on Mexico, Salomon Brothers had told its clients that "although we believe that an eventual more rapid depreciation of the peso may become necessary, the probability of a one-off devaluation is virtually nil." Not only had Purcell received assurances from top Mexican officials during a recent visit to Mexico City that there would be no devaluation, but his economic projections — based on Mexican government figures monitored by international financial institutions — showed that the country's foreign reserves were high enough to withstand pressures for a devaluation in the near future. All of a sudden, the "virtually nil" possibility had become a dreadful reality.

Within hours, U.S. investors who had bought peso-denominated Mexican stocks had lost $10 billion, a figure that would climb to more than $32 billion in coming weeks. Americans who had put their money into mutual funds run by firms such as Fidelity Investments; Alliance Capital; Scudder, Stevens & Clark; Goldman Sachs; and Salomon

Brothers were now facing huge losses. This time, unlike in the 1982 Latin American debt crisis that had also been ignited by Mexico, the big losers were not a few giant U.S. banks, but hundreds of thousands of small American investors — retirees, nurses, and office employees throughout the country — whose pension and retirement plans had placed part of their savings in the Mexican stock market. In Mexico, the impact was even worse: an estimated $70 billion loss in the stock-market value of Mexican corporations, an avalanche of bankruptcies, and nearly a million layoffs over the next twelve months.

The telephones at Salomon Brothers began to ring off the hook. Purcell and his aides tried to reach their contacts in Mexico's Central Bank and the finance ministry, people they had just had lunch with in Mexico City earlier that month, but nobody would come to the phone. A low-level official they finally reached was of no help — he didn't know what to say. Purcell and his aides called their colleagues at other New York securities firms, some of which were suffering much bigger losses in Mexico than Salomon Brothers. Everybody on Wall Street was frantically calling everybody else, but nobody seemed to be getting any answers on what Mexico had done or how it would affect U.S. investors. The herd was extremely anxious. By noon, normally blasé Wall Street brokers had lost their cool. The pack was on the move. Purcell began telling the irate Salomon Brothers clients who were calling him from across the nation, "I don't like what's going on!" To most, that could only mean one thing: "Sell!!!!"

Weeks later, amid escalating fears that the massive pullout of U.S. investors from Mexico would extend to markets as far away as Italy and Singapore, President Clinton rushed to put together a $50 billion international bailout package for Mexico, including $20 billion in U.S. loan guarantees. In nominal dollars, it was the world's largest rescue program ever, dwarfing the Marshall plan or any financial help Washington, D.C., had ever granted Europe, Israel, or post-Communist Russia. It was a matter of national security, U.S. officials explained: A Mexican collapse would trigger a full-fledged Latin American financial crisis, which would possibly extend to Eastern Europe and Southeast Asia. And America would be hit like no other country: Mexico was already vying with Japan to become the United States' second largest trading partner, after Canada, and hundreds of thousands of U.S. jobs would be lost if Mexico were forced to stop buying U.S. goods. Furthermore, U.S. Treasury officials said, a Mexican financial crunch was likely to drive up by 30 percent the number of illegal immigrants crossing the border to California and Texas — an additional 430,000 illegal immigrants a year.

Of course, there were also domestic political considerations. Clinton, already with an eye on the 1996 elections, could ill afford to allow Mexico to go under. It was his pet project. He had gambled part of his political future on Mexico, helping push the North American Free Trade Agreement (NAFTA) through Congress over the objections of angry labor unions and many domestic producers. Only two weeks before the latest Mexican devaluation, at the thirty-four-nation Summit of the Americas in Miami, Clinton had praised Mexico as a model for economic development and had proposed expanding the U.S.-Canada-Mexico trade agreement into a hemisphere-wide free-market area. Now, his grandiose plans seemed shattered, and the president was facing political sniping from all sides for bailing out Mexico at a time of dramatic budget cuts at home.

But while Mexico's financial collapse took Wall Street and the rest of the world by surprise that Tuesday morning, it did not happen overnight: It was preceded by a series of spectacular events over the previous eleven months, most of them unprecedented in Mexico's history since the turbulent days of the 1910–1917 Mexican Revolution. The first of a string of devastating blows to Mexico's much-cherished economic and political stability had taken place nearly a year earlier, on an eventful night that seemed borrowed from the opening page of a Hollywood script, but was only too real.

▼

President Salinas de Gortari and his wife, Cecilia Occelli, couldn't have been in a better mood on December 31, 1993, as they dressed up for the New Year's Eve party they were hosting at the presidential residence of Los Pinos. It was to be their last New Year celebrated at the presidential palace — Salinas was about to complete his six-year term in December 1994 — and they had decided to spend it with their families and best friends. Salinas, a short, prematurely bald man with ears that seemed disproportionately large for his head, looked tanned and rested after returning earlier that day from his first real Christmas vacation in years. He had spent a week playing tennis and jogging with his children in the southern resort of Huatulco, after returning from an official visit to Asia during which he had been enthusiastically received by the Japanese government and business community.

The New Year's Eve party was to be Cecilia's occasion to play hostess — dispelling rumors that Mexico's first couple was living in virtual separation since word had gone out that the president was dating a soap opera star with whom he was alleged to have conceived a child — and to invite all the relatives and friends who for one reason or other had been left out of the president's official schedule during the year. It was not only to be a party to get together and have a good time, but also to celebrate Salinas's phenomenal success.

As he entered his last year in office at only forty-five, Salinas was on top of the world. Few Mexican presidents had approached the end of their terms enjoying such popularity. Salinas had just won approval of NAFTA, the groundbreaking commercial treaty with the United States and Canada that was to go into effect at midnight — only a few hours away. The deal, which would gradually eliminate customs duties between the three countries over a fifteen-year period, was to propel Mexico into the big leagues of international trade. From now on, Mexico and its two business partners would become the world's single largest trading bloc. Mexico, long stereotyped as a backward country of peasants napping under cactus trees, was about to make a dramatic leap into the First World.

▼

"Carlos Salinas de Gortari is reversing Mexico's history," *Time* magazine had proclaimed in naming the Mexican president 1993 International Newsmaker of the Year for Latin America. "Salinas has almost single-handedly energized a nation that used to be jealous and resentful of the dynamism exhibited north of the border."

A Harvard-trained public administrator who according to his aides was so impressed by Asia's economic success that he had sent his children to a Japanese school in Mexico City, Salinas had dazzled Wall Street and Washington, D.C. The Harvard label was tagged to him so often in U.S. press reports that amused Mexicans were joking that

"Harvard-trained" had become their president's first name. Salinas was seen in the United States as the first of a new breed of Mexican leaders, the kind of young, pragmatic, U.S.-educated politicians who jogged every morning, wore Cassio plastic watches, Timberland heavy-duty shoes, and signed their government decrees with generic ballpoint pens, in sharp contrast with the pompous, visibly corrupt leaders of the past. The Mexican press had dubbed him *la hormiga atómica* — the atomic ant — because he seemed to be everywhere, moving like an insect, showing up at half a dozen meetings a day and generating more headlines than newspapers could accommodate.

A man of the nineties, Salinas seemed determined to challenge some of Mexico's age-old ideological hang-ups. He was somebody U.S. officials and foreign investors could talk to — in their own language. Shrugging off a century of troubled U.S.-Mexican relations — and recent economic fiascoes such as Mexico's 1982 nationalization of the banking industry — Wall Street investment firms had finally found a Mexican leader they could trust.

▼

The figures indeed were looking great. Foreign investment in Mexico's stock market had risen by a whopping 98 percent in 1993. Wall Street and London brokerage houses were pressing their clients to buy as many Mexican stocks as they could and take advantage of the economic miracle led by Mexico's young president. The country could boast record international reserves of $24.5 billion, up 25 percent from the previous year. Inflation had dropped to 8 percent from a record 160 percent a year when Salinas had taken office. New York brokerage houses were forecasting economic growth rates of more than 3 percent a year for the foreseeable future. *Forbes* magazine's ranking of the world's wealthiest people had just included thirteen Mexicans — placing Mexico right after the United States, Germany, and Japan as the country with the most billionaires. "You can't any longer think of Mexico as the Third World," the magazine had declared.

President Clinton, after wavering during his presidential campaign on whether to support NAFTA, had wholeheartedly embraced the plan for a new trade partnership with Mexico. Following the steps of President Bush, he had used the image of Mexico's U.S.-educated president to push the free-trade agreement through Congress — suggesting that the United States faced a now-or-never chance to bring Mexico into its fold. Clinton proclaimed his "enormous admiration for President Salinas and for what he is doing," and called the Mexican president "one of the world's leading economic reformers." Salinas was ecstatic. It was about as much praise as any foreign leader could get from a U.S. president.

This new image wasn't just good public relations, for which the Salinas government was doling out more than $11 million a year just in the United States. The president had in fact changed Mexico's economic course over the past five years. A man who had a foxy grin to match his shrewd personality, Salinas had built on free-market measures begun by his predecessor to launch a full-fledged economic opening, reversing several decades of nationalistic and statist policies. He had privatized 252 state companies, including Mexico's biggest commercial banks, the telephone monopoly, and hundreds of money-losing firms, netting about $23 billion in government reserves while reducing massive government subsidies to these enterprises. He had also accelerated Mexico's transition from a country that had relied on state-run oil exports for 78 percent of its foreign income in the early eighties to a nation that now made 81 percent of its income from private-sector manufactured goods exports, even if critics pointed out that such change resulted largely from lower international oil prices. At the same time, he had opened the doors to foreign investments in previously off-limits areas of the Mexican economy, which had rapidly changed the face — or at least the facade — of the country.

Almost overnight, the main streets of virtually all Mexican cities had been dotted with the neon signs of brand-new McDonald's, Domino's Pizza, and Pizza Hut outlets. Even Taco Bell had opened a franchise to do the unimaginable — push U.S.-made tacos down Mexicans' staunchly nationalistic throats. Mexico City restaurants once filled with laid-back government bureaucrats were now teeming with energetic young businessmen glued to their U.S.-made cellular phones while making deals over lunch. U.S.-style department stores had moved en masse to Mexico, offering every American consumer product imaginable.

The fact that massive U.S. imports were causing Mexico to run increasingly higher trade deficits seemed no cause for alarm: Government figures showed that enough foreign investment was flowing into the country to help it pay for its imports. Besides, hadn't Japan run trade deficits for fifty years before becoming one of the world's leading exporters? the confidence-brimming president asked skeptics. And if there were any doubts left, Salinas could even boast about a feat that would have been ridiculed only a few years earlier: The same country that had played the role of a Third World leader only a few years earlier was about to be accepted as a full member of the Organization for Economic Cooperation and Development (OECD), a select group of the world's richest nations. Salinas was almost universally hailed as the man who had carried out a second Mexican revolution, the biggest transformation of his country since the 1910–1917 Mexican Revolution.

▼

The night of the party, Salinas had even more reason to be happy. Only five weeks earlier, he had managed to impose his long-term protégé Luis Donaldo Colosio as the presidential candidate of the Institutional Revolutionary Party, the state party commonly known by its Spanish initials, PRI, that had ruled Mexico for sixty-four years.

Colosio, another U.S.-educated public administrator, wore a subdued Afro hairstyle, loved motorcycles, and was only two years younger than Salinas. He had made his entire political career under Salinas's wing. Salinas had first recruited him as a young economist, had appointed him as his presidential campaign manager, and had later placed him at the helm of the ruling party and of the social development ministry — two key jobs for a young politician with presidential aspirations. Although the two men jogged together, shared a passion for attractive women, and talked to one another in private in the Spanish-language familiar *tu*, Colosio would always walk one step behind Salinas when the two appeared in public and would refer to him as *"el señor presidente"* even when Salinas was not around. Colosio was the president's political son.

Considering the circumstances, Colosio's appointment had gone down smoothly. There had been growing criticism within the PRI and among democratic-minded opinion leaders of Mexico's political tradition whereby outgoing presidents single-handedly picked their successors. Critics demanded that Mexico start picking its presidential candidates through primary elections. In the early nineties, when the Soviet bloc had collapsed and the PRI remained as the world's oldest ruling political party, the critics argued that the least the PRI could do was to start a democratic process within its ranks. Mexico's political system of a strong party that placed its president in power and replaced him every six years had been variously described by critics as a "rotating dictatorship" and a "six-year-long inheritable monarchy." But, owing to Salinas's amazing popularity and Colosio's easygoing, unassuming character, Salinas's decision to continue the tradition of picking the PRI candidate by himself had been largely accepted by the party bosses. The PRI had once again rallied behind its new hand-picked nominee. Colosio seemed a sure winner of the August 21, 1994, elections. And his six-year term was almost sure to guarantee the continuity of Salinas's economic reforms into the year 2000.

As a smiling Salinas and his wife, Cecilia, prepared to make their appearance at the Lopez Mateos ballroom of the Los Pinos presidential residence at ten P.M., it was hard to imagine that anything could derail Mexico from its new path of economic modernization. The guests, who had been sipping cocktails in another room and were beginning to move toward the ballroom, were chatting cheerfully as they awaited the presidential couple. There was a buoyant mood in the air.

The talk over tequilas and margaritas before dinner had stayed away from politics. There were plenty of other things to talk about, all of them auspicious. Mexico's national soccer team had just qualified for the 1994 World Cup in the United States. The team's victories over the American and Canadian teams in prechampionship training games had triggered massive celebrations in Mexico City. Almost simultaneously, Mexico's world boxing champion Julio César Chavez, who publicly stated his admiration for Salinas whenever he could, had just won his eighty-ninth consecutive fight. Marathon runner Andrés Espinosa, a Mexican-born steelworker, had won the twenty-third New York City marathon. The movie *Like Water for Chocolate*, written by Mexican novelist Laura Esquivel, had beat all box-office records for a Spanish-language film in the United States.

It seemed Mexico was taking off on all fronts. Polls showed that the

Mexican people were more optimistic about the future than they had been in years. For Salinas and his guests that night at the Los Pinos palace, things seemed almost too good to be true.

▼

They were, but the president would not find out until later that night. When Salinas and his wife made their triumphal entry into their New Year's Eve party at ten P.M., he was smiling from ear to ear. The first lady, a somewhat introverted woman, was unusually elegant in a two-piece beige dress with a cotton top covered with spangles, low-cut enough to display a necklace with two big pearls in its middle.

A twelve-musician marimba band playing a huge synthesizer raised the volume of the music to announce the arrival of the presidential couple, to the applause of everybody. Salinas and his wife nodded to the crowd, walked across the dance floor, and took their seats at the presidential table standing on a small podium against the wall across the room. From there, they oversaw about twenty round tables laid out around the dancing area, filled with nearly two hundred guests.

The president was sitting with his recently widowed father, Raúl Salinas Lozano, a former minister of Industry and Commerce, and his three siblings with their spouses. There was his elder brother, Raúl Jr., a former leftist who with other Mexico City student activists had unsuccessfully attempted to ignite a social uprising in Chiapas in the early seventies. Raúl had since fully converted to capitalism, becoming an increasingly prosperous businessman-politician in various government administrative jobs. He sported a square-shaped mustache that accentuated his physical resemblance to his younger brother and served as a constant reminder of his status as the Mexican president's all-purpose assistant. From his successive jobs as manager of government food distribution programs he had been appointed to by the president, Raúl was known to have been making the most sensitive business and political deals for the Mexican ruler, while somehow finding the time to write short-story books with titles such as *Muerte Calculada* ("Calculated Death"). Then there was Enrique, an introverted business consultant who shunned the limelight; Sergio, a bohemian sociologist who moved in academic circles; and Adriana Margarita, whose bitter divorce from Salinas's former classmate and close adviser José Francisco

Ruiz Massieu had long been the focus of mutual recriminations within the family.

It was one of the most joyful parties ever hosted at Los Pinos — not the least because there had seldom been such a crowd of cheerful teenagers at a presidential palace dinner, several guests would recall later. Salinas's four siblings and the first lady's nine brothers and sisters had all come with their children. The president's teenage children — Carlos Emiliano, named after revolutionary leader Emiliano Zapata, Juan Cristóbal, and Cecilia — had also invited several friends each. It didn't take long after they had swallowed the main course — a choice of salmon or steak — for the crowd of cousins to take over the dance floor and form a conga-style lambada line that wriggled ecstatically through the tables.

"It was a family-and-friends sort of thing, where we grown-ups were a minority," recalls Nuevo León state governor Sócrates Rizzo, one of the handful of politicians who had been invited to the party as friends of the family. "There was a lot of enthusiasm, a feeling that things were going well. We all expected that with the start of the new year and the free-trade agreement there would be a massive increase of foreign investments."

Even the most serious-looking guests — Rizzo and fellow governors Manlio Fabio Beltrones of the northern state of Sonora, Otto Granados of the central state of Aguascalientes, and Rubén Figueroa of the southern state of Guerrero, who were sitting with their wives in the back of the room — soon joined in the dancing. The presidential couple danced to five songs in a row, laughing and joking easily with the other couples between songs.

At two minutes to midnight, a smiling Salinas stood up from his chair and looked at his digital watch, waiting to kick off the new year. The whole room exploded in laughter when a waiter behind him, who had been given the go-ahead by the president to uncork an extralarge bottle of champagne, found himself unable to do the job. The man was fighting with the cork, growing increasingly nervous as the seconds went by and midnight came closer. When he finally got the cork to fly in the air, everybody applauded, and the buoyant crowd began to count backward. *"Diez, nueve, ocho . . . ,"* they chanted, champagne glasses in hand. At the count of zero, everybody lifted their cups and — amid shouts of *"Viva México!"* — toasted right and left wishing everybody a good year, kissing one another on the cheeks and embracing their children.

It was nearly two A.M., and Salinas was dancing a Mexican *corrido* with his daughter, when a somber-looking presidential aide entered the room. The man walked straight to the dance floor, whispered something in Salinas's ear, and handed him a typewritten card. Still smiling, the president stood up and left the room. He had to take a phone call, he told his wife. General Antonio Riviello, the Defense minister, had an urgent message. He would come right back.

Salinas came back five minutes later. His face had changed, and so had Mexico. A near breathless Defense minister had gotten the president out of his New Year's party to tell him there had just been a guerrilla uprising in the remote southern state of Chiapas. More than two thousand Mayan Indians, carrying everything from machetes to AK-47 rifles, had taken the city of San Cristóbal de las Casas shortly after midnight and were reported to have also seized the nearby cities of Ocosingo, Altamirano, and Las Margaritas. They were calling themselves an Indian army — the Zapatista National Liberation Army — and were vowing to redress five hundred years of white exploitation of the Mayas.*

Whoever the Zapatistas were, they were threatening to march straight to Mexico City to topple the government. As absurd as that sounded, Salinas knew this was serious trouble. There had been dozens of deaths, perhaps hundreds. The reports were still sketchy because top military officers in Chiapas were out celebrating the New Year. The army commander in Chiapas had gone with his family to visit the ruins of Palenque and had not yet been located. The Interior minister, a former governor of Chiapas, was vacationing somewhere near the rebel-held area and had not been reached. But there had been dozens of calls from lower-level officials and private citizens in the

---

* In an interview with the author during a June 15, 1994, visit to Cartagena, Colombia, Salinas said he received the first news about the Chiapas uprising at 3:30 A.M., when he was already at his living quarters and was about to go to sleep. But his account contradicts that of several guests at the party who witnessed the president's brief exit and subsequent change of mood, as well as the testimony of a presidential aide who confirmed the guests' version of the story.

area. A shaken Salinas asked for an update later that night and went back to the party.

It all seemed like a bad joke. Mexico had not had a massive peasant revolt since the beginning of the century and had been virtually free of guerrilla violence over the past two decades. All potential rebel groups — including those in Chiapas — were thoroughly infiltrated by government security agents or had been bought out. It sounded weird, absurd, almost impossible.

When Salinas reentered the room, the crowd on the dance floor had doubled, and the euphoria had grown accordingly. The president tried his best to dance and posed for some guests who had brought their video cameras. But minutes later, at about 2:10 A.M., the presidential aide walked into the room and interrupted the president once again — it was Interior minister Patrocinio Gonzalez Blanco Garrido on the phone. Salinas excused himself and left the room. He would not come back.

"The laughter in the room soon began to die down," recalls another state governor who attended the party. "Half an hour later, there was a feeling of awkwardness in the air as we prepared to leave. We were waiting for the president to say good-bye, but he was nowhere to be seen." At about 2:30 A.M., some people began to leave. Soon the band stopped playing. The last guests left in silence.

A few days later, a Mexico City daily carried a cartoon showing Salinas in his tuxedo, sporting a big smile, raising his cup of champagne to celebrate the New Year — as a bullet coming from a window was about to break his glass in pieces. Other cartoonists evoked images of the 1959 Cuban revolution, when Cuban dictator Fulgencio Batista had learned of Fidel Castro's guerrillas' advance on the city while celebrating the New Year at a lavish party in the presidential palace and had left the country immediately. Like Batista's relatives, Salinas's wife, Cecilia, and their children had taken off early January 1 for the United States. Presidential aides said they had left on a long-planned skiing trip, but in light of the unprecedented events of the day, many Mexicans found that hard to believe. The Zapatista rebellion had shattered Mexico's illusions of peace and stability. The party was over.

CHAPTER 2

The Scepter of the Seven Forces

Deep in the Lacandon jungle, near the border with Guatemala, more than a thousand Indian rebels clad in military uniforms were standing firm, their right hands raised in a military salute, their eyes fixed on the distance. At a sign from one of their commanders, they began to sing the Zapatista anthem, "The Horizon." *"Ya se mira el horizonte, comba-tiente Zapatista!"* ("One can see the horizon, Zapatista combatant!"), the rebel troops intoned with devotion. Then, about a dozen Mayan leaders clad in their respective costumes — the Tzeltales in their white shirts and black ponchos, the Tzotziles with their distinctive red ponchos, the Choles with their black slacks, and the Tojolabales in their all-white clothing — stepped forward and handed over the staff of command, a scepter made out of an ocote tree branch, to a white man standing in front of them.

It was Subcommander "Marcos," a pipe-smoking leftist revolutionary who had come to Chiapas ten years earlier, and who had managed to do what no other Latin American leftist revolutionary had achieved in decades: blend into the native population. He had learned to communicate with the various Mayan tribes in their respective languages and had united a sizable part of half a dozen Mayan tribes that had been at war with each other for centuries with his plan to fight jointly for land, liberty, and justice.

The guerrilla leader, a man in his late thirties with a bushy beard, a prominent nose, and delicate hands, was an imposing figure next to the

Mayans: He was about a head taller than most of the Indians and also stood out because of his black attire. He wore a black poncho, black slacks, munition-filled bandoliers, and a revolver and an Ingram submachine gun tucked in his belt, a Rambo-style outfit that stood out immediately amid the assortment of red and white clothes worn by the Mayan leaders standing in front of him. He humbly lowered his head and took the ocote branch with both hands, stressing the significance he attached to the moment. The Mayan leaders were formally commissioning him to lead them in a revolution against the Mexican government.

With the scepter in his hand, Marcos sat down on a bench and received, one by one, seven war symbols from as many tribes: a Mexican flag, a red-and-black Zapatista flag, a rifle, a bullet, a container with human blood, a piece of corn, and a handful of clay. The first four were emblems of combat, the other three reminders of life. One of the Indian chiefs closed the ceremony with a prayer in Tzeltal: "Seven words, seven forces, seven roads. Life, truth, men, peace, democracy, freedom, and justice. Seven forces that empower the staff of command. Take the scepter of the seven forces and hold it with honor."

The solemn Indian ceremony, carried out about four weeks before the Zapatista uprising, marked the beginning of the rebels' preparations for their final offensive. It was partly Indian tradition, partly Mexicans' age-old fondness for ritual, and partly Marcos's own penchant for theatrics. But the presentation of the staff of command to Marcos had been a key moment: In Mexico, a long history of deceptions had taught people not to trust words and to seal their commitments through symbols and rituals. Marcos had borrowed from ancient Mayan rites to help give the new Zapatista army a fervent sense of mission.

▼

The Zapatistas' New Year attack on San Cristóbal de las Casas, a picturesque colonial city of 74,000 that was a favorite attraction for U.S. and European tourists, began with a shrewd diversionary tactic four days earlier: Small groups of Zapatista Mayans began hijacking trucks on December 27 in the city of Ocosingo, about sixty-two miles east of San Cristóbal. They had picked the time and place so as to fool authorities into believing that something was about to happen in that city.

Sure enough, Chiapas military region commander General Miguel Angel Godinez, a tall, imposing man in his early sixties, rushed to Ocosingo on December 28. After spending the day in Ocosingo checking on the reports of unusual criminal activity in the area, the general and his aides concluded that there was nothing extraordinary going on. They thought Mayan peasant groups were probably preparing for one of the many land seizures that dispossessed Indians in Chiapas launched periodically to claim acreage they had been granted, but never given, under Mexico's agrarian reform laws.

For many years, leftist Mayan peasant groups had been seizing property in Chiapas or reclaiming lands from which they had been unfairly evicted by government officials in the payroll of wealthy Chiapas ranchers. It was not unusual for the Mayans to carry light arms during their land invasions — they could be purchased with relative ease from corrupt army troops or drug traffickers. Eventually, after fierce legal battles and nasty protests, Mexican presidents would often grant Mayans land titles, usually at election time. It had happened hundreds of times — so often that Godinez and his aides could only conclude after their visit to Ocosingo that the peasants were hijacking vehicles to use in a land seizure, something that would surely happen after the New Year. The whole state was already in a year-end mood. Nobody was likely to interrupt the fiestas with violence.

As the army sent reinforcements to guard Ocosingo and its nearby lands, the Zapatista rebels — following a plan they had been rehearsing for months — crossed the hills toward San Cristóbal. Hundreds went by regular bus, hiding their military uniforms in small bundles Mayan women carried on their backs, mixing with the thousands of Indians who were traveling to visit relatives for the year-end holidays. Others carried guns in old, battered suitcases.

By the afternoon of December 31, as army general Godinez was presiding over a year-end toast with his top officers at the Rancho Nuevo military barracks on the outskirts of San Cristóbal, the Mayan rebels had silently surrounded the city and were waiting for nightfall. At nine P.M., as members of the mostly white — and wealthy — San Cristóbal elite were beginning to celebrate the New Year, the rebels began to hijack buses and trucks with which they would soon make their triumphant entry into the city. Most of the rebel troops were boys and girls in their teens, wearing olive green slacks and brown shirts with red bandannas around their necks. Only a handful of rebel officers had their faces covered with black ski masks or bandannas and wore one or two red stars over their shirt pockets.

Near midnight, when San Cristóbal streets were nearly deserted, the first buses packed with rebel Indians began to move into the city. Hundreds of other Zapatista troops sneaked their way into town through the underground drainage system, whose tunnels — mostly dry at that time of the year — led to various city suburbs. Their officers were carrying U.S.-made AR-15 rifles and World War II–vintage shotguns. Some of their troops were only armed with machetes or toy guns made out of carved wood. The Zapatista rebellion had begun.

▼

At about four A.M., a man in a black ski mask began to drive a blue Volkswagen van around the square giving out rifles. It was rebel leader Subcommander Marcos, in his black uniform, carrying a light Ingram submachine gun and a walkie-talkie tucked in his belt, escorted by two women. The weapons in the van had just been seized from the local police headquarters by one of the Zapatista elite teams under his command. Marcos was clearly a high-ranking rebel officer, but there were no visible clues at the time that he was the *"jefe máximo"* of the Zapatistas.

A rebel leader emerged from the crowd in front of San Cristóbal's municipal palace and gave the Zapatistas' first press conference, for two representatives of the San Cristóbal daily *El Tiempo* who were already at the scene, cameras in hand. It was an Indian in his fifties, with his face uncovered, a straw hat covered by a nylon plastic sheet on his head, and a red bandanna around his neck. He identified himself as Comandante "Felipe," a member of the Clandestine Indian Revolutionary Committee, a group of Indian chiefs that he described as the top authority within the Zapatista movement. Surrounded by fellow Indian chiefs, Comandante Felipe took a crumpled hand-written piece of paper from his black jacket's pocket and began to read with the obvious difficulty of a semiliterate peasant. Marcos, hiding behind his black ski mask, was watching from a few yards away.

"We have come to San Cristóbal de las Casas to do a revolution against capitalism," Comandante Felipe said in an outburst of ideological fervor that the rebels would downplay in front of the international media in coming days. "We have fought peacefully for years trying to get a solution, but the government has never cared to solve our big problems about land rights and other problems."

His statement stressed that the Chiapas peasants were the utmost symbol of Mexico's uneven distribution of wealth. Chiapas was one of Mexico's richest states in natural resources, yet its population was ranked along with that of Oaxaca and Guerrero among the country's poorest. Chiapas supplied nearly 60 percent of Mexico's hydroelectric power, 47 percent of its natural gas, and 21 percent of the country's oil, and was one of Mexico's top producers of lumber, coffee, and beef. Yet about a third of all households in the state did not have electricity, and half of its population did not have access to drinking water. In some cities seized by the Zapatistas, such as Ocosingo, 70 percent of the homes did not have electricity.

Now taking a printed pamphlet from his pocket, Felipe proceeded to read the rebels' formal "declaration of war on the federal army of Mexico, basic pillar of the dictatorship we suffer under, led by the party in power and headed by the executive power that today is in the hands of its maximum and illegitimate leader, Carlos Salinas de Gortari."

He said the rebels had just taken the cities of Ocosingo, Altamirano, and Las Margaritas, and that "our objective is to march to the capital of the country," freeing every city along the way and calling democratic elections to pick new authorities in each of them. A few intrigued San Cristóbal residents craning their necks over the reporters to catch the gist of the rebels' demands could not believe their ears. They looked at one another from the corners of their eyes with amazement. Were these Indians serious about trying to overthrow the government?

At seven A.M., when the last column of rebels had arrived at the central square, Comandante Felipe talked to the Zapatista troops that assembled around him at the steps of the municipal palace, by then scattered with debris from the all-night looting of the building. He talked to the rebels in a Mayan language, then raised his arms and shouted in Spanish:

"Long live the Mexican Revolution!"

"Viva!" shouted the rebels, raising their weapons.

"Long live the Zapatista National Liberation Army!"

"Viva!" responded the troops.

"Long live the Indian people in arms!"

"Viva!"

▼

Comandante Felipe — not Marcos — was supposed to have been the Zapatistas' spokesman and most visible face to the world according to the rebels' long-rehearsed war plan. Marcos, the group's military chief, was to stay away from reporters and not to draw attention to himself — much less become the sex symbol, media star, and guerrilla cult hero of the nineties. The Zapatistas could not fully claim to be a peasant Indian army if their leader was a white-skinned, well-educated young man with a Mexico City accent.

Comandante Felipe's public appearances were meant to convey the notion that the rebel army was led by an all-Indian Clandestine Indigenous Revolutionary committee. Officially, members of the committee, who like Felipe held the rank of comandante, made all major political decisions. Marcos, a subcommander, claimed that his role was limited to leading the peasant army's military operations, and that he followed orders from the Mayan committee on strategic issues.

"One of our main priorities will be to make sure that none of us becomes too much of a protagonist," Marcos told reporters minutes after Comandante Felipe's press conference, while asking photographers not to take pictures of him. "We want to remain anonymous so that we won't become corrupt. . . . This masked man's name is Marcos here today, but tomorrow his name will be Pedro in the town of Margaritas, Josue in the town of Ocosingo, Alfredo in the town of Altamirano, or any other name."

Yet Marcos's unscheduled rise to celebrity was as much the product of an accident as of his own craving for publicity. Even as he was stressing the Zapatistas' decision to follow a collective leadership, Marcos was already drawing attention to himself. When reporters at San Cristóbal's central square asked him why he — unlike Comandante Felipe — was covering his head, he answered with a smile, "Well, those of us who are the most handsome must protect ourselves." He later added, "Don't believe what I told you about me being so handsome. I was just making propaganda for myself."

As often happens in history, a minor episode would wreck the Zapatistas' original plan to have a Mayan commander as their most visible leader. In the confusion of the early hours of January 1, a group of wide-eyed American tourists were roaming around San Cristóbal's central square, growing increasingly anxious about their fate. They were terrified. They had come to Chiapas to visit the ancient Mayan ruins of Palenque and had found themselves in the middle of a revolution. Not speaking a word of Spanish, they were approaching anybody who looked like an English speaker to find out what was going on. When Comandante Felipe began to read the rebel proclamation, and local photographers began to take pictures of him, the Americans headed for the group.

After Comandante Felipe had finished reading the Zapatista statement in his Mayan Indian dialect and Spanish, an American tourist asked him what would happen to him and his fellow American tourists in San Cristóbal. Were they hostages? Could they leave the city? Were they supposed to go to any particular place? The Indian comandante, for whom Spanish was already a second language, looked at the English-speaking tourist with perplexity: He didn't understand a word of what the tourist was asking. Neither did any of the Indian leaders surrounding him, nor anybody nearby. They needed a translator to help calm down the more than a dozen American tourists at the site.

"I wasn't even supposed to show up at the central square," Subcommander Marcos told me months later in an interview. "My job was to lead the attack on the police headquarters. The members of the Clandestine Committee were the ones supposed to talk to the press. What happened was that one Zapatista officer whose job was to carry the weapons from the police headquarters to the central square — where our forces had the fewest weapons — got wounded. So I had to take his place. As soon as I got there, the Zapatista officer in charge of the seizure of the municipal palace walked toward me and told me, 'There is somebody there, a gringo, asking things that nobody can understand.' I said, 'OK, I'll take care of him.'"

Subcommander Marcos recalled with amusement, "It was a tourist who was scared that we were going to rob him, rape him, or who knows what. So I told him not to worry, that we wouldn't do anything to him, that this was a movement to achieve better living conditions for the Indians, and not against anybody, etcetera. As I was explaining this to him in my rudimentary English, people began to gather around us. Soon, a few journalists arrived and started asking questions, and I began to talk. That was at about eight A.M."

Within hours, news organizations from throughout the world were rushing to Mexico City to catch the first plane down to Chiapas and a glimpse of the charismatic Mexican guerrilla leader who had staged Mexico's largest peasant rebellion since the 1910–1917 Mexican Revolution. Comandante Felipe would give a second press conference at the San Cristóbal central square at eleven A.M. that morning. But reporters were already looking around for the more articulate, white-skinned Marcos. Within days, San Cristóbal street vendors would begin to sell Subcomandante Marcos T-shirts. A legend had been born.*

▼

But as often happens in Mexico, nothing was as it seemed. Salinas was no more a lifelong pro-American, free-market crusader than the Zapatistas were an all-Indian peasant army fighting mostly with sticks, handmade bayonets, and make-believe guns, as they were soon to be portrayed throughout the world.

In fact, Salinas had converted to free-market economics only recently, and it was open to question whether his move had been the result of new convictions or sheer political necessity. The fact was that only a few years before taking office, Salinas — who as a college student had often accompanied his brother Raúl to leftist meetings, and who had named one of his sons after peasant leader Zapata — was enthusiastically defending former president José López Portillo's nationalistic

---

*Comandante Felipe, meanwhile, faded into obscurity. According to Mexican Army radio intercepts and author's interview with Rancho Nuevo military barracks commander General José Rubén Rivas Peña, San Cristóbal de las Casas, July 20, 1994, he died a few months later, killed by a fellow Zapatista rebel in a fight in the jungle after a night of heavy drinking. Subcommander Marcos denied the report in an interview with the author in July 1994.

economic policies. In a little-known 1981 series of four articles in the daily *Excelsior*, Salinas — already a rising government economist at the time — had lambasted a recent book by economist Luis Pazos that called for a full-fledged economic opening: "Mr. Pazos displays an individualism and extreme pro–free market views that finally lead to fascism. His persistent effort to corrode the base of the current state and replace it with a free market 'laissez faire' system can only lead to the formation of a repressive and authoritarian system," he wrote. "Mr. Pazos devotes his harshest criticism to state-owned enterprises. He considers that nationalizations are thefts. . . . History has proven that the social cost of the free market and the extreme individualism that he proposes has been exploitation, neo-colonialism and the loss of national independence."

Salinas may have written his words under pressure or may have changed his views over the next few years, but his enthusiastic embrace of the free-market credo after he took office was at least partly motivated by political needs: He had won the most dubious election in recent memory — the official result giving him 50 percent of the vote over left-of-center candidate Cuauhtémoc Cárdenas was widely dismissed as fraudulent — and Mexico was rocked with opposition protests in the weeks that followed his inauguration. It was only through an unabashed courtship of the U.S. Government, the Mexican business elite, and the Roman Catholic Church — three institutions that had been kept at arm's length by recent Mexican governments — that Salinas managed to overcome the original sin of the dubious election that had placed him in power. Whatever his true beliefs were at the time, Salinas's free-market crusade was in part a desperate effort to win Washington's seal of approval.

By the same token, the images of landless Indian peasants rising up with toy guns against a well-equipped Mexican army that were beamed worldwide by television networks — and drew emotional support from human rights groups everywhere — did not tell the entire story. In fact, the Zapatista rebel army was a well-trained guerrilla force led by white middle-class intellectuals from Mexico City, who were much better armed than the poorly equipped peasants whose pictures made the airwaves.

What the world saw in the first days of January was only one part of the Zapatista army — the most improvised one. As Zapatista military leader Subcommander Marcos himself would concede to me later, his military strategy consisted of surrounding San Cristóbal with elite troops armed with AK-47 rifles, Uzi submachine guns, grenade launchers, and night vision devices, which he placed in the four major access roads to the city, while allowing lesser-armed rebel foot soldiers — some of them only armed with sticks, machetes, and hand-carved wooden toy guns — to march toward the center of town and take the municipal palace.

The idea was to provoke the army into trying to recover San Cristóbal, attacking the elite rebel positions on the outskirts of the city, which would have caused large numbers of civilian casualties and would have exposed the army to charges of massive human rights violations. If the army attacked, it would lose the propaganda war. If it didn't, it would lose as well: The television cameras would focus on the takeover of San Cristóbal's municipal palace by a ragtag army of landless Mayans mostly armed with toy guns. And it worked exactly as planned.

Reporters who headed to the city's central square with their video cameras in the early hours of that ice-cold January 1 to record the uprising would soon run into hundreds of uniformed Mayans milling around with their aged rifles and makeshift bayonets made out of sticks with knives tied to the ends. They had their faces uncovered and were sitting around bonfires erected on the square or walking back and forth to keep warm. It was hard not to feel sympathetic toward a rebel army so under-armed, and so hungry for justice.

▼

What the hell was Marcos doing?! the tall, silver-haired man who was the Zapatistas' real commander in chief would find himself asking aloud shortly after the uprising in a Mexico City safe house. Who did he think he was? He was going to ruin in one week what their military organization had been building for decades!

Commander in Chief "Germán" — the man whom the government would later identify as the head of the Zapatistas' secret Mexico City–based politburo — was in a state of fury as he watched Marcos speaking to reporters on national television, rebel defectors and sources close to the Zapatistas would assert months later. A highly disciplined revolutionary in his early fifties, he was a robust man who walked around in blue jeans and Guayabera shirts when he was not inspecting his troops in the jungle in his rebel commander uniform. He had little patience for breaches of discipline within his organization. Subcommander Elisa's mind was somewhere else. She had other things to worry besides the proletarian revolution, Zapatista sources would recall later.

She was thirty-eight, and the dour lines in her face hinted a tragic past she had probably not envisioned when she had first joined the guerrilla movement as a teenager. She had been first arrested in 1974, at age nineteen, in a bloody army raid on a rebel safe house in the Mexico state town of Nepantla, where five guerrillas — including her husband — had been killed. She had been tortured and raped in prison, and had rejoined the rebel movement after her release, only to shortly thereafter lose her second husband in another guerrilla battle, and her baby daughter in Chiapas, where bad medical attention in a rebel camp caused the child's death.

A committed revolutionary, she had later found a new companion within her rebel group, Subcommander Vicente, and after several years of trying to have a child they had just had a beautiful baby boy. As she had requested, Elisa had been appointed operations director in Mexico City — far away from the jungle, and the fighting. She was living with her baby, a dog, and a cat in an unassuming two-story house with a green iron fence at 32 Tenayuca Street in the middle-class neighborhood of Letrán Valle. From there, she handled part of the rebel underground propaganda network, faxing the Zapatista communiqués around town and making sure they got to the proper newspapers. She would be later identified by the government as the number three in the Zapatista hierarchy. By comparison, Subcommander Marcos was the number four: As leader of one of the organization's rebel fronts in Chiapas, his rank was equivalent to that of other subcommanders in charge of the group's other guerrilla fronts elsewhere in Chiapas and in other parts of the country.*

---

*After her arrest in 1995, Elisa signed a statement conceding that she was a senior officer of the National Liberation Forces — the guerrilla organization that had created the Zapatista army — and as such had helped launch the January 1, 1994, rebellion. After

Unbeknownst to the world, there were deep cracks in the Zapatista guerrilla organization even as it was making its spectacular international debut, rebel defectors would reveal later. Germán was becoming increasingly annoyed by Marcos's ego trips. A few weeks before the uprising, during a crucial vote held at the rebels' Chiapas jungle camp, Marcos and his Indian fighters had won a key victory over their commander in chief in a debate over when to launch the Zapatista attack. Marcos, the enthusiastic military commander, had called for starting the Zapatista rebellion January 1. He was under growing pressure from his Mayan rebel officers, who had promised their troops land seizures and greater political freedoms, and were now starting to suffer defections from Indians who had grown tired of the endless military training.

Germán, the cold, seasoned commander in chief, had wanted to launch a much wider attack six months later, when the group would have more sophisticated weapons, active support from other armed groups that were training for combat in central and northern Mexico — and a better chance of starting a war that would threaten the central government. Germán spoke from experience: He had been a top officer of the guerrilla group that had been destroyed — and its leaders, including Elisa's husband, killed — in 1974. He had been building up a new guerrilla army for the past two decades and did not want to repeat the mistakes that had led to the group's annihilation two decades earlier.

After losing the vote over the uprising's date, Germán had returned to Mexico City to oversee the planned uprising from there, and take care of the fund-raising and arms supply for the rebellion. He was still the commander in chief, but despite the semblance of civility in their radio messages, he could not help suspecting that his field commander

---

her release months later, she claimed that she had signed her testimony under torture, and that she had not participated in the Zapatista uprising. Two sources close to the Zapatista leadership conceded to the author, however, that she had indeed played a role in the Zapatista rebellion. Asked why she was denying it, the sources said Elisa would have subjected herself to new government charges if she admitted her Zapatista affiliation. In addition, the sources suggested Elisa and other middle-class NLF leaders had decided to deny their participation in the uprising in order not to contradict the Zapatistas' claim that they were an Indian-led movement.

in Chiapas had staged an internal coup d'état at the very moment he had held the jungle ceremony where he had received the Indians' staff of command. Germán knew that, as in any army in combat, it was the officers who commanded troops who had the upper hand. Marcos had rallied his Indian troops behind him, and seemed to be acting with growing independence of his Mexico City superiors.

▼

While Marcos was seizing San Cristóbal de las Casas, other rebel columns were taking the nearby towns of Las Margaritas, Chanal, Altamirano, and Ocosingo.

In Las Margaritas, a few hundred rebels made their entry into the city at about one A.M. and headed straight to the municipal police headquarters. Not far from there, hundreds of people were attending a Miss New Year pageant at the local Lions Club when the lights suddenly went off. One of the guests, Raúl Salazar, went out to catch some fresh air just as the shooting started. He was dead within minutes. "He was outside, and he was hit by a bullet," one of his brothers would tell reporters hours later. "We heard shooting, and there was a commotion among everybody at the party."

The small police contingent fled municipal headquarters in panic after the Zapatistas killed police agent Gabriel Arguello and wounded several others, making it clear that this was not just another street demonstration. The rebels soon took control of the police garrison and the Lions Club, where the remaining guests and the band were told to go to their homes.

The bloodiest combat took place in Ocosingo, a sixteenth-century city of about twelve thousand people. Contrary to widespread belief that the city's police force would suffice to quell an Indian attack that had been expected there since the abduction of several trucks four days earlier, more than five hundred rebels arrived from the jungle at about four A.M. and took the municipal palace in a fierce shoot-out about an hour later. José Luis Morales, the commander of Ocosingo's Judicial Police, and at least four police agents who were holed up inside the palace died in the battle. The rest of the town's small police force raised a white flag and abandoned the place with their hands up at sunset.

From there, the Zapatistas went to the XEOCH radio station and forced its operators to run a tape containing the rebels' "Declaration of the Lacandon Jungle." It would be heard several times that morning throughout the Chiapas jungle. The rebels wandering through the streets of Ocosingo, many of them teenagers, would echo the Zapatista declaration in conversations with reporters in their half-broken Spanish: They were fighting for jobs, land, justice, and freedom. Some of the older rebels, most of them in their late twenties and thirties, said they had sold their pigs and chickens — their lives' savings — to purchase their weapons. It didn't matter, some of them asserted with moving candor: The revolution would only last a few weeks, and then everybody would live a better life with a better government in power.

By January 2, there was little question that the Chiapas uprising amounted to the biggest Indian insurrection since the Mexican Revolution at the beginning of the century. As previously forgotten jungle towns became the focus of international attention, Indian street vendors discovered they could sell much more than Marcos T-shirts. Weeks later, they would be selling Zapatista dolls — the same cloth dolls Indian women used to sell on the street, but now with black ski masks covering their heads — and even a new brand of condoms offered under the name Alzados ("those that rise up") with the image of a masked rebel on the envelope. In a country where even the president worshiped Zapata, the Zapatistas had won a public relations coup.

▼

What few people outside Chiapas knew is that the Zapatista paraphernalia craze wasn't the truly spontaneous phenomenon that most foreign correspondents found ourselves reporting with wide-eyed amazement. Rather, it was a textbook case of self-fulfilling media coverage.

Once the fighting had died down in San Cristóbal, the hundreds of war correspondents from throughout the world who had arrived there hours earlier were wandering through the city in Banana Republic outfits, frantically looking for new angles to keep the story in the front pages. That was when we began writing about the Zapatista dolls, pens, and other souvenirs. What viewers didn't know — and many reporters found inconvenient to acknowledge — was that the merchandising phenomenon had been created by ourselves.

The tourism industry in San Cristóbal was hurting badly since thousands of foreign visitors had fled the city after the Zapatista uprising. Although a small army of foreign correspondents had moved into the city, they were fewer and less prone to shop than the German and Italian vacationers who had left. As days went by, the Indian women hawking dolls and other souvenirs grew increasingly frustrated with the reporters' disinterest in their merchandise. As a result, their sales pitches became more aggressive.

One Indian woman in particular was tireless in her efforts. Tired of the constant harangue, Joaquin Ibarz, a congenial correspondent for the Spanish daily *La Vanguardia*, came up with a brilliant marketing ploy, which he volunteered free of charge: Why don't you put ski masks on your dolls? Two days later, the woman showed up at her corner selling her usual Indian dolls along with several Zapatista dolls. Another foreign correspondent passing by saw them, bought them all, and rushed full of excitement to the press center at the Diego de Mazariegos hotel to report his discovery. The Indians were selling Zapatista dolls!

Those of us at the press center raced to the street — television crews elbowing their way out to get there first — to witness the new phenomenon. Soon, we were all buying Zapatista dolls, pens, T-shirts, and all kinds of souvenirs — and filing dispatches about the Zapatista paraphernalia rage that was taking over Mexico.

Next thing we knew, television viewers across the world were learning about the Marcos mementos' sales. Never mind that we were the only people in San Cristóbal who were buying them. Even in other parts of the country, where Marcos had gained widespread acceptance in intellectual circles, few had the spare change to buy Zapatista dolls beyond the foreign correspondents who were so happily reporting the trend.

▼

It took more than fourteen hours for Washington, D.C., to start taking the news of an Indian uprising in Chiapas seriously. The U.S. capital was a ghost town January 1. President Clinton was spending the New

Year weekend in Hilton Head, South Carolina, and Congress was in recess. The capital's movers and shakers were out of town, and so were the armies of lobbyists, public relations people, and journalists that revolve around them.

Robert Felder, the head of the State Department's Mexico desk, was the first U.S. Government official to be informed about the Chiapas uprising, and he thought it was a prank. Felder, a bright career diplomat who had served in Latin America and Africa, was having a late breakfast with his Argentine-born wife when he got the phone call at 11:45 A.M. A man identifying himself as an official with the U.S. embassy in Mexico's operations center told him a guerrilla war had just broken out in southern Mexico. Felder thanked the caller for the information with polite skepticism. He informed his boss, U.S. Deputy Assistant Secretary of State Alexander Watson, several hours later, after he had confirmed the story with political officers at the embassy in Mexico City.

"At first, I thought it was a joke," Felder recalls. "I thought some old friend who hadn't touched base with me in years was calling me up on New Year's Day to pull my leg with this story about an uprising in Chiapas. It just sounded too weird." It was a reaction that reflected Washington's generalized optimism about Mexico. As the Bush administration before it, the Clinton administration had been so consumed by its cheerful rhetoric about Salinas's economic reforms that it was caught totally off guard by the Chiapas uprising. U.S. intelligence agencies had warned about the possibility of political trouble in the poverty-ridden southern Mexico state, but the classified reports did not foresee a serious political challenge to the Mexican regime. It just didn't fit Washington's image of the "new" Mexico.

A classified CIA report dated September 1991 that had been distributed to all senior State Department and National Security Latin American experts at the time had warned about the social tensions building up in Chiapas. The fifteen-page report, entitled "Mexico's Troubled South: Being Left Behind," had cited the proliferation of drug trafficking and leftist rebel groups along the Guatemalan-Mexican border in Chiapas. It said that "high level corruption, reportedly including the governor of Chiapas," was "undermining local authorities and contributing to sporadic violence," and concluded that declining living standards and mounting public frustration "in our view will lead to increased political discontent."

But the report had failed to prompt any action in Washington, D.C., because it predicted that the possible acts of violence would be isolated and would not result in a serious guerrilla threat to the Mexican government. As was often the case, the CIA had done a decent reporting job, but a terrible one of analysis. In its concluding paragraphs, the report said that "southern states have a tradition of tumultuous local politics. But because grass roots groups defend highly parochial interests, they don't present a cohesive region wide threat to the ruling party."

The CIA report hardly sounded as a red alert at a time when civil and religious wars were erupting in Eastern Europe and Africa, most of them triggered by the disintegration of the Soviet bloc. Predictably, it was shelved within days by the State Department and NSC officials who had received it and quickly forgotten. Even the CIA dismissed its findings about political strife in Chiapas as of little relevance in the context of world affairs: The agency didn't even find it necessary to focus its surveillance satellites on Chiapas. The U.S. embassy in Mexico, too busy promoting NAFTA and the wonders of Salinas's economic reforms, did not write a single line in its reports to the State Department about the chances of a peasant uprising. "We were caught with our pants down," a U.S. embassy official assured me a few weeks after the Chiapas uprising. "We didn't have a clue."

▼

Long after the Zapatista uprising, President Salinas would also claim that the rebellion had taken him by surprise. He blamed the uprising on "a total failure of the state's intelligence systems." In fact, nothing could have been further from the truth.

The Zapatistas' active military training had been reported by Mexico's intelligence services to the top echelons of the Mexican government as early as November 1990. By 1993, the rebels' presence in Chiapas had become such an open secret that it was repeatedly reported by independent Mexican media.

But the Salinas government had firmly denied the reports of a guerrilla presence in Chiapas. By then, it was fighting every single vote in the U.S. Congress to get the approval of NAFTA and it didn't want any bad news to spoil the enterprise. Salinas, on the advice of his NAFTA negotiators, had concluded that news of a guerrilla force in Mexico would amount to precious ammunition for those seeking to scrap the accord on the argument that Mexico would be an unstable, dangerous U.S. partner.

In May 1993, seven months before the Zapatista uprising, there was a bloody fight between the rebels and the army in Mount Corralchén, near the village of San Miguel. An army patrol was checking reports about guerrilla activities in the area on May 22 when, at five P.M., it was attacked by the rebels. The patrol had accidentally arrived at the rebel camp Las Calabazas, headquarters of the Zapatistas' Fifth Regiment. A six-hour battle ensued, until Subcommander Marcos radioed a message to the rebels to destroy the camp and leave. Near midnight, the rebels abandoned the area, leaving behind at least one dead guerrilla, a teenage Tzeltal Indian who was known as Rafael. Also killed was Mexico City–born army sublieutenant José Luis Vera. He was twenty-two.

When the army moved into the rebel camp, officers were stunned: It was huge, with enough space for two hundred guerrillas, and was equipped with electricity, television sets, kitchens, and even a volleyball court. At the rebel training field, the army found cardboard replicas of army tanks and military barracks in Ocosingo. It was obvious that the guerrillas were planning to attack army barracks.

A few days later, the army captured ten armed suspects — eight Mexican Tzeltal Indians and two Guatemalans — who were arrested on charges of homicide and "treason to the fatherland." Chiapas prosecutors said in court documents that the suspects carried eleven weapons of various calibers, radio equipment, and "subversive propaganda," but all references to subversive activity disappeared from subsequent government communiqués. The charges against the Indians were quickly changed to "banditry," and the army — much against its will — put out a statement asserting that the fighting in Mount Corralchén had been "against a group of individuals, whose number has not yet been determined, that presumably carried out illegal activities."

"There is definitely no guerrilla activity in Chiapas," Patrocinio

Gonzalez, Mexico's Interior minister, told me with a straight face in an interview at his office a few days after the Mount Corralchén battle in Chiapas. Puffing on his Cuban cigar, displaying a magnanimous smile, Patrocinio — a balding, chubby man in his late fifties who was related to the Salinas family through his wife — explained to me that he had been governor of Chiapas until a few months earlier and thus knew the situation in Chiapas better than most other people. "There are land invasions and clashes that leave injured and even dead, but that's a far cry from a guerrilla problem. These are internal conflicts, not an insurgency."

Of course, he was lying. The first of several Mexican government reports on the Zapatistas had been written November 30, 1990, by the Center of Investigation and National Security, the Interior ministry's intelligence agency known by its Spanish initials, CISEN, under the hardly equivocal title of "The Presence of Guerrilla Groups in Chiapas."

The sixteen-page classified report, which was given to me by a Mexican Interior ministry official more than a year after the rebellion, was filled with names, political affiliations, and training ground locations of the rebels, and left no doubts about their preparations for war. It estimated the guerrillas' strength at "600 armed individuals" and quoted displaced peasants as asserting that the rebels had received their radio-communication equipment from the bishop of San Cristóbal, Msgr. Samuel Ruiz.

Over the next three years, there would be stacks of CISEN and military intelligence reports on the rebels' presence in Chiapas. The most compelling one was a May 1993 report written by Chiapas's military commanders shortly after the Mount Corralchén battle, where they informed their superiors about the mock military facilities they had found in the seized guerrilla camp.

Looking back at that clash, Marcos would tell me months later that he had been puzzled by the government's inaction. He said that, in the days that followed the fighting, "the army proceeded the way armies proceed: They started to deploy their troops, to position themselves to finish with the guerrillas. But, suddenly, after a few days, they withdrew. That wasn't a military decision — it was a political decision. . . . On the eve of the NAFTA vote, that withdrawal could not have been a mistake by the federal army. I'm convinced that it was a political decision coming from the very top. It couldn't have come but from the president of the republic."*

Salinas thought he would be able to avert a guerrilla outbreak in Chiapas by dramatically increasing government funds to rebel-controlled towns and — if that didn't work — perhaps by cracking down on the rebels once NAFTA's approval had been fully assimilated in the United States. But the Zapatista rebellion caught him off guard in that it took place before he could set in motion his plans to thwart it.

One of the top government officials who had repeatedly discussed the need to avert an uprising in Chiapas with the president was future government party candidate Colosio, at the time Salinas's Social Development minister. Colosio had good information, not the least because several of his aides were former leftist activists who had worked as peasant organizers in Chiapas and knew the inside workings of the state's leftist peasant groups better than most.

In an interview a day before his tragic March 23, 1994, death, Colosio conceded to me that he had received a confidential memo in mid-1993 from his delegate in Chiapas, Juan Manuel Mauricio Legizamo, asking him for an urgent $13 million for emergency social programs in the state. The memo, dated June 16, 1993, demanded the immediate creation of hospitals, roads, and sewage systems, to help offset "the growing presence of armed movements" in the Lacandon jungle.

When I asked Colosio whether he had passed on that information to the president, he raised his eyebrows and opened his hands — of course he had.

So what had gone wrong? Salinas had authorized the funds, and had agreed to send Colosio to visit Chiapas in August 1993 to distribute the

---

* In an interview with the author, Cartagena, Colombia, June 14, 1994, Salinas said he had not known about the extent of the armed rebel movement in Chiapas and cited as evidence of this the fact that he had visited the Chiapas town of Guadalupe Tepeyac, which would later emerge as the rebels' headquarters, on September 5, 1993. But there was no way he could have ignored it: In addition to the intelligence reports that according to Salinas's aides reached his desk, Mexico's independent newsweekly *Proceso* had carried a cover story June 7, 1993, reporting the sightings of at least six guerrilla training camps in Chiapas. The news was even beginning to draw the attention of international media: the *Miami Herald* published a front-page story June 28, 1993, under the headline "Guerrillas in Chiapas?"

money among the most restive Indian communities, Colosio said. The president had further instructed Colosio to meet with the rebel front organizations and give them a say in how the money would be spent — the first step toward trying to co-opt their leaders. Colosio made the trip, but it didn't help much. "Looking back and considering the levels of suffering and the demands of the people we found there, it's obvious that we arrived too late," Colosio concluded.

▼

The Zapatista uprising had left a toll of at least 145 dead, hundreds wounded, and more than 25,000 war refugees. In its rush to catapult Mexico into the First World — and in its fear of alarming the United States — the Salinas government had covered up widespread evidence of the guerrilla insurrection. In a system without checks and balances, where the government had always been able to buy off the most influential media and write history at its will, Salinas thought he could get away with describing any potential incidents of violence in Chiapas as isolated clashes stemming from age-old land disputes. His policy of denial would cost Mexico dearly.

CHAPTER 3

Chiapas: Opera and Revolution

I knew things were bad in Chiapas from the very moment I arrived there. It was January 2, 1994, a day after the Zapatista uprising. Like hundreds of reporters from all over the world, I had taken the first Mexicana Airline flight out of Mexico City to the Chiapas capital of Tuxtla Gutiérrez. We had arrived there with a two-hour delay because of bad weather — which I was assured was a pretty good showing for that flight.

From the air, the Tuxtla airport was a small speck on a barren, hilly place. But seen on the ground, it turned out to be a modern building, pretty fancy for what was supposed to be one of the most backward corners of the world. It had spit-clean marble floors, fancy cedar ceilings, and a huge cafeteria with a panoramic view of the runways. Other than that, I didn't notice anything extraordinary about the Tuxtla airport until I took a cab and headed for the city.

We had been driving for more than five minutes on a highway, when I became curious about not seeing any houses — or any other sign of civilization — on the road. After ten minutes, there still wasn't any sign of human life around us. A few minutes later, I couldn't help asking the cabdriver how long it would take us to get to the city. The man turned around and said, with an unflappable face, "Right away. . . . It'll be half an hour at the most. . . ."

Half an hour?! Driving through the middle of nowhere?! Whose idea had it been to build this airport so far away from the city? What was the point of it? The taxi driver raised his eyebrows with a knowing smile, almost laughing at the innocent foreigner in the backseat. The airport had been built twenty miles from the city because a former Chiapas governor had sold the land to the state, he said. The former governor — a surgeon with no political experience who according to the popular wisdom had been given the governorship as a prize after operating on President Echeverría — was believed to have made a fortune out of the deal. So had his friends who got the contracts to build the highway on which we were driving, he said matter-of-factly.

That by itself wasn't such a big deal, the taxi driver went on. The trouble was that the airport was useless. It was placed on high ground and near a huge dam that produced a thick layer of fog that covered the airport — and paralyzed air traffic — every morning for more than six months a year. Hadn't my plane been delayed in Mexico City because of poor weather conditions here? Yes, I said, somewhat astounded. At least twice a week, the morning flight from Mexico City had to be delayed because of the fog. Often, flights had to be diverted to nearby states.

The airport had been built there despite scores of studies recommending against that location. Jokes about it were legendary, I would soon learn. According to one story residents swore was true, the fog was so heavy one day in 1979 during the airport's construction that two earthmovers had crashed because of the poor visibility, and one of the drivers had been badly wounded. Soon after the surgeon-governor's departure, his successor had joined the generalized criticism of the airport while conceding that he had had no alternative but to complete its construction. Instead of calling it by its name, Llanos de San Juan, or "plains of San Juan," he had used a play on words to rename it Ya No Se Vé, or "Can't See It Anymore."

The airport's location had been such an embarrassment to future Chiapas governors that none of them had ever dedicated it. The airport had been opened for traffic August 22, 1980, but there had never been an opening ceremony or an inaugural plaque: No Chiapas governor had ever wanted his name on a sign that would associate him with the infamous Tuxtla airport. So, more than a decade later, the airport remained perhaps the only one in the world that had never been officially dedicated, or named after a national or local hero.

Had corruption diminished under future Chiapas governors? I would get sarcastic smiles when posing that question to prominent citizens in the days that followed. The airport construction saga was only the first of many blackly humorous tales of government ineptitude and bad faith in that remote corner of Mexico.

In 1992 then–Chiapas governor Patrocinio Gonzalez had announced with great fanfare that he had obtained permission from the military garrison in Tuxtla Gutiérrez to use part of the city's military airport for civilian flights. Tuxtla residents and frequent travelers to the city were ecstatic: At long last, they would no longer have to make the tedious trek to the remote airport.

Thanks to Patrocinio, as the governor was commonly known, one airline — Aviacsa — was given permission to land at the city airport. Aviacsa immediately built a new passenger terminal and a 500-yard extension to the military airport's runway. By 1993, when the terminal was completed, most passengers had switched from Mexicana — which still landed, when it could, at the faraway airport — to Aviacsa. It was a major political triumph for the governor. Whatever you thought of him, people said, Patrocinio got things done.

It wasn't until a year later, in February 1994, that Chiapas residents read with amazement in the financial pages of Mexico City newspapers that Patrocinio had long been a major shareholder of Aviacsa. After making the airline's business boom during his governorship, Patrocinio was reported to have sold his stock to a Monterrey group for $5 million shortly after moving to Mexico City to take up his new job as interior minister. Now, the Chiapas capital had two airports and two extremely happy former governors.

▼

Buried amid the stories of the Zapatista uprising on January 2, 1994, I found a small item in the local newspaper that immediately caught my attention. It was a story reporting, almost in passing, that former governor Patrocinio Gonzalez's police chief was under investigation in connection with the murders of twenty transvestites.

For the past two years, Tuxtla Gutiérrez's most notorious transvestites had been killed in execution-style murders. Many had been picked up at Central Avenue, where transvestite prostitutes used to wait for prospective clients, and taken to deserted roads outside the city, where they were slain in a hail of gunfire. A cross-dresser known as La Gaby had been found with nine bullet wounds in the chest. Another one, known as Chentilla, was found with a bullet hole in the head and nine others in his body. Several others had followed.

When terrified transvestites ceased walking the streets, the mysterious killers began shooting homosexual men. The former governor had played down the issue, saying that the reports of twenty murders of homosexuals were grossly exaggerated — to the best of his knowledge, there were only seven such cases. Furthermore, the soon-to-become Interior minister used the occasion to congratulate himself for his law-and-order measures, suggesting that much of the scandal was being caused by increasingly outspoken gay groups, "who over the past few months have not been able to carry out in liberty their sexual deviations along Central Avenue."

For two years, until the case had begun to draw attention from international human rights groups, the Chiapas police chief had branded the killings as "passional crimes." Now, the police chief himself was under investigation. It seemed he had always hated gays, I was told — without a trace of outrage, as if explaining a fact of life — by local government officials. Chiapas was Mexico's Wild West — the land where everything goes.

▼

By the end of the second day of the uprising, the previously unknown Zapatista National Liberation Army, known by its Spanish initials as EZLN, had abandoned San Cristóbal and was surrounding the Rancho Nuevo military battalion on the outskirts of that city. Before leaving San Cristóbal, they had taken over the prison, freeing all 179 prisoners, whom they said were victims of discrimination against Indians (including a lucky American anthropologist locked up on charges of having raped and savagely beaten the thirteen-year-old Chamula Indian woman he had recently married).

Now, the Zapatistas were heading in various directions. They had already seized the towns of Oxchuc, Chanal, Huixtla, Altamirano, and Las Margaritas. Some reports said they were heading to the state capital. They had taken with them a ton and a half of dynamite stolen from the state oil monopoly, Pemex — enough to blow up any major oil installation in the country.

By January 6, the crisis had spread beyond Chiapas, drawing growing alarm in the international financial community. Newspapers reported that unidentified rebels had blown electricity towers in the states of Michoacán and Puebla, and classified Interior ministry memos read to me months later asserted that an additional twelve electricity towers had been downed or severely damaged in other parts of the country. On January 7, a powerful car bomb exploded in Mexico City's University mall. There were fears of a guerrilla uprising across the nation.

▼

In Mexico City, Salinas was facing a rebellion within his own cabinet. His top aides were deeply split among those favoring a swift military crackdown, led by Interior Minister Patrocinio Gonzalez, and those recommending a peace agreement with the rebels, headed by Foreign Minister Manuel Camacho Solis. The latter, an ambitious politician who was hurt by not having been picked by his close friend Salinas for the PRI's presidential nomination, was threatening to quit. His private appeals for negotiations with the rebels during the first days of the Chiapas rebellion had been ignored by Salinas. Now, Camacho's resignation at the peak of the wave of violence could turn the Chiapas conflict into a national political crisis, exactly what Salinas was trying to prevent.

The foreign minister, a slender, boyish looking man in his mid-forties who had made friends in left-of-center intellectual circles during his years in academia, was granted a private audience with Salinas January 8. It was a Saturday morning, and Salinas received him at his presidential quarters. Camacho started out by stating his disagreement with the government's attempt to minimize the Zapatista uprising as a problem limited to a small corner of a remote province, and to describe the rebel leaders as "professionals of violence."

"My point is simple: Over the past week, Mexico has lost almost all the international prestige it has won during this administration," Camacho told the president, laying on the coffee table a thick folder of U.S. and European press clips he was carrying. "Here I have a detailed analysis of the situation. All the front pages, all television networks around the world are stressing what has happened in Chiapas and are condemning the Mexican government. I think the financial repercussions of this will be imminent. This will be the last weekend of tranquility in the stock market. We are facing massive and sudden capital flight."

Salinas listened attentively.

"But that's not the main thing," Camacho continued. "The country is in a profound crisis. The army can resist an attack and could even win the war, but the political implications of such a course of action would be a different story. Can Mexico win a war against its own Indians? That's where the government's current position is taking us." Camacho went to the point: He wanted the government to drop its hard-line stand, and to be assigned to lead efforts to resolve the crisis peacefully. "There's nothing I can do to resolve the Chiapas conflict from the foreign ministry. I could appear on one, two, or ten U.S. television shows, and what would that achieve? What's more, what would I say? What would I defend? . . . Carlos, I'm not willing to be a foreign minister to argue before the world whether there were ten more deaths or ten fewer deaths. I don't believe in that. I'm not willing to defend that."

The conversation lasted hours. Camacho made a persuasive argument in favor of launching a peace offensive. It was critical for the government to turn the tables and to be seen as the force of moderation, peace, and national reconciliation. Camacho volunteered to leave the Foreign Relations ministry immediately and to become the government's peace negotiator. The president ended the meeting with a promise to make a decision within the next few days. He had mixed feelings: Camacho, who was said to be still hoping to become a presidential candidate with or without the PRI's backing, was eager to be at the center of the new crisis for his own political reasons. And there was the question of Camacho's ties to the left during his recent tenure as Mexico City mayor: Hadn't he — consciously or unknowingly — provided financial aid to some of the same leftist militant groups, such as Mexico City's Route 100 bus drivers, who were supporting the Zapatista rebels?

Two days later, on January 10, Salinas appointed Camacho as the government's peace negotiator. Public opinion polls were already showing growing support for Subcommander Marcos and his demands of justice for Mexico's Indians. On the advice of doves within his cabinet and two unlikely outside advisers — Nicaraguan Sandinista army chief General Humberto Ortega and former Salvadoran guerrilla chief Joaquin Villalobos, who made secret trips to Mexico to provide the government with their insights as one-time guerrilla leaders — the president announced on January 12 a unilateral cease-fire, and shortly thereafter an amnesty for the guerrillas.

Salinas's image handlers said the president was touched by the Indians' demands for social justice and had acted accordingly. Members of his inner circle knew that at least part of the president's turnaround was triggered by Camacho's rebellion, and by fears that his disgruntled foreign minister would add to the national political crisis by resigning in protest.

▼

Camacho's appointment as peace commissioner fell like a cold shower on Colosio's campaign. As was to be expected, the ambitious peace negotiator soon began to grab the headlines, at Colosio's expense. Political columnists soon began to pose a nagging question: Would Salinas pick Camacho to replace Colosio as the PRI candidate if the Chiapas mediation effort ended successfully?

Among the most worried was Colosio campaign manager Ernesto Zedillo Ponce de León. In a confidential memorandum to his boss dated March 19, 1994, Zedillo warned Colosio that the campaign conditions had changed: President Salinas, increasingly isolated and deserted by his top aides as he was approaching the end of his term, could no longer be counted on as their unconditional ally. Until the Chiapas rebellion in early January, Salinas's top priority had been ensuring that his candidate would be elected, Zedillo wrote. Now, the president's top priority was solving the Chiapas problem and ending his presidency successfully. "All of this bolsters Manuel Camacho's temptations, and underscores the risk that the president may distance himself [from Colosio's candidacy]," Zedillo wrote.

Long after Colosio's death, when the Zedillo memo was leaked to the daily *Reforma*, conspiracy theorists had a field day: They claimed it helped prove that Salinas wanted to get rid of Colosio, and that members of his inner circle may have ordered his killing. There was nothing in the memo to support their conclusion. But Zedillo's words left little doubt that tensions were rising within the ruling elite. The Zapatista rebellion had — perhaps unintentionally — reopened the power struggle for the presidential succession.

▼

To what extent were the Zapatistas an ideologically vague army of landless Indian peasants demanding their basic rights, as they were first portrayed by most of us in the media? Was their leader, Subcommander Marcos, a true democrat? Or were they just one more well-trained Marxist guerrilla force, only different from others for their image-conscious commander's seemingly moderate public statements?

The way millions of Americans got the story, the Zapatistas were a new phenomenon — a prodemocracy Indian uprising with no ideological overtones. Even CBS's *60 Minutes* devoted an opening story to a glowing profile of Subcommander Marcos, portraying him — as most of us did, some more than others — as a virtual Boy Scout. "What Robin Hood was to the people of Sherwood Forest, Subcomandante Marcos has become to the people of Mexico — a fighter for the rights of peasants who are trapped in poverty by large landowners," *60 Minutes* correspondent Ed Bradley said in the opening lines of the show on August 21, 1994, without even raising the possibility that Marcos could be a fighter for a one-party proletarian state.

"We want democracy, I mean, the right of the people to choose the government and the way of this government," Marcos told Bradley. "We want liberty. I mean, every people have the right to choose one way or another way. We want justice."

Bradley: So basically, what it is you're asking for are basic individual rights?

Marcos: Yes.

Bradley: What we call in the United States life, liberty, and the pursuit of happiness.

Marcos: Yes.

▼

The Zapatistas wanted that, and much more. What most U.S. and European newspapers simply referred to as an "Indian army" was in reality one of the armed wings of Commander in Chief Germán's Mexico City white-dominated Marxist guerrilla group. There was nothing improvised about the Zapatista leaders' ideological background: It was class struggle, in its most radical fashion.

Judging from the Zapatistas' initial communiqués, internal rebel documents, and Marcos's own response when I asked him about it, there is little doubt that the Zapatistas grew up as a traditional Marxist guerrilla group, which changed its rhetoric after the January 1 rebellion, when its media-savvy leader discovered the advantages of playing up the Indian participation in his uprising — the one aspect of his revolt that had captured the world's imagination. The difference between the Zapatistas and previous Latin American leftist guerrilla groups was that they had succeeded where "Che" Guevara and so many others had failed: The white middle-class Mexican rebel leaders had won the allegiance of scores of Indian communities.

The Zapatista army was the rural wing of the National Liberation Forces (NLF), one of Mexico's oldest guerrilla groups. The NLF was born on August 6, 1969, in the northern industrial city of Monterrey, as a pro-Cuban offshoot of another Marxist rebel group, the Mexican Insurgent Army. In the seventies, the new guerrilla group had made headlines with urban actions such as bank robberies and attacks on big department stores in Monterrey, but had at the same time begun to develop peasant support groups in Chiapas. By 1980, according to internal documents released by the government, the NLF had adopted a five-pointed red star as its symbol and had — at least in writing — set up a four-tier organization: a national directorate, a politburo, an urban front named Students and Workers in Combat, and a rural front named Zapatista National Liberation Front.

According to the NLF's documents, Zapatista defectors, and sources close to the movement, the group had by then adopted a Maoist strategy of "prolonged popular war," which would combine urban and rural guerrilla actions throughout the country with massive protests by the civilian population to wear down the government and ultimately topple it. Following that plan, a group of young Marxist philosophy and sociology graduates from the Autonomous Metropolitan University of Mexico (UAM) had moved to Chiapas in the early 1980s to set in motion the NLF's rural guerrilla front.

Other groups of leftist militants who had spent time in Chiapas in the seventies — like Salinas's older brother, Raúl — were in their forties and fifties, and had already returned to the capital with government jobs to run various social programs. But many of the peasant leaders they had trained had remained in the jungle, and soon teamed up with the newly arrived leftist militants from Mexico City. Over the years, they infiltrated militant Roman Catholic peasant groups created by San Cristóbal de las Casas's bishop, Ruiz, the activist priest whom right-wing Chiapas ranchers called "the Red Bishop."

By the early nineties, the Mexico City guerrilla group led by Commander in Chief Germán had built a sizable rebel army in Chiapas, made up of Mexico City intellectuals, Mayan peasant leaders, and officials of San Cristóbal Archdiocese lay groups. The pillars of the NLF's military wing in Chiapas were three subcommanders — Subcommander Marcos, who was in charge of the Ocosingo area; Subcommander Daniel, who headed the Altamirano region; and Subcommander Pedro, who led the troops in the Las Margaritas area — all of them white-skinned intellectuals from Mexico City. The Zapatista leaders were idealistic young men, but hardly Robin Hood–style fighters for U.S.-styled democracy: Their original goal, as stated in their internal documents, had been establishing a "dictatorship of the proletariat."

▼

Indian rights had never been a central part of the NLF's rhetoric: Like other hard-line Marxist groups, the rebel group was fighting for the workers and peasants to take power and "create a single political party based on the principles of Marxism-Leninism." Its main enemies, according to its statutes, were "north-American imperialism, and its local partners, the Mexican bourgeoisie," the Mexican government, and its armed services.

The Zapatistas' first official communiqués after the January 1, 1994, uprising, had only made marginal references to Indian rights. The *Mexican Awakener*, the group's first known official publication, had virtually ignored Indians as an ethnic group. The Zapatista revolution, it said, was being carried out by "the poor, the exploited and the miserable of Mexico" against "the oppressive government, and the big national and foreign exploiters of the people."

Was it an oversight? It didn't look that way. In its "Declaration of the Lacandon Jungle," the Zapatista army's official statement of purpose released by the rebels on the day of their uprising, the group declared war on the "Salinas dictatorship" and listed eleven basic demands: "work, land, roof, food, health, education, independence, liberty, democracy, justice and peace." The 2,500-strong rebel group, which had taken arms against Mexico's 170,000-strong army, was announcing its quixotic plan to "advance to the capital of the country, overpowering the Mexican federal army," and vowed to hold summary trials on treason charges against army officers "who have been advised or trained by foreigners, within or outside our fatherland." It also promised to "suspend the sacking of our natural resources" by foreign multinational companies and to confiscate all sizable rural properties.

Only after the first week of fighting, when the Zapatista rebels had made headlines worldwide, would Subcommander Marcos start playing down their calls for class struggle and begin to emphasize the Indian nature of the rebellion. Mexico's intelligence services would soon draw their own conclusion: Somebody — perhaps Zapatista friends in the Roman Catholic Church or rebel sympathizers in the United States or Europe — had read the international reaction to the uprising and had advised Marcos to forget the socialist mumbo jumbo and play up the Indian card. That was what was drawing attention in New York, Paris, Madrid, and Mexico City, and what helped turn the Chiapas rebels into media stars.

Marcos made no bones about the fact that he adjusted his political message after the rebellion. "The change resulted from a decision by the [Zapatista] Committee to respond to government charges that we were foreigners and 'professionals of violence,'" the guerrilla leader told me in an interview months later, citing the term with which the Salinas government had referred to the rebels in the first days of fighting. "The Committee said, 'We must emphasize our Mexican and Indian roots and show that this is not a movement financed by foreign governments, Castro, or anything of the sort. We have to show people that this is a Mexican and Indian movement.'"

As days went by, Marcos would further fine-tune his discourse to portray the Zapatista uprising as an ideologically vague rebellion with no other guiding light than the desperation of Chiapas's poverty-stricken Mayans. The new line proved a smashing success: Enthusiastic support letters from international human rights groups began to flood the rebel headquarters. Many leftist intellectuals, hurt by the collapse of the Soviet bloc and disappointed by Cuba's progressive march toward totalitarian capitalism, hailed the arrival of what they quickly called the world's first post-Communist rebel movement. Just as the 1910 Mexican Revolution had been the first social uprising of the twentieth century, preceding the Russian Revolution by seven years, the Indian uprising in Chiapas would make history as the first ethnic rebellion of the twenty-first century, they said.

Marcos, a Mexico City leftist intellectual whose identity would remain a mystery until more than a year later, rejected time and again the idea that he was a Marxist. When I asked him about Comandante Felipe's January 1 statement that the Zapatistas were socialists, Marcos shrugged: The Indian leader had been grilled by reporters during the first days of fighting on whether they were capitalists or socialists and he had responded the latter "for the simple reason that we are not capitalists," he said. As for himself: He was just fighting to open up Mexico's authoritarian system.

Unbeknownst to me at the time, Marcos had reaffirmed his Marxist vows as late as January 1993. He had been among the top NLF leaders who had participated at a meeting in the jungle town of Prado, where the organization had issued a "Declaration of Principles" that would make future Zapatista communiqués look like icons of moderation. It stated, more than a year after the collapse of the former Soviet Union, that the NLF's goal was to "establish the dictatorship of the proletariat, understood as a government of the workers that will stave off counterrevolution and begin the construction of socialism in Mexico."

Marcos's personal library was hardly that of a new age democrat. Among the few books he could keep at his jungle hideout, he had chosen classic revolutionary manuals and computer manuals. Near his bed at the six-room rebel headquarters he abandoned in a hurry after an army offensive more than a year later, reporters found *History Will Absolve Me*, by Fidel Castro, and *Revolutionary Works*, by Che Guevara, next to Microsoft Windows manuals and a pipe.

And even when his public statements departed from the radical language of previous Latin American guerrilla leaders, he periodically slipped into positions that were hardly examples of political tolerance. Once, he told the daily *La Jornada* that Mexico faced the threat of a government takeover by the "fascist right [embodied by] the most organized expression of that right, the PAN." Never mind that the National Action Party had been fighting for representative democracy since before Marcos's birth. It sometimes seemed that Marcos only accepted one kind of democratic government — one led by the revolutionary left.

When I mentioned to a Mexican source with close ties to the Zapatista leadership that the NLF's Declaration of Principles was hardly that of a group committed to representative democracy, he played down the significance of the document, without denying its authenticity. It was a morale-boosting internal document aimed at the Zapatistas' Mayan troops and written in a Marxist rhetoric that Indian political activists had become used to hearing for the past three decades, he said. You could not change that language overnight, throwing your troops into ideological confusion at a time when you were preparing to launch your all-out offensive.

That may have been the case. The Zapatista army leader may have convinced himself at the time of his uprising that Communism's days were over. But he had been high-ranking officer of the Maoist NLF till the very day of the uprising, which raised legitimate questions as to whether the subcommander's more moderate post-insurrection rhetoric was not just a public relations strategy. In any event, while the Zapatista rebellion could not be explained away as the work of a small group of Mexico City radicals, it wasn't a spontaneous indigenous rebellion either. It was a carefully planned offensive by a white-dominated Marxist guerrilla group that had found considerable support among long-exploited Mayan communities.

▼

I did not have to look far to find the misery the Zapatista rebels were talking about. Traveling on the sinuous mountain road that linked the Chiapas capital with San Cristóbal de las Casas, in between the army roadblocks that would stop vehicles intermittently to prevent their access to the war zone, I could see the Indian women walking barefoot on the side of the roads, bent by the heavy loads of wood they were carrying on their backs.

They were amazingly small, four foot three inches tall at the most.

Because they had no drinking water or electricity in their villages, they had to make five-hour-long treks just to carry the water and wood they needed for cooking. Their men — those who had not migrated to the United States to make a living — worked in the fields, fighting a losing battle against economic reality. The drastic cuts in state subsidies and the rapid shift toward free trade that Mexican and U.S. leaders were heralding so enthusiastically were hurting Indians — the most unprepared to compete in the global market — like nobody else.

Everything was going against them. Land reform, one of the main legacies of the Mexican Revolution, had never been fully implemented in Chiapas. Large numbers of Mayans had lived for several generations in their villages but were still fighting for their land. They had copies of presidential decrees granting them land titles, some of them dating from several decades back, and had spent years trying to get the *ingenieros* — or "engineers," as they referred to government officials — to recognize them, but to no avail. Wealthy Chiapas ranchers had blocked their efforts by appealing such decrees in the courts and using their political clout to make sure that they would never be enforced. On other occasions, large landholders would skip land reform regulations by subdividing their land into legal-sized parcels and registering them in the names of friends and relatives.

When frustrated Indians protested, ranchers would use their influence with the governor to send state troops to crack down on them, or would hire private gunmen — who became known in Chiapas as *Guardias Blancas*, or "White Guards" — to repress them. Hundreds of Indians had been killed in such land disputes in recent years, and few — if any — of the murderers had ever been brought to justice. The ranchers had the law on their side: Article 225 of Chiapas's Criminal Code called for sentences of up to four years in prison for those seizing land, buildings, public squares, "or obstructing communication arteries," which meant that Mayans risked long terms in jail just for taking their demands to the streets.

Even those Mayans who possessed legal land rights had run out of land for their children. In the sixties, thousands of Chamula Indians had resettled in the Lacandon jungle, most of them Evangelicals who had split from their Roman Catholic–dominated communities. They had founded new villages in the jungle and given them biblical names such as Jerusalém, Jericó, and Betania. Over the next two decades, they were followed by landless Tzeltal, Chol, Tzotzil, and Tojolabal Indians from the northern and eastern part of the state, who saw the jungle as a new land of opportunity, where they could find work as lumberjacks and eventually get a piece of land for themselves. The names they chose for their new villages reflected their hopes: Wherever you went in the Lacandon, you found places with names such as El Triunfo ("The Triumph"), La Esperanza ("The Hope"), and El Porvenir ("The Future").

There had also been a mystical motivation behind the silent migration of thousands of Indians to the Lacandon jungle. Under the leadership of militant bishop Ruiz, the Roman Catholic diocese of San Cristóbal de las Casas had organized up to four thousand lay workers to help spread the gospel of liberation theology among Chiapas Indian communities. The church workers' main evangelization text was the book of Exodus, which in many communities was the only part of the Bible translated into all Indian languages. The church's message was that the oppressed Indians of northern Chiapas were the people of Israel, who were fleeing a corrupt regime that was equivalent to that of the Egyptians in biblical times, and who were to build a new society in the unpopulated lands of the Lacandon jungle. Catholic Church –steered communities had been thriving in the jungle for years, with their priests and lay workers preaching resistance against ruthless coffee barons and corrupt government officials.

Now, even those Mayans who had some land risked losing it as a result of a new constitutional change: The Salinas government had dropped an age-honored constitutional norm whereby peasants living on cooperative farms had lifelong property rights over their lands and could thus not be forced to sell their properties. By the early nineties, many Chiapas Indians were finding themselves deeply indebted to their suppliers and bankers, who were about to claim their properties to collect their loans.

The constitutional revocation of lifelong land titles could not have come at a worse time: Coffee prices had dropped by more than 60 percent since the mid-eighties, the cattle-raising business had collapsed after meat processing plants nationwide had stopped buying from

Chiapas because of official reports of a plague in Ocosingo, and the state's lumber business was hurting badly after Salinas declared a new ban on tree cutting on the eve of his trip to the Earth Summit in Rio de Janeiro, Brazil. The president's environmental decree had drawn applause in world capitals but provoked panic in Chiapas.

Meantime, Chiapas's population was exploding: While the country's overall population was growing by 2.1 percent a year, the state's population growth was 5.4 percent. In some of Chiapas's poorest Indian villages, population growth rates were going as high as 7 percent. Ignorant of birth control methods or discouraged from using them by Bishop Ruiz — who was extremely conservative on birth control issues — Indian women often had seven, eight, or nine children. The combination of a plunging economy and soaring population growth had left many Indians with little choice but to leave their communities and join the ranks of the urban homeless. They could not easily find work as field hands elsewhere in Mexico: A flood of cheap corn and wheat imports from the United States since the start of NAFTA was hurting Mexican farmers badly, and driving many of them out of business.

By the end of the Salinas government, the Mayans who had moved to the jungles of Chiapas had not only failed to find the promised land, but found themselves in even greater misery than that they had originally left behind. Most Indian communities in the jungle had illiteracy rates of more than 50 percent. In the city of Altamirano, 75 percent of the households lacked electricity. In Las Margaritas, 73 percent of them were without drinking water. And the farther one ventured into the countryside, the more of a rarity it became to find such luxuries as homes with tin roofs, concrete floors, or nearby schools or hospitals. Thousands died every year from curable diseases such as diarrhea.

Chiapas was, as Marcos was saying, "Mexico's basement" — a part of the house where none of the glitz of northern Mexico reached and that was rarely seen by outsiders. It was in this context that Marcos and a handful of white leftist militants had found fertile ground to recruit soldiers for their peasant army. Bishop Ruiz's missionary work had run into a major contradiction: He had supported active resistance against the exploitation of the Indians, with arms if necessary, but he was disapproving of guerrilla warfare as a way to topple the government. As Salinas's free-market reforms plunged the Indian communities into even greater hopelessness, Marcos's peasant army became a more appealing option than Ruiz's calls for active — but peaceful — resistance.

▼

Mixed among the rambunctious crowd of khaki shirt–clad foreign correspondents and human rights activists that had arrived in Chiapas in those early days of the Zapatista rebellion was a petite Philippine American woman wearing blue jeans, white sneakers, and carrying a sure-shot camera hanging from her neck. Her name was Josephine Jimenez: She was neither a journalist, nor a human rights activist, nor a secret agent for a foreign government, but a money manager for one of the large U.S. emerging markets funds who was traveling incognito as a tourist.

Jimenez had read all about the Zapatista rebellion at her Montgomery Emerging Markets fund bay view offices on the seventeenth floor of San Francisco's pyramid-shaped Transamerica Building, but wanted to take a personal look at the situation. While most of her competitors were staying at five-star hotels in Mexico City learning about the Chiapas crisis over dinner with U.S.-educated Finance ministry officials, Jimenez had decided to become a financial community war correspondent: After spending three days in Mexico City, she took a domestic flight to Tuxtla Gutiérrez and made the two-hour trip by taxi from the Chiapas capital to San Cristóbal de las Casas.

Jimenez, an MIT-educated financial manager whose fund had about $1 billion invested in more than two dozen emerging markets, had already slightly reduced her exposure in Mexico before the Zapatista rebellion after concluding that Mexican stocks were overvalued. But she still had $70 million invested in Mexican stocks when she set out for the war zone, and wanted to decide whether to leave the money in Mexico or transfer it elsewhere. On previous trips to Mexico, she had spent most of her time visiting individual companies in search of undervalued stock purchasing opportunities. Now, she wanted to see where Mexico as a whole was heading.

She got scared from the very start of her trip: A few miles from Tuxtla, she was stopped for the first time at an army roadblock, where heavily armed — and seemingly nervous — young soldiers asked her to get down from her taxi and began to ask questions. Before boarding her cab again, she was able to ask one of the soldiers if he was from Chiapas, and was surprised by his answer: He turned out to be from Tijuana, at the other end of Mexico. The army had brought in troops from other states to crack down on the Chiapas rebels.

On the remainder of the trip to San Cristóbal, Jimenez had been surprised to see how fertile the land on both sides of the highway was. At the San Cristóbal public library, she learned that Chiapas supplied a large chunk of Mexico's electricity needs, and that the Pemex national oil monopoly depended heavily on the state's natural gas output. She also learned that most of Chiapas's lands were held by a small number of landowners. The combination of Chiapas's role as a key supplier of energy to the rest of Mexico and its explosive social conditions made her increasingly anxious about the country's future. "We had already seen the guerrillas blowing up oil pipes in Colombia," Jimenez would reflect later. "Whoever had organized the rebellion in Chiapas had not chosen that state by chance: After all, there were poverty-ridden Indians in many regions of Mexico. They picked Chiapas because they had the leverage to disrupt the country's economy from there."

Back in San Francisco, Jimenez gradually began to unload her Mexican stocks. A few other fund managers quietly followed her steps. Months later, when the Mexican stock market crashed and other American funds that had left their investments in the country were badly hit, Jimenez would be seen as a visionary among her colleagues. For Mexican and U.S. officials, however, she would be considered part of the problem: A new brand of fund manager who got easily scared by unexpected political events and whose pack reaction could deplete a country's foreign reserves in a matter of minutes. Unlike their predecessors — the Citibanks, Chase Manhattans, and other New York banks that accounted for the bulk of U.S. deposits in Mexico in the past — the new money managers had no business history or long-term commitments in the country. They could shift their stock and bond investments across the planet at a stroke of their keyboards, and turn a bad situation into a far worse one.

▼

Had the Salinas government neglected the Indians, as Subcommander Marcos was claiming? Not really. Rather, its sin had been allowing the massive resources it sent to Chiapas to be squandered by a clique of corrupt PRI officials that had long run the state at their whim — often spending millions on pharaonic projects that looked surrealistic to outside observers.

The Salinas government had poured more money into Chiapas — relative to the size of its population — than any other Mexican state. You could see it with your own eyes. On the road from Tuxtla Gutiérrez to San Cristóbal de Las Casas, there were dozens of freshly painted signs with the logo of Salinas's "Solidarity" social works program. Behind them, there were entire neighborhoods of newly built concrete homes, or schools in the process of being expanded with new wings.

When Salinas claimed weeks after the uprising that his government had increased by ten times economic assistance to Chiapas during his term in office, he may not have been exaggerating. Although his programs could not even start redressing the centuries-old conditions of misery in which Indians were living, the government had brought electricity to twelve hundred villages, refurbished about four thousand schools throughout the state, and built four new hospitals.

But many of these projects were extravagant public works — aimed more at being captured in a picture that could be played on the front pages of Mexico City newspapers than at addressing the needs of the Indians. Just three months before the Zapatista uprising, for instance, Salinas himself had flown to the village of Guadalupe Tepeyac in the very heart of the Lacandon jungle to dedicate what is probably the world's biggest — and perhaps most useless — jungle hospital. The $5.5 million hospital was gigantic in comparison to the four hundred wooden shacks scattered over two hills near the border with Guatemala that made up the village. It consisted of a 10,000-square-foot ultramodern building, with another 5,000-square-foot area for manicured gardens and a paved parking lot for visitors.

Meanwhile, the village didn't have a single paved road, much less cars to use on one. The air-conditioned hospital had a state-of-the-art surgery room, X-ray facilities with a darkroom for film development, and a reading room for its ninety-two-person staff. The outside walls were painted in an elegant beige with huge red, white, and green Solidarity signs. But soon after Salinas descended on the hospital in a helicopter and had his picture taken cutting the ribbon of the giant facility, many physicians had left the place. They were mostly interns from Mexico City who had found excuses to return to the city.

By the time I visited it, the Guadalupe Tepeyac hospital was chronically empty, largely because of the small population in the area. Far from a sign of government concern for their needs, the magnificent jungle hospital had been received by the increasingly militant Indians of Guadalupe Tepeyac as a reminder that the Zapatista guerrilla leaders and Bishop Ruiz had been right all along: There was little that could be expected from the central government.

▼

Among the government public works I found most intriguing were the basketball courts for the Indians. You could see them from any road: In every Indian village, next to the wooden shacks surrounded by pigs and stray dogs, you could see a regulation-size concrete basketball court.

With 3,700 basketball courts across the state and 12,000 basketball teams — most of them made up of Indians and organized by government or religious workers — Chiapas had been turned into Mexico's most basketball-intensive state. Why was the government encouraging five-foot-three-inch-tall Indians to play basketball with professional-size ten-foot basket rims? Was it some kind of sadistic joke? Why wasn't the government encouraging Indians to play soccer, which was the most popular sport elsewhere in Mexico anyway, was much more attuned to the Indians' physique, and did not require building costly concrete courts?

It turned out that General Absalón Castellanos, a Chiapas governor in the 1980s, was a big basketball fan. Accordingly, he had included among the key elements of the federal government–sponsored 1982–1988 "Chiapas Plan" construction of a basketball court in every Indian community. The general had decided that Indians needed sports, among other things, to help them stay away from drinking, although skeptics would later speculate that he had built the courts to use as landing platforms for military helicopters, as they would be used during the Zapatista insurrection. The fact was, however, that Mayans found themselves almost overnight with brand-new basketball courts in the center of their villages, and with legions of government social workers encouraging them to make use of them.

I stopped on the road one morning to watch one of these games. It was a peculiar scene. Many of the Indian youths were barefoot, and could only reach the basket rim towering above them by throwing up grandma shots, heaving the ball with both hands from below their waists. Some players made amazingly good outside shots, but what they played looked more like a three-point tournament than a basketball game. They must have ended the day with stiff necks from keeping their eyes on the sky-high basketball hoops.

Gonzalo Ituarte, the militant Roman Catholic vicar of San Cristóbal de las Casas, was not amused when I told him of my amazement at the proliferation of basketball in Chiapas's Indian communities. To him, the basketball courts were a symbol of the government's insensitivity to the Indians' needs. "They made these beautiful courts so that our undernourished Indians could play basketball after working fourteen hours a day," he told me sarcastically. "Meanwhile, they don't have drinking water, electricity, or sewage systems."

▼

But the most extraordinary public works project in San Cristóbal de las Casas was not a waterworks, a new power plant, or even a water treatment facility. It was a giant $11 million world-class opera house, busily under construction at the time the Zapatistas launched their armed rebellion.

As I arrived in San Cristóbal a day after the Zapatista uprising, I was stunned to see hundreds of helmeted construction workers putting the finishing touches on the new theater complex not far from where the fighting was taking place. They seemed totally oblivious to the guerrilla war that was drawing world attention. Their mission was to finish the building — by far the tallest in the city — in time for its scheduled dedication a few weeks later, and they had no time for distractions, political or otherwise.

A huge sign in front of the building proclaimed: Theater of the City: For the well-being of the people of Chiapas. The thousand-seat state-of-the-art theater and opera complex was to serve a city and several surrounding Indian towns that together had fewer than a hundred thousand residents, most of whom couldn't even afford a pair of shoes to enter a theater. As if its builders had wanted to emphasize the contrast between the rich and poor in Chiapas, the new theater was being built right next to a run-down government building where hundreds of homeless Indians from the nearby town of San Juan Chamula had taken refuge.

They had been recently expelled from their town in a religious dispute, mainly because they had embraced evangelical religions and given up alcohol — a decision that was hurting the pockets of the PRI-affiliated Indian chieftains who controlled the alcohol business. They were sleeping on the floor, cooking on improvised wood ovens in a crammed patio, and killing time idly watching the progress of the giant construction project next door. Two young Indian children — one a year old, the other a few days old — had just died at the refugee center: A doctor had certified they had died of cold, for lack of proper housing facilities.

The state government seemed more worried about completing the theater on schedule, so it could be dedicated in March for the annual Fair of San Cristóbal, a tourist attraction that had been peddled in promotional brochures for months. Authorities had spared no resources for the new theater: It had a sunken pit for a hundred-member symphony orchestra, a separate rehearsal hall, an elaborately landscaped parking lot for 250 cars, doors and window frames made out of the finest mahogany, and the latest in lighting and sound systems. Although the construction firm, ICA — headed by Gilberto Borja, one of the president's closest friends — had recommended installation of air ventilation rather than an air-conditioning system in the theater because of San Cristóbal's cold weather, the government had overruled it.

"They ordered us to put in a full-fledged air-conditioning system," a young Mexico City–born ICA engineer at the project site told me, shaking his head disgustedly. "We told them it wasn't necessary, because the weather is always cool here at night, but they wouldn't listen."

What the heck. It would only cost a few million more. What was worse, the young engineer told me, was that the new theater had been built on a swamp. Its foundations had required several thick layers of concrete that had significantly elevated construction costs.

As the young engineer walked me through the giant new theater, it was clear that he was feeling a mixture of professional pride at the quality of the project and embarrassment for what he clearly saw as a costly government extravaganza in one of the world's poorest corners. Toward the end of our tour, almost as a side comment, he mentioned that the new theater would not be San Cristóbal's first, nor its only one. The city was simultaneously remodeling its old colonial theater at a cost of several million dollars. San Cristóbal would soon have two state-of-the-art theaters. As we parted ways, I couldn't help speculating that considering the few hundred San Cristóbal residents who could probably afford a theater ticket, the city would soon be able to present itself as a cultural center ahead of Paris or New York in the number of seats per capita for potential theatergoers. The young engineer nodded, raising his eyebrows with a sad smile.*

▼

What could you do? Chiapas residents would ask me with a shrug. Who were you going to complain to about a governor selling his land to build a fog-covered airport, a police chief repressing gays, or the state building a world-class theater in one of the world's most hunger-stricken places?

Salinas had won with 90 percent of the vote in Chiapas in the 1988 election, a figure that revealed more about the PRI's electoral shenanigans in that remote spot than about its popular support. In the 1991 legislative elections, some districts in Chiapas reported official results that could have been included in the *Guinness Book of Records* if anybody had believed in their fairness: In La Trinitaria, for instance, the PRI scored 18,114 votes, the opposition, 0. The new governor who had succeeded Patrocinio was from the PRI. The city mayor was from the PRI. The PRI ruled all but one of the 110 Chiapas municipalities and controlled the state congress at will. All judges were from the PRI, and so were the police and military authorities. There was nothing anybody could do. That's the way things were.

Chiapas was the epitome of everything that was wrong with Mexico. It was the most corrupt, authoritarian, backward area of a country that was being hailed abroad for its dramatic steps toward modernization.

The Zapatistas wanted to correct the unfair treatment Chiapas was

* The San Cristóbal theater opened its doors to the public June 24, 1994. Its first show was a comedy named *Adorable Enemies*. Its first classical music season began a year later.

getting from the country's capital, just as they wanted to correct the unfair treatment they felt Mexico was getting from the world's financial centers. As Subcommander Marcos put it when asked about his ideology, "There is a law in guerrilla warfare according to which a guerrilla column can only move as fast as its slowest man. Well, the same should be true of this country. How fast should this country's economy move? As fast as its poorest state."

Subcommander Marcos was questioning the very premise of Salinas's economic modernization program — that Mexico had to join the big leagues of international trade to strengthen its economy and thus be able to build a better future for its people. His armed challenge to trickle-down economics touched a chord in Mexico. Mexicans began to ask themselves a new question: Was the Zapatista rebel uprising the last aftershock of Latin America's guerrilla wars, or the first revolution of the post–Cold War era?

Would the Zapatistas go down in history as the rebels who changed the course of Mexico's economic reforms, or as a fleeting symptom of the country's growing pains on the road to modernization?

CHAPTER 4

Marcos

Several months after the uprising, when I set off to interview Subcommander Marcos in the guerrilla-held mountains of Chiapas, near the border with Guatemala, the mysterious rebel leader was at the peak of his political prominence. His Zapatista rebellion had managed to expose the shortcomings of Salinas's economic and political "miracle," shattering almost overnight the Mexican government's image at home and abroad. Suddenly, in the eyes of the world, Mexico had turned from a model of political stability and economic modernization into a nation of growing social tensions, on the verge of civil war. Screaming headlines talked about the sightings of guerrilla training camps in other states, the collapse of the stock market, a possible wave of capital flight, and other calamities that threatened to lead to a popular uprising or a military coup.

Only days after the January 7 car bomb in Mexico City, another three terrorist bombings were reported across the country, including one that rocked the government palace of Acapulco. Billionaire banker Alfredo Harp Helú, one of Mexico's richest men and a close friend of Salinas, was kidnapped March 14. His abductors' demands for $90 million sent shock waves through the business community, and sent the stock market tumbling.

Then, on March 23, Mexico was rocked by the news of the assassination of Colosio, Salinas's hand-picked presidential candidate, by a seemingly deranged gunman who shot him in the head during a campaign swing through Tijuana. While a man of the system, Colosio was seen by many as an open-minded politician. Less than three weeks before he was killed on March 6, Colosio had made a speech that had annoyed his party's old guard: He had criticized Mexico's "excessive concentration of power" in the hands of the president, and had promised a series of democratic changes "to end any vestige of authoritarianism."

Colosio's death shook the country like no other news in recent history. It was the first murder of a presidential candidate since a gunman had taken the life of General Alvaro Obregón in 1928, and it buried Mexico's pretension of being immune to the political violence that had long shaken Latin America. What was worse, the government-appointed special prosecutor would soon disclose that there had been a "concerted action" to carry out the murder, fueling speculation that the hit had been commissioned by powerful establishment figures. Based on videotapes and photos showing confessed killer Mario Aburto Martinez communicating with other men seconds before the murder, investigators detained seven suspects, including several retired members of the notoriously corrupt police services who had volunteered to help protect the candidate. Many newspaper columnists and radio commentators drew the conclusion that only top officials of the PRI, or of the government, could have had the money, connections, and motivation to eliminate Colosio. Had it been the PRI "dinosaurs" — members of the party's old guard who were resisting Colosio's proposed reforms?* Or had the orders come from members of Salinas's inner circle who had decided to remove Colosio from the presidential race?

A month later, on April 28, 1994, Tijuana police chief José Federico Benitez was killed in Tijuana, not far from where Colosio was slain. It was as if the Zapatista rebellion had unearthed a multitude of long-repressed political tensions. Mexico was bordering on chaos.

---

* Weeks later, the same special prosecutor, Miguel Montes García, would release all the suspects except Aburto, citing lack of evidence against them. Then, on July 12, Montes García virtually closed the case, stating that a follow-up investigation had proven that Aburto had acted alone. Government critics charged that Salinas had ordered a *"carpetazo"* — a slamming of the folder — to cover up a war within the upper echelons of his regime.

▼

When I finally met Marcos in person at a prearranged site deep in the Lacandon jungle, the first thing that struck me was his physical appearance: He was much smaller than I had imagined. At five feet seven, he was a much less imposing figure than the larger-than-life black-robed guerrilla leader — a mixture of the Lone Ranger, Batman, and Darth Vader — who had appeared on the covers of international news-magazines, showing him at least a head taller than most of the Mayans surrounding him. Marcos had an incipient pot belly and delicate hands. The soft voice coming from the opening of his ski mask — big enough to reveal a grown black beard around his lips — made him look much younger than the forty years old he was believed to be.

Unlike Cuba's Castro, Marcos didn't talk or walk with the pomposity of someone constantly playing the role of a world figure. On the contrary, he was as casual as he could be. His charisma was that of an antihero: someone who seduced his audiences by combining the macho aura of a guerrilla leader with the self-deriding sense of humor of a sensitive male of the nineties.

He owed much of his popularity to his talent for making fun of the government and turning to his favor every accusation against him made from the presidential palace. When the government, partly in an effort to disqualify him as a legitimate leader of the Indians who made up the bulk of the EZLN's fighters, described him shortly after the eruption of the war in Chiapas as white-skinned, blond, green-eyed, and athletic, Marcos joked in a January 13, 1994, letter to Mexican newspapers that he feared such description would lead to the arrest of the handsome star of a popular soap opera, Corazón Salvaje.

A few days later, after a magnanimous-looking Salinas had appeared on national television to announce a change of heart and offer the Zapatista rebels a pardon if they laid down their weapons, Marcos responded with a January 18 letter that turned the issue upside down and left the government speechless. The rebel leader said it was the government that had to ask to be forgiven for five hundred years of neglect of Mexico's Indians, a charge that not even the most conservative members of the ruling elite could dismiss as preposterous. "What do we have to ask pardon for?" Marcos asked. "For having refused to starve to death? For not remaining silent in the face of our misery? . . . For having risen up in arms when all other roads were closed? . . . And who has to ask for pardon, and who has to grant it? Those who for years and years have sat in front of a table full of food?"

Like a judo fighter who used the energies of an enemy's attack to strike back at him, Marcos would time and again turn government blows into public relations wins. When the Salinas government called him a coward for wearing a ski mask and hiding his true identity, Marcos responded with a metaphor that touched a soft spot in most Mexicans: The whole country, he said, was hiding its national reality behind the mask of an Americanization process that gave it a false illusion of prosperity. "I propose the following," Marcos continued, responding to the government's challenge. "I'm ready to take off my mask if Mexican society takes off the mask that those with alien vocations have placed on it. . . . What would happen? The expectable: Mexico's civic society would discover . . . that the image of itself it has bought is false, and that reality is much more terrifying than it thought. We would both show one another our faces, but the difference will be that Subcommander Marcos has always known what his face really looks like, while society will only begin to wake up from its long and dozing 'modernity' dream."

It was a combination of bravado, chutzpah, and self-mockery that worked marvels, and that he used as a powerful weapon to seduce visiting journalists. After the first few minutes of conversation, I couldn't help enjoying the man's sense of humor.

▼

It was past ten P.M., and Marcos had invited me to sit on a fallen tree covered by dense jungle foliage, on the outskirts of Guadalupe Tepeyac. Marcos was puffing his pipe under his black wool ski mask, topped with an olive green cap with three stars. He had a pistol tucked in his belt and was wearing a black plastic Cassio watch on each wrist: The left one had what he referred to as "Zapatista time" — one hour ahead — while the one on his right arm had Mexico's real time. Conscious of the sensitivities about U.S. stereotypes of Mexicans or Indians, I decided against asking him if his troops were so unpunctual that they needed to function on a one-hour advance schedule. (In fact, he had earlier told me that the January 1 attack had been delayed for one hour because a key Zapatista column had not arrived in time at San Cristóbal de las Casas.) I contented myself with his poetic explanation that Mexico would achieve peace the day Mexican time caught up with Zapatista time.

Throughout our chat late into the night, Marcos kept emphasizing that the Zapatistas were a different kind of rebel army — the first one that was not seeking power, but only to press the government to make the necessary reforms to turn their country into a democracy. He maintained a prudent distance from the Cuban revolution — referring to its military leader as "Castro," rather than "Fidel," as was customary among Latin American leftists — and denied any links to what remained of the international left.

Okay, I said, that's what many rebel movements have said before taking power, only to remain for decades afterward. But what if, by some accident of history, he became Mexico's president? What could the leader of an Indian uprising do in an increasingly interdependent world, where — despite the Zapatistas' objections — free-market policies were becoming the worldwide norm?

Marcos looked at me wide-eyed, raising his eyebrows: "What? Me president of Mexico?" he asked, smiling at his own words. "You must be crazy! It would be a disaster. I'm a guerrilla leader, a poet, a dreamer. Can you imagine what would become of this country if I became president? It would go down the drain."

▼

Getting to see Marcos was a painful exercise in journalistic tenacity. You had to spend days driving through the jungle, leaving messages for the guerrilla leader at various rebel checkpoints, and packs of Marlboro cigarettes to ensure they would be passed on. It was a highly uncertain venture — and Marcos made sure to leave the impression that not every reporter would get an interview with him.

Some journalists had managed to see the Zapatista leader over the previous three months, but many more had returned to the Chiapas capital without success. It seemed to depend partly on the timing — more than twenty thousand army troops were surrounding the guerrilla-dominated territory, and the guerrillas seemed to interpret any seemingly hostile government declaration as a sign of an imminent attack that moved them to retreat deep into the jungle — and partly on Marcos's whim. Although he played the media masterfully, he did not necessarily grant interviews to prominent media at the expense of smaller ones. It was one of the many ways in which Marcos established that it was he — not the outside world — who was calling the shots.

Driving a double-traction Jeep I had rented at the Chiapas airport for the take-it-or-leave-it rate of $150 a day, I had made my first approach to Marcos at the town of San Miguel, a dirt-road village with no electricity or running water on the threshold of Zapatista-held territory. I had just passed the village when I ran into an improvised roadblock made of a tree held by two fork-shaped branches. A few seconds after I had stopped, four young peasants — clad in civilian clothes, three of them in worn-out Chicago Bulls T-shirts — popped up casually from the woods and walked toward my vehicle.

They had an air of curiosity about them, as if they were peasants who happened to be hanging around the place rather than Zapatista sentinels running a checkpoint. When I told them I wanted to see Marcos, they looked at me with blank eyes, as if not knowing what I was talking about. It was only after more than half an hour of insistence — and handing over several packs of Marlboros — that one of them agreed to relay my message. He took a handwritten note with my name to a nearby shack and radioed my request to the guerrilla leadership. When he came back, he carried an ironclad response: *"No hay paso."* ("There's no passage.") He repeated it several times in response to my pleas, as if it were a celestial mandate beyond any man's power of appeal. I should try again some other day, the leader of the Chicago Bulls squad said. Today, there was no passage.

It was only after several of these parleys, and after sending more than half a dozen messages to Marcos, that I got a positive answer from the subcommander. The message said he would see me three days later in Guadalupe Tepeyac, in the southernmost corner of Chiapas near the Guatemalan border. It was a small village of about forty shacks at the end of one of the world's most spectacular mountain roads. It was reminiscent of postcards of the Himalayas: From the winding jungle road high up in the mountains, you could look down to steep valleys crossed by a constantly moving sea of white clouds.

Even on that road deep in Zapatista territory, I would still run into several more checkpoints. They did not seem to correspond to a single, well-disciplined rebel command. The most memorable one was a giant fallen tree that blocked the narrow jungle road just a few miles before I got to Guadalupe Tepeyac. I had stopped my Jeep and was wondering how to remove the big tree when a teenager came running down from a hill. With a stern demeanor, he asked me where I was going. I identified myself as a journalist and proudly told him the subcommander had granted me an appointment. Maintaining his firmness, he demanded my identification. My heart was pounding. Had a counterorder arrived? Would the young man force me to turn back? The youth scribbled down my name, walked up the hill, and — much to my relief — came back to say he had received orders I could pass. By the way, was I carrying any cigarettes? And crackers? And any extra T-shirts, by any chance? I gave him everything he wanted, excited by having crossed what seemed to be the last hurdle in the excruciating march to see the subcommander. But an hour later, I hit another roadblock at the entrance of Guadalupe Tepeyac. A half dozen guerrillas came to check me out. When I protested that a colleague of theirs had already cleared me — and cleaned me out of several belongings — a few miles up the road, the rebel guards at the village entrance laughed. The kid was not a Zapatista, they told me. He was an *oportunista*.

▼

The Zapatista sentinels at the Guadalupe Tepeyac checkpoint escorted me down the village's main road to a brand-new house next to a giant concrete building. It was the guest house beside the town's towering hospital. That was where I was supposed to wait until somebody came to lead me to Marcos. I sat on the floor and began to wait. One hour, two hours, three hours. After four hours, I walked back to the checkpoint to ask — as politely as I could — how much longer I would have to wait. The answer was *"al rato,"* "anytime."

That measure of time ended up being twelve hours. To fight boredom, I asked my guards for permission to walk to a nearby shack where I was told one could buy a soda. Guadalupe Tepeyac, with its dirt roads and its huts built on two hills surrounded by mountains, had its charm. I counted three vehicles in the whole town — one pickup car and two old trucks, all of them parked — and more than a dozen tin roofs, a measure of prosperity in a region where most peasants couldn't afford more than adobe ceilings. It even had a movie theater, the soda vendor told me. When it dedicated the hospital, the government had extended a few electricity lines to the town's population. One of Guadalupe Tepeyac's coffee growers had immediately purchased a VCR, and periodically traveled to the nearby city of Las Margaritas to purchase secondhand tapes. His home had become the town's movie theater: There were shows every night, for the equivalent of about fifty cents.

The night had already fallen on the jungle, and I had lay down to sleep on the floor, when I felt somebody shaking my shoulder. It was a female Zapatista soldier, with her face covered by a hood and a rifle strung across her back. The subcommander was waiting for me, she said. I had been lucky, she commented as we were walking away: Most visitors had to wait four or five days before being received by the subcommander.

It was vintage Marcos: Like Fidel Castro, he had a habit of letting reporters and prominent visitors wait for days at a time as a way to soften them up. After days of driving over flooded jungle roads and another long wait once they had reached their meeting place, few visitors — no matter how high their frustration — decided to turn back. Even the most hard-nosed reporters were turned into lapdogs by the time a Zapatista soldier came for them at the hospital guest house to take them to the long-sought interview.

It was pitch dark in the jungle when we left the hospital's guest house. The rebel soldier asked me to board the back of a truck with an EZLN sign on each door and a powerful spotlight mounted on its roof. We drove for about ten minutes outside the town through a narrow path covered by palm trees when we ran into nearly two dozen heavily armed Zapatista guerrillas blocking the road, waiting for us.

They asked me to get down. They didn't look friendly. "Hands up!" one of them yelled at me from behind his black ski mask as soon as I hit the ground. I tried to smile, hoping to break the ice, but it didn't seem to help. The rebels, who judging from their short height were all Indians, pointed their AK-47s at me and subjected me to an unusually thorough body frisking. They checked my clothes, and asked me to empty every pocket and take my shoes off. One guard twisted my shoes several times back and forth. I first thought they were looking for a knife, but later learned they were looking for some sort of metal tracking device that could help tail the rebel leader.

They then asked me to take off my socks, demanding that I raise my hands while they were examining my bare feet. Did they fear an attempt on Marcos? Since I had already gone through several body checks, I could only conclude that the rebels were putting on a little show. They were eager to show foreign reporters that they were not an improvised guerrilla group, but a rebel army. They may have been instructed to act like a military force just to make their point.

▼

But the extraordinary security precautions surrounding Marcos revealed a much more significant aspect of the Zapatista movement. It demonstrated that, far from the loyal subcommander who reported to a committee of Indian leaders he claimed to be, Marcos was the Indians' undisputed supreme leader. Once in a Zapatista village, if you wanted to find any member of the allegedly ruling Clandestine Committee, you only had to ask and you would be pointed in the right direction. To talk to them, you just needed to walk over, tap their shoulders, and introduce yourself. They were walking around rebel towns without any escorts or other special security precautions. Marcos was a decidedly different story. He was guarded like a king.

Even the body language of the Indians guarding Marcos revealed their unswerving loyalty to the white, middle-class man they had adopted as their leader. The Zapatista column of five Indians that led me to Marcos along a short jungle path stopped its march, stood firm, and — judging from the wide eyes behind the ski masks — waited full of expectation once we arrived at the fallen tree covered by jungle vegetation where the subcommander was to meet me. One could only wonder what the Mayans saw in Marcos. Was he a new version of the Ah K'in, or master-saint sun, as the ancient Mayans had venerated some of the white Franciscan priests who had lived among them? Were they seeing in his all-black robes some of the Roman Catholic priests they had revered for centuries? Or had he simply touched a sympathetic chord by evoking the memory of Zapata, the legendary fighter whom most Indians associated with their age-old land claims? All of these thoughts were going through my mind when Marcos showed up, out of nowhere, a few seconds later. The Indians clicked their heels and looked up, waiting for his orders.

"*Hola, soy Marcos,*" the subcommander said casually, emerging from the jungle foliage. Puffing his pipe, he made a slight nod to the rebel officer in charge of the column. The guards relaxed and took up positions around us. Marcos, the genial host, motioned for me to sit on the fallen tree, which he obviously used as a visitors' sofa.

The rebel officer in charge of the column that had led me to Marcos stayed next to us throughout the interview. He was Major Moisés, and he was a virtual Marcos clone. A small man with a bowler hat atop his ski mask, he walked like Marcos and talked like Marcos. What's more, he was the only Mexican Indian I ever saw who smoked a pipe. He stood next to us, puffing his pipe and nodding approvingly at almost everything that came out of Marcos's mouth.

The subcommander was not only bigger than Moisés and the other rebel soldiers, but was also much better dressed. It was hard to keep one's clothes neat in the jungle, but Marcos looked impeccable in what must have been a Banana Republic multipocket vest and black slacks. I myself was a wreck: Exhausted from several days of driving in the jungle, drenched from the intermittent rain, and itching from a two-day-old beard, I could have easily passed for a rebel. Marcos, however, looked spotless. He wore two bandoliers of ammunition that criss-crossed his chest over his neatly ironed vest, and his black slacks looked as if they had just come out of the dry cleaner's. I couldn't help thinking that he must have had a small army of cleaning ladies behind the trees, keeping his wardrobe ready for his next public appearance. Marcos was well taken care of.

He reminded me of Lawrence of Arabia, in that he was a well-read white intellectual leading a rebellion of mostly illiterate Indians with whom he had little in common, but whose blind trust he had won through a combination of courage and wits. He shared a common political purpose with his Indian troops, but it was clear to anybody spending some time in the Zapatista camp that he must have felt lonely among them.

He wrote poetry, quoted philosophers and writers, and was tremendously nostalgic for city life. When we talked about life in the jungle and about what he — as a city person — was missing the most from civilization, he did not pretend to have overcome the rigors of guerrilla life. On the contrary, speaking like an amateur camper rather than as a revolutionary leader in a clandestine interview, he volunteered his biggest weaknesses. "Chocolate," he said, his eyes lighting up. "That's the only thing you can't find in the jungle. When you can't buy a chocolate, you start remembering it, and it can become an obsession. It's something that can hit a city guy like me really hard. The other thing is light: In the jungle, you can't read after dark. You really miss an electric light to read at night."

Above all, he was desperately hungry for approval from Mexico City intellectuals. He had read almost every book by Mexican writers such as Carlos Fuentes, Carlos Monsivais, and Elena Poniatowska, and had written about them — and to them — since becoming an international celebrity. He sent them personal letters urging them to back the rebel movement or at least come to Chiapas to listen to their demands — an invitation he did not bother to extend to Mexico's politicians, whom he regarded with visible disdain.

"I must do everything possible to convince you that, in order to silence the guns, ideas must . . . speak louder than guns," Marcos wrote to Fuentes in a June 1994 letter dotted with quotes from Shakespeare's *Macbeth* in which he implored the writer to participate in a Zapatista-convened political conference. "I must convince you, also, that we do not want to be alone raising the flag; that we want others, better and wiser than us, to raise it with us." When writer Elena Poniatowska asked him why he was so eager for the intellectuals' support, Marcos said, "Because they are public opinion leaders." His rebellion was carried out by oppressed, malnourished Indians, but his audience — and some of his biggest fans — were in Mexico City.

In addition to poems, Marcos cranked out short stories, children's tales, and political essays about the latest events at a feverish pace. He sent them regularly to *La Jornada*, which tripled its circulation in early 1994 thanks to its newest correspondent.

"It's the kind of life I'm leading now that makes me want to write," he told another visitor, drawing a line on the dirt floor with his finger. "On one side is life and on the other is death. And since January 1, I'm right on the line. I can easily pass to the other side any day now. So I can't have any ambitions to write the great novel or to have some great career. . . . So I write as if every day were my last."

Marcos spent much of his day writing, trying to make the best use of sunlight, and received visitors late at night. Afterward, he would catch up with the latest world news, both political and artistic. "I listen to the Voice of America, the BBC, and Radio France International," he told me when I showed surprise at his detailed knowledge of the latest world events. "We can't tune in AM Mexican radio stations here in the jungle. But you get a lot of news from shortwave radio stations."

▼

Marcos conceded that he had come to Chiapas in the early 1980s as one of many leftist activists who wanted to spark an uprising in the most backward corner of the country. Unlike many other activists who helped organize labor unions or Indian rights groups, Marcos said he began organizing a rebel army from the very minute he arrived in Chiapas. He started out by creating a self-defense group to help Indian peasants protect themselves from the "White Guards" hired by wealthy Chiapas landowners to drive the Indians off the ranchers' lands, and who often harassed the Mayans. With time, the self-defense groups developed into the Zapatista army, he said.

"When we started, we did so as a small vanguard group, with the classic idea that with our example we would lead the rest," Marcos told me when I asked him how a white intellectual from the city had become a leader of the Mayans. "But when we started getting in touch with Indian collective societies, it was a shock. We ended up subordinating ourselves to them."

It hadn't taken the activists long to discover that the Indian peasants would not follow a group of city people. Among the Mayans, all decisions were made collectively, even the most innocuous ones. It had been like that for centuries, and it hadn't changed a bit. So Marcos soon began to submit every one of his plans to the Indians, and to accept their collective decisions.

"I have the honor of having as my superiors the best men and women of the Tzeltal, Tzotzil, Chol, Tojolabal, Mam, and Zoque tribes," Marcos had written shortly after the Zapatista uprising, when the media was pressing him to disclose his relationship with the Indians. "With them I have lived for more than ten years, and I am proud to obey them and serve them with my weapons and with my soul. They have taught me more than what they are now teaching the country and the whole world. They are my commanders, and I will follow them through the roads they choose. They make up the collective and democratic leadership of the Zapatista National Liberation Army."

But when I asked him to expand on his alleged submission to the collective leadership, it became clear that it lay somewhere between a formality and a sincere dialogue in which he — as the Zapatista leader who best knew the outside world — had the upper hand. "I was always the military chief, from the very start," Marcos told me. "I was also in charge of drafting the committee's written communiqués, although I was not supposed to show up on television or talk to the press. But on political issues, I have always reported to the committee. The main decisions are made by them. I only make the military decisions."

But if you were always the military chief and also wrote the Zapatista communiqués, what decisions were left for the Clandestine Committee? I asked. Could he cite any example of an instance when he was overruled by the committee?

It took several seconds for Marcos to come up with an example. He said the committee had ordered him to rewrite the Zapatista communiqué announcing they would free General Castellanos, the former Chiapas governor who had built the basketball courts, and whom the rebels had taken hostage at the start of the uprising. The committee had demanded that the statement be much harsher on the former governor, citing the many crimes he had committed during his term in office, he said. It was hardly a policy decision, or one that changed the thrust of the statement at all.

Noticing that I wasn't impressed by his example of the group of Indian leaders' alleged powers, Marcos said the Clandestine Committee had even seriously considered demanding that he take off his mask and reveal his identity. "In January, when the government began to refer to the Zapatistas as 'professionals of violence' and 'foreigners,' and it became clear that I was the 'foreigner professional of violence' it was talking about, the committee considered that perhaps it would be convenient for Marcos to reveal his identity and show that he was an average Mexican," he said.

But the fact was, the committee had in the end decided against the idea. Marcos had prevailed, and demonstrated once again that — perhaps unbeknownst to himself — he had become the Mayans' maximum leader. He almost conceded as much when I asked him how his relationship with the Indians had changed since the January 1 uprising. "They see me like they always have." Marcos shrugged, smiling. "They make fun of my ski mask. They crack jokes about it all the time: They say women in Mexico City say I'm handsome because they haven't seen me without my ski mask." Then, turning serious, he conceded that the Mayan guerrillas treated him with near veneration — the kind of respect only awarded to indisputable leaders. "When it comes to military affairs, I have taught most of them whatever they know," he explained matter-of-factly. "They came to the mountains after I did."

This was no ordinary subcommander. Rather, it was Supercommander Marcos.

▼

Marcos laughed when I began asking him about his past: One of his major public relations achievements had been keeping his identity a mystery, and making Mexico's intelligence agencies look foolish by not being able to solve it. He had given reporters erratic responses about his upbringing, telling some he had traveled extensively in South America and others that he had lived in the United States. He had even been quoted as saying he was gay and had worked at a gay restaurant in San Francisco. I asked him about the latest published reports, which had quoted him as saying he had spent time in Peru.

"You visited Peru, didn't you?"

"No, that was a lie. Look, what happens is that when a Chilean comes to see me, I tell him I visited Chile. When somebody comes from Los Angeles, I tell him I was in Los Angeles. When a Frenchman comes, I tell him I was in France. . . ."

"So you make things up, to drive the army intelligence crazy?"

"Sure. When people start asking personal questions, I ask them, Where are you from? Oh, from Veracruz? I was in Veracruz. You are from Monterrey? Ah, I've been in Monterrey. You are from San Francisco? I've been there; I've even worked at a gay bar there. Whatever they ask me, I've been there. . . ."

I had intended to ask him whether his name was one of about half a dozen that Interior Ministry intelligence officials were periodically leaking to the press, but I decided it would be of no use: He would have lied anyway. His standard response was that he had been born when he arrived in Chiapas ten years earlier, that his parents were the Indians who had accepted him as one of them, and that his real name was Marcos. He was Mexico's biggest mystery, and he wasn't about to give away his secrets.

▼

What did the Zapatistas really want? Why had they turned down February 1994 government offers of drastic increases in health and education funds for the Chiapas Indians? Weren't they fighting for better living conditions for the poor?

Marcos shook his head, frustrated at what he clearly saw as a foreigner's lack of understanding of the Indians' drama. When the Salinas government offered a massive package of public works and cash transfers to Chiapas following the February 1994 peace talks with the Zapatistas in San Cristóbal, the Zapatista Indian base communities had overwhelmingly turned down the offer. Only somebody who knew the history of the Chiapas Indians' relations with the government could understand why the Mayans had rejected the offer, he said.

"They saw it as another government ploy to build a few roads and schools, get the people to calm down, and go back to normal," he said. "They said that unless there is a profound change, these government offers will be useless."

The Indians had been cheated time and again, Marcos said, and there was little question that he was right on this one. He pointed his index finger in the direction of the Guadalupe Tepeyac hospital, at whose guest house I had been waiting earlier in the day. "Take the case of that hospital, the hospital there in Guadalupe Tepeyac," he said. "It was dedicated by Salinas last year. He arrived in a helicopter, with trucks full of equipment. They unloaded the trucks, dedicated the hospital, and left. Once Salinas left, they took the equipment away, and the doctors left. The hospital never worked as it should have.

"If we had agreed to the government offer, the same thing would have happened to the roads, schools, and bridges. They would allow the roads to deteriorate, they would have left us with schools without teachers. They would have given us all kinds of things to calm us down, but it wouldn't be of any use to us. We know that, because the government does that all the time, because it has already done it too many times to us."

But wasn't it unrealistic to ask that the government resign, as the Zapatistas were doing? After all, as we were talking, the guerrillas were surrounded by tens of thousands of federal troops.

It wasn't unrealistic, he responded emphatically. The Zapatistas had changed the course of Mexico January 1 by drawing national and world attention to the plight of Mexico's poor, and had set a new agenda for the country's politicians. The eleven points of their program — especially justice and democracy — had by now become the main issues of Mexico's political debate. In his view, the Zapatistas were winning the political war, which was the only one that counted. If the Mexican people supported the Zapatistas' demands, the government would not dare launch an all-out attack to kill them.

"Look, we think we have succeeded in getting the country to take off its ski mask and show itself as it is. The Salinas group had tried to present to the world the image of a stable and prosperous Mexico. It had also tried to convince Mexicans that we were doing well, on our road to the First World. But on January first, we brought the mask down and showed the country's real face to the world. People began to look at Chiapas, at Guerrero, at Oaxaca, and to realize that there is an underground Mexico, a basement of the country that was invisible in political, social, or economic terms, but that existed all along."

Marcos was convinced — and had convinced his troops — that there could be no improvement in the living conditions of Mexico's forgotten ones as long as the PRI remained in power. Mexico was ruled by a political dynasty glued together by family and business ties that would never relinquish power voluntarily. Through the PRI, it would continue rigging elections indefinitely. He talked about the close ties between the PRI and more than two dozen Mexican billionaires who had been listed in *Forbes* magazine among the world's richest people, and of the fabulous contributions these business tycoons were making to the ruling party candidates. He virtually ruled out the possibility that Ernesto Zedillo, the PRI presidential candidate picked in the aftermath of Colosio's assassination, would meet his campaign promise of re-forming the system from within.

"Zedillo is backed by the hard-line of the party, which is gaining ground," he said. "Zedillo arrived at his candidacy without a political personality and was given one by the hard-liners. They created his per-sonality of toughness and intolerance. We think that's not the real Zedillo, but that he is being controlled by the hard-liners. Behind him we see, among others, [billionaire Agriculture minister] Carlos Hank Gonzalez and his group."

▼

When Marcos talked about ridding Mexico of the "PRI dictatorship," he was not just talking about the party leadership. He was referring to a political dynasty that had ruled Mexico for the past six decades.

His vision of Mexico's ruling elite was not exaggerated. In fact, the PRI was only an electoral machine used by a well-entrenched ruling class. Rather than a classic party with a defined ideology, it was closer to a political tribe that clung together to defend its interests. The PRI was only the visible face of Mexico's political aristocracy. In sharp contrast with the former Soviet Union or other strong-party systems, the PRI's Central Committee was little more than a facade and had virtually no power. Rather, the party was run by a maximum leader — the Mexican president — and an inner circle of about twenty favorite sons who in many cases did not even come from the higher echelons of the party. In most cases they were the maximum chief's political disciples, who had joined the ruling elite as sons or followers of other top members of the tribe.

Marcos and other government critics were quite serious when they said Mexico was run by a "revolutionary family" that had held power since the days of the revolution. A close look at the men — there were relatively few women — who occupied the top positions in Mexico's last three administrations showed that most of them had a distinct po-litical pedigree. It was as if members of the tribe's inner circle passed on their positions from generation to generation.

Salinas's predecessor President Miguel de la Madrid's cabinet was a case study: His government secretary, Manuel Bartlett, was the son of a powerful Tabasco state governor; Secretary of Foreign Affairs

Bernardo Sepúlveda was the nephew of a prominent government adviser on international law and son of a physician to various presidents; Finance Secretary Jesús Silva Herzog was the son of one of Mexico's most respected intellectuals; Energy and Mining Secretary Alfredo del Mazo was the son of a former secretary of Water Management; and Planning Secretary Carlos Salinas de Gortari was the son of a former secretary of Industry and Commerce. The president himself was a distant relative of a family of governors and had been the protégé of his uncle, former Bank of Mexico director Ernesto Fernandez Hurtado.

Under Salinas, the tribal nature of Mexico's inner circle had changed very little. Government Minister Gonzalez Garrido, the former Chiapas governor who had built the new civilian airport wing in the state capital, was the son of a former minister of Labor and the nephew of a governor; Foreign Affairs minister and former Mexico City mayor Manuel Camacho Solis was the son-in-law of a Chiapas governor; Education Minister Manuel Bartlett was the son of a Tabasco state governor; Foreign Minister Manuel Tello was the son of a foreign minister and the brother of an ambassador; and Finance Minister Pedro Aspe was the grandson of an undersecretary of Finance.

The new generations of PRI politicians, mostly educated in the United States, were modern and cosmopolitan — but they were still scions of the tribe's caciques. Even Salinas's top rival in the 1988 elections, leftist PRI dissident Cuauhtémoc Cárdenas, was a prime example of the trend: He was the son of former president Lázaro Cárdenas.

If Mexico was being rocked by the murder of its leading presidential candidate, and there were suspicions that his murder had been ordered by fellow ruling party politicians, it was because the tribe was far from united. After more than six decades in power, the ruling elite was showing signs of growing internal tensions, primarily over business affairs. Foreign correspondents, under time and space limitations to explain the intricate nature of Mexico's politics, usually described the ruling party as a tribe divided in three: the "dinosaurs," or members of the party's old guard; the "babysaurs," who belonged to the new generations of PRI leaders who spoke a more modern language but generally adhered to their forerunners' policies; and the reformers. In fact, the way things functioned was more complex: Members of the ruling family were more often united by business ties and promises of mutual protection than by their ideological affinities.

Mexico's ruling class was divided into camarillas, or clans, which responded more than anything else to joint business interests or partnerships in corruption. These clans had often originated from ideological allegiances, but had over the years incorporated dinosaurs, babysaurs, and reformers alike in defense of their interests. And as the Mexican government's economic pie shrank with hundreds of privatizations in the early nineties, there was growing competition among the tribe's clans for dwindling resources. If PRI politicians were behind Colosio's murder, as some Mexican newspaper columnists were speculating, they were most likely members of an ideologically mixed camarilla that feared its business interests would be threatened by other camarillas likely to acquire power under Colosio's future government.

A second level of power, after the tension-ridden political class, was made up of a few hundred representatives of the financial world, industry, and perhaps the military, who did not formally belong to the PRI. Business leaders had long had easy access to the Mexican president and often influenced his decisions — but never with the peace of mind of being a formal part of the ruling elite, and always subject to the *jefe máximo*'s sudden changes of mind.

Ironically, the PRI bureaucracy — including the party leaders — appeared only in the third tier of the hierarchy of Mexico's power elite. Once the PRI's political machine accomplished its mission of putting its candidate in the presidential house, the party immediately became a docile tool of the maximum leader for the next six years.

In fact, virtually all Mexican presidents over the past four decades had picked their successors from their inner circle — which was most often made up of family friends or technocrats with no position of power within the party. Between 1928 and 1971, only 14 percent of the Mexican government's successive cabinet ministers had held top positions within the party. The ratio didn't change much afterward. President Salinas's top policy makers — his chief of staff, José María Cordoba, and Finance secretary, Jaime Serra Puche — had only joined the PRI four years and ten years respectively before their appointments to top government jobs. This curious relationship had led many historians to conclude that the PRI was not really a "ruling party." It didn't really rule the country — it was the president who ran the party and channeled government funds to it in order to keep the tribe's electoral machine well oiled for the next election.

So when the Zapatistas called for Salinas's resignation and a new transitional government to set new rules for the August 21, 1994, election, they were not just trying to oust a president whose free-market ideas they thought were hurting Mexico's poor. They wanted to end Mexico's quasi-imperial presidency, which ensured the system's continuity by bankrolling the PRI and appointing a successor at the end of each presidential term.

▼

Were the Indians ready to follow Marcos to their deaths? Many of them were. It wasn't just a matter of ideological commitment. Rather, it was because — as a result of their geographic isolation from the rest of Mexico, their proximity to Central American guerrilla groups, and their long exposure to El Salvador's rebel radio Farabundo Martí and Nicaragua's Radio Sandino — they had come to live in a political fantasy world.

I learned that from Major Rolando, a rebel Indian officer who was the commander of the Zapatista-run hamlet of La Garrucha, not far from the town of San Miguel on the threshold of Zapatista territory. Rolando must have been in his mid-twenties. Although he said he had only gone to school through third grade, he spoke fluent Spanish and was highly articulate when it came to discussing the Zapatistas' political goals. It was a few weeks before the August 21, 1994, presidential elections, and Rolando was enthusiastically explaining the rebels' decision to give civilian society a chance to repudiate the PRI regime in the polls.

"If there is fraud or if the people are not allowed to win the elections, there will be a massive uprising of civilian organizations throughout the country," he told me, seemingly convinced of what he was saying. "The Mexican people will take to the streets to get the bastards out."

The idea that the PRI could win without fraud did not even cross Rolando's mind. The Zapatista uprising had shaken Mexico like nothing before, he said. He knew it firsthand: Reporters from all over the world had descended on Zapatista territory to interview them. Foreign journalists had brought newspapers and magazines with Marcos on their front pages. Mexico and much of the world had woken up to the plight of the Mexican Indians, he said. Mexicans would change history by voting massively against the PRI in the upcoming elections, or by toppling the government if the voting was rigged.

Really? I voiced my skepticism. I told Rolando I had just spent three weeks in Mexico City, and there was only one thing people were talking about. It wasn't the plight of Mexican Indians, but the World Cup soccer tournament that had just finished in the United States. It wasn't only the official media: The whole country was in a state of euphoria over the Mexican team's better-than-usual performance. More than a million people had taken to the streets in the capital to celebrate the national team's passage to a new round of the competition. Tens of thousands of people had painted their faces with Mexico's national flag and roamed Mexico City's main avenues waving flags and chanting hurrahs for their team. There was little else people on the street were talking about.

Rolando looked at me, somewhat surprised. "Well, we don't know much about that here because we live pretty isolated from the rest of the world." He shrugged. "We don't have electricity in our villages, so we don't get to watch television. Newspaper vendors don't get to the jungle and even if they did, it wouldn't be of much use because most Indians are illiterate." Lifting his hand and pointing in the direction of the last village before Zapatista-run territory, Rolando said with a resigned smile, "My world ends in San Miguel. I can't see much farther than that."

Rolando did not make any connection between his conviction that Mexico was about to explode in a massive Zapatista uprising and his admitted news quarantine. While Marcos was up to date on the latest news — if only by listening to the Voice of America and the BBC — Rolando and his troops were relying for their information on Central American rebel radio stations, liberation theology priests, and what Marcos was telling them. Rolando didn't seem to mind having missed the World Cup: It was a trivial matter at a time when Mexico was witnessing a new Mexican revolution for peace and justice. You will see, he told me as we were about to leave, Mexicans will prove to care more about social justice than about soccer.

I asked him, almost in passing, whether he knew who had won the World Cup. Only a few days earlier, virtually all Mexico had come to a halt to watch the final game between Brazil and Germany, and to celebrate the Latin American team's victory.

Rolando took some seconds to think about it. "Germany?" he asked, looking at me for an answer. As I said good-bye to him, I couldn't help but fear for his life, and those of the teenage Indian soldiers at his side. Isolated from everything beyond the next town, they nonetheless seemed confident that the entire world would back them in their struggle against the oppressive PRI regime. Would their blind belief in the people's support for them hurl them into a suicidal attack on the Mexican Army, in hopes that others would follow them? Would hundreds of Indians die with toy guns in their hands, as some had done during the New Year's Day offensive?

Judging from Rolando's words, it seemed so. The Zapatista soldiers — most of them illiterate, desperate, and alone — were not aware of the sad reality that most Mexicans were unwilling to do anything for them. I couldn't help thinking that if the government really wanted the Zapatistas to lay down their weapons, it should bombard them with television sets and radios. As things stood now, the Indians' world, as Rolando had said, ended in San Miguel.

CHAPTER 5

The Banquet

Nothing made Zapatista leader Subcommander Marcos's claims that Mexico's political system was hopelessly corrupt more apparent than a private dinner party held at the home of former finance minister Don Antonio Ortiz Mena to raise funds for the ruling party's 1994 campaign. It was one of those high-level, top-secret meetings that seem to exist only in the minds of conspiracy theorists — but that turned out to be real.

The party, attended by President Salinas and Mexico's top billionaires, was supposed to have remained a confidential affair. It had taken place on a Tuesday evening about ten months before the Zapatista uprising, on February 23, 1993. It was 8:30 P.M., and one by one, the thirty wealthiest men in Mexico (there were no women in the group) began arriving in their limousines at the mansion of Ortiz Mena at Tres Picos Street Number 10, in Mexico City's exclusive Polanco neighborhood. Their invitations had asked them to attend "a small dinner party" — a code for no wives included and no word out to the media — with President Salinas.

The agenda of the secret meeting, as specified in the invitation letter, was to discuss a five-point program to help prop up the PRI for the 1994 elections. After more than six decades in power, the PRI had become rusty. It was in urgent need of updating its ideological platform and campaign strategies to confront a growing challenge from the left. Among the points to be discussed were rewriting the party's platform to reflect the new closeness with the United States and support for free-market policies, shoring up the party's grass roots support, and discussing the upcoming electoral campaign fund-raising drive. The key proposal to be discussed called for getting the PRI to raise its own funds instead of continuing to receive massive government financial aid. Mexico could no longer afford to be described by critics at home and abroad as a state party system. The time had come for the PRI to sever its financial ties with the government and help give Mexico a democratic image.

PRI president Genaro Borrego had organized the dinner with the help of two business leaders close to Salinas — banking tycoon Roberto Hernandez and construction magnate Gilberto Borja. Borrego and the two businessmen had met several times at the PRI headquarters and for breakfast at the University Club. They had planned everything to the last detail, from the list of the guests to the order of the speakers to the menu. Now, after weeks of preparations, their banquet was about to begin.

A uniformed watchman guided the guests, most of them overweight, folksy-looking men in their late fifties, to the elevator that took them to the second-floor dining area. It was a big room, decorated with sixteenth-century French furniture and original paintings by muralists Diego Rivera, David Alfaro Siqueiros, and José Clemente Orozco worth several million dollars. In the middle of the room was a U-shaped table, with the guests' place cards in alphabetical order. Facing the center of the table, between its two open wings, was a small table for three: Salinas, PRI president Borrego, and the host.

None of the visitors looked at the paintings: They had them by the dozens. Among the guests were television tycoon Don Emilio Azcarraga, known as El Tigre ("The Tiger"), described by *Forbes* magazine as the richest man in Latin America (the magazine estimated his net worth that year at $5.1 billion); telecommunications czar Don Carlos Slim (net worth: $3.7 billion); cement baron Lorenzo Zambrano (net worth: $2 billion); Bernardo Garza Sada (net worth: $2 billion); Jerónimo Arango (net worth: $1.1 billion); Angel Losada Gomez (net worth: $1.3 billion); Adrian Sada (net worth: $1 billion); and Carlos Hank Rohn, whose multimillion-dollar fortune was almost entirely in family-owned businesses and thus unaccountable. Mixed with the guests were party organizers Borja and Hernandez, who had — as an additional show of support for the party — provided the Paris-trained kitchen personnel of his Banamex bank to cater the event.

Last to join the party, at nine P.M. sharp, was President Salinas, according to several of the guests. Everybody applauded the minute he entered the room. After greeting most of those present with ear-to-ear grins and bear hugs, Salinas took his seat at the smaller table. Dinner was served. There was smoked salmon as an appetizer, followed by steak au poivre. The atmosphere was joyful. Word had gotten out that the business leaders would be asked to raise funds for the PRI, and the government leaders and the business tycoons were exchanging barbs about the project in front of an amused, good-spirited president.

"Well, how much are we supposed to collect?" Borrego was asked by one of the business leaders shortly after they had begun to eat.

"Mucho" ("a lot"), Borrego responded, smiling.

"But how much?" the business tycoon insisted.

"Muchísimo" ("a whole lot"), Borrego responded, drawing laughter from around the table.

Nearly an hour later, when everybody was having dessert — vanilla ice cream topped with melted chocolate — Ortiz Mena, the host, stood up. He hit his spoon several times against a wine glass and asked for silence. Ortiz Mena introduced the first speaker, Borrego, who quickly ran down the five-point party modernization program. The August 1994 presidential election was getting close, and the PRI faced a serious challenge from the left, the PRI president concluded. It was crucial that all the business tycoons around the table make major contributions to save the PRI — and the country, he said. Salinas, his eyes on the ceiling, nodded. Ortiz Mena followed suit, recounting the PRI's history and stressing the ruling party's role as a social glue that had prevented Mexico from exploding into chaos and bloodshed throughout the country's history. Salinas closed the presentation, saying he wholeheartedly supported the proposed reforms to re-energize the party.

Okay, the business leaders said, nodding to one another. There was general support for the idea of stopping the flow of money from the government to the PRI and getting the party to raise money from the private sector. But how much were the business leaders supposed to fork out? The conversation went back and forth. Officials at the head table at first avoided giving a figure, then suggested that the PRI needed a campaign chest of at least $500 million. Then, Salinas's friend Roberto Hernandez, the banker, threw out the figure that had been previously agreed upon between the three banquet organizers during their breakfast at the University Club.

"Mr. President, I commit myself to making my best effort to collect twenty-five million," Hernandez said.

There was an awkward silence in the room.

"Mexican pesos or dollars?" one of the billionaire guests asked.

"Dollars," responded Hernandez and Borrego, almost in chorus.

Twenty-five million dollars each?! There were hmms and ahhs around the table. Don Garza Sada, of Monterrey's Visa soft drinks empire, said he agreed — it was the business community's responsibility to support the party. Telecommunications magnate Slim, who had won the government bid to privatize the national telephone monopoly, supported the motion, adding only that he wished the funds had been collected privately, rather than at a dinner, because publicity over the banquet could "turn into a political scandal." In a country where half the population was living under the poverty line, there would be immediate questions as to how these magnates — many of whom had been middle-class businesspeople until the recent privatization of state companies — could each come up with $25 million in cash for the ruling party. Charges of massive corruption under the Salinas administration were bound to surface.

At that point, department store magnate Angel Losada took the opportunity to voice more personal concerns about the proposed contributions, witnesses say. Collecting $25 million was an exorbitant task for somebody like himself, he said. He was small compared to others at the table. He couldn't even dream of coming up with that kind of money for a political contribution. He had just formed a joint venture with U.S. investors. What would his American partners say if he pledged $25 million for the PRI?

Before other reluctant contributors could join Losada in voicing their opposition to the enormous sum that was being requested, television baron Emilio Azcarraga stood up, full of enthusiasm, to make his pledge. The minute he rose from his chair, the room went silent. Azcarraga was the biggest among the big — not only financially but physically. An imposing man of six feet two inches, he commanded instant attention — and some fear — wherever he went. He could be brutal with his aides and would often publicly embarrass almost anybody but the president. He gave a vintage Azcarraga performance: loud, arrogant, and grandiose.

"I, and all of you, have earned so much money over the past six years that I think we have a big debt of gratitude to this government," Don Emilio said. "I'm ready to more than double what has been pledged so far, and I hope that most in this room will join me. We owe it to the president, and to the country."

Everybody raised his eyebrows. Azcarraga was talking of pledging more than $50 million. President Salinas, smiling broadly, applauded. Others followed suit. A few did their best to smile, still dumbfounded. Don Carlos Slim, trying to break the ice, said he would be delighted to give as much as Azcarraga — if he had his money. The room broke into laughter as many wondered aloud whether Slim wasn't conveniently playing down his fortune. The men around the table began to tease one another about who was in a position to give more and who was making more money at the expense of whom. But whatever protests had been uttered about the size of the pledges were clearly obscured by generalized acceptance. Ortiz Mena and Salinas looked pleased.

By midnight, when the president left, Mexico's wealthiest businessmen — had committed themselves to contributing an average of $25 million apiece to the ruling party, for a total of about $750 million. The men swore themselves to secrecy, slapped each other on the back, exchanged the last jokes of the evening, and walked out to their limousines.

▼

The PRI needed the money badly, and not just because it wanted to avoid an embarrassment during the electoral race over the massive financial help it had long received from the government. After decades of functioning like a de facto government agency that got its money directly from the Finance ministry, the PRI was discovering that the flow of government funds was running dry. A few months earlier, Finance Secretary Pedro Aspe had sent a memo to party president Borrego informing him that the central government would no longer finance the party's needs.

The memo didn't put a complete stop to the flow of government aid to the PRI. But Borrego was under growing pressure to find new sources to cover an estimated $1 billion in government funds that was wire-transferred every year to the party headquarters, most often disguised in the government's budgets as disbursements for public works. In the past, the PRI president had only needed to ask for the money to get it. And if for some reason or other the transfer was delayed, there was always the national lottery. "The national lottery is the party's petty cash," a top PRI official familiar with the party's finances explained to me matter-of-factly. "Whenever we need a few million from one day to another, there's where we get it from."

Aspe, a conservative economist with top connections in the world financial community, had explained his memo to Borrego as part of the government's overall policy of reducing public expenses. Just as the government was privatizing state enterprises and reducing subsidies across the board, it needed to make drastic cuts in its financial support to the PRI. The party needed to generate its own resources. Borrego, a reform-minded economist, supported the idea — even though it would make his life as party president more difficult, according to participants in the talks. He was sensitive to criticism from Mexico's opposition that the country would not be democratic until the ruling party became independent of the government and allowed a fair competition among all parties. Like many young party leaders, Borrego believed that Salinas's bold economic reforms had to go hand in hand with political reforms to turn Mexico into a truly modern democracy.

Borrego had heard that the PRI's local chapter in Mexico state had created a blind trust to which the state's most powerful businessmen had contributed enormous sums, making it virtually independent from government resources. After discussions with Salinas and separate meetings with Hernandez and Borja, he had instructed an aide to mail the invitations for the banquet. There was no time to waste. The finance secretary was threatening to shut off the flow of funds, and the August elections were nearing. What none of the fund-raiser's organizers suspected at the time was that it would become a major political scandal.

The banquet at Don Ortiz Mena's residence created a public uproar over the months that followed, when details of the meeting began to make their way to the press, not the least because the pledges made that night were a mind-boggling sum by international standards. How could these billionaires pledge so much so fast? Mexicans from all walks of life would ask themselves. What kind of favors would these chosen few get in return for their political contributions? The billionaires' pledges were a startling symptom of the massive corruption in Mexico's official circles — a world where publicly disclosed funds amounted to a small fraction of the fabulous sums that were moved under the table.

Mexico's gross domestic product barely reached 5 percent of the U.S. economy and amounted to that of the state of Ohio, yet Ortiz Mena's guests had pledged more than five times what the Democratic Party had spent in the 1992 U.S. presidential elections. Compared with the largest single contribution to the Democratic Party that year — $398,876 from the United Steel Workers of America — Azcarraga's single offer to donate $50 million was gargantuan.

But, more importantly, the pledges were obscene in light of Mexico's generalized poverty and of the rapidly growing gap between the rich and the poor. Under Salinas, the concentration of economic power had reached record highs, and little effort had been made to increase the new billionaires' contributions to society through increased taxes or charity ventures. The privatization of hundreds of state enterprises — and their purchase by a select group of presidential friends — had led to the creation of giant business empires and to an increasingly skewed distribution of wealth.

By the early nineties, the wealthiest 20 percent of the population was receiving 54 percent of the country's income, while the bottom 20 percent was getting only 5 percent of it, according to the government's Institute of Statistics, Geography and Information (INEGI). Fewer Mexicans were having more; growing numbers were having less; and it looked as if the country's business tycoons were spending much more in political contributions to preserve their influence with the ruling party than to help alleviate ever-growing poverty rates.

▼

The "Mexico twelve," as the best-known billionaires became quickly known in Mexico's political and business circles, had mostly benefited from Salinas's radical measures to get Mexico out of its $96 billion foreign debt crisis. Building on a timid economic opening begun by his predecessor Miguel de la Madrid, Salinas in early 1990 signed a much-heralded debt pact with creditor banks to ease Mexico's debt payments over a thirty-year period. But it soon became clear to him that the agreement — which became known as the Brady plan, for U.S. Secretary of the Treasury Nicholas Brady — would only make a small dent in the $10 billion Mexico was paying its foreign creditors annually.

Bolder moves were needed to stop the financial hemorrhage and lure capital back to Mexico. It was a time of a world economic slowdown. International investors, fascinated with the collapse of the Soviet bloc, were fantasizing about fabulous business opportunities in Eastern Europe. Salinas had discovered with shock during a visit to Davos, Switzerland, to address the World Economic Forum, that his announcements of drastic free-market reforms were generating little interest: His presentation had drawn a small audience compared to the enthusiastic crowd that Russians and Poles had attracted. European investors were too busy studying the new markets of the former Soviet bloc to spend time looking into faraway Mexico.

"It's becoming clear that our future lies closer to home," Salinas told his aides with resignation on the plane back. Mexico could only emerge from its hopeless foreign debt quagmire if it took drastic free-market steps to draw the attention of the world's financial community — especially that of the United States.

Salinas would soon make his mark by announcing the privatization of Mexico's eighteen commercial banks, which had been expropriated in 1982 by President José López Portillo. He also announced the privatization of Telmex, Mexico's giant telephone monopoly, and dozens of other state companies, while stating Mexico's intentions to sign a free-trade treaty with the United States that would among other things bind future Mexican governments to the new free-market policies. Salinas's economic revolution had an immediate psychological and economic impact: Slowly at first, faster later, massive capital inflows began to return to the country. Mexico would take in nearly $20 billion over the next three years through the sale of more than three hundred government companies to the private sector.

Salinas's reversal of the nationalization of the banking industry a decade earlier marked the end of a policy that had severed the bond between the PRI and Mexico's business class. But Salinas did much more than mend a strained relationship. He extended such an array of privileges to a small group of businesspeople — many of them close to him — that he elevated them into a power clique married through a commonality of business and ideological principles to the new leadership of the PRI.

In his bid to increase capital inflows, Salinas had put state banks on the block at three times their book value and often more. Contrary to the criticism of leftist politicians and popular belief in Mexico, the state enterprises were not sold at bargain prices. But in exchange for high prices, Salinas offered their buyers sweet regulatory deals and longterm promises of fabulous riches through NAFTA, which would soon allow some of the new private owners to sell their monopolies to multinational corporations at record profits. More importantly, in the short run, he offered them a new climate of government–big business cooperation that, in its best form, translated into new opportunities for the private sector in an environment of growing deregulation, and, at its worst, a series of behind-the-scenes government favors that would guarantee the profitability of the new owners' investments.

Through a policy of "directed" deregulation or selective liberalization, Salinas paved the way for the formation of more than a dozen monopolies that would control industries such as copper mining and telecommunications. They were meant to be strong enough to compete with U.S. firms in a free-trade environment, and perhaps even become the first Mexican multinationals to make it big in the U.S. market.

To the United States and the rest of the world, Salinas sold his privatization program as the biggest turnaround in economic policy since the 1910–1917 Mexican Revolution. What he didn't say is that to get

Mexican entrepreneurs to buy government companies at several times their book value, he had to offer them generous rewards under the table. Shortly after the government's Telmex telephone monopoly was sold to Slim, the son of a Lebanese merchant who had made a fortune in real estate and the cigarette business, Salinas authorized spectacular tariff increases without demanding corresponding improvements in the telephone service. In 1991, Telmex was allowed to increase telephone rates by 247.4 percent, while wages that year were allowed to rise by 18 percent. When the announcement of the telephone rate hikes triggered massive protests, the company withdrew its announcement and agreed in a compromise to raise rates by a mere 170 percent. "With wage increases of 18 percent and telephone rate increases of 170 percent, you don't need to be a financial genius to make it in the business world," wrote political scientist Lorenzo Meyer at the time. "And since the telephone service in Mexico is a monopoly, there is no free competition to benefit the consumer."

What's more, the government assured several of the new business barons a longterm monopoly over their respective industries and overt or disguised government protection well into the NAFTA era. Under the free-trade agreement that went into effect January 1, 1994, key Mexican industries — mainly those of the Mexico Twelve — were assured government protection for up to fifteen years. Television baron Azcarraga's Televisa network, which had more than 90 percent of Mexico's viewing audience and acted as a virtual mouthpiece for the PRI, was protected from foreign competition for twelve years. Telecommunications czar Slim was assured protection against foreign competitors for ten years under the NAFTA deal. Banamex banking tycoon Roberto Hernandez, the Salinas friend who had catered the PRI fundraiser at Ortiz Mena's home, was protected from foreign competition for the next fifteen years.

Of course, the whole point of NAFTA was to prevent protectionism, but the government–big business alliance in Mexico would take advantage of the years before the full effects of the treaty kicked in. The selected tycoons were given a head start in the new game of free trade — not an unreasonable principle in a deal between very unequal partners. But their considerable privileges would allow them to position themselves so strongly in the Mexican market that no foreign competitor was likely to make a dent in their businesses before they were forced to compete openly with U.S. and Canadian firms at the beginning of the next century. Free trade had created its own brand of protectionism, and the Mexico Twelve were to be its main beneficiaries.

Mexico in the early nineties was similar to American capitalism in the late 1870s. Azcarraga, Slim, and Hernandez were not much different from railroad and steel magnate Andrew Carnegie or oil trader John D. Rockefeller. Like the American "Robber Barons" of their time, the Mexico Twelve were making a fortune from their close partnership with the government. And, to their immense relief, Mexico was not contemplating anything like the 1890 Sherman Anti-Trust Act, which had broken up U.S. monopolies through forced sell-offs.

"They discovered how convenient it was for them to use the government's power in favor of their enterprises, and to thus accumulate fabulous fortunes," Meyer said of the Mexican billionaires of the nineties. "Government leaders walk around arm in arm with them, for the benefit of both of them, and for the detriment of society."

▼

The business tycoons who attended Don Antonio's banquet were far from strangers to one another. They all belonged to a small, secretive organization called the Council of Mexican Businessmen (Consejo Mexicano de Hombres de Negocios, CMHN). It was a private group made up of Mexico's thirty-six wealthiest industrialists that met with the Mexican president and his top ministers several times a year to discuss the issues of the day.

The council had been created in 1962 in an effort to fight Mexican president Adolfo López Mateos's increasingly antibusiness policies and the socialist rhetoric that shrouded them. After the president had stepped up distribution of land to peasants and refused to join other Latin American governments in breaking ties with Cuba's new revolutionary government, the council made its political debut by placing an ad in the newspapers under the headline "Which way are we going, Mr. President?" It turned out to be amazingly effective in scaring the government into toning down its populist rhetoric, not the least to stop a growing wave of capital flight that had been — perhaps unwittingly — encouraged by the ad. Since then, the council had met with every Mexican president and had had a growing behind-the-scenes influence over state affairs.

Under Salinas, it had reached the peak of its clout. It had advised the president at every step of his tortuous struggle to push NAFTA down the throats of skeptics on both sides of the U.S.-Mexico border, while assuring that its members' business conglomerates would not be affected by the proposed free-trade environment.

The council, which had never had a headquarters and met mostly at the home of the daily *Novedades* publisher, Rómulo O'Farril, was now moving into its first formal headquarters — its political weight had become too obvious to continue exercising it from the shadows. But the council's membership — a virtual carbon copy of the list of guests at Don Antonio's fund-raiser — had fresh memories of the 1982 nationalization of Mexico's banking system and other impetuous presidential measures against the business class. It was eager to transform its variable influence into more permanent and structured political clout.

▼

Don Gilberto Borja, sixty-four, was the prototype of the Mexican business tycoons whose companies had long lived from sweetheart contracts with the government. A tall, silver-haired, and aristocratic-looking man, Borja presided over Mexico's biggest construction and engineering firm, the 30,000-employee ICA Group, which among hundreds of other public projects had built the $11 million opera house in San Cristóbal de las Casas. The firm's board of directors and advisers read like a who's who of Salinas's closest friends in the business world: ICA's two main outside advisers were Telmex chief Carlos Slim and banker Roberto Hernandez.

Under Salinas, ICA had helped build, among other projects, the Highway of the Sun between Mexico and Acapulco (a megaproject that according to some was the costliest in the world per mile), another highway linking Mexico City to Guadalajara, several legs of the Mexico City subway system, and a huge pipeline system for the national oil monopoly, Pemex, serving the city of Guadalajara. By 1994, ICA officials said theirs was Latin America's largest construction firm, with public works in Colombia, Turkey, the Philippines, China, and the United States, where it was building, among other things, the City of Miami metro stations.

Several months after he had helped organize the secret fund-raiser at Ortiz Mena's house, Borja had adopted a more public political position as head of the PRI's Células Empresariales, or "business committees." In his new capacity as special adviser to candidate Ernesto Zedillo on business matters, Borja was leading a nationwide drive to get owners of small and medium-sized businesses to become active PRI contributors. Borja said he had come up with the idea of forming the committees as a way to gather the businesspeople's concerns and pass them on to the candidate. He had already chaired more than forty such meetings, many of them in a tent he had specially built for that purpose in the garden of his Mexico City home. In reality, it was a little-disguised fund-raising drive, whereby small groups of businesspeople were invited to offer their advice before being asked to make a pledge for the candidate.

"I think I'm putting about thirty hours a week for Zedillo, and about fifty hours for ICA," Borja told me with obvious pride during a May 17, 1994, campaign tour with Zedillo to Acapulco. "I travel about two days a week with Zedillo and hold the meetings at home in Mexico City on the other days. But I try to travel with Zedillo and hold the meetings after I leave the office at six P.M., when I can work it out."

"When you hold the meetings at your home, do you just talk about business problems? You don't discuss politics?" I asked.

"The main purpose is to listen to their concerns," Borja responded. "But I must say that at the end of each meeting, I make the concluding remarks. I have to confess that I make the personal reflection that Mexico's political system is being severely questioned, that we are in a time of growing political competition, that the people demand more democracy, that we have the duty to make a careful analysis on to whom we are going to give our vote. It's at this point when I express my personal support for Zedillo: I tell them that because of his capacity, because of his background, because of his moral standards, Zedillo is the person who must carry on this country's economic program."

"But isn't your whole involvement as a PRI liaison with the business community a huge conflict of interest?" I asked as politely as I could. "If Zedillo wins the election and ICA wins the bids on major roads and highways during his term, won't there be a generalized suspicion that his government would be returning your favors?"

Borja looked at me with amazement, cracking a forced smile. He shook his head, saying no. "Why?" he asked, as if he didn't understand what I was talking about. "I don't see it at all that way," he went on. "I don't mix the activities of ICA with those of Gilberto Borja. . . . I'm not doing it in my capacity as ICA president, I'm doing it as Gilberto Borja."

More than angry, Borja looked baffled by the question. In the world of Mexico's big business, where the government had long been the biggest client and political connections counted more than anything else, it hadn't even crossed his mind that his increasingly visible role in the ruling party could be seen as a source of favoritism. The ICA Group president was wearing his new title of official adviser to Zedillo on business matters as a feather in his cap. In fact, his business committees were largely created as a new way to come up with campaign funds for the PRI's presidential campaign following the scandal over the Ortiz Mena banquet.*

▼

Mexico's business tycoons had not always been that cozy with the ruling elite. At first, they had supported it reluctantly, as the best alternative against chaos. In the aftermath of the 1910–1917 Mexican Revolution, a web of regional peasant and middle-class revolts that were hardly coordinated and had left the country in a state of anarchy, a sizable part of the business sector had begun to view the victorious revolutionary government of Venustiano Carranza with a sense of relief. Even if he was establishing himself in a semidictatorial role and creating a personality cult, at least he was an antidote to the virtual anarchy left behind by the internal rivalries among the revolutionary

---

* Borja retired from ICA shortly after the August 21, 1994, elections. He was resurrected a few weeks later as a government official when Zedillo appointed him president of NAFIN, the government's huge financing bank.

caudillos. Carranza brought a semblance of stability to the country, and the business barons had blessed it accordingly.

As Mexico's Nobel Laureate Octavio Paz said, the Mexican Revolution became a "compromise between opposing forces: nationalism and imperialism, workers' rights and industrial development, state-managed economy and free market, democracy and state tutorship." Ironically, the new revolutionary state's main reason for being had soon become the maintenance of law and order. Its major accomplishment was of a negative nature: preventing the cycles of dictatorships and bloody revolts that had shaken Mexico throughout history.

To put an end to politicians' temptations of unlimited power, Mexico's post-revolutionary rulers created a system of elections every six years, with no reelection. The creation of the ruling party, in turn, offered a guarantee of peaceful continuity. The revolution became an institution — a revolving dictatorship that, while not providing an effective system of checks and balances, guaranteed peace and a predictable future.

▼

But how could Mexico's billionaire industrialists support a self-proclaimed revolutionary government that worshiped Zapata, a guerrilla leader who had done the same thing that Subcommander Marcos was doing now? Even if they couldn't afford to break their ties with the ruling party in a country where politics and business were so intertwined, how could they support a regime that glorified the 1910–1917 Mexican Revolution as the century's first social uprising and to this day was one of the most ardent — and last — allies of the Castro regime in Cuba?

The answer was that Mexico's business class had never taken the revolutionary credo too seriously. They knew better. Much of the government's cult of the Mexican Revolution was aimed at making Mexico's leftists feel better — despite being systematically ignored in almost anything that counted — about their country's ideological stands.

In Mexico's official culture, the Mexican Revolution was everywhere. Mexico City's main avenues bore names such as Revolución, Héroes de la Revolución, and Obrero Mundial ("International Worker"). There were monuments to revolutionary heroes everywhere, and portraits of Zapata — looking at the camera with an air of amused defiance, his right hand holding his rifle, his left hand resting on his spade, and bullet-filled *cananas* crossing his chest — in almost every government office. Elementary school textbooks extolled the glories of virtually all revolutionary heroes — winners and losers alike — and built much of Mexico's modern history around the U.S. military interventions that had resulted in the annexation of Texas and California in the 1830s and 1840s, respectively. While American schoolbooks gave only perfunctory treatment to what some of them referred to as "the Texas incident," generations of Mexican students had grown up with maps on their school walls showing Texas and California in different colors and with the legend "Territories usurped from Mexico by the United States" — as if to remind them that the wounds opened by that war had not healed.

Mexico's official rhetoric had long been aimed at building mental defenses against the ever-threatening Colossus of the North. A reform of the Constitution's Article Number 3 shortly before the presidency of Lázaro Cárdenas had mandated that "the education imparted by the state shall be socialist." Even long after that principle was abrogated in the late forties, official school textbooks in the fifties and sixties — by which many of Mexico's current political leaders were formed — dedicated half a page to Buddha, one page to Jesus Christ, three pages to Mao Tse-tung, about the same space to Cuba's Castro, and ten pages to the Russian Revolution.

Mexico's official cult of nationalism was best symbolized by the government-commissioned murals of Diego Rivera, David Alfaro Siqueiros, and José Clemente Orozco glorifying Mexico's pre-Hispanic past and questioning the Spanish conquest and the capitalist and imperial powers that had tried to enslave the Mexican people since. Even Mexican presidents who had turned their backs on the nationalist and statist policies the revolution was supposed to have stood for felt compelled to state in their speeches that they were acting to uphold Mexico's national sovereignty and the spirit of the Mexican Revolution. Mexico's business elite had come to accept nationalism and a portion of leftist rhetoric as the state religion, whose rites you had to follow even if you did not believe in its contents, or knew they were based on myths.

Most of us who covered Mexico's politics as foreign correspondents, like our Mexican counterparts, had long fallen into what may have been an ideological trap: looking at Mexican politics as a struggle among the forces that were trying to resurrect a supposedly unfulfilled Mexican Revolution and the "reformers" — U.S.-trained technocrats such as Salinas and Zedillo — who were trying to propel the country into the global economy. In fact, this was only partly true. It was a vision of Mexico that had long been encouraged by the ruling elite to present itself to foreigners as the last line of defense against an allegedly barbarian leftist-nationalist Mexico that was lurking behind the surface. Private opinion polls in the hands of Mexico's business tycoons showed they needed not lose sleep: The country was much less nationalistic and revolutionary than outsiders were led to believe.*

▼

In fact, surveys showed that by the early nineties Mexicans were less nationalistic than Americans. In a poll asking Mexicans whether they considered themselves "very proud" of being Mexicans, only 56 percent of those questioned had responded affirmatively. By comparison, 75 percent of Americans had declared themselves "very proud" of being Americans.

Other polls asking Mexicans about the United States had shown amazingly positive reactions for a country whose history had been built around fear and suspicion of its northern neighbor. In a 1991 poll commissioned by the respected magazine *Este País* on Mexicans' attitudes toward the United States, Mexicans were asked if they would be for or against forming one single country with the United States if that would result in an improvement in their living standards. To the pollsters' amazement, 59 percent of those questioned responded positively.

Years later, Market & Opinion Research International (MORI), the firm that had conducted the poll for *Este País* and had also worked for center-left presidential candidate Cárdenas, asked in a confidential poll of 1,450 people who was to blame for the December 20, 1994, devalu-

---

* When asked about their political leanings in a 1991 poll, 18 percent of Mexicans who responded said "right" or "center-right," whearas only 12 percent responded "left" or "center-left." Source: *Los Valores de los Mexicanos*, volume 2, by Enrique Alduncin, Fomento Cultural Banamex, Mexico, 1991.

ation that had rocked Mexico's economy. An overwhelming 48 percent of those questioned said "the government," while 18 percent blamed Zapatista Subcommander Marcos, 7 percent "foreign investors," and only 5 percent "the United States."

Another survey sponsored by the Banamex Bank Foundation had shown that poor Mexicans were as sympathetic to America as wealthy ones. Asked, "Which country would you like Mexico to be like?" Mexicans polled ranked the United States first after "none." Twenty percent of those who named another country picked the United States, and they were evenly divided among working-class and wealthy Mexicans. "I used to think that only upper-class Mexicans had favorable views of the United States, but I was wrong," MORI director Miguel Basañez told me as he was showing me the figures at his office. "The polls show that there is support for America among the rich and the poor, while there is apprehension in the middle class, especially among people who come from the public education system's universities."

The rich were pro-American because they skied in Aspen and had their summerhouses in San Diego. The poor, because they spent years working as farmhands in the United States — or had close relatives who did — and, despite being chased as illegal aliens and discriminated against, came back home with surprisingly good memories — and dollars — from their years in America.

So what about Mexico's historic anti-American feelings, that hidden repository of resentment that was said to be part of the national character?

"It's a myth," Basañez said. "The idea of a fervent nationalism and anti-Americanism has been exploited by the Mexican government to enhance its negotiating position with the United States. It has been a weapon used by Mexican governments time and again, but is not supported by the facts."

▼

There was even a serious question as to whether the Mexican Revolution had been — as the government's school textbooks suggested — a Zapata-led uprising by landless peasants that amounted to the century's first popular rebellion, preceding by seven years the Russian Revolution. Most of Mexico's most prominent historians agreed that the official story of the Mexican Revolution was one-sided and probably wrong.

In fact, the Mexican Revolution had been a chaotic struggle among various armies that had been ultimately won by the more conservative armies of northern Mexico, led by Carranza and Alvaro Obregón. At the very least, as writer Carlos Fuentes has noted, there hadn't been one Mexican Revolution, but at least two: one led by professionals, intellectuals, ranchers, and merchants from an emerging middle class who were seeking a modern Mexico ruled by a strong central power, and a peasant revolution led by guerrilla leaders Emiliano Zapata and Pancho Villa, who had fought for land rights, social justice, and local governments. After years of battles, what we know today as the Mexican Revolution was won by Carranza and his armies of the north, a force supported by a coalition of business and professional sectors that soon made it among its first priorities to quell Villa and Zapata's peasant movements.

The final battle between the two Mexican revolutions had taken place in 1915, when Carranza's commander, Alvaro Obregón — who would later become president himself — defeated Villa's forces at the battle of Celaya. Four years later, the northern forces would end the last vestiges of the peasant revolution when Zapata was killed by a government officer disguised as a renegade. On April 10, 1919, Zapata had gone to a ranch in Chinameca to meet Colonel Jesús Guajardo, an officer who had allegedly defected from Carranza's army. When Zapata made his entrance to the ranch at two P.M. that afternoon, Guajardo's guards presented arms to the guerrilla leader. At that point, at the sound of a trumpet, the guards aimed at Zapata, who was only thirty-nine, and shot him to death. It turned out that Guajardo had never really defected, and been promised a handsome reward for the killing. He was soon promoted to general and given a fifty-thousand-peso reward by the government. The ploy, according to some historians, prompted General Obregón's famous dictum — which would be repeated for generations — that no Mexican general can resist a cannonade of fifty thousand pesos.

Yet it was Zapata who was turned by future Mexican governments into the hero of the Mexican Revolution. Eager to appease the peasants who had supported the popular guerrilla, the winning forces wrote many of Zapata's demands into the new constitution and erected monuments to the fallen rebel across the country. Since then, the cult had taken a life of its own. Even U.S.-educated Mexican presidents such as Salinas and Zedillo had given the name Emiliano — Zapata's first name — to one of their sons. Visitors to the presidential house couldn't help but notice the images the two presidents and their predecessors chose to decorate their offices: They didn't have portraits of Carranza or Obregón, but of the cocky-looking Zapata. For many decades, successive Mexican governments had adopted a rewritten history of the Mexican Revolution that made Zapata and Villa — the rebel leaders who had not only lost in the battlefield but were killed in the process — look as if they had been part of the winning team.

Mexico's business elite had long accepted the image of a rebellious Mexico as a useful tool for Mexican leaders in their relations with the United States: By feeding the illusion of a victorious peasant revolution, Mexican presidents had conveyed the idea to their friends in Washington, D.C., that they were the best U.S. allies they could possibly find, and that they were the only ones standing between a modernizing, pro-American Mexico and an insurgent Mexico lurching dangerously in the backdrop of the country's psyche. In fact, as the opinion polls showed, it was the government's version of Mexico's history that — more than any inborn Mexican feeling — was keeping old wounds open.

▼

One of the classic examples of Mexico's government-promoted myths was the story of the "Niños Héroes," or "heroic children." From their very first year of elementary school, Mexicans learned the story of the children who had wrapped themselves in the Mexican flag and thrown themselves to their deaths during the 1847 U.S. attack on the castle of Chapultepec in Mexico City. The heroic children had committed suicide rather than turning themselves in to the invading U.S. forces. The story was repeated year after year and was the focus of endless speeches by Mexican presidents.

Yet I couldn't find one single historian — left or right on the political spectrum — who would tell me that story was true. In fact, there was unanimity among historians that the "heroic children" — however courageous they were — were not children, but young soldiers of the military academy, and that they had not committed mass suicide but had died in combat or been taken prisoner by the American invaders.

Yet no Mexican government had dared to correct the historical mistake in the country's history books: A timid attempt to refer to the "Niños Héroes" in school textbooks as "cadets of the military academy" during the Salinas years — while Zedillo was minister of Education — was quickly abandoned after a deluge of protests from old-guard members of the ruling party, leftist intellectuals, teachers' unions, and army officials.

"It's a cohesive myth," I was told by Alfonso Zárate, a respected political analyst and historian who was among the intellectuals battling against the textbook reforms. "The story may not be true, but all countries have their cohesive myths. And those that have been as battered as ours need them more than anyone."

▼

While blown out of proportion by the government propaganda machine, Mexico's quasi-socialist mythology could not be entirely dismissed by the super-rich. Mexicans were by nature contradiction-prone people — the product of Indian and Spanish ancestors, squeezed between the United States and Latin America — who could always resurrect a forgotten part of their character to suit the political needs of the moment. Just as the business tycoons had polls showing that Mexicans were more acquiescent than depicted in their monuments, most surveys also showed that there was another side to their character.

One U.S. marketing executive showed me a Coca-Cola company study that illustrated the point. The soft-drink giant had commissioned a survey in an effort to boost its Diet Coke sales in Mexico. While Coca-Cola's overall sales in Mexico were phenomenal — Mexicans are the world's top soft-drink consumers, downing an average of 306 eight-ounce bottles per person per year, in part because of the country's dry climate and limited supply of drinking water — very few Mexicans drank Diet Coke. The Atlanta-based company was puzzled: Diet Coke accounted for only 2 percent of its sales in Mexico, while it represented

30 percent of its sales in the United States. Why were Mexicans not drinking Diet Coke?

A comprehensive 1994 marketing study produced two conclusions: Mexican males perceived Diet Coke as a feminine product they would not drink in public, and — more interestingly — Mexican consumers in general were much more erratic than their U.S. counterparts when it came to loyalty to a particular soft drink. The study discovered that while U.S. consumers would steadily drink either Coke or Diet Coke, Mexicans would shift back and forth between the two products, often in the course of the same meal. The study branded a large number of Mexicans as "compensators," a category that was very small in the United States. Compensators overeat, repent, and try to undo the damage on the next day, only to revert to their old habits shortly thereafter.

"In the United States, you are either a Coke consumer or you are a Diet Coke consumer, but you really don't mix that much," said Alexandra Freeland, NutraSweet's marketing manager in Mexico, who helped coordinate the study for the Coca-Cola company. "Mexicans, on the other hand, will indulge one night, eating a lot and having fun, and then they will repent and drink Diet Coke on the next morning."

The Coca-Cola marketing study was focused on the soft-drink market, but it served as a metaphor for Mexico's political character. Mexicans were political compensators: They balanced their inborn conservatism with bouts of revolutionary zeal. Mexico's super-rich had to be on guard for such eventualities. They were making their presence felt in political circles — just in case.

▼

But the main reason for Mexico's billionaires' close ties to the government — despite their reservations about the state's revolutionary religion — was good business sense. Shortly after the revolution, the government had become the main source of business for Mexico's private companies. The same Mexican state that expropriated the petroleum industry created a network of private trucking firms to transport oil products, extended gasoline-station permits to private businessmen — most of them associated with the ruling party — and began to reward loyal supporters with government contracts for huge public works. It also began to give direct subsidies to thousands of companies that produced food and other basic products, and to protect virtually all industries against foreign competition. Behind its antibusiness revolutionary rhetoric, Mexico had created a wide business class of national industrialists whose fate was closely tied to the state's intervention in the economy.

Unlike many other Latin American countries, where the business elite put its friends in government and kicked its enemies out of it, Mexico's businessmen's political power had been much more limited in the early years of the revolution. Politics — not business — was the traditional way of reaching power and making money in Mexico. "Politics is the easiest and most profitable profession in Mexico," Jesús Silva Herzog, one of Mexico's foremost political analysts, had written in the 1940s.

And Mexican history was full of examples of businessmen making fortunes from their proximity to politicians without ever getting themselves involved in politics. The anecdote that best illustrated the business potential of closeness to power — no matter whether it was real or phony — told the story of when prerevolutionary dictator Porfirio Díaz was visited at his office by an old friend named Gonzalez, whom the president had not seen in years.

"What can I do for you? Ask whatever you want," the president is said to have told his friend.

"I don't want you to give me anything," Gonzalez responded. "The only thing I would ask is that every time you see me, you give me a big hug in front of everybody."

It wasn't until the early 1990s, amid the Salinas-sponsored sale of state corporations to the private sector, that businessmen found a formal place in the ruling party and a growing voice in national affairs. In its 1990 National Assembly, the PRI had added a new wing to its previous structure: In addition to the existing workers, peasant, military, and "people's" branches of the party, it created a "territorial" wing that would represent grass roots organizations throughout the country, including business groups. For the first time, business leaders could have a standing in the revolutionary party, even if it was without identifying themselves as such.

For the next few years, Mexico's business barons had lived a love affair with the ruling party, which culminated with the $25 million-a-plate fund-raiser at Ortiz Mena's residence.

▼

Yet everything that could go wrong with Don Antonio's private fund-raising dinner had gone wrong the morning after the party. As often happens, a trivial matter — the indigestion of one of the billionaires who had attended the banquet — allowed the affair to get out in the open and turn into a political scandal.

Luis Enrique Mercado, the publisher of the financial daily *El Economista* who broke the story, learned of the secret fund-raiser only hours later, on February 24, 1993, while attending a long-scheduled breakfast organized by a big-business lobbying group at Mexico City's Camino Real hotel. There were only four tables in the small conference room, enough to accommodate a select group of billionaires and a handful of outside guests like Mercado, who had been invited — perhaps in an oversight by the organizers — in his capacity as a successful businessman rather than as a journalist. Mercado took a seat next to Banco Atlantico chairman Alonso de Garay, one of the first to arrive at 8:30 A.M.

Mexico's wealthiest business tycoons began to show up shortly afterward. They looked uncharacteristically tired, many of them with red eyes. Cement czar Lorenzo Zambrano and Gigante-Kmart department-store tycoon Angel Losada took a seat at the table next to Mercado and began to exchange small talk with their neighbor. What a night! one of the business barons commented. He had arrived home near one A.M. One of the others cracked that he had gotten home earlier, but the pledge he had made had kept him awake all night. A third joked that for so many million dollars, Don Antonio could have offered a better steak — his stomach was still upset from something he had eaten at the dinner.

"I heard them talking, and didn't say a thing," Mercado remembers. "I was the only journalist there, but I had been invited as a businessperson. If I had asked anything, they would have made me promise that I would keep my mouth shut."

A day later, Mercado joined President Salinas for a three-day tour of the countryside. The president — a permanent campaigner — took about half a dozen personal guests, mostly journalists and businessmen, on each of his weekly trips to the interior. Mercado, whose trip had been scheduled several weeks earlier, had chosen to accompany the president to Guadalajara and Monterrey. He wanted to use the opportunity to touch base with the two cities' business elites, among the most prosperous of Mexico's business world.

As soon as the presidential party arrived in Guadalajara, Mercado jumped into the van of Raymundo Gomez Flores, the head of Guadalajara's giant DINA truck factory and the Banca Cremi banking emporium, who was at the airport to welcome the president.

"How was the dinner?" Mercado asked with a smile.

"Which dinner?" Gomez Flores asked, his eyes wide open, faking total surprise.

When the publisher responded with a knowing grin, Gomez Flores opened up. Figuring that Mercado had heard about the fund-raiser on the presidential plane from Salinas himself or his aides, the trucking magnate shook his head and began to comment about the dinner. The president himself had asked for $25 million from each of the guests, Mercado remembers him saying.

The story appeared on the front page of *El Economista* on Monday, March 1, under the byline of the newspaper's political reporter. The most explosive news — the fact that each guest had been asked to contribute $25 million was cited in the seventh paragraph — was well couched, but it only took hours for the story to become the talk of the town.

Leaders of the leftist Party of the Democratic Revolution (PRD) had a field day. The fund-raiser proved what they had long claimed: that Salinas was not propelling Mexico into a free-market democratic society, but into an oligarchic system wherein the party leaders and a few chosen business magnates were keeping a tight grip on power through a Mafia-style secret society. By then, the PRI could not deny the meeting. The story was out, and too many witnesses had already confirmed it.

"The whole thing had been well planned but badly handled," Borja told me later, talking about the dinner. "As all things that are not properly disclosed, it was perceived as a crime, as a Masonic affair, which it shouldn't have been. The goal was for the guests to seek twenty-five million each from their friends and associates. . . . The mistake was to shroud the whole thing in mystery. Today, the party is acting more frankly, more openly."

▼

After the scandal broke out, an embarrassed Salinas ordered PRI finance secretary Senator Miguel Alemán Velasco to shelve the billionaires' blind trust fund plan. Alemán, the son of former Mexican president Miguel Alemán and himself one of the country's wealthiest men, obeyed immediately. But when I visited him at his law offices and asked him about the affair, he insisted there was nothing wrong with the PRI's idea to solicit $25 million from each of the country's wealthiest industrialists. On the contrary, it was a sign of the party's determination to become independent of the government, he said. Wasn't everybody demanding that the PRI stop receiving government funds? Well, what were they complaining about now?

Alemán, a blue-eyed man with aristocratic manners, received me at his palatial Alemán and Alemán law offices on the most elegant leg of Mexico City's Reforma Avenue. He was one of the most visible members of Mexico's political aristocracy: In addition to being a senator and PRI finance secretary, he was a board member of Aeromexico, Grupo Industrial San Luis, Seguros América, Grupo Chihuahua, Grupo Novedades, Grupo Industrial Minera Mexico, Transportación Marítima Mexicana, Aluminio S.A., Almexa, and Diversified Metal International Corporation. Much of his fortune had been made by his father, who had presided over one of the most business-oriented — and corrupt, according to many historians — governments in recent history.

"Some people got scared the other day because somebody pledged twenty-five million at the fund-raising dinner. . . . I wish a lot more people would offer that," Alemán told me. "Sure enough, there was talk of contributing twenty-five, thirty, fifty, and even seventy million, because Mr. Azcarraga offered seventy million. But this wasn't the first nor the last time that we did it. We have already done eleven such dinners in the country and forty luncheons. . . . We need to collect a minimum of three hundred million, which is the minimum we will need for the 1994 congressional and presidential election."

It wasn't a big deal, Alemán said. The argument that the billionaires' pledges would give them extraordinary clout with the government was "absurd." First, money alone would not get votes, and the PRI would not have a greater debt toward its major contributors than to the mass organizations in charge of getting out the vote. Second, there were other interest groups that would provide as much or more than the businessmen. "Labor unions contribute more money, much more money. A well-organized labor union, such as the CTM or the CROC, can easily pledge a hundred million each, easily," he said. "And organized peasant groups can also offer lots of campaign funds."

▼

Ironically, what was intended to be an effort to make the PRI more independent from government resources had backfired and turned into a symbol of the Mafia-styled ways of Mexico's ruling elite. It didn't take long for the story to make the front pages of the *Washington Post*, the *New York Times*, the *Wall Street Journal*, and the *Miami Herald*, and for Ross Perot to use the banquet as new ammunition for his anti-NAFTA tirades. Three days after the scandal broke out, the PRI announced it would cancel the billionaires' contribution program and draft a bill setting strict campaign contribution limits of no more than $600,000 per person. Salinas, who had presided over the banquet, put out a statement erecting himself as an all-time champion of putting caps on political contributions. "On many occasions . . . have I noted that we need transparency in the process of fund-raising for the parties, as well as to guarantee a better access of them to the media, and to establish limits to campaign spending," Salinas said. "I commend the PRI's proposal to revise its fund-raising strategy, as the party has announced today. . . . Its campaign funds should come from society, represented by the diversity that the party seeks to represent, and not from any special [interest] group."

A few weeks later, PRI president Borrego and finance secretary Senator Alemán were ousted from their jobs. Much of the world interpreted Salinas's move as an effort to clean the party. In reality, the government move toward making the PRI more independent of the government — and more dependent on its friends in the business world — would continue, although less conspicuously. The fund-raising would continue openly through Borja's business committees, while big business would keep making its massive contributions under the table.

The government party's new fund-raising drive worked. Within months, the PRI had accumulated a $700 million campaign chest for the 1994 elections, more than twenty times the legal limit for campaign expenditures. The figure dwarfed the opposition parties' resources: The National Action Party only spent $5 million on the presidential race, and Cárdenas's Party of the Democratic Revolution said it had only come up with $3 million.

The PRI had more than enough money. Its problem — it would soon find out — was its candidate.

CHAPTER 6

The Accidental Candidate

Ernesto Zedillo could not hold back his tears. He was sad, frustrated, and angry. It was only a week after Colosio's murder, and he had been sitting behind a mock desk at the Qualli television studio for more than an hour under the heat of the spotlights, trying in vain to tape his first television advertising spot as the PRI's new presidential candidate.

Time and again, he had found himself raising his hands and asking for another take. He simply could not deliver his lines. His eyes were not conveying the self-assured look of a future head of state. The words he had memorized — a vow to fight street crime and improve Mexico's corrupt justice system — were delivered without conviction. He could not afford to come across as a poor speaker, reinforcing the criticism from his adversaries that he was a last-choice replacement candidate, a technocrat with no political talent.

His first photo session as a candidate a few days earlier had been a disaster. The photographer had tried to make him smile by cracking jokes — but to no avail. Heartbroken by the death of Colosio and overwhelmed by his new responsibilities as Mexico's most likely future president, Zedillo couldn't smile. The official campaign picture that had emerged from the photo session — the best they could come up with — had been awful. His smile looked forced, artificial, insincere, like that of a grim-faced man trying to show his canine teeth. Mexico City cartoonists had had a field day the following days portraying him as Dracula. It was a horrible picture and it was already hanging all over the city.

Now, at the television studio, Zedillo badly needed to redress the damage with a convincing television spot. It was programmed to be a straightforward ad featuring the new candidate's anticrime program. It was designed to introduce him as a man with his own agenda and dispel rumors that he was a lackluster nominee who would merely recite Colosio's campaign platform. Yet Zedillo couldn't bring himself to present a composed image before the cameras. He still had not been able to digest the recent events. He was in such a state of mental confusion that he couldn't look convincingly at the cameras. The harder he tried, the more frustrated he became. Furious at himself, he stood up and walked out of the studio without uttering a word. In a room down the hall, he embraced one of Colosio's top assistants, tears in his eyes. *"Pinche Donaldo, donde estás!"* ("Damn it, Donaldo, where are you!"), Zedillo was overheard saying. "Where are you when we need you the most!" Seconds later, the slain politician's aide was seen escorting Zedillo out of the building. The taping session was suspended.

The Zedillo campaign strategists met late into the night to devise a new television spot. They needed to put something on the air right away, but couldn't use any of the day's footage of the shell-shocked candidate. So they devised a series of four television ads relying on Zedillo's family album pictures and old press clips. The first one depicted the candidate's humble origins, showing pictures of his family in the northern city of Mexicali. Immediately, television viewers would see the back of a young boy running down a dirt road, selling newspapers. Through a computerized image effect, the boy — an actor — would turn around, and his face would be replaced with an elementary school picture of Zedillo. A second television spot a few days later, intended to stress Zedillo's government experience, was made up of old television footage of Zedillo's speeches as minister of Education.

Fortunately for the PRI campaign, the spots were so well made that nobody noticed that Zedillo was absent from them. But the people around him knew — and kept it a tight secret. Zedillo wasn't ready for the job. What's more, he was terrified.

▼

Zedillo was indeed an accidental candidate. Although he had been one of seven cabinet members and party leaders who had been thought to have a chance of being appointed by Salinas as the PRI nominee, he had never taken the possibility seriously. He was shooting for the year 2000.

While Colosio had been appointed to key political jobs by Salinas — he had been the president's campaign manager, a senator, and PRI president — Zedillo had never run for office or held any important political job. "I never thought I had a chance this time," Zedillo would concede later in a rare moment of candor.

Even in the days after Colosio's murder, Zedillo had not expected to replace the slain candidate, despite the fact that, as his campaign manager, he was certainly a top candidate for the job. At Colosio's funeral, Zedillo had remained sitting in a corner, head down, away from the clique of PRI governors and senators who were already discussing who would be the new party nominee. Two days later, Zedillo went to his campaign headquarters and — to everybody's surprise — began packing his belongings. With Colosio gone, he was convinced that his political career was over. The new party candidate would seek his own campaign manager, a man he could trust. "He started putting his stuff in boxes," recalls one of his closest aides. "He told me he would go into teaching, that there was nothing for him to do here anymore."

Zedillo was a follower, not a leader. Until Colosio's death, he had the reputation of a teacher's pet: a model student who had risen from a humble background to top cabinet jobs thanks to a combination of intelligence, hard work, and loyalty.

According to his official biography, he was the second of six children of an electrician and a medical school dropout, and grew up in the northern city of Mexicali, on the border with California. His family had moved there from Mexico City in search of a better future when he was only three years old, the official story went. They settled on a dirt road in the working-class neighborhood of Pueblo Nuevo, only a few yards away from the U.S. border. But Zedillo's father is said to have failed to find a steady job in their new home. His mother had to work as a secretary and supplement the family income selling candy at the Mexicali movie theater, while the older children shined shoes and sold newspapers on the streets. On the weekends, Ernesto picked up scrap metal in his neighborhood — beer cans, nails, any piece of metal he could find — and sold it to the local steel mill for ten pesos a sack, the official version went.

The official story may not have been a fairy tale. In fact, Zedillo's childhood may have been even tougher than stated in his biography. According to unconfirmed accounts of some former friends of the family in Mexicali, Ernesto and his older brother, Luis Eduardo, were not the biological children of Rodolfo Zedillo, but were the product of their mother's previous marriage to another man. Zedillo's mother, according to this story, was a fairly cultivated woman who had completed four years of medical school and fled Mexico City with her two young children after that relationship had gone sour. In Mexicali, she had married Rodolfo Zedillo, a soft-spoken electrical contractor who would later give his name to the boys.

"In elementary school, Ernesto and Luis Eduardo had another last name," one of their former classmates at the Teniente Andrés Arreola elementary school in Mexicali told me. "They changed it to Zedillo when they changed schools, in the second half of elementary school."

A top Zedillo aide rejected the story "categorically" when I asked him about it, hinting that such rumors may have arisen from the fact that the candidate's father was a distant parent who would occasionally leave the home for months at a time. But I was left wondering. There was a mysterious blank in Zedillo's official biography about the president's first and second elementary school years: It made no mention of the Teniente Andrés Arreola school, or any other institution he attended in his early childhood. The only known picture of Ernesto as a young child, released during his presidential campaign, showed him at age three, standing with his brother Luis Eduardo and their maternal uncle Guillermo Ponce de León at Mexico City's Zócalo Square.

The three are looking at the camera with a quasi-solemn expression, as if the children's outing with their uncle were a big social event. Uncle Guillermo is wearing a suit with a white handkerchief pouring out of his jacket pocket, resting his hands on the shoulders of the two boys clad in their Sunday attire. The picture was said to have been taken in 1954, presumably before the two boys moved to northern Mexico. Why hadn't the Zedillo campaign released a picture of the boys with their father? Perhaps, as the candidate's aide told me, because the poverty-stricken Zedillo family had no camera — and thus no photo album. But perhaps, as some former friends of the family in Mexicali speculated, it was because Zedillo — as a candidate who had stressed family values and campaigned on the slogan "Well-Being for Your Family" — may have rewritten the history of his first years to make it look more attuned to the image he was trying to project.

Whichever was the real story of his early childhood, there was little question that Zedillo was telling the truth when saying that he had grown up in a working-class environment. In sharp contrast with most children of Mexico's political families, who went only to elite private schools, Zedillo went to public schools throughout elementary and high school. "El Zedillo," as he was known by his high school classmates, was always among the best of his class. By the time he was in high school, his maternal grandmother had moved into the house, and she took care of the children while their mother was at work. "He was a little bit skinny, a little bit pallid, very tidy — always very serious for his age," recalled Rosalba Castro, who worked with Ernesto's mother and was one of her best friends in those days.

Socially, he was cordial but withdrawn. Most of his classmates remember him as somewhat of an outsider, perhaps in part because he was a kid from the capital in a place where the Chilangos, or Mexico City residents, were not especially liked. As in much of northern Mexico, the stereotype of the Chilangos in Mexicali was that of cocky newcomers who looked down on natives from the provinces. "In elementary school, we made fun of him because of the tone of his voice," recalled Fernando Prince, a former Zedillo classmate at the Leona Vicario elementary school. "He was a Chilango! He had a little accent!"

At age fourteen, Ernesto moved back to Mexico City to live with his elder brother, Luis Eduardo, and pursue his high school studies there, making the forty-eight-hour bus trip on his own. At first, the two boys stayed with their grandparents, then they moved to a small apartment where they lived by themselves. After graduating from high school, Zedillo went on to study economics at the state-run National Polytechnic Institute, a school that had been founded as a counterpart to humanist — and elitist — state universities. At age nineteen, he suffered a serious blow: His mother, whom he loved dearly, died of peritonitis when she was only thirty-eight.

Zedillo got his break in 1971, when — while still pursuing his college degree — he simultaneously joined the PRI and got a job at the government's Office of Economic Policy. The head of that office,

Leopoldo Solís, took him under his wing, and the young man soon became part of one of the many chains of loyalty within the ruling party. Thanks to his new protector and party connections, he would soon get government scholarships to study abroad, first at the University of Bradford in Great Britain, and later for his Ph.D. in economics at Yale University.

It was a Cinderella story that nevertheless left deep wounds in his character. A CIA psychological profile prepared in early 1995 concluded that the Mexican president harbored some "anger" and "resentment" against the privileged, according to U.S. officials familiar with the report. As a self-made man whose childhood had been marked by deprivation, he was quite likely to see the world as an unfriendly place. He did not feel he owed his success to anybody: He was distrustful of Mexico's political class, the privileged businessmen who had made billions thanks to their government contacts, and even had a distant — if friendly — relationship with most people who surrounded him. His emotional refuge was work — the all-out dedication bordering on compulsion that had made him succeed.

His staff viewed him as "cold, hard, rigid and humorless," and as a man who "considers preparation, discipline and punctuality non-negotiable," according to another report from the CIA's Leadership Analysis Section that circulated among U.S. diplomats in 1994 and early 1995. More concisely, some of his aides referred to him as "El nerd," the intelligence memorandum said.

▼

As a student at Yale, Zedillo was pretty much a bookworm. A lanky, serious young man with horn-rimmed glasses, he didn't smoke, didn't drink, and would only drop in briefly at parties. When I asked him about that, he said it was because he was one of the few Mexican students at Yale who was already married, and lived away from most of his classmates' dorms. He had married at age twenty-three, shortly before entering Yale, to Nilda Patricia Velasco, a former classmate at the National Polytechnic Institute.

"I led quite a monastic life," Zedillo told me, recalling his days at Yale. Unlike Colosio, another student from a working-class family who had obtained government scholarships to study in America, Zedillo didn't venture much off campus. His priority was completing his studies as fast as he could — and that didn't leave much time for anything else.

The difference between the two men's personalities was striking. When I once asked Colosio what had influenced him the most during his days as a graduate student at the University of Pennsylvania, he said it was Vietnam protests and the racial segregation he had seen in Philadelphia and other U.S. cities. When I asked Zedillo the same question a few months later, when he had replaced Colosio as the PRI's candidate, his instinctive response was to talk about Yale, as if he had never ventured away from the school's campus.

"The first year was very tough, because, as a result of the different kind of preparation I had received in Mexico, I was behind in mathematics, statistics, and economic theory," Zedillo said. "Also, it was tough because the very first semester we had a professor, William Brainard, who was an extraordinary teacher, but who spoke so fast that even my American classmates couldn't follow him. For me, it was a real predicament to follow him and take notes in his classes."

Back in Mexico, and with the help of his former boss, Zedillo joined the Banco de Mexico, the country's central bank, at age twenty-seven. He soon became an aide to Miguel Mancera, one of the bank's top economists, who would adopt the young economist as one of his protégés and place him in increasingly important government jobs in coming years. In 1983, Zedillo was appointed head of a government trust fund to help Mexican companies restructure their foreign debts, and in 1987 he was promoted to undersecretary of Programming and Budget. When Salinas took office in 1988, he appointed Zedillo as secretary of Programming and Budget and in 1992 as secretary of Education.

But throughout his career in Salinas's cabinet, Zedillo was best known as a Mancera protégé — one of several young technocrats from the Banco de Mexico who had impressive résumés but no political experience to speak of. Because of that, he was one of the few top cabinet ministers who was not considered a serious contender for the presidency. His political insignificance was such that Zedillo's name didn't even appear in the 1993 edition of the *Encyclopedia of Mexico*: It jumped from Zea to Zelis, skipping the then minister of Education and soon to become presidential candidate. When he was finally nominated to run for the government party, Zedillo's pollsters found themselves facing a shocking reality: Only about 10 percent of the Mexicans polled recognized him in name recognition surveys.

If Zedillo was known for anything within the ruling party, it was for his penny-pinching ways — both in his government jobs and in his personal life. Like most Mancera disciples, Zedillo was resented by the PRI's free-spending political class for his reputation as an inflexible budget-cutter, and as a man who prided himself on wearing unassuming plastic watches, driving inconspicuous cars, and leading an austere personal life.

Zedillo and Nilda Patricia, a stern-looking economist who had given up her career to raise their children, boasted about not having a live-in maid — a real eccentricity for a Mexican government official, much more so for one with a cabinet job. Nilda Patricia claimed that ever since they had returned from Yale and moved to a middle-class neighborhood in Mexico City, they had preferred not to have a strange person in their home. Even as a cabinet minister, Zedillo claimed he made his own bed, and that his wardrobe consisted of half a dozen suits, mostly gray and black, "one for each day of the week." At work, while other bureaucrats ordered espresso coffee or fresh orange juice from their office waiters, Zedillo would ask for *agua al tiempo* — water at room temperature. Zedillo was one of the most austere — and honest — PRI candidates for the presidency ever: Certainly none of them had reached that position with such modest economic assets.

But what Zedillo regarded as an exemplary way of life for a public servant, many fellow officials — long used to spending freely at the government's expense — saw as a symptom of stinginess. "The joke among us was if Zedillo invites you to lunch, make sure you take some money," a senior Mexican official told me, recalling Zedillo's days as a Salinas cabinet minister. "When it was time to pay the bill, it always turned out he had forgotten his wallet, had run out of cash, or came up with some other excuse."

▼

Hours after the Colosio assassination, as the country began to absorb the shock, word started to spread in Mexico's political circles that the tragedy could propel Zedillo into the PRI's candidacy. Under Mexico's

Constitution, no cabinet members, state governors, or other public officials could run for office for six months after they had left their last government jobs. The rule, aimed at ensuring that government officials would not use their offices to help their personal election drives, in effect prohibited Salinas from picking any of his top aides to replace Colosio.

Salinas could either postpone the election, and get Congress to change the Constitution so he could pick an experienced successor at the risk of unleashing an extended power struggle within the ruling party — a dangerous move at the time when Zapatista guerrillas and mysterious political assassins were trying to destabilize the country — or choose the party candidate from outside the government. If he went for the latter option, there was only a handful of people he could appoint. The two most obvious candidates were Zedillo, who had left the government several months earlier to become Colosio's campaign manager, and PRI president Fernando Ortiz Arana, a party bureaucrat with no international flair or economic experience. They weren't remotely the best-prepared men Salinas could think of to lead Mexico through the turbulent times the country found itself in. But he didn't have much of a choice.

Salinas needed to make a decision right away. The growing speculation of a political conspiracy behind Colosio's murder was threatening to cause the collapse of the stock market and a wave of capital flight by the time the banks opened for business after the Easter holidays. Political infighting within the ruling party was escalating dangerously. "Only a few hours had passed from the painful death of my dear friend Luis Donaldo Colosio when, amid the tragedy and the mounting economic uncertainty, a tremendous struggle for his succession broke out," Salinas recalled later. The pressures were coming from all sides. In the days that followed Colosio's murder, Salinas was working late one night at his office when former president Luis Echeverría arrived at the presidential mansion and requested a meeting with him. Echeverría, the old-guard party leader who had championed Third World causes during his 1970–1976 administration, "showed up unannounced, with great urgency, to propose 'his' candidate," Salinas recalled. Echeverría, like other party bosses who had mixed feelings about Mexico's economic opening, was pushing for somebody who would restore order and veer the country back to its hard-line nationalist course — perhaps somebody like Don Fernando Gutiérrez Barrios, a former Interior minister who had commanded Mexico's intelligence services for more than two decades.*

Salinas was not only pressed to pick his candidate before such lobbying efforts turned into open political warfare, but had to come up with a decorous way of presenting him to the world. To protect his own legitimacy, he had to maintain the fiction that PRI candidates were elected by the party's leadership, rather than handpicked by the outgoing president. As a self-proclaimed supporter of democratic reforms, he could not afford to be seen as perpetuating the monarchic traditions of Mexico's previous rulers.

Salinas gave the first clue about his choice shortly after Colosio's funeral, on Sunday, March 27, 1994, but Zedillo would not fully realize it at first. As usual within the ruling elite, Salinas's decision was not spelled out even to his closest aides — not the least in order to avoid leaks that would have once again exposed the undemocratic nature of Mexico's presidential successions. Mexico's political world was one of courtesies, symbols, and unspoken messages, where — in the absence of candid talk — political insiders had to read the president's mind from a telling smile or a casual remark.

It was Sunday morning, and Salinas had phoned Zedillo at his home with a seemingly routine assignment. There were reports of uneasiness in the military. The generals were concerned that Colosio's murder and rumors of a possible postponement of the elections would create further political instability. In his capacity as Colosio's campaign manager, Zedillo was to meet with the armed forces' high command that same afternoon and brief them about the constitutional provisions for the presidential candidate's succession, and was to reassure them that the president was determined to avoid a messy internal fight over the nomination.

Zedillo carried out his mission. It was somewhat ironic that he

* Salinas did not specify in his December 3, 1995, written statement to the media who Echeverría had proposed as a substitute candidate. The daily *Reforma* reported a day later that Echeverría's candidate was former Communications and Transportation minister Emilio Gamboa Patrón, while *La Jornada* said it was Gutiérrez Barrios.

would find himself briefing the military: Only a little more than a year earlier, when he was still Education minister, he had been at the center of a political scandal for having authorized new elementary school history books that had infuriated the military and the teachers' unions, among other powerful groups. The textbooks' section about the Niños Héroes and their suggestion that the armed forces were responsible for the 1968 massacre of students at Mexico City's Tlatelolco Square had created such an uproar among the military that Zedillo was forced to withdraw them from circulation.*

But that Sunday afternoon, the meeting with the military had gone reasonably well. In light of the country's dramatic situation in the aftermath of the Colosio murder, the history books affair seemed like a trivial matter.

The next morning, while discussing the situation at his home with Manlio Fabio Beltrones, a young governor of the northern state of Sonora who was credited with having one of the sharpest political noses among his peers, Zedillo began to see the Sunday meeting with the military in a different light.

"Don't you see? It's you! You are going to be the candidate!" Beltrones told him, opening his hands and smiling broadly.

Zedillo fixed his eyes on the governor. What made him so sure of that?

"It's crystal clear: If they sent you to talk to the military, it means something," Beltrones went on. "It's not for nothing that they would send Colosio's campaign manager rather than the PRI president to brief them."

Salinas had asked Zedillo to brief the military to test the generals' reaction, the governor said. The president would not risk asking the armed forces' high command whether Zedillo was an acceptable candidate to them — especially after the history textbooks affair. Things were never done that openly. Instead, Salinas would ask the generals after the meeting if they had been properly briefed, and if everything had been all right. He would take their positive answer, or their failure to

---

* The 6.8 million books, which had cost $4.05 million, ended up gathering dust in a government warehouse, according to *Proceso* magazine, April 4, 1994.

raise any objections about Zedillo, as an indication that they had not vetoed him.

Zedillo nodded. The governor's interpretation of the previous day's events was beginning to seem plausible, even persuasive.

Having received no complaints from the generals following their meeting with Zedillo, Salinas went to work on his next most difficult task: getting a reluctant PRI leadership to announce its wholehearted support for Zedillo. It was an open secret that the party bosses supported their president, Ortiz Arana, for the job — in part because he was their protector and in part because they were convinced that Mexico needed a leader with great political skills, rather than a technocrat, to solve a crisis that was of a clear political nature.

Fortunately for Salinas, the Sonora governor would come to his rescue with a brilliant idea. In an audience with Salinas at the presidential palace Monday afternoon, an enthusiastic Beltrones informed the president that he had found in his video library the film of the November 29 Colosio press conference in which the slain candidate had appointed Zedillo as his campaign manager. In it, Colosio had lavishly praised Zedillo as a "true patriot" and a "great Mexican."

Why not play the tape in front of the PRI leadership and have the late Colosio himself make the nomination? Who would dare go against the words of a martyr of the fatherland? By playing the tape, the president would avoid being accused of imposing Zedillo's nomination and of perpetuating the authoritarian succession practices that had earned Mexico the label of an inheritable monarchy. In fact, Salinas would never have to pronounce Zedillo's name. He would be able to tell the nation that it had emerged from the heart of the party.

The president smiled, lightening up perhaps for the first time since his friend's murder. "Very interesting . . ." he said, nodding slightly several times and then thanking the governor for his time. Beltrones knew what he had to do the next morning.

In conversations with several members of Salinas's inner circle before his meeting with the president that afternoon, Beltrones had become convinced that Zedillo would be the chosen one — and that his own political future would be tied to the new candidate. So the governor, sensing which way the wind was blowing, had decided to step ahead of the pack to support Zedillo's nomination. And in Mexico's quasi-oriental world of subtleties, Salinas's nod, or his failure to stop the governor upon hearing his plan, amounted to a clear sign of approval.

"Politics has its signs, messages, and tacit understandings," Beltrones told me several months later. "It was very obvious that the president, like many of us, thought Zedillo was the best man for the job."

▼

On Tuesday, March 29, 1994, at 7:45 A.M., barely six days after Colosio's assassination, twenty-seven state governors of the PRI arrived with an air of urgency at the presidential residence of Los Pinos. Most of them had been called by Beltrones's office Monday evening, and by the presidential office later that night. The meeting, they were told, was to discuss the party's new presidential nomination — a code word for getting a briefing on whom the president had chosen. The governors would then make their decision, so to speak, and their verdict would later be rubber-stamped by the PRI leadership. Much as the president was the party's de facto leader nationwide, the state governors were the de facto PRI bosses in their respective states. As such, they were the party's backbone and needed to be onboard.

The PRI governors and a handful of other party leaders were standing in the Miguel Alemán residential quarters of the presidential palace, forming a half circle around Salinas. Much like when the Vatican council gathered in secret to elect a new pope, an entire nation awaited the outcome of this meeting. Beltrones was the first to raise his hand. As governor of Colosio's home state of Sonora and as "a Mexican grieved by the murder," he wanted to make a proposal that would best represent the slain candidate's wishes, he said. He pulled a videotape out of a box he had been holding and passed it to the president. A poker-faced Salinas took the tape, placed it in a videocassette machine, and turned it on. The governors looked on in silence.

When the tape was over, and the president had pulled it from the video recorder, Beltrones raised his hand. "Our proposal has been made in the voice of Luis Donaldo," he told the audience. Salinas made a slight nod. To everybody in the room, it became apparent that Salinas was behind the motion. Beltrones would not risk committing political suicide by going out on a limb, they reasoned. He had to be acting on behalf of the president.

"Any other suggestion?" Salinas asked.

There was no response.

"Any other suggestion, gentlemen?" Salinas asked for the second time.

Fidel Velazquez, the ninety-three-year-old head of the PRI's labor wing and longtime symbol of the party's dinosaurs, for whom party discipline was the most sacred principle, said in his frail voice: "That, Mr. President, is our suggestion as well."

Case closed. The governors and other party leaders were immediately escorted to a bus waiting for them outside the presidential palace. They were kindly asked to turn in their cellular phones before boarding it as a measure to prevent leaks to the media and allow the party to control how the news would be delivered. The PRI leaders were deposited at the party headquarters, where Zedillo had been nervously waiting since early in the morning at his semi-abandoned campaign manager's office. In a matter of minutes, the party leaders drafted a short communiqué and announced on national television that the PRI had "unanimously and wholeheartedly" picked "our comrade and friend Ernesto Zedillo" as the party's new candidate.

For the next several days, Mexico's television stations would show a parade of seemingly ecstatic PRI and government officials hailing the nomination of Zedillo — whom each of them said had been his first choice all along. Salinas would categorically deny that he had influenced — much less proposed — his successor's candidacy. The PRI leadership had done it, in a truly democratic internal process, the government said. What's more, Salinas had never even pronounced Zedillo's name, party leaders told skeptical reporters. Technically, that was the case. But Mexico had picked a new leader in its old authoritarian way, only slightly camouflaged by the magic of video, a thirty-second sound bite that carried Mexico's future in it.

▼

Less than an hour after Zedillo's *destape*, or unveiling, the PRI's time-worn political machine was once again put to work. Hundreds of government workers were bused to the PRI's headquarters in downtown Mexico City to hail Zedillo's nomination.

As I walked among the chanting crowd on the patio of the PRI's magnificent central offices — the party occupied four big buildings — I was surprised to see various groups holding Zedillo banners. How could they have manufactured them so fast? Had they known something in advance? Looking closer, I noticed that *Zedillo* was the only freshly painted word on the banners. The signs, reading Zedillo for President and Long Live Zedillo, had obviously been written some time ago, leaving a blank space for whoever the party — actually, the president — picked. Judging from the mechanical chanting from those who had come to celebrate the nomination, it was obvious that it really didn't matter who the new candidate was. The only thing that counted was that he would lead the party from now on — and assure that it would continue rewarding its supporters' loyalty with government jobs, gifts, or secret subsidies.

Many in the crowd didn't even know who Zedillo was. One man holding a freshly painted Zedillo for President sign standing next to me under the scorching sun told me that if the party had chosen Zedillo, it was because he probably was the best man for the job. Party bureaucrats who had rooted for Ortiz Arana were standing by, clapping as enthusiastically as they could. One of them, a man who had told me several times in private conversations that he didn't think Zedillo was up to the job, whispered to me the latest joke making the rounds among the party's reformers: "In Mexico, we have a true power sharing system," he said. "The president has just shared with the rest of us that Zedillo will be our new candidate."

▼

That evening, Zedillo gave his emotional acceptance speech at the government party's headquarters. Clad in a black mourning suit, reading nervously from a typewritten text, the bespectacled economist did little to hide that he was unprepared for the job. He did not sound like a man accepting his party's nomination for president. He sounded like a man lost in grief. "This is not the beginning of a campaign, but the continuation of a campaign," Zedillo said, reading from his text. "I accept this nomination with the absolute certainty that the best man to lead the party to victory, and the country to its aspirations, has always been Luis Donaldo Colosio."

He mentioned Colosio's name an astounding thirty-eight times in his twenty-minute speech.

"At that moment, I was going through a very strange mixture of feelings," Zedillo told me months later. "I think the dominant ones were anger, pain, and indignation over the murder of Luis Donaldo. I had worked on the speech the whole night, without getting any sleep. My wife had helped me to give it the finishing touches. It was a speech that reflected, more than anything else, a personal feeling. . . . At that moment, I think I was thinking more about Luis Donaldo than about the country."

▼

Zedillo was not only ill-prepared for the presidency, but was also one of the most improvised candidates the government party had ever entered in a presidential race. A wooden speaker who had a hard time smiling naturally for the cameras, he did not fare well in the first focus groups assembled by his image-makers in their efforts to find a way to package him for the public.

One of the first focus groups conducted by Estudios Psico Industriales (EPI), a private firm hired by the Zedillo campaign to conduct confidential surveys, showed that the candidate's efforts to crack jokes failed miserably with his audiences. "Nobody laughed," recalled a participant in the focus groups. "When people were asked why, everybody said the candidate was trying to be funny because that's what his advisers were telling him to do. It wasn't working. . . . Most of us suggested that he stop making jokes."

To make things worse, the government candidate was also a virtual stranger to the party's local leaders throughout the country — the men and women who had to get out the vote in their districts. During his campaign, Colosio had moved from town to town slapping the backs of thousands of local officials, most of whom he knew by their first names: As PRI president and later as Development minister, Colosio had been meeting with them regularly on his weekly trips to the countryside. But Zedillo hardly knew any of them — his previous jobs had rarely taken him to rub elbows with party bosses in the interior.

Making things even tougher for the new candidate, the August 21, 1994, elections loomed as the most difficult ever for the PRI. Bowing to escalating pressures for a more democratic system, especially since the Chiapas rebellion, Salinas had agreed to rewrite election rules and make it much more difficult for anybody to rig the vote. For the first time, the elections would not be run by the government but by a semi-independent agency, the Federal Electoral Institute, which in turn would be overseen by a six-member board that would include several members of the opposition. There would be campaign financing limits, tamper-proof identification cards, national election monitors, and unofficial foreign observers, who had been allowed into the country under the ambiguous designation of "international visitors." The outgoing government had also authorized political parties and citizens' groups to conduct their own exit polls. If these polls showed an opposition win, the government would find it difficult to claim a victory after the counting of the votes.

There was only one way in which Zedillo could overcome his weaknesses and win the election without breaking the new rules — with massive resources, a lot of help from progovernment television networks, and the full support of PRI dinosaurs who were still in control of the party's apparatus. In the absence of a strong candidate, the PRI had to campaign on the strength of its political machine — and the mistakes of its adversaries.

CHAPTER 7

The Cleanest Election

It was a few weeks before the August 21, 1994, elections, and I had turned on Televisa, Mexico's largest television chain, to get the latest news from the campaign trail. Not that I had much of a choice: Of the five freely broadcast television channels in Mexico City, four were owned by Televisa. It was the network of Don Emilio "El Tigre" Azcarraga, the man who had bid $50 million for the PRI at the private fund-raising banquet a year and a half earlier, and whom *Forbes* magazine had ranked as the wealthiest businessperson in Latin America. Azcarraga's Televisa had a 95 percent audience share in Mexico — a virtual monopoly of the airwaves. By comparison, the combined circulation of all Mexican newspapers didn't reach 3 percent of the network's daily viewers.

In addition to running a parallel newspaper and magazine empire — which seemed mainly aimed at promoting Televisa stars — the network ran an around-the-clock news channel. The chain's ECO news station was beamed to the United States, Europe, Latin America, and Africa, and — with eighty-five correspondents around the world — had long since surpassed CNN's Spanish-language broadcast as the most widely seen news station in Latin America.

That day, ECO's top news of the hour was from Bosnia. The Serbs had attacked a United Nations arms depot in a place called Ilidza, north of the Bosnian capital of Sarajevo. A cocky-looking ECO correspondent was reporting from the war front, detailing the latest Serb troop movements, warning about the possibility of imminent NATO air attacks, and interviewing desperate refugees who were fleeing the area in anticipation of the fighting. With a map in his hand, the correspondent reported that the refugees were running toward two small towns, and followed up by providing a myriad of figures about the towns' sizes, populations, and income sources.

The camera then switched to another corner of the former Yugoslavia, where another ECO correspondent was interviewing a Serb official. As the screen filled with the image of a Serb official talking to an ECO microphone, the correspondent's voice-over quoted him as denying charges that his forces had violated NATO's heavy weapons exclusion zone around Sarajevo by seizing a T-55 tank from Ilidza. From there, the broadcast went to Naples, Italy, to show images of a NATO commander's press conference on the latest events in Bosnia. The story, several minutes long, ended with a stern-looking ECO anchorman in Mexico City shaking his head and making a seemingly impromptu closing comment on how fast the former Yugoslavia had fallen from being a peaceful and stable country into an image of hell on earth.

I couldn't help being impressed by ECO's coverage: The Mexican network seemed to have more correspondents on the Bosnian warfront and devote more time to the story than CNN or any other U.S. network I had seen. And it wasn't just that day or that channel. As I began to watch ECO and its sister Televisa station's *24 Horas* newscast regularly, it seemed there was a major story from Bosnia in every news program. Televisa's second most covered international story was the Middle East: Throughout the day, you would get regular reports from Israel, Jordan, or Egypt, offering each side's stand on the latest wrinkle — no matter how minuscule it was — in the Middle East peace agreement.

Since when did Mexicans care so much about Bosnia-Herzegovina? Or the Gaza Strip, for that matter? Was there a historic or economic link between Mexico and these faraway countries that I was missing? As hard as I tried to think of one, I couldn't come up with any. In fact, Mexicans did not seem particularly excited by news from places far away from home. I had never heard Mexicans engaging in an argument over Bosnia in a subway line or at a cocktail party. Why were ECO and

24 *Horas* spending so much time and money covering every detail of the Bosnia conflict, then?

Several weeks later, after the elections, a senior PRI adviser gave me his explanation. The man, an intellectually sophisticated politician in his mid-fifties who was a close adviser to the PRI president, was trying to convince me that the ruling party had won the elections without rigging the vote when he brought up Televisa's coverage amid several other factors that had helped sway Mexican voters toward Zedillo. The way he put it, Televisa's coverage of Bosnia or the Middle East had little to do with those regions' problems — and a lot to do with Mexico's own. The network had always covered political conflicts in faraway places and would continue to do so long after the 1994 elections, but had gone out of its way to do so in the months prior to the vote.

"After the Zapatista rebellion, Televisa bombarded viewers with stories about the former Yugoslavia, and about how Marshall Josip Broz Tito had built a prosperous and independent nation on the threshold of a great empire that had fallen apart within months because of political violence," the PRI adviser explained. "It was part of the government's overall strategy to scare the Mexican people, telling them that something similar could happen in Mexico if the PRI was voted out of office."

Was there an explicit agreement between the government and Televisa to create a climate of preelection angst? Or was Televisa's Bosnia coverage, as I was more inclined to believe, part of Azcarraga's grandiose way of doing things — an effort to show the world that he could beat the big international networks at their own game?

It was more than that, the PRI official said. There had been an agreement "at the highest levels" to intensify Televisa's coverage of political violence abroad, he said. A few months before the election, the government had awarded Azcarraga licenses to operate sixty-two new television stations throughout Mexico, thanks to which Televisa had been able to set up its fourth nationwide television network. Azcarraga's financial contributions to the PRI and Televisa's routine manipulation of the news to help the ruling party were not an act of pure political generosity. "Considering the help he has given us, we should have rewarded him with even more television licenses," the PRI official said, opening his hands and smiling broadly.*

▼

If Televisa used its foreign news to send subliminal messages to its audience, it was less subtle in its coverage of the presidential race at home. In the months preceding the elections, Televisa gave most of its airtime to the Zedillo campaign. Meanwhile, it equated coverage of Zedillo's main rivals, the center-right National Action Party (PAN) and the center-left Party of the Democratic Revolution (PRD), with that of some half a dozen minuscule parties, many of which had been created by the government for the purpose of splitting the legitimate opposition vote.

A study of television campaign coverage by the Federal Electoral Institute, the independent government agency created by Salinas to monitor the elections, showed that Televisa's prime-time *24 Horas* nightly newscast had devoted 40.6 percent of its campaign coverage to Zedillo. By comparison, PRD candidate Cuauhtémoc Cárdenas had received 7.8 percent of the newscast's coverage, while PAN candidate Diego Fernandez de Cevallos had received only 7.6 percent.

What was even more telling was the amount of time that Televisa was giving to tiny political parties, most of which were financed by the government and had never won more than 1 percent of the vote in a national election. Televisa's top news program had devoted more time to each of the candidates of the Green Environmental Party of Mexico (PVEM), the Mexican Democratic Party (PDM), and the Authentic Party of the Mexican Revolution (PARM) than to Cárdenas or Fernandez de Cevallos. If you watched Televisa without knowing much about Mexico, you would have concluded that any of the three small parties was more important than Cárdenas's PRD, which according to govern-

* Televisa's anchorman Jacobo Zabludovsky says ECO and *24 Horas* had been covering news from the former Yugoslavia long before the Mexican elections and continued doing so after the vote. Denying the PRI official's story, he told me in a telephone interview, Mexico City, November 2, 1994, "Our only strategy is that of providing information to our viewers: We reported these conflicts because they were news. We did not have any ulterior motives."

ment critics had won as many votes as Salinas — if not more — in the murky 1988 presidential elections.

Granted, Televisa was more balanced than it had been in the previous presidential race, when it had virtually kept Cárdenas out of public view. At the time, it would only occasionally show silent images of the leftist opposition candidate on the campaign trail, with the off-camera voice of a reporter paraphrasing what Cárdenas had said — in effect never allowing his voice to reach the television audience. But even if Televisa was now airing image-and-sound footage of the strongest opposition candidates, it was often aimed at embarrassing them.

A few weeks before the August 21 election, virtually all independent polls had concluded that Zedillo's main rival was not Cárdenas, but Fernandez de Cevallos. The PAN candidate, a charismatic lawyer with a grave voice and a conquistador-style beard, had crushed a wavering Zedillo in Mexico's first-ever televised debate in May and had climbed steadily in the polls. Some surveys, including one conducted by Indemerc–Louis Harris, were even showing Fernandez de Cevallos more than five points ahead of Zedillo after the debate. Not surprisingly, Televisa spent the last weeks of the presidential race trying to shoot down the PAN candidate's chances by every means at its disposal.

On Wednesday, August 17, Televisa's nightly news program devoted only a few seconds to covering — almost in passing — Fernandez de Cevallos's campaign, and it didn't do him any favor at that. Fernandez de Cevallos had given his closing campaign speech before an estimated twenty thousand followers in his stronghold of Monterrey, stressing some of his favorite themes — Mexico's lack of democracy and its need for change under the leadership of a conservative party that would not throw the country into chaos. But Televisa's spot only showed a fragment of his speech, in which he appeared raising his index finger and saying, "I challenge the leaders of the PRI and the PRD to come up with evidence to support the charges they are leveling against me." It wasn't clear from the newscast what charges he was referring to, but the audience was left with the impression that he had been accused of a serious crime, possibly involving corruption. In fact, there was nothing of the sort: He had referred to routine campaign allegations from Cárdenas, who was alleging that the PAN had made a secret deal with Salinas to help crush the leftist opposition. But Mexico's television viewers had no way of knowing that.

A few months earlier, when Cárdenas had loomed as the most formidable opposition candidate, Televisa and its rival Television Azteca network had helped shoot down the leftist presidential hopeful's campaign. The two networks had, among other things, helped publicize a smear campaign against the PRD candidate following his awkward encounter with a group of transvestites from the Bum Bum cabaret in Xalapa, Veracruz. The incident was dirty politics at its worst. It started when, to the surprise of an estimated one hundred fifty guests at a campaign fund-raiser at the Hotel Fiesta Inn, the group of transvestites — in miniskirts, high heels, and feather ornaments — made it into the room chanting, *"A la bio, a la bau, todos estamos con Cuau!"* ("Say bio, say bau, we are all with Cuau!") Within seconds, the performers had made their way to the head table, introduced themselves as members of Les Femmes 2,001, a group performing at the Bum Bum nightclub, and proceeded to kiss the candidate on the cheeks. Meanwhile, photographers worked feverishly to record the scene.

The next morning, images of Cárdenas surrounded by the performers were all over the country. Progovernment newspapers stressed that Cárdenas had been endorsed by gay organizations and portrayed him as the candidate of Mexico's fringe groups. The independent weekly *Proceso* and the left-of-center daily *La Jornada* would later expose the whole affair as a plot by Veracruz PRI officials to embarrass Cárdenas — *Proceso* said each of the transvestites was paid about three hundred dollars for the job — but Mexico's millions of television viewers would never get the full story.

"We won't have accurate, balanced, and diverse information as long as the bulk of the television news that saturates our homes pursues the political ends of the state party, and as long as one single company controls ninety percent of the audience," a furious Cárdenas complained. "Televisa, let's state it clearly, has become one of the pillars that sustains the authoritarian regime that we are suffering."*

---

* To Televisa's anchorman Jacobo Zabludovsky's credit, he aired Cárdenas's quote criticizing Televisa on that night's *24 Horas* broadcast.

At other times, the various campaign rallies were covered in such a way that — even if there was no visible effort to smear them — public appearances by Fernandez de Cevallos and Cárdenas were bound to look anemic in comparison with Zedillo's. The ruling party candidate's campaign rallies were covered by both Televisa and Television Azteca from the air, with helicopter shots showing huge crowds acclaiming him. By comparison, campaign speeches by Zedillo's main rivals were shot from the ground, showing little more than the first row of their audiences. Images such as these, repeated night after night, would help leave a clear impression that Zedillo was running the most successful campaign.

Postelection television coverage studies left little doubt about Televisa's manipulation of the news. In addition to giving Zedillo eight times more airtime than any of his adversaries, the network seemed to consciously play opposition candidates up or down according to the PRI's daily needs. After giving scant coverage to the Cárdenas campaign for several months, Televisa suddenly began to prop up the center-left candidate two weeks before the elections. In the final week of the campaign, Cárdenas got 6.1 minutes of airtime on *24 Horas*, much more than Fernandez de Cevallos's 3.2 minutes. The other five leading television news programs on both networks showed a similar — and equally sudden — pattern of increased coverage of Cárdenas. It wasn't a last-minute act of repentance: By then, Cárdenas had fallen far behind in the polls. Fernandez de Cevallos was the biggest threat to the Zedillo campaign.

Long after the election, and after a barrage of criticism from all corners of the opposition, "El Tigre" Azcarraga would reject allegations that Televisa newsmen were soldiers of the ruling party. "We are soldiers of the president of the republic, not of the PRI," he corrected. One could accuse Azcarraga of many things, except of not being frank.

▼

"Hi," said a kid's voice in a radio spot that was broadcast constantly during the five days prior to the election.

"Hi," responded another child.

"What's wrong?"

"Nothing. . . . "

"What's wrong?" insisted the first child.

"I'm scared."

"Why?"

"Because my father is scared."

Then, an adult male voice presented the kicker: "At no time, in no place, for any reason, should a child grow up with fear. Because we believe in the force of reason, we reject violence."

The ad, without party identification, was sponsored by the Mexico City Municipal Government and the Association of Mexico City Radio Broadcasters, an owners' association with strong ties to the government. Because it was ostensibly not tied to any party, it could run during the five-day blackout period prior to the elections. As if Televisa's scary reports from the world's most horrendous trouble spots weren't enough, the radio spots were helping to remind Mexicans that — in the aftermath of the Zapatista uprising and Colosio's assassination — there was nothing their country needed more than political stability.*

▼

While the total readership of Mexican newspapers was relatively small — Mexico City's twenty-three daily newspapers, of which only half a dozen had a real readership, had a combined circulation of fewer than 500,000 copies — newspaper coverage of the election wasn't left to chance either. Early in the presidential race, the ruling party had secretly paid millions to Mexico's largest dailies to publish Zedillo campaign propaganda disguised as news.

Through the separate "*convenios,*" or secret contracts with newspapers, the PRI had paid about $800,000 each to Mexico's largest newspapers — including the progovernment dailies *Excelsior* and *El Universal,* and the leftist opposition daily *La Jornada* — to regularly carry Zedillo campaign news on their front pages. In addition, various PRI state governments signed their own *convenios* with the same news-

---

* Campaign coverage was even more tilted toward Zedillo on radio stations than on television, according to the Federal Electoral Institute report. The study said that Zedillo got 50.1 percent of radio airtime, compared with 49.9 percent for the remaining eight candidates together. The study monitored radio stations in the week from June 22 through 28, 1994.

papers to obtain sympathetic coverage for their local candidates, in effect elevating to about $3 million the figure each of the newspapers was getting from various government and party agencies.

Reporters weren't terribly upset about these deals: About 10 percent of each contract went directly to the reporters covering the campaign — meaning that a journalist covering Zedillo got about an $80,000 commission, not bad in a country where most reporters made a miserable salary of $12,000 a year. Considering the fat checks the publishers and a few chosen reporters were getting, it was not surprising that few would blow the whistle on the deals, which were common knowledge in the newsrooms.

In some cases, the confidential contracts signed at election time amounted to a lifeline for small newspapers. Hundreds of Mexico's estimated eleven hundred newspapers were government propaganda sheets with no advertising and virtually no readership, or apparently independent newspapers aimed at keeping former leftist activists or potential troublemakers employed.

In a memorable scene from *Galio's War*, a political novel by Héctor Aguilar Camin focused on Mexico's leftist intellectuals, an opposition newspaper hosts a year-end dinner for its writers and contributors at an elegant Mexico City restaurant. One of the newspaper's editors, in a toast to the crowd, makes his favorite self-mocking joke: "Our goal for the coming year is to have more readers than writers." It wasn't that much of an exaggeration: Some government-funded dailies had hundreds of contributors and readerships of only a few dozen people in government offices that received them for free.

▼

Regino Díaz Redondo, the silver-haired publisher of the 100,000-circulation *Excelsior*, one of Mexico's largest newspapers, jumped from his seat when I asked him about his newspaper's secret advertising agreements with the government. "There aren't any!" he yelled at me, banging his hand against the desk. "I challenge you to show me any evidence that we have any kind of secret *convenios* with the government!"

"But, Don Regino," I replied as graciously as I could, trying to protect a high-ranking PRI official who had just given me details about the party's deals with *Excelsior.* "Everybody knows that *Excelsior* publishes government press releases disguised as news stories. It's *vox populi.* And not just *Excelsior,* virtually all Mexican newspapers do it. . . . Why deny it?"

Suddenly, Díaz Redondo raised his eyebrows and threw back his head in an apparent sign of relief.

"Aahhh, you are talking about stories; that's different," he replied. "We sometimes publish up to one hundred lines of government-paid stories on our front page, but we always demand an advertising receipt from them. We don't have any long-term agreements, nor do anything under the table."

Don Regino's initial outburst, it seemed, was in response to allegations that the management of *Excelsior* was somehow making lucrative deals behind the backs of its employees. Because the newspaper was a cooperative of its twelve hundred employees, Díaz Redondo was especially sensitive about claims of that sort. We were talking in Díaz Redondo's office in *Excelsior*'s building on Mexico City's Paseo de la Reforma Avenue, one of the country's prime real-estate locations. The building and its presses had been built with a low-interest loan from the de la Madrid administration, on which *Excelsior* only made the first two of its fifteen monthly payments, causing its debt to the government to grow to more than $5 million by the early nineties.

Wealthier than other newspapers thanks to the government's blind eye to its debt, *Excelsior* had been Mexico's most influential newspaper for nearly half a century, and for some time in the 1970s — under the helm of Julio Scherer García — had also become one of the most independent. But after Scherer García's ouster in a government-orchestrated internal maneuver, the newspaper had come to rely increasingly on government-paid "news." Despite its old-fashioned look and chaotic layout — it somehow managed to cram two dozen stories on the front page — it had managed to keep part of its readership through the years. It was only recently that *Excelsior* had begun to lose many of its readers to the more modern-looking *La Jornada* and *Reforma,* which were more independent and had thus become appealing to sophisticated readers.

What about reporters' commissions for the advertising they sell to government agencies? I asked.

"It ranges between seven and fifteen percent," Díaz Redondo said matter-of-factly. "But there are no hidden subsidies of any kind."

Wouldn't Excelsior do better by rejecting government advertising and taking a more confrontational line? I asked.

Once again, Don Regino became impatient. Every Mexican newspaper, even the most rabid government opponent, depended on official advertising for its livelihood, he said, standing up from his desk once again.

But shouldn't *Excelsior* tell its readers when it published government-paid news on its front page? Wouldn't that help improve the newspaper's credibility?

"We sometimes alert readers when a story is paid by the government, but very seldom," he conceded. "I plead guilty to that. We should tell our readers when a story is an ad. . . . We will do it in the future."

▼

Even *La Jornada*, the leftist opposition newspaper, published front-page headlines with straight — and sometimes openly favorable — accounts of Zedillo's campaign speeches. In a gesture that set it apart from *Excelsior* and other recipients of hidden government advertising, *La Jornada* most often published the headlines of its government-paid front-page news stories in italics to differentiate them from the newspaper's regular headlines. Connoisseurs knew that the italics stood for paid ads disguised as news, but the general public was unaware of it. One of the newspaper's top editors once told me that 70 percent of *La Jornada*'s advertising came from the government and that about 20 percent of it was published in the form of news.

"I wish one day we will be able to reject all government advertising," the editor said. "For the time being, we can't."

▼

I got a taste of the ruling party's largesse with the media during a tour with the candidate to the countryside. I boarded the PRI's chartered Boeing 727 jets with about two hundred Mexican journalists who traveled with the candidate five days a week. It was a fast-breaking, well-organized campaign swing: In two days, we touched several states, running from planes to buses to catch up with the candidate's street rallies and speeches. All along, we stayed at the best hotels, eating in the classiest restaurants. And wherever we went, we got a new kit with Zedillo paraphernalia: T-shirts, watches, baseball caps, and even Zedillo-labeled apple-cider sodas.

I started getting nervous. Under my prearranged agreement with the PRI press office, I would be charged for the trip's expenses on my return. I made some quick mental calculations, and the looming bill promised to be exorbitant. But when I asked my Mexican colleagues how much they thought it would be, they shrugged off the issue, saying they didn't know, that their papers would eventually pay the bill or reach an agreement with the party to cover the expenses by offering it free ads. It soon became clear that few — if any — on the plane were paying for their own travel expenses.

On our return to Mexico City, when I went to the PRI offices demanding to pay my share of the trip, I couldn't find anybody to take the money. They all told me to forget it: I could make up for it some other time. Were they expecting me to invite Zedillo for a two-day trip to the countryside? When I finally convinced one official to make an estimate of my expenses, he could not find any PRI form to charge journalists for their travel expenses — there weren't any.

Somewhat irked by my insistence, the official went to various offices to consult with his superiors. He finally came back — suddenly showing a smile — saying they had come up with a solution. He pulled a blank sheet of PRI letterhead, wrote down the amount we had calculated for a week's worth of campaign traveling, and signed it. As I turned over several hundred-dollar bills in cash, I could not help detecting a self-contained elation in the man's smile. In all likelihood, he had just become that few hundred dollars richer.

Thanks to age-old government subsidies and the generous donations of sympathetic billionaires, the PRI's resources were inexhaustible — and so was everybody's appetite to get a slice of them.

▼

As election day neared, a sea of white-and-red plastic flags began to cover Mexico City's streets. At first, the small flags appeared attached to telephone poles. Then, one day, millions of them materialized overnight, hanging from electricity and telephone wires and flapping in the wind overhead wherever one looked. It was as if the whole city had been blanketed with small plastic flags. Contrary to what one could have suspected, they were not campaign propaganda for the well-funded ruling party — they were ads for the small, little-known Labor Party.

To the amazement of Mexicans in the capital and several other major cities, the Labor Party, which had only won 1 percent of the vote in the 1991 legislative elections, seemed to have deeper pockets than any other opposition party. In addition to the flags, it had brand-new white vans with the party's logo on their doors crisscrossing the country, blaring campaign propaganda from loudspeakers mounted on their roofs. Labor Party volunteers were giving out free T-shirts and caps in working-class neighborhoods as if money had never been a problem to them. Where was Cecilia Soto, the party's attractive and highly articulate presidential candidate, getting all her money from?

Teodoro Palomino, a teachers' labor union leader and cofounder of the Labor Party, told me over breakfast in a Mexico City restaurant what I had heard from dozens of politicians from other parties: The money came from the government. He said President Salinas had helped create the Labor Party and was now funding the Soto campaign for two reasons: to further divide the opposition and steal votes from both Cárdenas and Fernandez de Cevallos — even 1 percent of the vote could make a difference in a close election — and to have an ostensibly antigovernment party in place to help validate a Zedillo victory in the event of disputed electoral results.

How did Palomino know? Because he was right there when it all started, he told me matter-of-factly. The Labor Party was born at a 1989 meeting in Monterrey's Ambassador Hotel between Salinas and several leftist labor leaders led by the president's former college classmate and good friend Alberto Anaya, a former leftist activist who had recently moved toward the moderate left. "Anaya made a long presentation proposing the creation of a new party, and Salinas agreed, saying that this would help strengthen Mexico's democratic system," Palomino said. "Next thing I heard, we began to get funds for whatever we needed. The money was falling from the sky."

The Labor Party soon got a permit from the Interior ministry to import duty free about two hundred U.S.-made vans and pickup trucks, and $4 million to run a social development program in Monterrey. As the 1994 elections neared, its campaign offices throughout the country began to display brand-new computer equipment and growing numbers of secretaries. Most of the funds came from the government's Solidarity public-works program, while other contributions were funneled through Salinas's brother Raúl, also a college classmate of Anaya's, Palomino said. Labor Party leaders were acting on the assumption that they needed a costly campaign to spread their ideas nationwide, and that if the government was willing to fund part of it for its own purposes, they should take advantage of the opportunity. In politics, you made strange bedfellows — and you tried to keep your affairs with them hidden from the public.

In 1993, when it was time to pick a presidential candidate, Interior Minister Patrocinio Gonzalez had suggested at private meetings with Labor Party leaders in his office that they nominate Soto, according to Palomino. The fact that Soto had never been a member of the Labor Party — she was a congresswoman for another government-funded opposition party, the Authentic Party of the Mexican Revolution, or PARM — didn't seem to matter. As the Labor Party's major contributor, the government was entitled to suggest a candidate. Soto got the job a few weeks later, and Palomino quietly left the Labor Party protesting the government's excessive meddling in the group's internal affairs.

Labor Party leader Anaya smiled gently when I confronted him with Palomino's allegations a few weeks after the elections. Anaya, a middle-aged political fox who was surrounded by four aides and seemed glued to a cellular phone, confirmed that he had discussed the Labor Party's creation with Salinas, and that the president had encouraged him to form the new party. As to where his party's funds had come from, Anaya smiled again and proceeded to give me a lesson in Mexican political party history. "In this country, all political parties are subsidized by the government," he responded, in an apparent reference to the legal campaign funds given by the Federal Electoral Institute. "None of them is in a position to play holier than thou.

"If you don't understand that Mexico is a Napoleonic, paternalistic state, you don't understand anything," he explained to me amiably. "In this country, the government pays for everything — even to be criticized."*

▼

He was right. In its limitless preelection generosity, the government was even funding the most unsuspected group — the Zapatista National Liberation Army. Unbeknownst to his leftist devotees, even Subcommander Marcos — the very bulwark of Mexico's social conscience, the leader of an armed insurrection against the state — had knowingly accepted government funding for his own political offensive in the weeks preceding the 1994 elections.

Marcos desperately needed the funds for the National Democratic Convention, an ambitious national meeting he had convened for August 8, two weeks before the elections, in the Lacandon jungle. His plan was to unite for the first time all of Mexico's authentic opposition groups, including conservative government critics, behind a common prodemocratic agenda.

He hoped the meeting of about five thousand representatives of hundreds of labor and civic opposition groups would among other things set the base for the creation of a transition government, or at least position them to form a parallel government should the upcoming national elections be shamelessly fraudulent and trigger a wave of protests. But Marcos lacked the funds to invite his thousands of guests — much less transport them to the jungle or house them.

By the time the Zapatista convention opened, Marcos had solved his problem: Chiapas governor Javier López Moreno and several government agencies, with the green light from President Salinas, had secretly funneled to the Zapatistas $173,000 in equipment and vehicle rentals to help carry out the antigovernment meeting in the jungle hamlet of Aguascalientes, next to Guadalupe Tepeyac. The government provided the sound system from which Marcos would address the outdoor convention — seven tower speakers that were posted on both sides of the

---

*The Labor Party came in fourth in the 1994 elections, obtaining 2.8 percent of the vote, substantially more than the other smaller parties.

podium from which Marcos spoke and four smaller ones that were placed underneath it — dozens of latrines, trucks carrying drinking water, a giant plastic roof to protect visitors from the rain, and technical assistance to extend electricity wires from Guadalupe Tepeyac to the improvised jungle auditorium.

"I decided to provide support for the meeting because if the Zapatistas concluded that the government was boycotting it, they would have had more reasons to oppose the general elections," López Moreno told me in an interview months later. "I believed that a conciliatory attitude on the part of the government would help the peace process."

"Our biggest priority was to avoid violence during the elections," a close aide to Salinas told me in a separate interview, conceding that the funds for the Zapatistas had been approved by the president himself. "The convention was planning to adopt a wait-and-see stand about the elections. We naturally wanted to encourage that, because it would send a strong message to other hard-line leftist groups not to disrupt the voting."

Journalists puzzled by the Zapatistas' display of economic strength during the convention were told that European support groups had contributed generously to the meeting and that most delegates had paid for their own expenses. Neither the government nor the Zapatistas ever disclosed the real source of the funds, which helped Marcos to impose his idea of not disrupting the elections without raising suspicions from the most radical among his fellow revolutionaries. As Labor Party leader Anaya had put it, the Mexican government loved to pay its critics. But, far from an act of political masochism, it was pure politics — and it paid handsomely.

▼

If the PRI could spend lavishly to buy media coverage and fund friends and foes, it was because it had an almost bottomless campaign chest. And this wasn't because Mexico was awash in dollars: In fact, foreign investors were quietly beginning to withdraw their money from Mexico, both because of nervousness over the Colosio and Chiapas affairs, and because of the lure of rising interest rates in the United States. Mexico's foreign reserves had plummeted from $29 billion in February to $17 billion in April. Yet the Salinas government kept churning out rosy financial projections: The president would not allow any bad news to spoil Zedillo's election or his own campaign for the newly created World Trade Organization. "The level of our [foreign] reserves allows us to bolster the solvency of our currency," Salinas continued to brag in his last state of the nation address in October 1994, two months after the elections. A few weeks later, Mexico and its foreign investors — most of them American — would pay a dramatic price for Salinas's failure to address the country's financial strains.

There seemed to be no limit to what the ruling party could spend. Just on officially reported campaign expenditures, the PRI had spent $105 million — or nearly 80 percent of what all political parties had doled out for their presidential, congressional, and municipal races, according to official figures that were released several months later. In addition, the ruling party had resorted to part of the $700 million it had collected from private contributions through its businessmen's fund-raising cells without reporting it. On top of that, the Zedillo campaign was getting a little-disguised financial push from various government agencies.

According to PAN estimates, the government spent about $4 billion in social development programs — mainly in opposition-dominated areas — over the two months preceding the elections. The funds were delivered by the government's Solidarity and Procampo programs: Solidarity built schools, hospitals, and drainage systems, while Procampo — suspiciously launched toward the end of the Salinas term, shortly before the elections — doled out cash subsidies to financially strapped farmers. Often, Solidarity and Procampo disbursements came with a catch — recipients were told that if the PRI lost the elections, nobody could guarantee that the incoming government would honor what was left to pay. I got a glimpse of the ruling party's vote-getting schemes during the electoral race in San Miguel Xicó, a working-class town about forty miles east of Mexico City, where residents candidly explained to me the bizarre circumstances that were leading them to vote for the PRI, even if they despised the government party.*

---

* The Solidarity public-works program disbursed $15.1 billion in more than 523,000 public works during the Salinas administration, according to President Salinas in his

▼

San Miguel Xicó was one of the several poverty-ridden towns in the Valley of Chalco, a district that had been the showcase of Salinas's Solidarity social works program, where the president had once taken Pope John Paul II and other world dignitaries to show his government's works for the poor. The road to the town was paved — and for some reason littered with an amazing number of dead dogs — but that was almost the only public work that had been completed.

The town was a mess. Its streets were filled with pool-sized potholes filled with water, which made them look like never-ending canals. Neighbors had built narrow concrete sidewalks on their doorsteps, which forced one to walk linearly, almost with the back against the walls, to avoid falling into the water. What was worse, the stagnant water had long putrefied, was littered with floating plastic bags and empty cans, and had become a friendly habitat to vast colonies of insects and frogs. Residents swore to me that there were fish in there, and that their children had caught many, although — perhaps because of the campaign-related activities — there didn't seem to be any fishermen the day of my visit.

The most striking thing about the scene was that there were huge piles of concrete sacks emerging from the water on almost every corner and pieces of heavy construction equipment scattered all over town. What was going on? Who had abandoned the works, and why?

Two men who were chatting on the street explained to me what had happened. Solidarity had provided the funds and equipment to pave the entire town about a year earlier. Huge steamrollers and cement trucks had actually arrived in town and begun to flatten its dirt streets. But then, the work stopped all of a sudden. Party bosses said it was a temporary delay and that construction would resume soonest. But the months went by, the streets began to crack, the water began to fill the potholes, and the neighbors began to raise hell. It turned out that the road workers had forgotten to build a drainage system. With the rainy season, San Miguel Xicó first turned into a poor man's Venice,

Sixth State of the Nation address to the Mexican Congress. The Procampo program disbursed $1.5 billion to 3.4 million peasants in 1993 and 1994, according to President Salinas's Sixth State of the Nation address to the Mexican Congress.

then into a huge swamp. Shortly before the elections, the PRI bosses announced the good news: The Solidarity funds to build the drainage system had finally been approved and were on their way.

"They told us, 'Vote for us, and the drainage system will be completed within two or three months,'" said one of the men, who ran one of the town's small grocery stores. "They obviously delayed the works on purpose, to keep us under their grip. And they will win a majority of the vote, because we all know that only the PRI can get the job completed."

There was no question that if the opposition won, residents of San Miguel Xicó risked being told that there were no funds for the project: Opposition parties had their own constituencies to satisfy in the towns they controlled, and this was not one of them. Residents of San Miguel Xicó had little choice but to continue voting for the PRI: The water was — not so metaphorically speaking — reaching their necks.*

▼

But the ruling party's most shocking mechanism of political control was the near forceful recruitment of millions of workers to build up the crowds at the party's campaign rallies. Although the government party had long been supported by corrupt labor unions, I wasn't fully aware of how this relationship worked until I discovered it almost by chance one day, when I set out to get a shoe shine.

It was a few days before the 1994 election, and I couldn't find any shoe shiner on the streets. Where had all of them gone? Where was Pedro Mendoza, the veteran *bolero* — as shoe shiners are known in Mexico — who was usually posted on the corner of Genova and Hamburgo Streets in the touristic Zona Rosa district? I looked for the *boleros* at their customary stands along Reforma Avenue and in the Zona Rosa, but they were nowhere to be found. It was as if they had all vanished overnight.

It turned out that the shoe shiners, along with lottery ticket vendors, newspaper hawkers, street marketeers, mariachi musicians, and most other independent workers, had been recruited by the PRI to build up

---

* On election day, the PRI swept San Miguel Xicó with 56 percent of the vote, followed by the PRD with 23 percent, and the PAN with 13 percent.

the crowds at Zedillo's closing rallies. In addition to money for propaganda, the ruling party had used its age-old mechanisms of political control to fill the downtown Plaza de la Constitución with more than a hundred thousand people for Zedillo's closing campaign rally August 14. Tens of thousands of street vendors had been coerced to attend the nationally televised event.

They didn't have a choice. The PRI mobilized the workers through authoritarian mechanisms that were largely invisible to outsiders, but that had long been crucial to maintaining the party's hold on power. The shoe shiners and other independent workers — including taxi and bus drivers — made up a giant captive army of party activists: Because they needed government licenses to conduct their businesses, they depended heavily on the PRI officials who handed them out. For decades, such licenses had been given out in exchange for political work for the ruling party, and this didn't seem to have changed a bit despite Zedillo's new talk of democratizing the country.

I learned how the party controlled the lives of hundreds of thousands of independent workers a few days later from Mendoza, the fifty-six-year-old *bolero* who had been posted for four decades at his Zona Rosa corner, and who counted me among his occasional clients. Like virtually all the six thousand shoe shiners in Mexico City, Mendoza was an active member of the PRI. To be able to work as a *bolero*, you couldn't just buy your tools and start working wherever you pleased, he explained to me. You needed a permit, which was only given out by the PRI-affiliated Union of Shoe Shiners. When you joined the Union of Shoe Shiners, you automatically got a PRI membership card and — depending on how big a bribe you paid the union's boss — the corner of your choice. From then on, the party would give you several social benefits, including subsidized health care, a pension plan, and two blue uniforms a year — with the PRI logo emblazoned on the chest. Your only obligation as a union member was to occasionally show up at political rallies, especially during election time.

What happened if you didn't go? You had to go, Mendoza replied candidly. If you failed to show up, the union suspended you for three days, and you could not work at your corner during that time. Since most *boleros* lived hand to mouth — Mendoza had won the lottery twice and thus felt somewhat less intimidated by the threat of losing three days' worth of work — it was a luxury they could not afford. And how did the union know who attended the rallies? Very easily: Each union boss was given a geographic space at the square where the rally was taking place and checked the names of the *boleros* at their preassigned spot as their party-rented buses arrived. Each *bolero* would then get a stamped ticket with the date on it. On the following day, union inspectors would visit the shoe shiners at their respective street stands and check the tickets. Whoever failed to produce a stamped ticket was suspended on the spot. That was what had happened during Zedillo's closing rally, and that's why most *boleros* had abandoned work to attend it.

I shook my head, scandalized by what I was hearing. I hadn't seen that kind of political control in any place but Cuba, I commented to him. But Mendoza, who prided himself on having a pragmatic mind when it came to politics, didn't seem to share my outrage. Look, he said, the PRI was subsidizing all kinds of social benefits to the shoe shiners. Where else would they get a work license, subsidized health care, uniforms, and even a free burial for a monthly fee of less than two dollars? "Showing up at a rally once in a while is not such a big deal compared with the kind of services you get in exchange," Mendoza assured me. "Even if you don't give a damn about the candidate, you do it as part of the job."

Eager to know more about the PRI's tools of political control, I went to the Shoe Shiners' Union. It was a three-story building in a somewhat run-down section of the old part of Mexico City, not far from the cathedral and the Plaza de la Constitución where the Zedillo rally had taken place. In the lobby, there were four big shrines, each containing an image of the Virgin of Guadalupe, the *boleros'* chosen protector. In the first-floor administrative offices, there was a flurry of activity, with functionaries coming and going with papers in their hands and an air of urgent business about them.

The union's president was David Betancourt, a fifty-two-year-old former *bolero* who wore a leather jacket, a gold chain, and a prominent gold ring. His union activities had propelled him to serve briefly as an alternate government party congressman ten years earlier, and he had since been appointed secretary-general of the PRI's Federation of Organizations of Non-Salaried Workers. The federation, one of the dozens of labor umbrella groups run by the ruling party, was made up of fourteen unions of independent workers. In addition to the shoe shiners, it included the 3,000-member Mexican Union of Mariachis, the 800-member Union of Streetcar Washers and Keepers, and the 1,500-member Union of Photographers of Church, Social and Official Ceremonies (which Betancourt pointedly warned me not to confuse with the 600-member Union of Five-Minute Photographers, which was also part of the federation but had its separate statutes and executive committee).

Betancourt proceeded to show me around the building. With great pride, he took me to the classroom where 120 *boleros* were getting an elementary school education thanks to scholarships from the ruling party. From there, we walked to another room where the union had its clinic, and to a music room where the union's twenty-five-drum, twenty-five-trumpet military band practiced for its performances at party rallies. We ended the tour at the building's top-floor cafeteria, donated by President Salinas after an official visit to the union, where Betancourt reviewed the social benefits the *boleros* were getting, including free burial from a funeral home with the astonishing name of the Final Solution.

Toward the end of the interview, I asked him point-blank: Did the union really check on which of its members attended Zedillo's campaign rallies? Were there penalties for those who didn't show up?

"Yes," Betancourt responded naturally, apparently unaware of any criticism of such practices. "We call their names and give out a small ticket to those who show up. We have about a hundred inspectors who later visit union members at their respective corners and ask for the tickets. If members don't come up with them, they are punished with a three-day suspension."

There was nothing wrong with that, Betancourt said. On the contrary, it was in compliance with the union's statutes, which — like other unions' charters — called for members to support its ruling party–run umbrella organizations. Betancourt asked an employee — who turned out to be his wife — for a copy of the union statutes. Chapter 1, Article 7, of the shoe shiners' statutes stated that the union was joining as a full member two of the PRI's labor federations. The ensuing articles demanded that members follow these groups' guidelines and warned them that they would lose their union rights if they were found "collaborating with organizations of contrary ideology, or defaming the federations to which we adhere."

Betancourt's battalions of shoe shiners, newspaper hawkers, and mariachis were only the lower end of the ruling party's captive army of unionized workers. In the closing weeks of the Zedillo campaign, the PRI had mobilized the five-million-strong Confederation of Mexican Workers, as well as dozens of party-run professional and peasant organizations. There was virtually no profession, job, or occupation for which the ruling party had not created or adopted a labor union, and from which it didn't demand a quota of political work at election time. Just like the *boleros*, there were thousands of lawyers, physicians, economists, veterinarians, and bank workers who had joined PRI-run unions to obtain a wide variety of government permits from well-connected labor leaders in their respective fields. Now, it was time to pay them back.

Not surprisingly, the Plaza de la Constitución was packed for Zedillo's campaign closing rally. Each section of the plaza had been previously assigned to a labor federation, which had committed itself to bringing a certain number of people — and had bused them in accordingly. To some international observers, Zedillo's closing campaign rally was living proof that Mexico's ruling party still enjoyed widespread popular support. To those who knew better, it served as evidence that it had not shed its coercive methods.

▼

As if the PRI didn't have enough of an advantage, it got some precious help from Cárdenas: His fiery speeches in the closing days of the campaign played right into the ruling party's scare tactics. In what amounted to a string of bizarre political miscalculations, the leftist opposition candidate made a pilgrimage to the Lacandon jungle to meet with Subcommander Marcos shortly before the election and began to raise the Zapatista conflict in speeches that made him look like an advocate of violence.

I could hardly believe my ears when, addressing tens of thousands of sympathizers at Mexico City's Zócalo Square in his televised closing campaign speech, Cárdenas brought up the Zapatista uprising and lashed out against the government for its failure to come to terms with the Chiapas rebels. It was Cárdenas's only occasion to reach a huge audience on television with a live speech and his best opportunity ever to woo undecided voters. Yet he blew it. The very moment he began to talk about Chiapas, the crowd at the square — or at least the people standing in the front rows whose voices could be heard on national television — began chanting, "Marcos! Marcos! Marcos!" Cárdenas had not only allowed the masked rebel leader to upstage him at his own rally, but had alarmed millions of violence-fearing Mexicans.

My next-door neighbor at the apartment I rented at the time in Mexico City's Del Valle neighborhood, a housewife in her mid-fifties, was one of them. When I ran into her later that morning at the elevator and asked her about Cárdenas's speech, she was shaking her head in disgust. Like millions of Mexicans who cared more about their pocketbooks than about an Indian rebellion in a remote border state, she was scared by what she had seen on television. "That man will lead us to civil war," she repeated again and again. "If he wins, we will have *el gran desmadre* — all hell will break loose."

▼

One person who couldn't have been happier every time Cárdenas brought up the Zapatista struggle in his speeches was Jorge Matte Langlois, the Chilean-born pollster who conducted the behind-the-scenes public-opinion surveys for the Zedillo campaign. A short, stocky man who shunned the public limelight — most of Mexico's best-connected political columnists didn't even know of his existence — Matte was best known in Mexico's corporate world. His polling company, Estudios Psico Industriales, worked mainly for Mexican and multinational corporations, but had also periodically conducted sensitive public-opinion surveys for the Mexican government.

Matte's special talent was being a Renaissance man: A Sorbonne-educated psychologist, sociologist, and theologian who played amateur polo in his spare time, he was seen by his clients as a man with a wider view than other pollsters who just worked with numbers. Matte's surveys for the Zedillo campaign — which included 25,000 personal interviews and 400 focus groups — were among the most comprehensive ever done in Mexico. It was the kind of mammoth, invisible job that only the government party could afford.

Matte's confidential polls, which he showed me following the elections and after we obtained a formal authorization from Zedillo's office, showed a Mexico that was very different from the country Cárdenas was addressing. The pollster's massive surveys, which I later found out coincided with PRD internal polls that Cárdenas refused to take seriously at the time, revealed that most Mexicans cared little about politics, got most of their information from progovernment television networks, and — if anything — were more conservative than generally believed. Mexico was in no mood for a social upheaval.

In sharp contrast with the image projected by crowds of youths holding Che Guevara and Marcos posters at Cárdenas's campaign rallies that were captivating part of the Mexican and foreign media, Matte's polls showed that political issues such as democracy and fair elections ranked low among people's concerns. Mexicans cared most about jobs, better education, better protection against crime, and even traffic jams. One of Matte's largest polls, conducted July 26–29, 1994 — at the height of the presidential campaign, when issues such as democracy were at the center of the political agenda — was particularly telling. When asked, "Which do you think are the most important issues facing the country?" Mexicans placed their country's lack of democracy near the bottom of the list. Their answers, measured in total number of mentions, were as follows:

1)	Unemployment	21.8 percent
2)	Economic problems	17.7 percent
3)	Social problems	9.9 percent
4)	Poverty	8.2 percent
5)	Corruption	7.6 percent
6)	Lack of security	4.3 percent
7)	Crime	4 percent
8)	Low wages	3.8 percent
9)	Lack of democracy	3.4 percent
10)	Messy government	2 percent

When Matte posed the same question in a different way, asking Mexicans what were the most important problems they faced personally, issues such as the Chiapas conflict didn't even make the top ten answers.

In fact, the Zapatista rebellion ranked lower than traffic jams. Their most pressing problems were:

1)	Not enough money	30.6 percent
2)	Don't know	22.5 percen
3)	Unemployment	15.5 percent
4)	Lack of police protection	4.8 percent
5)	Low wages	4.6 percent
6)	Family disintegration	3.4 percent
7)	Bad public services	2.2 percent
8)	Pollution	1.8 percent
9)	Crime	1.7 percent
10)	Traffic	0.4 percent

When asked what issues should become the top priority for the next Mexican president, the issues that Cárdenas had stressed in his closing campaign speech ranked in nineteenth and twentieth place. Mexicans responded that they wanted their next president to focus on the following tasks:

1)	Create new jobs	52 percent
2)	Improve wages	23 percent
3)	Improve education levels	22 percent
4)	Fight crime	17 percent
5)	Fight corruption	16 percent
6)	Focus on social problems	13 percent
7)	Fight poverty	12 percent
8)	Economic stability	12 percent
9)	Improve public services	9 percent
10)	Develop rural areas	9 percent
11)	Pay attention to marginal sectors of the population	9 percent
12)	Reduce inflation	6 percent
13)	Unite Mexicans	6 percent
14)	Meet government promises	6 percent
15)	Stabilize the country	6 percent
16)	Be fair	5 percent

17)	Improve the government's administration	4 percent
18)	Take better care of the youth	4 percent
19)	Improve housing conditions	4 percent
20)	Improve health care	3 percent
21)	Control pollution	3 percent
22)	Help industry	3 percent
23)	Solve the Chiapas conflict	3 percent
24)	Democracy	2 percent

▼

Analyzing his preelection polls over lunch, Matte told me with a cordial smile that both Cárdenas and we foreign correspondents had gotten it all wrong. "If you look at U.S. newspaper and television networks' coverage of the elections, you will find that they most often quoted leftist politicians, intellectuals, or journalists, as if Cárdenas had been the most serious contender to the presidency," he said. Some leading U.S. newspapers had run stories asserting that Cárdenas had a serious chance of becoming Mexico's next president. Commenting on our work as reporters, Matte said we were writing our dispatches under the influence of pro-Cárdenas street rallies in downtown Mexico City, oblivious to the fact that they represented a tiny fraction of Mexico's public opinion.

So where was the support for Mexico's leftist causes coming from? I asked. Who were the tens of thousands of leftists who filled Zócalo Square every time Cárdenas held a rally? And the thousands of devout readers of the leftist daily *La Jornada* one saw on Mexico City buses every day?

"It's a very minuscule sector of the population, whose center can be almost geographically located in the southern Mexico City suburb of Coyoacán," Matte responded. "It's a sector of the population that is very politically active and makes a lot of noise, but whose real impact in public opinion is very small."

▼

What was even more interesting in Matte's confidential polls was that, when the population was broken down according to age groups, it turned out that young Mexicans were even less interested in democracy than their parents — only 2.8 percent of the youths had cited the issue at all. The enthusiastic college students in blue jeans with pro-Marcos signs who filled Cárdenas's street rallies posed no serious electoral threat to Zedillo.

Other surveys conducted for U.S. and Mexican corporations at the time coincided with Matte's conclusions. The Yankelovich Monitor, a 548-page-long wide-ranging nationwide survey conducted by the Yankelovich Mexico polling firm, had concluded that most of Mexico's youth were highly materialistic people who cared mostly about their economic status and personal gratification. It was older Mexicans — especially those who had gone to school in the sixties — who were more idealistic and concerned about social issues.

Mexicans who could be defined as materialistic minded were mostly young people and accounted for 28 percent of the Mexican population, the study said. "They believe that money is important, and they want it in large amounts. They do not think that society places too much emphasis on money. They believe money can give them happiness, and that money is the best measure of success."

By comparison, it described the oldest group of Mexicans, averaging about forty years of age, which accounted for 14 percent of the population, as idealistic. This group believed that society was placing too much importance on money and shared "a high sense of patriotism and support for everything that is Mexican," it said.

What did young Mexicans read the most, the survey asked? The answer was the *Reader's Digest*. Where did they get most of their news? From Televisa's *24 Horas* newscast — Cárdenas's worst foe. What's more, most regarded Televisa's newscast as fairly reliable. Judging from the polls, Cárdenas was totally out of sync with Mexico's reality: Even young Mexicans, once the most rebellious sector of the population, were in no mood for radical change.

▼

Intrigued, I decided to pay a visit to the National Autonomous University of Mexico, the giant state-run campus in the country's capital that had produced generations of radical student activists and staunchly nationalistic government officials for decades. It was by far Mexico's biggest — and by some standards still the most influential — university.

The university, known by its Spanish acronym UNAM, had opened a modernistic campus in Mexico City's southern outskirts of El Pedregal in the early fifties that would become a key center of Latin American leftist thinking in coming decades. Its buildings were decorated with giant murals depicting Mexico's Aztec past, revolutionary heroes such as Zapata, the Soviet socialist revolution of 1917, and the proletarian masses of the world. The school's auditorium was named for Ho Chih Minh. Even in the nineties, billboards at the university's various schools reflected its political climate: There were solidarity committees with Castro's Cuba, fund-raisers in support of the Zapatista rebels in Chiapas, and weekly protests against real and imagined U.S. interventions in various parts of the world. This had long been leftist territory — the place where Cárdenas gathered the most enthusiastic crowds, the university that had produced, among its most recent celebrities, Subcommander Marcos.

Once on campus, I headed for the School of Economics. The vast majority of its professors came from Mexico's hard-line left, and many were still known to describe themselves as Marxists, explaining the collapse of world communism as a failure of implementation of "real socialism" in the former Soviet Union. Until the early 1990s, the bulk of the school's courses were of a Marxist orientation, and Marx's *Das Kapital* was still the main text throughout the program.

But what I found on the evening I ventured into the UNAM's School of Economics belied the Marxist trappings. In the lobby, facing the entrance and hanging from a second-floor balcony, there was a huge sign in English reading, Opening New Frontiers, and promoting a new English-language course that students were encouraged to take.

Juan Pablo Arroyo, the dean of the School of Economics, laughed when I mentioned the English sign. New winds of pragmatism were blowing through the school, he admitted, shrugging. A forty-six-year-old man who sported a beard and was one of the few people at the school wearing a tie, Arroyo had gone through his school's various phases: A former Communist Party member, he had graduated from the school and taught various Marxist courses there for several years.

Up to 1993, he explained to me, a total of twenty-two of the School of Economics's fifty-three courses taught Marxist theory. They carried names such as Class Struggle and Marxist Theory of the State and The State in the Transition from Capitalism to Communism. But that year, the school had changed its programs rather than face a continued loss of students: Enrollment had gone down from 6,000 students in the mid-seventies to 2,300 in the early nineties, only partly because of the proliferation of new economics schools throughout the country.

"We were facing a tremendous crisis," Arroyo said. "At one point, we discovered that more than eighty percent of our new enrollments were rejects from the schools of law, medicine, or accounting who had not been able to keep up with their academic standards. Very few students were choosing our school voluntarily: The education we were offering was of little use in the job market."

In a gradual overhaul of the school's academic program that was completed in 1995, Arroyo fired many of the school's 735 professors, reduced the number of Marxist courses to about 10 percent of the total, and introduced new courses teaching the basics of free-market economics. Under the new academic program, students could choose during their last two years one of five subjects in which to major: Four of them were business or trade oriented and the last one — History of Economic Development — was made up largely of Marxist theory. More than 85 percent of the students had picked the first four subjects to major in, Arroyo said. The school's tilt was still overwhelmingly leftist, but — more than half a decade after the collapse of the Soviet bloc — it was beginning to acknowledge that there was such a thing as a free-market trend in much of the world.

"We didn't turn into a free-market school, but into a pluralistic one," Arroyo said. "Today's young people are more pragmatic, more mature. . . . They are looking for an education that can help them succeed in today's world."

What was happening at the UNAM's economics school was a long-delayed echo of what had been happening on campuses all over Mexico for nearly two decades. In recent years, there had been a massive exodus to private universities by middle-class students who saw no future for themselves as socialism-wise UNAM graduates. Despite often prohibitive tuition fees, enrollment in private universities had grown by 190 percent over the past decade, while the number of admissions at the UNAM had only gone up by 17 percent. Whenever the subject of the state university came up among well-to-do families, they immediately brought up stories of help-wanted ads for professionals that read, "UNAM graduates, please abstain." The ads reflected a widely held view in the private sector that the state university produced nothing but coffee-table ideologues — and outdated ones at that.*

In sharp contrast with the pre-1960s generations, the ultimate status symbol in 1980s and 1990s academic circles had become earning a postgraduate degree from a U.S. university. The number of Mexican graduate students in U.S. universities had soared from a few hundred in the seventies to more than six thousand in the early nineties, according to U.S. figures. U.S. doctoral degrees had become a near must for the young technocrats who had begun filling Mexico's cabinet jobs in the late 1980s. Mexico's college students were far ahead of both the government and the Mexican left's pseudonationalistic rhetoric.

▼

Unbeknownst to the world, Cárdenas had his own secret Chilean consultant — the only difference was, he didn't pay any attention to him. Chilean pollsters and political consultants had become hot stuff in Latin America, especially among center-left parties: They had overcome formidable odds to win the 1988 plebiscite against right-wing strongman General Augusto Pinochet, and had become experts in circumventing tricky electoral rules. After years of exile in Mexico and Europe, most had resettled in Chile and were working for the new democratic government, or had become successful advertising or marketing executives in the private sector.

A well-known Chilean pollster, fifty-year-old publicist Juan Forch, had arrived in Mexico on April 16, 1993, more than a year before the Mexican election. He had been invited by Cárdenas's spokesman

---

* A probusiness trend was also evident in the career choices of college students within state and private universities. Enrollment in accounting schools grew from 5,375 students in 1980 to 25,378 in 1993, while enrollment in business administration schools rose from 4,406 in 1980 to 8,846, according to Anuarios Estadisticos de ANUIES, the National Association of Universities and Superior Education Institutes. By comparison, new admissions in philosophy schools only grew from 454 students in 1980 to 602 in 1993.

Adolfo Aguilar Zinser, a U.S.-educated political activist who was deeply impressed by what he had seen as an international observer during the Chilean plebiscite. To Aguilar Zinser, there were many similarities between Chile's 1988 elections and Mexico's 1994 vote: In both cases, opposition parties faced a huge government propaganda machine designed to convince voters that they would face a future of chaos and violence if the left were allowed to win. In Chile, the opposition had won by dissociating itself from the images of violence and persecution that had marked its recent past and running an upbeat campaign with optimistic television spots. Aguilar Zinser hoped Forch's recommendations would help Cárdenas win with a similar counterpropaganda strategy.

But, much to Aguilar Zinser's dismay, Cárdenas didn't believe in polls. He felt that, in an authoritarian country like Mexico, people would never tell the truth to a pollster. Nor did he think much of U.S. or Chilean political consultants. "He saw the [U.S.] electoral process as a circus, and presidential candidates as meek puppets of marketing and media experts," Aguilar Zinser recalled after the elections. "To him, [the leftist daily] *La Jornada* was the bible, thermometer, and mirror of his campaign."

In the candidate's mind, he had won the fraudulent 1988 elections by sticking to his principles. He was, after all, the son of Mexico's most popular recent president, the hero who had nationalized the country's oil industry and had given land and dignity to Mexico's peasants. Only the government's electoral fraud — this time made more difficult by greater international scrutiny — could stop him from winning, he thought. And his hard-line advisers reassured him constantly that the enthusiastic support he was getting from leftist students and labor activists was only a hint of the avalanche of votes he would get from the population at large.

After a brief tour of Mexico to study the country's electoral arena, Forch presented Cárdenas with his conclusions. Cárdenas could not expect to be seen as a responsible presidential candidate and at the same time behave as a revolutionary in constant confrontation with the state, the Chilean said. If Cárdenas wanted to win the elections, he had to try to expand his electoral base and reach the widest possible audience. At first, Cárdenas seemed to accept Forch's analysis and agreed to commission an independent public-opinion poll.

But when the poll's results came in and showed him far behind — when asked whether they would be better or worse off if Cárdenas won, 27 percent of Mexicans had responded "worse" and 18 percent "better" — Cárdenas quickly reverted to his original skepticism about political consultants. Surrounded by a small clique of hard-liners who reinforced his conviction that the polls were unreliable, he intensified his campaign of agitation and mobilization. Cárdenas's distrust of packaged candidacies was such that he declined to change his suit and take a makeup professional with him to the television studios for the nationally broadcast presidential debate in May, his spokesman would lament after the elections. Forch was sent home, and his recommendations were soon forgotten.

"Instead of turning our entire resources and Cuauhtémoc Cárdenas's endless energies to capture the vote of the undecided, and even try to gain some ground among those who rejected him, our campaign stepped up the mobilization of those who were already on our side," Aguilar Zinser concluded after the election. "The enterprise clouded our vision."

▼

Two days before the election, on Friday, August 19, an upbeat U.S. Ambassador James Jones gave the Zedillo campaign something new to be happy about. In what amounted to a U.S. blessing to the electoral process, he told a briefing of U.S. correspondents that the Clinton administration was pleased with the election's preparations. Neither the PRI's schemes to circumvent campaign spending limits, nor the unfair television coverage, nor the strong-arm tactics to coerce workers to attend party rallies seemed to prevent U.S. officials from applauding Mexico's electoral process.

"We are optimistic," Jones told a handful of American correspondents after a press briefing at the U.S. embassy auditorium. "We don't see any evidence of a pattern of systematic irregularities or abusing of the system. There may be operational glitches, but [there is] no systematic pattern of irregularities." Jones, the Oklahoma-raised former head of the New York Stock Exchange and Clinton's former point man to sell NAFTA to a skeptical U.S. Congress, was focusing on the positive: There was little question that the 1994 election was shaping up as much fairer than previous ones.

New electoral rules and the presence of tens of thousands of observers — Mexicans and foreigners — would make it significantly more difficult for the PRI to engage in its old tricks. A new electoral roster supervised by independent auditing firms would keep the ruling party from tossing to the streets thousands of *"ratones locos,"* or "crazy mice," as Mexicans described breathless voters who in previous elections had been forced to run from place to place because their names had been deleted from voter registration lists. Under the old practice, PRI officials would routinely strike from the lists the names of thousands of people living in opposition-dominated areas to reduce the numbers of likely antigovernment voters.

And the introduction of transparent ballot boxes and the presence of election observers would prevent government party electoral engineers from fixing the ballot boxes. In previous elections, the ruling party had made widespread use of what Mexicans had come to call *"urnas embarazadas,"* or "pregnant ballot boxes" — wooden ballot boxes with special compartments that had been stuffed with progovernment votes before the start of the voting.

Buoyed by these steps toward electoral fairness, the U.S. embassy in Mexico had sent a confidential cable to the State Department two weeks before the vote, stating that the PRI faced a "very competitive election" in six of Mexico's top ten states and that — while the embassy's assessment was that the ruling party would win with between 40 and 45 percent of the vote — "we would not be surprised by any [other] outcome in this election." The cable added that if there was an upset, the most likely winner would be the PAN.

The voting procedures had been changed in such ways that U.S. officials were vouching for them even in their confidential reports. Days before the voting, the 1994 elections had already gained wide acceptance as the cleanest in Mexico's history — no matter that they were, with the exception of Cuba's, the ones resulting from the most unfair electoral process in Latin America's present.

CHAPTER 8

A Bittersweet Victory

At six P.M. on Sunday, August 21, 1994, about an hour before the polls had closed in all Mexican states, I was invited by Zedillo's top aides to a "small chat" with the candidate and a handful of foreign correspondents. By then, we all knew that Zedillo had won: The first exit polls by U.S. television networks had just been released in Washington and Miami, and had shown the ruling party candidate well ahead. Like my other colleagues invited to the meeting, I dropped whatever last-minute election reporting I had left and showed up at Zedillo's campaign headquarters within minutes.

To my surprise, Zedillo showed no outward signs of elation or even fatigue. He looked impassive, almost as if it had been just another day at the office. Wearing a heavily starched white dress shirt, tieless and unbuttoned at the neck, a navy blue jacket, and gray slacks, Zedillo took a seat at the end of a coffee table and fielded our questions for forty-five minutes. He responded obliquely when asked what he would do once in office — it would be poor form to acknowledge his victory before the polls closed.

But his cautious speech was more than politically correct. It was detached, distant, like that of a knowledgeable university professor analyzing political events in a foreign land. By comparison, Zedillo's two aides — his private secretary, Liébano Sáenz, and soon-to-become foreign minister, José Angel Gurría — were on the edge of their seats, hardly able to contain their smiles, looking as if they were only waiting for us to leave to start jumping around the room.

I stayed on for a few seconds with Zedillo after the meeting was over, and commented to him that I couldn't help being surprised by his un-emotional demeanor. He had just achieved the unthinkable: rising from a poverty-stricken family without political connections to become Mexico's president! And he was only forty-two! Wasn't he excited about it?

"I have an elephant's skin," Zedillo told me, rubbing his forearm with his index finger and smiling for the first time. "I have learned not to allow either the good news or the bad news to go to my head. It has proved to be a good policy so far."

As I left the room, I couldn't help wondering whether Zedillo was such a cold technocrat that he would not allow himself a celebration on what any other politician would have considered the happiest day of his life. Or, perhaps, whether there wasn't another, more ominous explanation: that despite four months of campaigning that had amounted to a crash course in big-time politics, he was as nervous at the task ahead of him as when he had first been picked as the government party's accidental candidate.

▼

In fact, the president-elect had no shortage of reasons for not being ecstatic. Foreign reserves had fallen sharply since the Colosio assassination, not the least because of a gradual rise in U.S. interest rates, and there was no sign that his election victory would stimulate investors to return to Mexico. The country's economic policy had fallen into disarray as Salinas's attention had been absorbed by the political crisis: The number of Salinas's economic policy cabinet meetings had plummeted from an annual average of fifty-six over the previous five years to only seven in 1994 — and none over the previous three months. Worse, the Salinas government had issued large amounts of high-interest, short-term bonds indexed to dollars — known as *tesobonos* — after each political crisis in an effort to maintain the flow of foreign investments. After the Chiapas uprising, and again after the Colosio assassination, when many nervous investors had begun to pull their deposits out of Mexico,

Salinas had issued new *tesobonos* to help make up for the foreign reserve losses. Trouble was, Mexico would have to pay back these short-term bonds — and very soon. And the country's accumulated short-term debt was coming dangerously close to its total foreign reserves.

"The government reacted to each political event as if it would be the last one, but none of them happened to be the last one," Salinas's Trade minister and future Zedillo Finance minister Jaime Serra Puche commented to me months later, referring to the progressive sale of *tesobonos*. "Governments don't base their decision making on catastrophic scenarios."

▼

The only part of the economy that was booming was one that the president-elect would rather see collapse: the drug trade. U.S. intelligence reports that had landed on the president-elect's desk showed that the porous two-thousand-mile Mexican-U.S. border was rapidly becoming the world's biggest drug smuggling route. U.S. officials estimated that about 75 percent of all cocaine shipments entering the United States were coming from Mexico, and that Mexican drug mafias were earning annual profits of between $10 and $30 billion. It was a phenomenal booty that was polluting Mexico's political system — much as had happened in Colombia before — with a combination of bribery and terror.

What had happened? In the 1980s, most of the Colombian cocaine was taken to Mexico in small Cessna planes. Now, Colombia's cocaine barons were using old passenger jets — Boeing 727s and DC-7s — to transport shipments of up to ten tons to Mexico. Because these aircraft were bigger and faster than Mexico's fleet of small drug-interception planes, mostly Cessnas, they could not be stopped. In addition, the attention of Mexico's armed forces for the past year had been centered on Chiapas, leaving the drug traffickers more leeway to conduct their operations in northern Mexico.

There was another, potentially more ominous new development in Mexico's drug trafficking business as well: In the past, Mexican drug mafias had been working on contract for Colombia's cartels, earning a fee for transporting drugs across the border. Since the late 1980s, with the U.S.-Mexican border replacing Florida as the main passage for drugs to the U.S. market, Mexican drug barons had been going into business by themselves. They were buying cocaine cargoes from the Colombians, paying for them in cash, shipping them to the United States, and even creating their own distribution rings on the other side of the border — making hundreds of millions more in the process.

Even before their transition to junior versions of the Colombian drug barons, Mexican narco traffickers had corrupted much of their country's law enforcement apparatus. A chilling example of the drug mafias' growing penetration of Mexico's police forces had come on August 4, only a few weeks before Zedillo's election, when a French-made Aeroespatiale Caravelle jet carrying an eight-and-a-half-ton cocaine shipment had made a forced landing on a semiabandoned airstrip near the desert town of Sombrerete in the north-central state of Zacatecas. Federal highway police officers had seized the aircraft and reported that the cargo had been taken away by federal and local police agents — yet only two and a half tons of the drug were recovered. Days later, packages of cocaine with the same markings as those found in the Caravelle jet had turned up in seizures at the U.S. border. There was little question that local or federal Mexican authorities had kept the bulk of the cargo.

Zedillo had received alarming intelligence reports about the fabulous fortunes the new Mexican drug lords were amassing, and how they were laundering billions of dollars — sometimes in partnership with ruling party politicians — through Mexican banks and investments in beach resorts, housing developments, and shopping centers. The question was, had the newly powerful drug mafias already turned Mexico into a narco-democracy, a country where drug lords had become untouchable? Had they been behind the killing of Guadalajara cardinal Posadas Ocampo, whose city had become the Wall Street of Mexico's money laundering business? Had they killed Colosio?

Zedillo did not have the answers at the time, but it was clear to him that the Mexican drug rings could easily become — if they hadn't already — a major destabilization factor.

▼

Despite what appeared to be a major triumph for him and the ruling party, Zedillo knew that he was not about to take office with a mandate.

On the surface, the election results looked quite favorable. A record 78 percent of eligible voters had turned out to the polls, much more than anybody had expected. Official results had given Zedillo 48.8 percent of the vote, while Fernandez de Cevallos had obtained 25.9 percent and Cárdenas 16.6 percent. What was more, the United States and other international observers seemed pleased with what they had seen on election day.

A delegation of U.S. observers from the National Democratic Institute and the International Republican Institute had concluded that while the group had witnessed serious irregularities, it had found "no evidence to suggest that they would have affected the outcome of the presidential race." In a similar vein, the Civic Alliance, which had been previously accused by government officials of a pro-Cárdenas slant, concluded that widespread irregularities had probably altered the correlation of forces in the Congress and may have changed the outcome of state elections, but "were not massive enough to affect the final result of the presidential election." Unlike Salinas, Zedillo would take office without a debilitating stain: His election had been validated by much of the international community.

Even Mexico's largest opposition party was grumblingly accepting his victory. In his concession speech late that night, a crushed Fernandez de Cevallos denounced the ruling party's use of government buses to load workers and carry them to the polling places as if they were sheep, the various mechanisms of political control at state enterprises, and the flagrant use of the government's Solidarity and Procampo funds for electoral purposes. In addition, he lashed out against the pro-government television networks that had been pressed to "deform the truth." In view of these and other irregularities, he had concluded that "this process has been deeply inequitable." But Fernandez de Cevallos's party, unlike Cárdenas and the Zapatistas, had refrained from denouncing the election as a sham. The government could state that the two parties representing nearly 80 percent of Mexican people endorsed the election results.

Zedillo's victory had come as no surprise to him: He had long taken it for granted. By nightfall on election day, he knew from exit polls that things were not as rosy as they seemed. A closer look at the exit polls revealed that he had been voted into office with the lowest percentage ever won by a PRI candidate, and that he had been shunned by the most rapidly growing and influential sectors of society: the young, the well-educated, and large sectors of the urban population. He would inherit a financial and political house of cards at a time when the glue that bound Mexico's social fabric was cracking, and not just because of the Zapatista rebellion in southern Chiapas.

Exit polls showed that Mexico's youth — the fastest-growing sector of the population — had voted in substantial numbers for Fernandez de Cevallos's conservative PAN, the probusiness party founded in 1939 by disenchanted supporters of the Mexican Revolution, anticommunists, and Roman Catholic activists. A surprising 45 percent of all PAN voters were under twenty-nine. By comparison, only 38 percent of all PRI voters were that age or younger, and 37 percent of the center-left PRD voters belonged to that age group.

The PAN's popularity among the young was an ominous sign for the ruling party: More than half of Mexico's population was below the voting age of eighteen in 1994, and a sizable number of Mexico's young would be ready to cast their ballots for the first time in the 2000 elections.

José Luis Salas, the PAN's presidential campaign manager, told me that Mexico's young had turned out in large numbers for his party because its presidential candidate had best interpreted their yearnings for peaceful change. In its internal polls, the PAN had found that, unlike their parents' generation, which had been shaken by the government's 1968 massacre of leftist students in Mexico City's Tlatelolco Square, young Mexicans had no romantic ideas about the left. They were not longing for a revolution. They wanted change, but a social transformation that would make Mexico look more like the developed nations of the north.

"The young people of 1968 were the sons and daughters of a postwar generation who rebelled against rigid, conservative parents," Salas said. "The young people of today are sons and daughters of the 1968 generation: They don't long for freedom; they long for order and economic progress."

Mindful of the changes, the PAN had come up with a slick campaign slogan: "Change with stability." It was this motto that best expressed the feelings of young Mexicans and that — coupled with Fernandez de Cevallos's charisma — helped explain their massive vote for the conservative PAN.

▼

But Zedillo's party was also losing ground in almost every other corner of society:

• Urban Mexicans, who were rapidly becoming the majority of the population, had voted for the ruling party in much smaller numbers than residents of rural areas. While the PRI had trounced its rivals by more than fifty points in the countryside, in most major cities it had won by a narrow margin. Mexico's rapidly changing demographic picture was bound to hurt the government party in the future: About 70 percent of Mexico's population was projected to live in urban areas by the time of the 2000 elections, up from 51 percent in 1960.

• Well-educated Mexicans had voted for the PAN, and to a lesser extent for the leftist opposition, relegating the government party to a distant third place. Among voters who had completed college, the center-right opposition party had come out first with 21 percent of the vote, followed by the center-left opposition party with 20 percent, and the ruling party with 13 percent. By comparison, the government party had won 42 percent among the largely peasant voters who had only completed elementary school. The growing inroads of Mexico's public education system among the population were likely to further erode the ruling party's hold on the electorate. According to government projections, Mexico would have for the first time in history a higher percentage of its population in high school than in elementary school by the year 2000, and the number of college students was projected to soar from 196,569 in 1980 to 280,000.

• The growing number of Mexicans working for the private sector had also voted in large numbers for the PAN, especially in Mexico's northern states. With fewer state enterprises under its control and less money in its pocket, the government had lost hundreds of top jobs with which to reward the PRI's political bosses and the thousands of loyalists who depended on them. Zedillo would start his term without the powerful political machine that his predecessors had used so effectively to consolidate themselves in power. Its ability to buy votes was bound to diminish.*

In most other countries, such voting trends would not amount to a big deal: After all, the government party's adoption of free-market economic policies in recent years had blurred much of its differences with the center-right opposition. But in Mexico, ideology was the least important aspect of political competition: The preservation of economic privileges and — perhaps more importantly — impunity from past abuses were much more critical issues for ruling-class politicians. The government party's dinosaurs and their disciples, the babysaurs, would not sit idly by while the opposition gained political ground.

The 1994 election's official results had been the worst ever for the ruling party. In fact, its share of the vote had been declining steadily ever since its creation in the late 1920s, when it used to run unopposed. In those good old days, General Alvaro Obregón had made history by winning an election with 1,670,456 votes in favor, and an astounding 0 against. Decades later, when the party had grudgingly allowed a semblance of opposition under heavy international pressure, its votes had dropped with each presidential election: The PRI's share of the vote had fallen to 86 percent in 1964 to 80 percent in 1970 and 1976, 69 percent in 1982, 50 percent in 1988, and 48.8 percent in 1994.

▼

While Mexicans had rejected Cárdenas's confrontational style and firebrand leftist rhetoric, Mexico was showing signs of an increasingly vigorous civic society that was beginning to challenge the government on virtually all fronts. The number of nongovernmental citizens' groups and political organizations had soared from a few hundred in the early eighties to thirteen hundred in the mid-nineties, according to the Inte-

---

* The number of state-owned enterprises had dropped from 1,155 in 1982 to 213 by the end of the Salinas administration, according to Finance Minister Pedro Aspe, quoted in *Reforma*, July 13, 1993, "Concluye la Privatización." Critics point out, however, that the state's role in the economy didn't shrink much in terms of assets or employment because giant firms such as Pemex remained in government hands.

rior ministry's Directory of Civic Organizations. But because many independent groups didn't even bother to register with the government, the figure was likely to be much higher. Reliable estimates put the number of nongovernmental groups at more than five thousand nationwide.

The Chiapas rebellion had reenergized human rights and Indian affairs watchdog groups, and hundreds of grass roots citizens' organizations were springing up everywhere to challenge the government on a variety of issues. Despite the government's blocking efforts, and in part as a result of the NAFTA negotiations, Mexico could no longer shield itself from outside scrutiny by invoking the principles of national sovereignty: Growing numbers of Mexicans did not buy such government excuses anymore, and U.S. and European nongovernmental organizations were beginning to provide technical and material cooperation to their increasingly assertive Mexican counterparts.

For the first time, citizens' groups from across the political spectrum had organized themselves to set up the largest ever nongovernment election monitoring system. More than fourteen thousand Mexicans had checked voting procedures at more than five thousand polling stations in the just-completed elections. Their umbrella group, the Civic Alliance, had learned from civil rights groups in Chile and the Philippines, and had formed a sizable army of prodemocracy volunteers — coached by United Nations experts and partly sponsored by the U.S. National Endowment for Democracy — that soon acquired considerable weight in the eyes of the international media and the U.S. Congress. Far from fading away after the election, groups such as this were spreading in numbers and in their scope of action.

Civic leaders such as Civic Alliance head Sergio Aguayo had become an influential political force in their own right, and not just because they commanded respect and admiration abroad. They were getting growing press coverage at home as — in addition to the left-of-center daily *La Jornada* — a new independent newspaper, *Reforma*, increasingly covered their activities. The new daily was beginning to profile civic leaders and to publish exposés of government corruption from a secure vantage point: Its owners — the publishers of Monterrey's daily *El Norte* — had deep pockets and could not be easily cowed with threats of financial punishment.

Aguayo, a Johns Hopkins University–educated political scientist and president of the Mexican Academy of Human Rights, had been instrumental in creating an umbrella organization for various citizens' groups and in getting them active in election monitoring. Many of these groups had sprung up in the aftermath of the 1985 Mexico City earthquake, when official rescue efforts had proven totally inept at solving basic city services problems, and had gotten reenergized following the 1988 elections that many of them felt had been stolen from Cárdenas. In 1991 Aguayo helped gather three hundred volunteers to monitor the 1991 gubernatorial election in San Luis Potosí, and soon spread his effort nationwide with the enthusiastic support of Canadian and U.S. foundations. In the years that followed, as Salinas tried to win U.S. congressional approval of NAFTA, it became increasingly difficult for the Mexican government to repress such civic initiatives. Aguayo and other civic leaders had made the most of the circumstances. They were here to stay.

A separate middle-class rebellion of small ranchers and merchants who had defaulted on their debts and were protesting against bank seizures of their properties was spreading like wildfire around the nation. The El Barzón movement, named after the wooden yoke used to attach oxen at their necks, had started when a group of bankrupt small ranchers in Zacatecas had taken their twelve tractors to the streets of the city of Fresnillo to demand a renegotiation of their debts and prevent the banks from seizing their working tools. Since then, El Barzón had grown to one million farmers, merchants, industrialists, and credit card holders who were challenging the banking system with building occupations, sit-ins, and legally assisted defiance of the banks' repossession orders.

In Mexico City's poor neighborhoods, Superbarrio, a masked man clad in a red-and-yellow wrestling costume who had already become a fixture of the city's cultural landscape, was leading daily occupations of properties by tenants about to be evicted by their landlords. Superbarrio, who worked closely with pro-Cárdenas grass roots groups, had been emulated by more than half a dozen other masked activists — including Superanimal, a defender of animal rights; Superecologista, a champion of environmental causes; and Ultrapoli, a fighter against police corruption — who led daily protests along the capital's downtown streets and often made front pages with their imaginative publicity stunts. In recent months, they had launched a string of unlicensed radio stations throughout the city — with names like Radio Pirata, Radio Verdad, and Radio Vampiro — to seek support for their struggle and challenge progovernment radio networks.

The day I met Superbarrio, the top news was that Washington, D.C., was pressing the Mexican government to impose new austerity measures, and the masked political activist was preparing his next move: a mock fight on Mexico City's busy Reforma Avenue with El Gringo Empinado — "the Bent-Over Gringo" — a new wrestler who would make his debut on the occasion. "Social struggle shouldn't be formal or dull; in addition to effective, it should be fun," Superbarrio said.

Other new civic groups were planning to fight government corruption in a variety of ways. One of them, inspired by U.S. watchdog groups such as Common Cause, was hoping to establish itself as an anticorruption monitor by launching a peculiar campaign: "Adopt a Government Official." The group called for each of its member organizations to "adopt" a government official and to look into his or her finances, spending habits, and work attendance. The new group planned to publicize any corrupt practices it found, much as other groups reported human rights violations.

Progovernment media didn't find the idea amusing. The main political column of *Excelsior* said the new program was aimed at "manipulating public emotions," and that it contributed to a "postelection destabilization project." Supporters of the adoption project, however, responded by quoting Don Quixote's famous words to his trusted aide, "They're barking, Sancho — a sign we must be galloping." This was a new Mexico.

▼

Was the PAN Mexico's party of the future? Were the new generations of Mexicans turning their backs on their country's history of staunch nationalism and big government, or had they just reacted more positively to Fernandez de Cevallos's powerful television presentations than to Cárdenas's lethargic image?

There was little doubt that just as the ruling party was losing electoral ground, the PAN was winning positions throughout the country and becoming the most serious contender for the presidency in future elections. The PAN had grown steadily from 7.8 percent of the vote in the 1952 elections to 27 percent in 1994. It was already governing the states of Baja California, Guanajuato, and Chihuahua, and would soon win the 1995 elections in the key state of Jalisco.

The party's decades-old practice of focusing on local races and of building up national support little by little was paying off handsomely: After the 1994 elections, PAN state governors and mayors were ruling over nearly 20 million Mexicans. The PAN had seen its number of elected mayors across the country soar to 156, its federal congressmen go from a few dozen to 119, and its senators from none to 25. The conservative party was on a roll, not the least because it did not have a history of corruption and most of its elected officials had turned out to be cleaner than their ruling party predecessors — a quality that would surely be a political asset in future elections.

The PAN's growing popularity — which had also benefited from Salinas's chivalrous relations with party leaders, as opposed to his open hostility to Cárdenas — posed a serious problem to Zedillo. It was almost sure to provoke a strong reaction from old-guard politicians within the PRI, who were not likely to risk losing their positions of power and the fabulous business deals that went with them. For the first time in their lives, the dinosaurs were seeing their government allow an opposition party to take over growing numbers of neighborhood associations, municipalities, and even states across the country.

Now, the PAN was suddenly well positioned to win the 2000 elections. The PRI dinosaurs could be expected to fight tooth and nail — behind the back of their president, if necessary — to prevent this from happening.

▼

Manuel "El Meme" Garza, a legendary figure of what critics called the ruling party's "Jurassic Park" wing, told me with his brightest smile that he didn't mind being called a dinosaur. "On the contrary, I even have a dinosaur pin that I often wear on my lapel," he added with an amused shrug.

"El Meme," as he was known by friends and foes, was a wealthy rancher-congressman from the northern border state of Tamaulipas who had occupied dozens of senior PRI positions over more than forty years of political activity, but who was best known for his reputation as an "electoral alchemist," or election fixer, for the PRI. Now in his early sixties, he had been dispatched all over the country over the years to help the PRI win elections, and he had always delivered — a record attributed by government officials to his extraordinary political skills, and by his enemies to his use of a wide variety of tricks to rig the vote. As far as he was concerned, he had always acted within the law, he said: If he had used government resources to help party candidates, he had done it at a time when that was not illegal under Mexico's laws.

After hearing so much about the party dinosaurs, I was eager to meet El Meme. When he kindly invited me to his Mexico City home for lunch, thanks to the intervention of a common friend, I half expected to meet a Tyrannosaurus rex of Mexican politics — an old-fashioned politician who would recite blatant lies while looking me straight in the eye. Instead, I found a witty man with enormous political acumen whose arguments for slowing down the pace of political reforms would most likely be hard to dismiss by the new president.

I arrived at El Meme's place in Mexico City at about two P.M. — a little bit early for what was to be a 2:30 P.M. Mexican lunch. His house looked like a transplant from his Tamaulipas ranch. Its rooms were filled with huge stuffed animals fixed to the walls — a giant Great Kudu he had hunted in Uganda dominated the living room, next to more than a dozen antelopes of all sizes and a big jaguar — and the ceilings were crossed by Swiss chalet–style wooden beams. As the decor suggested, El Meme's passion was hunting, and his entire political vocabulary was peppered with hunting metaphors: "Before I go to a meeting, I always ask what we are going to talk about," he told me when referring to a call he had just made to a leading government official. "One must always know what weapons to carry for each occasion."

At about three P.M., perhaps noticing that I was starved, El Meme's wife, Luz Marina, brought a silver tray filled with tamales to the living room. They tasted funny — quite different from the corn tamales I was used to eating in Mexico. They were deer tamales, made out of smoked deer. I had two, saving my appetite for lunch. But at four P.M., we were still talking under the Great Kudu's seemingly inquisitive look, and there was no sign of lunch. The clock marked 4:30, and I was really getting hungry. It wasn't until five P.M. that El Meme's elegant wife walked smiling into the room and announced that lunch was ready.

"The plane came in late," El Meme explained as we walked toward the dining room. The plane? I asked, not understanding what he was talking about. "Yes, whenever we have a young goat to eat, we have it slaughtered at seven A.M. at our Tamaulipas ranch, put it in an icebox, and fly it to Mexico City that same morning." He added matter-of-factly, "You have to do it that way or it loses its flavor." Aaah. I nodded, as if taking note for the day when I had a ranch across the country and servants to hunt a young goat, put it on a plane, pick it up in Mexico City, and cook it.

Over lunch, while eating the exquisite milk-marinated goat with a 1984 Château-Lafite-Rothschild, El Meme explained to me what he saw as wrong with Mexico's democratic reforms: Their breakneck speed was shattering the political stability that Mexico had managed to maintain for so many decades and that had been the basis for the country's economic development, he said. Mexico should not allow hastiness to destroy what it had built over several decades. The government had to carry out all the democratic reforms that the modern times required, but gradually. Otherwise, society would crumble under the kind of political violence that had cost so many lives at the beginning of the century.

"If you are going to turn this house into a school and begin knocking down the walls, doors, and windows, you must make sure that you are not destroying the columns and bridges that keep the building together," he said. "The same thing happens in politics: You must make sure not to break the structure, and if you are going to unite different structures you must allow time for the concrete to dry, or the whole building will collapse."

One of El Meme's main concerns was Zedillo's campaign vow to become a "passive member" of the party, which amounted to giving up the historic presidential practice of handpicking future PRI local and national leaders. Going out of his way not to appear critical of the president-elect, El Meme said this could be dangerous, and possibly even damaging to the country's democratization goals. In Mexico, the president had always acted as the "maximum umpire," he explained. They traditionally received input from all PRI factions before appointing a candidate and picked the one who would suit the most. Without such arbitrage — and new party regulations to replace it — the party would become even more autocratic: A handful of powerful regional bosses would run the country at their will, he said.

"The political bosses of Mexico's big states, such as Jalisco, Michoacán, Mexico state, Mexico City, Puebla, Veracruz, and Nuevo León, which amount to nearly seventy percent of the country's vote, could easily impose their will over the rest of the nation," El Meme said. "Five or six political bosses of major states could impose their candidates, and there would be no higher authority to say, 'What are the other twenty-five states saying?' "

These were the kinds of arguments that Zedillo was getting from the men who ran his party's political machine, and thanks to whom he had just won the elections. The dinosaurs were not just a clique of reactionary politicians terrified about losing their economic privileges, as they were often portrayed by the press. Some of their arguments made perfect sense to the president-elect, even if he agreed with the social demands — and Zapatista requirements — for turning Mexico into a full democracy. His own party's old guard could become as formidable an adversary to the new president as some of his most rabid political rivals.

▼

Few of the old-guard politicians inspired more apprehension than Don Fernando Gutiérrez Barrios, the shadowy figure who had run Mexico's intelligence apparatus on and off for nearly three decades and commanded one of the most powerful political camarillas in the country. Don Fernando, as he was known by everybody who was anybody, was already sixty-seven and had stepped down from his last government job as Salinas's Interior minister in 1993, but he was still very much at the center of Mexico's political life: Several governors, Interior ministry officials, and ruling party leaders across the country were known to be members of his clan, and to follow his suggestions as if he were still in office.

All kinds of rumors surrounded the mysterious Don Fernando: The most benign ones asserted that he ran a giant private intelligence service; that he had just bought a $15 million cellular telephone interception system that was more sophisticated than the government's own; that he had highly compromising dossiers on every politician and businessman in town; and that he protected leftist guerrilla groups throughout Latin America in exchange for information and their promise not to export their revolutions to Mexico.

Some of it was undoubtedly true. A military school graduate who had retired from the army with the rank of captain, Don Fernando had joined the government as an intelligence agent in the fifties and had risen through the ranks of the Interior ministry to serve for twelve years as undersecretary of Interior and another four years as Interior minister. Don Fernando's trademark was having forged close ties with Latin America's revolutionary left since the day when, as a young government intelligence officer, he had interrogated a young Cuban rebel named Fidel Castro who was preparing an expedition aimed at toppling the Fulgencio Batista regime in Cuba. Gutiérrez Barrios had set Castro free, and their original meeting turned into a warm friendship following the Cuban rebel leader's 1959 revolution.

Over the next several decades, he was viewed by U.S. officials as a key facilitator of Mexico's warm ties with Cuba and Latin America's revolutionary movements. By providing a safe haven in Mexico for Cuban-backed Latin American rebels, Don Fernando had become an important figure in Mexico-Cuban relations and had thus helped spare Mexico of the leftist violence that had swept most of the region. Castro, indeed, supported most leftist revolutionaries in Latin America — except the Mexicans.

In the mid-nineties, Don Fernando remained a commanding figure for old-guard PRI members. Their argument: Mexico had fallen apart since Don Fernando had been removed from the government's intelligence apparatus in early 1993. The country had since been rocked by the Zapatista insurgency and had plunged into its worst cycle of violence since the beginning of the century. Some even speculated privately that the former Interior minister may have tacitly allowed — or perhaps even encouraged — some of Mexico's recent incidents of violence, either to stop democratic reforms or to make himself once again indispensable to the government. Don Fernando rejected such claims as outrageous.

It was not exactly clear what Don Fernando was doing for a living now, but when I visited his offices in a three-story townhouse under a bridge in downtown Mexico City it was clear that he was keeping busy: A telephone operator at the entrance managed a switchboard with twenty-four lines, and more than two dozen men were sitting around in various offices, sipping coffee, pasting newspaper clippings, and looking busy. After being led to a man who identified himself as Major Félix — one of several guards holding walkie-talkies at a security booth near the entrance — I was escorted to Don Fernando's offices upstairs.

Don Fernando looked just as I had imagined him: a seasoned, wealthy gentleman who projected an image of power, real or imagined. He walked with his head up, like most men with a military background; combed his snow white hair with a loop, as was fashionable in the sixties; and kept carefully manicured nails. He was clad in a starched double-breasted navy blue suit with a matching tie, and his spit-shiny shoes looked as though they were brushed every other hour. Don Fernando made no bones about his belief that Mexico was on the wrong track, and that the U.S.-educated technocrats who had ruled the country in recent years were responsible for part of the current instability. Not only had they tried to change things too fast, they had broken long-standing rules that helped guarantee social peace in the country, he said.

In the past, when a government official or ruling party politician stole $10 million, a small group of top officials would summon the suspect and demand that he pay back the missing money the very next morning, Don Fernando explained. "There were ways of dealing with things, in which we all respected one another and fixed our problems among ourselves," he said, with what I interpreted as obvious nostalgia. "Later, in the late seventies, Mexico's political class got into a progressive pattern of self-flagellation by venting these problems publicly, at a time when Mexican society was awakening thanks to the proliferation of schools, roads, and information media. As a result, the people began to perceive their authorities as corrupt and ineffective."

From where Don Fernando stood, Mexico had functioned much

better in the good old days when those in power fixed their problems behind closed doors. Too much openness too soon, he seemed to suggest, was plunging the country into chaos.

▼

Just as Don Fernando commanded universal reverence for his real or imagined wealth of secret information, billionaire Agriculture minister Carlos Hank Gonzalez elicited general deference within Mexico's ruling class for his fabulous fortune, and the generosity with which he used it to buy loyalties within the party.

Hank Gonzalez, who proudly accepted the nickname of "the Professor" that dated back to his days as an elementary school teacher in a rural town, was the leader of the Atlacomulco Group, one of the most influential power cliques within the ruling elite. Its main feature, aside from the fabulous fortune the Professor had amassed since his days as governor of Mexico state, was that its own leader denied its existence, as well as the fact that his loyalists were peppered all over Zedillo's team. The Professor's well-oiled political machine within the PRI had been crucial to helping Zedillo win the election, and that — according to the unwritten laws of Mexican politics — was bound to give his group a powerful say in the new government. The Atlacomulco Group was set to become a strong wall of resistance against drastic political reforms.

"Noooo, Don Andres, I can assure you that there is no such thing as the Atlacomulco Group," the Professor told me, opening his hands, during a breakfast interview at his mansion in the plush Mexico City neighborhood of Las Lomas. That group was a creation of the media, he said. True, the president of the PRI, the party's finance secretary, and Zedillo's chief of staff were known to be close to him, but that didn't mean they operated as a group or that they responded to him. "They are just my friends. Why are they my friends? Because, Don Andres, I've been a PRI activist for the past fifty years. I joined the party's youth wing in 1944 and I know virtually everybody. I'm not an influential person within Dr. Zedillo's group, nor in any other, but I am an old PRI member with a very long militancy and, fortunately, a lot of friends within the party. It's as simple as that."

The Professor was, as I had been warned before meeting him, one of the most charming men you could possibly run into. A tall, white-haired man who looked younger than his sixty-seven years, he was legendary for his public relations feats. It wasn't just doling out money: When the mother of a young and relatively unknown reporter had been diagnosed with cancer, the Professor had immediately ordered her sent to Houston — all expenses paid — for state-of-the-art treatment; when the father of a junior ruling party member died, the Professor personally attended the funeral and offered his help to the family; when a senior PRI leader was axed from his job and everybody else deserted him, the Professor invited him to his home for dinner with other celebrities and rescued him from political ostracism. These were gestures that were not easily forgotten, and that created lifelong loyalties.

The other thing for which the Professor was legendary was the fabulous wealth he had amassed during his years as Mexico state governor, Mexico City mayor, minister of Tourism, and minister of Agriculture — $1.3 billion, according to *Forbes* magazine. He and his children ran, among other companies, the Hermes Industrial Consortium, which sold Mercedes-Benz vehicles, power generators, and oil industry equipment, mainly to the government. Much of the Professor's fortune dated from his days as Mexico state governor and Mexico City mayor, when he allegedly purchased millions of dollars' worth of garbage trucks, tractors, and buses from a company run by his sons. When he was asked at about that time how he had risen from a penniless rural teacher to a multimillionaire, he had smiled and quipped, *"Un político pobre es un pobre político"* — "A politician who is poor is a poor politician."

Mexico's opposition leaders and U.S. officials saw the Professor as a symbol of much of what was wrong with Mexico. How could somebody who was born poor, had never inherited anything, and had always worked in the government have made so much money? they asked. "He has accumulated a fortune of $1.3 billion on a salary that never exceeded eighty thousand dollars," a senior U.S. official told me in Washington, D.C. "He has become a face that illustrates Mexico's problems."

The Professor shook his head once again when I asked him about his fortune. Sitting across the table from me in his dining room decorated with million-dollar paintings by nineteenth-century Mexican painter José Maria Velasco, as we picked our breakfast choices from a hand-written menu offered by his white-clad waiter, the Professor asserted that he had begun to build his fortune before becoming governor of Mexico state. "Nooo, Don Andres," he repeated with a warm smile as he rejected claims that he had profited from his closeness to power. "When I was very young, I decided to take care of my family's economic problems before plunging into politics. So I founded a little candy factory in my town, Atlacomulco. Then I became a distributor for Pepsi Cola in that region and began other businesses." Over the next few years, as he was rising in his town's local politics, he had begun purchasing a few "little trucks," which had developed into a "small trucking company," which had in turn allowed him to start other allegedly modest business ventures. "I did it because I never wanted to depend on a politician's income to make a living. I like to have my own income sources that are independent from politics, so that I can act with total freedom."

Toward the end of our breakfast, the Professor told me he planned to retire from the government and would thus not take any job with the incoming Zedillo government. He didn't need to: Zedillo was surrounded by his loyalists. In or out of government, the Professor led an old-guard wing of the PRI that the new president would find hard to ignore.

▼

As I watched the president-elect at his campaign headquarters during our election evening interview, I got a hunch that he would end up becoming a hard-line president. He had a short temper that could be taken for an authoritarian streak. I had seen him lose his temper in public at least twice during the weeks prior to the election — once rudely cutting off a reporter whose question at a press conference he clearly didn't like. A no-nonsense technocrat with not much of a sense of humor and little political flair, he had the kind of personality that could lead him to become an autocratic ruler. In addition, he could possibly be forced to become one: He was viewed with suspicion by the PRI's political machinery, which had only supported him as a candidate of last resort, and was disliked by much of the center-right and center-left opposition. He had had no time to develop a political staff and was about to take office as the most isolated president in recent memory. Probably, he would only be able to assert himself by force.

During the casual chat at the end of the interview, after we had talked about his plans for handling the Chiapas crisis, I mentioned to him — only half jokingly — that I had the hunch that he would become a *"presidente duro,"* or hard-line ruler. Zedillo laughed and shook his head.

"You're wrong," he said, repeating his assertion twice. "Very much to the contrary. . . . You'll see."

CHAPTER 9

Murder in the Family

The more than two dozen personal guards of former president Salinas, who by now had been out of power for nearly three months, jumped into their bullet-proof Jetta vans. As the vehicles dashed off at full speed, they loaded their Uzi submachine guns and 9 mm Browning pistols. They were going to the southern Mexico City neighborhood of Las Aguilas: Salinas had just ordered them to rush to the home of his sister, Adriana, at 62 Costa Street, where their brother Raúl was staying. Their orders: to stop Raúl's impending capture by government agents. More than seventy elite troops of the Federal Judicial Police and the Presidential Guard, clad in black uniforms and bullet-proof vests, were approaching the house from all directions. Civilian-clad police sharpshooters, who had arrived in the neighborhood hours earlier, were beginning to take up positions on the roofs of nearby buildings. They were armed to the teeth, just in case Raúl tried to resist arrest — or the former president's guards tried to prevent his capture.

It was Tuesday morning, February 28, 1995. For a few moments, as the two armed convoys zigzagged their way through Mexico City's traffic-congested streets toward Adriana's house, it looked as though Mexico were headed for a small civil war. It was a key moment in Mexico's contemporary history: Salinas, one of its strongest presidents in recent times, the architect of Mexico's economic opening, was widely believed to be the real power behind the country's rookie president. More than half of Zedillo's cabinet was made up of Salinas loyalists, and the former president had spent the previous weeks touring the world to promote his U.S. and Mexico–backed candidacy to head the World Trade Organization. Salinas's bodyguards, who were also members of the Presidential Guard, the military unit in charge of protecting current and former government officials, had not thought twice when Salinas ordered them to protect Raúl from the other government troops, including some of their own comrades. It did not cross their minds at the time that their boss was no longer calling the shots: For as far back as the young military men could remember, Salinas had been the most powerful man in Mexico, in or out of office.

But Salinas's guards were only a few blocks away from their destination, ready to jump out of their Jettas and set up a defensive cordon in front of Adriana's house, when a stern voice over their vehicles' military radio system forced them to come to a sudden stop. It was General Roberto Miranda, chief of the Presidential Guard, with orders that left no room for misunderstanding. "Stop that action!" General Miranda recalls having shouted over the radio. "It's an order!"

The operation to arrest Raúl Salinas had been approved from the very top — by President Zedillo himself. Raúl's own bodyguards, also members of the Presidential Guard, had just been ordered to leave their positions and allow the Federal Judicial Police officers to carry out the arrest. The Jettas carrying the troops that were to defend Raúl stood still for a few seconds, their engines still idling. Then they turned around and slowly began to head back to where they had come from. Minutes later, a defeated Raúl Salinas was led out of the house escorted by prosecutors and police agents. Clad in a gray suit and tie, he kept his head down, holding his hands behind his back even though he had not been handcuffed. A bloody confrontation between Salinas's guards and Zedillo's Federal Judicial Police, which could have triggered a wider conflict, had been averted by a matter of seconds.

▼

Zedillo's dramatic break with his predecessor and former mentor would have been hard to imagine a few weeks earlier, when the new president received the red, white, and green sash of office from a proud Salinas at his December 1, 1994, inaugural ceremony at the Mexican Congress. The whole Congress and more than a dozen foreign dignitaries — including U.S. vice president Al Gore, Cuban president Fidel Castro, and Argentinian president Carlos Menem — had stood up and applauded as Mexico's young new president walked down the hall of the building's main auditorium toward a two-level podium.

A small but telling episode captured my attention while I was watching the scene from the press balcony: As Zedillo was about to reach the stage, he had mistakenly headed for the lower-level table, where the leaders of Congress sat. He was quickly rescued by a protocol official, who led him to an upper-level pulpit where Salinas was waiting for him. Zedillo shook his head and laughed, as if joking to himself that he would be better off taking the lesser job. It looked as if Salinas would continue running Mexico for some time.

But minutes later, in his inaugural speech, Zedillo would raise some eyebrows by giving a personal touch of candor to a new government that looked largely like a continuation of the previous one. Looking at the audience, Zedillo tacitly admitted that the August 21 elections could have been "more equitable," and that Mexico needed new electoral reforms that would include "party funding, ceilings for campaign expenditures, access to the media, and the autonomy of electoral authorities." This would be a pluralistic government, he vowed. To prove it, he had appointed Antonio Lozano Gracia, until then the leader of the opposition National Action Party in Congress, as his new attorney general. The new administration would launch a head-on offensive against corruption, Zedillo said — no matter from how high up it came.

Turning his eyes to the right of the podium, where his full cabinet was sitting, Zedillo said, "The government is not a place for amassing wealth. He who has such aspirations should do so outside my administration and in accordance to the law." While even the most corrupt of Mexico's previous presidents had made great rhetorical gestures against corruption, Zedillo's warning to his top aides drew applause from legislators across the political spectrum.

At the high point of the ceremony, when Zedillo took the sash of office from his previous boss, the whole country could see Salinas whis-

pering something in the new president's ear, away from the micro-
phones, as the two men embraced. Zedillo acknowledged the outgoing
president's private words with an appreciative smile and a prolonged
handshake.

"I wish you good luck, Ernesto," Salinas had said, according to government officials who were standing by. "Because if the president does
well, Mexico will do well."

▼

But Zedillo did miserably during his first weeks in office — and so did
Mexico. Within days of Zedillo's inauguration, Mexico plunged into
one of its worst political and economic crises ever. Political infighting
within the ruling elite escalated to dangerous levels; capital flight de-
pleted the country's foreign reserves; the stock market fell 44 percent;
more than five hundred thousand people were laid off; and the new
president was forced to announce a 35 percent devaluation of the currency that reverberated through international financial markets and
moved President Clinton to announce a $50 billion bailout program
— including $20 billion in U.S. funds — to get Mexico back on its
feet.

Even the Popocatepetl, the long-dormant volcano south of Mexico
City, started to emit huge clouds of steam and ash — evoking ancient
Aztec stories that its tremors presaged great disasters, and driving the
new authorities to evacuate more than fifty thousand terrified residents
of small villages at the foot of the mountain. Certainly no reasonable
observer could blame Zedillo for the volcano. For the rest of it, Zedillo
was only partly responsible. The economic and political crisis that
marked his first weeks in office — and led to his dramatic break with
Salinas — had been unleashed by a September 28, 1994, killing in
downtown Mexico City that had rocked the country eight weeks before
the change of government.

▼

The young man in faded blue jeans, a black shirt, and tennis shoes had
been leaning against the wall of the Casablanca Hotel for about an
hour, pretending to be reading a newspaper. To the hundreds of people

who passed him on their way to Sanborn's, one of Mexico's most popular department stores, he was probably invisible, one of the thousands of poor peasants who roam the streets of the biggest city in the world. Certainly nobody noticed that beneath the newspaper he concealed a 9 mm mini-Uzi submachine gun.

Finally, his accomplice, standing across the street, nodded. It was the sign the man in faded blue jeans had been waiting for. His target, a short man with a mustache, emerged from the building next to the hotel surrounded by larger men in dark suits. He was José Francisco Ruiz Massieu, the general secretary of the ruling party, who was scheduled to become the new majority leader of Congress when the new government took office. Perhaps more importantly, he was a close friend and former in-law of President Salinas, who still called him by his nickname, Pepe.

As he was leaving, Ruiz Massieu announced that he didn't want to be late for his next meeting with two leading politicians who were likely to go for one another's throats. "I may have to intercede, for the good of the country," he joked. It was the last joke Pepe, known for his acerbic wit, would ever make. Still laughing, he stepped into the driver's seat of a gray Buick parked across the street, while his bodyguards boarded the vehicles behind him. The assassin, a twenty-eight-year-old semiliterate farm worker named Daniel Aguilar, calmly crossed to the car. It was 9:32 A.M. Ruiz Massieu took off his jacket, placed it on the backseat, and turned on the engine. Aguilar pulled the 9 mm from under his newspaper and fired one shot at his sitting target. The bullet pierced Ruiz Massieu's neck and went straight into his heart. He would die at a nearby hospital less than an hour later.

Within minutes of the shooting, Mexico was near panic. After all, this was the country that had prided itself on being Latin America's most stable nation, free for nearly seventy years of the political violence that had rocked its southern neighbors so often, and at such high economic and human cost. What stunned Mexicans about this murder wasn't only Ruiz Massieu's importance, but the pattern that seemed to be evolving. In the nine months before this latest violence, Mexico had faced its first guerrilla uprising since the 1910–1917 revolution and the first murder of a presidential candidate since 1928. Before September

28, many Mexicans were trying to believe that these shocks were some-how unrelated: The Zapatista guerrilla rebellion had been confined to a remote, poverty-stricken corner of Mexico, and Colosio's killing appeared to have been caused by a lone, deranged killer. But this was too much. Now even skeptics believed that — despite all government assurances to the contrary — a monstrous conspiracy was under way to bring the country into chaos.

Almost everyone had a theory about the killing. Were opposition groups trying to destabilize Mexico? Were the drug cartels taking revenge against the victim's brother, a senior government prosecutor who had vowed to crush Mexico's mighty Gulf cartel? Was it a crime of passion against a man who, according to a widespread rumor in political circles, was bisexual? Had the ruling party dinosaurs killed Ruiz Massieu to stop Mexico's gradual political opening?

There was one thing on which everyone agreed — if the Mexican power elite was behind this murder, the investigation would be a sham, as many others in the past had been. But hours after Ruiz Massieu died, a shaken President Salinas seemed to put that fear to rest: He announced the appointment of Mario Ruiz Massieu, the murdered politician's brother, who happened to be a government prosecutor, as chief investigator in the case. The message was clear: This case would not be allowed to fizzle in a cloud of contradictions — as the recent murder of Colosio had. Who could be more certain than the victim's brother, blood of his blood, to make sure that there would be no government cover-up? Who could be more determined that the masterminds of the murder would be brought to justice — no matter how influential they were?

There was another encouraging development: Aguilar, the gunman, was cooperating with the investigation. In his rush to flee the scene of the crime, he had stumbled and dropped his Uzi, and was grabbed and pinned to the floor by a bank guard. Within hours, he'd made a full confession, leading to the immediate capture of a dozen co-conspirators.

▼

The surviving Ruiz Massieu plunged into the investigation even more fearlessly than anyone could have hoped. Day after day Mario announced new findings in the case, each one more stunning than the last. The incriminating chain began with the lowly assassin. Aguilar said he had been promised $16,000 for the murder, and taken to the scene of the crime by a man named Fernando Rodriguez. Rodriguez was the top aide to PRI congressman Manuel Muñoz Rocha, a relatively obscure member of the party's executive committee. When Rodriguez was arrested a few days later, he confessed that he had recruited the gunman "on direct orders" of Congressman Muñoz Rocha. What was more, Mario revealed, Muñoz Rocha was working for an influential "political group" of PRI hard-liners who were seeking to stop Mexico's democratic reforms and people who were advancing them, such as Pepe Ruiz Massieu. Muñoz Rocha had once said that Pepe was part of "a list of political figures who had to be eliminated," Rodriguez later told prosecutors. For the first time in recent history, Mexicans were being confronted with evidence of a conspiracy to kill a leading politician — and the plot seemed to be coming from the very heart of the party that had maintained Mexico's stability for nearly seventy years.

But abruptly, Mario's investigation hit a snag. Muñoz Rocha, the key to finding the real masterminds, disappeared. On November 15, two months after the investigation began with such high expectations, Mario stood before Mexican television cameras to charge before the world that the PRI was blocking his investigation. "There were no conditions under which I could advance the investigation," he would say later in a public resignation letter. "The bullet fired September twenty-eighth killed two Ruiz Massieus: It took the life of one of them, and took the other's faith and hope that a PRI government would do justice."

▼

It was the first time in Mexico's recent history that a top government official had publicly accused PRI leaders of corruption and criminal behavior. Like virtually everyone watching this drama, I couldn't help feeling some sympathy for this courageous prosecutor. I had seldom seen something like this in Mexico. Few people had.

His tirade ignited an economic disaster. The foreign investors stampeded. More than $1.5 billion left the country the day after Mario's denunciations — much more than had been withdrawn from the banking system after the Colosio and Pepe Ruiz Massieu killings. The stock market plummeted. There had been earlier economic tremors at the news of the two political killings. But this was the big quake. The one thing that had kept the system together for decades — the monolithic unity of the ruling party — was now shattered, shortly before a new president was to take office. Mario's charges signaled open warfare within the PRI — precisely the kind of brutal infighting within the government that had triggered the Mexican Revolution.

I visited Mario Ruiz Massieu at his house a few days after his cataclysmic television speech, excited by the prospect of interviewing Mexico's man of the hour. The prosecutor was guarded by more than a dozen men clad in civilian clothes, armed with handheld radios and submachine guns. It was a spacious but unimpressive house by Mexican politicians' standards: no exotic furniture, no high-priced murals, no luxury cars in the driveway. It looked like it should look, but in Mexico rarely did: the house of a senior public servant, unembellished by luxuries obviously beyond the means of his salary.

Sitting on a black leather couch in his living room, where he kept thousands of CDs — mostly boleros and Latin American romantic songs — neatly lined against the wall in a music cabinet, Mario Ruiz Massieu recapped his story: Shortly after Salinas appointed him, he had questioned Aguilar, the killer, and obtained the names of more than a dozen people who had participated in the murder. Unlike Colosio's assassin, a reclusive young man who insisted he had acted alone, Aguilar had turned out to be a police interrogator's dream. Scared by the big city and the army of government investigators bombarding him with questions, he spilled his guts.

Within days, Mario Ruiz Massieu had arrested fifteen co-conspirators in the case — virtually the entire group of named suspects, with the significant exception of Congressman Muñoz Rocha, who was still at large. All those arrested had told the same story, he said: They had been working for a "high-level political group" that included the PRI senator from Tamaulipas, Enrique Cárdenas, and PRI congressman "El Meme" Garza, the old-guard party leader at whose home I had tried deer tamales and milk-sautéed goat airlifted for the occasion. Yet despite the co-conspirators' testimony, the ruling party had refused to strip the two legislators of their legislative immunity. What's more, Mario Ruiz Massieu told me, the PRI leadership had even refused to strip immunity from fugitive congressman Muñoz Rocha, getting the Congress instead to grant him a leave of absence.

That's when Mario publicly accused top PRI leaders of "being more concerned with trying to defend the criminals than trying to solve the case of their slain secretary-general." The PRI president had angrily denied the allegations, and government spokesmen had begun making off-the-record suggestions to reporters that the prosecutor was out of his mind. His hands tied, frustrated and angry with the system, Mario resigned a week after he broadcast his accusation to the world.

Given the circumstances, it did not surprise me that he seemed depressed. His voice was feeble and his face a stony blank as he went into the details of his confrontation with the almighty PRI leaders. "From the very moment I told the party president and the new secretary-general that the investigation was leading toward high-level figures, they began to put obstacles in my way," he told me. "They said this was going to stain the party's image and do irreparable damage to it.

"I told them the suspects were not being investigated in their capacity as party members, but as suspects in a murder investigation. But they didn't see it that way: They said the general perception would be that the crime had come from the top levels of the party. They argued that the testimony of a semiliterate farm worker was not credible, that we could not investigate somebody like Senator Cárdenas on the basis of statements by people like that."

His own boss, Mexico's then–attorney general Humberto Benitez, was part of the conspiracy to cover up the murder, Mario said. Files began to disappear. Resources for the investigation were suddenly withdrawn under various bureaucratic excuses. Key prosecutors began to call in sick. Mario said he could no longer fight a lonely battle against the state. He had quit his PRI membership and said he would start a political career with an opposition party. He would begin to write a weekly column in the independent newspaper *El Financiero* under the title "The Demons are loose, and have triumphed," and went on to write a book, *I Accuse.*

As I left Mario Ruiz Massieu's home, I couldn't help feeling excited about what I was about to write. In more than three hours of taped interviews, he had described to me in precise detail — months before his book would come out — the inner workings of a high-level conspiracy to kill his brother and thwart the democratic reforms he planned to launch as majority leader in the new Congress. It was Mexico's story of the decade. And Mario's theory of the crime made perfect sense. It fit exactly into what his brother had told me shortly before he was murdered.

▼

It was a Saturday morning in June 1994 that "Pepe" Ruiz Massieu had invited me for a breakfast interview at his home. Like his brother, Pepe lived in a comfortable but not ostentatious house, which like many in the city's middle-class or wealthy neighborhoods was hidden behind a huge front wall. He greeted me in his library, the place where he seemed to spend most of his time. It was a dark room with English-style furniture, books covering all walls from the floor to the ceiling, and a moving ladder hooked to the bookcase to help reach its upper shelves.

Pepe prided himself on being the PRI's leading intellectual. A lawyer, he had completed postgraduate studies at the University of Essex in Great Britain and had written several books on Mexico's political history. Shortly after a servant brought us coffee and we began to talk, he proudly presented me with one of his latest books, *New Political Class or New Politics?* Throughout the conversation, he kept going back to the book and pinpointing key sentences like, "We are living in times of transition, and whoever doesn't understand that will fall between the cracks."

Perhaps because he wanted to shed his image as a ruthless former governor of the state of Guerrero in the late eighties, he was eager to establish his credentials as a reformer. Pepe explained that Mexico had once been committed to truly free elections, but as communists and fascists ascended to power in Europe, the ruling party had adopted the

Zapatista officer Major Rolando and fellow guerrillas with the author at the Chiapas rebel camp of La Garrucha, July 20, 1994. *(Tim Padgett)*

Zapatista army leader Subcommander Marcos with the author at a guerrilla camp near Guadalupe Tepeyac in Chiapas, July 23, 1994. *(Tim Padgett)*

Mexican government–released picture of Rafael Sebastián Guillén Vicente, whom President Ernesto Zedillo identified as the masked Zapatista leader Subcommander Marcos. *(Courtesy of Mexico's attorney general's office)*

The rebel who would later be known as Subcommander Marcos, with Zapatista army lieutenant Cecilia, years before the uprising. Smiling in the back, a rebel officer whom government officials identified as Subcommander Elisa. *(Courtesy of Mexico's attorney general's office)*

Fernando Yañez, the Marxist rebel whom the government identified as Commander in Chief Germán, the behind-the-scenes Zapatista leader. *(Courtesy of Mexico's attorney general's office)*

Maria Gloria Benavides Guevara, the rebel leader whom Mexican officials identified as Zapatista army subcommander Elisa. *(Courtesy of Mexico's attorney general's office)*

"There are no guerrillas," the Mexican government statement echoed by Chiapas army commander General Miguel Angel Godinez Bravo, and written by the rebels at San Cristóbal's central square the day of the rebellion. *(Eloy Valtierra/Cuartoscuro)*

Comandante Felipe, the rebel who according to the Zapatistas' plans was to be the spokesman for the guerrilla army. His place was taken by Subcommander Marcos hours after the uprising.
(Courtesy of La Republica, *Chiapas)*

Some of the Zapatista paraphernalia that appeared in Chiapas days after the rebellion. The goods' initial market: foreign correspondents. *(Rodolfo Valtierra/Cuartoscuro)*

Bodies that the government identified as Zapatista guerrillas found in Altamirano, Chiapas, after the January 1, 1994, uprising. *(Eloy Valtierra/Cuartoscuro)*

Zapatista rebels guarding the ruling party headquarters in Altamirano hours after the uprising. *(Eloy Valtierra/Cuartoscuro)*

Zapatista guerrillas in San Cristóbal on the night of the uprising. Unlike Subcommander Marcos, most of the guerrillas had their faces uncovered. *(Courtesy of* La Republica, *Chiapas)*

Above: President Ernesto Zedillo (left) and the author, during a campaign trip to Guerrero, May 17, 1994. *(Courtesy of Mexico's presidential office) Below:* Late presidential candidate Luis Donaldo Colosio (right), during an interview with the author in Mazatlán, Sinaloa, March 22, 1994, the day before Colosio's assassination. *(Courtesy of the Colosio for President campaign)*

Mario Aburto Martinez, the gunman convicted in the killing of Luis Donaldo Colosio, in prison hours after the murder. *(Ricardo Reyes/Cuartoscuro)*

Ruling party secretary general José Francisco "Pepe" Ruiz Massieu after his murder in downtown Mexico City. *(Hector Mateos/Cuartoscuro)*

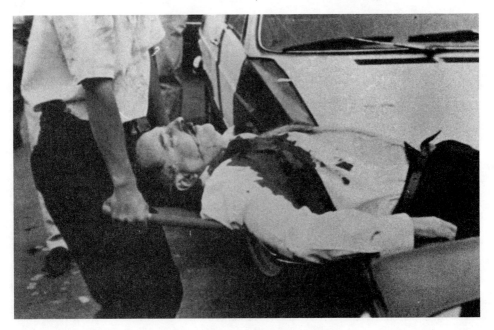

Former government prosecutor Mario Ruiz Massieu, at his home in Mexico City, January 24, 1995. *(Andres Oppenheimer)*

President Ernesto Zedillo (center right) seconds before taking office from President Carlos Salinas de Gortari (center left), December 1, 1994. Their close relationship would begin to sour days later. *(Pedro Valtierra/Cuartoscuro)*

Raúl Salinas de Gortari, former president Salinas's older brother, after his arrest on charges of master-minding the murder of Pepe Ruiz Massieu. *(Courtesy of Mexico's attorney general's office)*

Raúl Salinas in better days: with Maria Bernal, the Spanish woman with whom he was reported to have had an extramarital affair in recent years. (Courtesy of *Reforma*)

Sinaloa drug cartel baron Héctor "El Guero" Palma, arrested in 1995, had senior police officers in four states on his payroll. *(Courtesy of Mexico's attorney general's office)*

Graffiti in the iron fence along the U.S.-Mexican border in Tijuana, February 1995. *(Andres Oppenheimer)*

Superbarrio, the Mexico City citizens' rights activist. *(Andres Oppenheimer)*

Manuel "El Meme" Garza, one of the ruling party's self-declared "dinosaurs," surrounded by hunting trophies at his Mexico City home. *(Andres Oppenheimer)*

San Francisco investment banker Josephine Jimenez in Chiapas shortly after the insurrection. Alarmed by what she saw, she got her money out of Mexico. *(Josephine Jimenez)*

Billionaire former Mexico City mayor and Agriculture minister Carlos Hank Gonzalez, a major behind-the-scenes power broker of the ruling elite. *(Courtesy of Mexico's Agriculture ministry)*

Television baron Emilio "El Tigre" Azcarraga, owner of Televisa, the pro-government network that has a 95 percent share of the Mexican audience. *(Eloy Valtierra/Cuartoscuro)*

credo of "patriotic fraud" whereby — supposedly for the good of the country — it would never allow opposition candidates to win any elections. Now, he said, the federal government wanted to return to the democratic ideal, but the local PRI governments were desperately trying to maintain their absolute hold on elective power. "In most state governments, we are still living in the Stone Age," he said. "Patriotic fraud is seen as an honorable practice."

Pepe said he believed it was his mission to bring the party caudillos in the countryside into the twentieth century. In hindsight, Pepe's statement that morning fit perfectly with his brother's theory as to why he was murdered: Pepe Ruiz Massieu had been killed by the reactionary and corrupt regional party bosses he was challenging within the party — probably the "political group" including the Tamaulipas legislators that had been cited by the co-conspirators arrested in the case.

▼

My admiration for Mario Ruiz Massieu wouldn't last long. I was ready to start writing my big exposé on Mario's courageous battle against Mexico's corrupt power elite a few weeks after Zedillo's December 1 inauguration when I was hit by a screaming newspaper headline: "Mario Ruiz Massieu flees Mexico, arrested in Newark."

Stunned, I rushed to my computer to call up the latest wire stories. The news was more improbable than the plot of a political thriller: Mexico was seeking Mario Ruiz Massieu's immediate extradition, the wire agencies said. He had covered up the involvement of Raúl Salinas de Gortari, the former president's brother, as the mastermind of his own brother's killing, the new district attorney had announced. Raúl Salinas had ordered Pepe Ruiz Massieu's killing for personal reasons — a vendetta that had capped years of disagreements between the two former in-laws.

I was flabbergasted. Would a man cover up the killer of his own brother? It sounded like a Mexican government smear campaign to discredit the man who had exposed a top-level cover-up. But on the other hand, when Mario was arrested, U.S. authorities had found more than $7 million in bank deposits made by the former prosecutor at the Texas Commerce Bank in Houston. The money — a fabulous amount for an official making $70,000 a year — had been deposited between March and November 1994, starting several months before his appointment as prosecutor in his brother's death.

In the days that followed, there were new revelations about Mario's wealth: Authorities found a $700,000 house of his in Cuernavaca and two residences in Acapulco. Where had Mario Ruiz Massieu gotten the $7 million? How could he have honestly amassed that much money in an eight-month period?

CHAPTER 10

The Secret Meeting

"El Meme" Garza did not look like a man in panic when we met at the Sevilla Plaza hotel for breakfast at the peak of the Ruiz Massieu political scandal. I had not seen him since the day he had invited me to lunch at his home and had explained to me — under the glassy stare of his stuffed Great Kudu — why ruling party dinosaurs like himself were against hasty political changes. Since then, Mario Ruiz Massieu had made his denunciations, and El Meme's name had appeared in front-page headlines as one of the masterminds of the Ruiz Massieu killing. His vigorous denial of the charges had only made the final paragraphs of these stories. He was under intense public scrutiny and was the object of generalized suspicion.

An old political fox, he was putting the best face on dire circumstances. He walked into the room in a new suit and a fashionable Hermès tie, greeted other patrons as if nothing was happening, and gave me an affectionate hug as he sat at the table.

The story about his alleged involvement in the Ruiz Massieu murder was ludicrous, he said: Anybody who knew anything about politics in Tamaulipas knew that Senator Cárdenas and he, the two alleged leaders of the "political group" that had ordered Pepe Ruiz Massieu's killing, had long been bitter enemies. The prisoners arrested in the case had been induced by Mario to tell a story that had basic flaws. "They mixed water with oil," El Meme said with an explanatory smile. "The entire world knows that if Senator Cárdenas and I would kill somebody, it would be one another."

▼

If there was a part of me that still suspected that Mario was the victim of a huge frame job by the government and the PRI's dinosaurs, it suffered a severe blow a few days later. That was when Pablo Chapa Bezanilla, the new chief prosecutor in the case, revealed to me new details of the investigation that made Mario look more sinister than I could possibly imagine.

Chapa Bezanilla, forty-two, had been working as a government prosecutor for the past seventeen years. A white-haired, blue-eyed, and athletic man whose hobby was competing in thirteen-mile triathlons — running, bicycling, and swimming races — he looked like Paul Newman playing a New York cop. The new attorney general, Antonio Lozano Gracia, said he had chosen him because he wanted a real cop with long experience in police investigations to handle the case.

Chapa Bezanilla was indeed more of a policeman than an attorney: A virtual stranger to the corridors of power, he felt most comfortable on the street and never left home without a 9 mm Browning pistol tucked in his belt. His specialty had long been common homicides, store burglaries, and home-invasion robberies. His biggest source of pride was having attended criminal investigation courses at the FBI Academy in Washington and at the Los Angeles Police Department.

He invited me to sit on the couch in his office and pulled up a chair in front of a black bust topped with a hairpiece that stood beside his desk. The bust had a familiar face: It was the police-made statue of missing PRI congressman Manuel Muñoz Rocha, his white hair covered by a black toupee to make him look as though he were disguising himself — if he was still alive. "We call him 'Manolo,'" Chapa Bezanilla joked, using the Spanish nickname for Manuel, while stroking the bust's head as if it were a pet. Chapa Bezanilla's story left me openmouthed.

He said he had solved the Pepe Ruiz Massieu murder case — and discovered Mario's lies — by thinking of it as a routine murder. Rather than following the previous course of the investigation — trying to trace the missing congressman and the "political group" behind him, and risking reaching a dead end if he was not found — he decided to start from scratch, doing what cops do at the beginning of any murder case: finding out who the victim might have damaged in his professional or personal life, and who might have a reason for wanting him dead.

Chapa Bezanilla's investigators interviewed eighteen relatives, friends, and political allies of Pepe Ruiz Massieu: All of them had pointed out that the victim had very bad relations with Raúl Salinas de Gortari, brother of the former president, a shadowy figure who was known to handle Carlos Salinas's most delicate business and political missions. Putting the previous suspicions about El Meme and other old-guard politicians on hold, investigators began to take a closer look at Raúl. Among the stories they heard:

• Raúl, as the oldest of the Salinas brothers, had never forgiven Pepe for a bitter 1978 divorce from his sister, Adriana. The divorce was triggered, officials said, when Adriana found Pepe with a male lover. After months of often violent arguments, in which Raúl's side of the family claimed Adriana had been beaten by her husband, the couple divorced by mutual consent.

• When the older of Pepe's and Adriana's two daughters turned fifteen, her father invited her to travel with him to the United States as a present, while her mother invited her to travel with her to Europe. A family feud ensued. Raúl Salinas intervened on behalf of his sister, asking Pepe to give his written consent for the trip to Europe, without which the girl could not legally leave the country. Pepe refused, and the girl ended up stranded in Mexico. Raúl was allegedly heard telling friends he would never forgive Pepe for this.

• The president's brother had clashed with Pepe several times over business differences. In 1987, when Pepe was starting his six-year term as governor of Guerrero state, and Raúl working for a government food-distribution program, the president's brother had been furious when he was rebuffed in his efforts to obtain from Pepe a lucrative cornmeal production plant contract for a friend. The prosecutor showed me a copy of a letter Pepe Ruiz Massieu had sent to President Salinas, telling him about a nasty meeting he had had with Raúl over the cornmeal production project. The letter, dated June 19, 1987, and addressed to the president, read: "Dear Carlos: Yesterday, I had a meeting with your father and your brother Raúl. As far as the latter is concerned, I cannot say it was pleasant."

• Raúl Salinas de Gortari had long had a close relationship with the fugitive congressman Muñoz Rocha, the man whose bust was standing next to the chief prosecutor's desk. The two had been classmates at the National Autonomous University of Mexico's Engineering School three decades earlier, and Raúl had been Muñoz Rocha's main political protector in recent years. While relatives and friends were telling these stories, Chapa Bezanilla's police investigators found other evidence linking Raúl to Muñoz Rocha — and, they said, to the murder.

One of the first telephone calls the missing congressman had made after fleeing Mexico City September 28 had been to Raúl Salinas's home, investigators found. When investigators interrogated the friend who had helped Muñoz Rocha hide from police in the days after the murder, he admitted driving Muñoz Rocha to Mexico City. Asked where Muñoz Rocha had gone, he stated, "To the home of Raúl Salinas de Gortari." In addition, Raúl had been making telephone calls and holding private meetings with top members of the ruling party before the August elections, lobbying for a promotion of Muñoz Rocha to PRI candidate for senator or, if possible, governor of Tamaulipas.

Finally, Chapa Bezanilla had something to move on: Shortly after the murder, when asked to testify about Muñoz Rocha, the president's brother had stated under oath that he had not seen the congressman "in more than twenty years."

This was obviously a lie. Virtually all of Raúl's friends and political associates had told prosecutors that the congressman was in contact with Raúl and was one of his main protégés. Yet Chapa Bezanilla had read the testimonies of the fifteen suspected conspirators in prison and had found no mention of Raúl. It was time to go to prison and see Fernando Rodriguez, the top aide to Muñoz Rocha. Chapa Bezanilla expected that he would have to pry the truth out of him. To his astonishment, all he had to do was ask.

"We asked him who was the congressman's boss, and he told us: Raúl Salinas de Gortari." When Chapa Bezanilla asked the prisoner, and later his co-conspirators, why they hadn't named Raúl Salinas before, they gave the most startling answer: Of course they had!

In some cases, the government attorneys interrogating them had warned them it would be better for their own sake to erase all references to Raúl Salinas from their testimonies. Others had been blindfolded and threatened with the barrel of a gun stuck in their mouths. One prisoner was told his daughter would be raped unless he cooperated. In other cases, the prisoners had mentioned the president's brother's name only to find it missing from the official testimonies brought to them for their signature.

It seemed a wild story, Chapa Bezanilla told me, but part of it was undoubtedly true: When his men checked the tape recordings of the prison interrogations, they found several references to Raúl Salinas de Gortari that were missing from the official transcripts. "Mario Ruiz Massieu and his top aide, Assistant Prosecutor Jorge Stergios, had changed the text in the computer and later forced the prisoners to sign the doctored copies of their statements," Chapa Bezanilla said. "Mario Ruiz Massieu invented the whole story about the 'political group' behind the murder and wrote it into the documents to divert public attention away from Raúl. His whole personal campaign to charge the PRI leadership with a cover-up, his column 'The demons are loose,' his book, *I Accuse*, everything was a smoke screen aimed at hiding Raúl's involvement in the case."

▼

I left Chapa Bezanilla's office with more questions than answers. I couldn't reconcile the image of the courageous prosecutor willing to defy Mexico's almighty ruling class I had met with the cold-blooded criminal his successors were describing. Why on earth would Mario Ruiz Massieu protect the mastermind of his brother's murder?

The Ruiz Massieu brothers, it turned out, had not always been that close. Pepe, the elder one, had always been the family's shining star — the brilliant speaker, the prolific writer, the prominent politician. Mario had lagged behind, a lesser-known government prosecutor who was said to owe his better jobs — a senior Interior ministry position and a stint as Mexico's ambassador to Denmark in the early nineties — to his family's influence.

Scions of a family of government bureaucrats — their grandfather and father had been government officials, and their sister, Maricela, was a PRI legislator — the two were the eldest of five children who shared a tragic history. Their brothers, Wilfrido and Roberto, had been shot to death in 1965 by the furious father of a girl who was having a love affair with one of the teenage boys. Both were repairing their car's engine on the street when they were hit by the bullets and died instantly. Shortly after the tragedy, twenty-four-year-old Pepe had married Adriana, the daughter of prominent PRI politician Raúl Salinas Lozano, and begun his brilliant career within the party.

Mario had always envied his brother, prosecutors said. Envy led to hard feelings. At one point, relations between them were so bad that Pepe and Mario didn't speak for twelve years. Perhaps, the new prosecutors told me, Mario's affection for money was greater than his affection for his brother: Maybe he had protected Raúl for money — although much of the $7 million deposited in the Texas bank came in before Pepe's killing. Or perhaps Mario had agreed to screen Raúl Salinas in exchange for a top job in the incoming Zedillo administration. Toward the end of the Salinas administration, the conventional wisdom was that the outgoing president would have extraordinary influence over the Zedillo government, and that many of the new president's ministers would in fact be placed by the outgoing one.

The most likely scenario, according to Chapa Bezanilla's team: Days after the murder, when the prisoners began naming Raúl Salinas de Gortari as the mastermind of the killing, Mario Ruiz Massieu — who had told me that he was in constant touch with President Salinas and talked to him almost daily — must have told Salinas, "Mr. President, we have a problem: Your brother killed my brother."

"We think Mario Ruiz Massieu may have taken advantage of that situation to obtain political favors," Assistant Prosecutor José Cortés Osorio, Chapa Bezanilla's top aide, told me. "Assuming that Mario Ruiz Massieu told the president that Raúl had killed his brother, he probably added, 'I will help you out, but you must help me out.'"

When inauguration day neared, and it was becoming clear that Mario would not be appointed attorney general, he figured the next best way to protect himself was to become a hero to the opposition, the new prosecutors said. Prosecutors were looking into the source of Mario's $7 million Texas bank account. They believed it was the fruit of ordinary corruption — unrelated to the killing. In Mexico, there were many ways a senior prosecutor could get rich. First, Mario had been in a position to sell regional district attorney positions. In drug-rich areas such as Tamaulipas, where corrupt prosecutors could make millions in bribes and protection fees, an appointment could be sold for as much as $1 million, Chapa Bezanilla's prosecutors told me. There was also an opportunity to pocket drug money from unreported confiscations. Or perhaps Mario had direct links to drug traffickers, the investigators speculated.

▼

Attorney General Lozano Gracia faced an awkward task: telling President Zedillo that the mastermind of Pepe Ruiz Massieu's killing had been the former president's brother. It was an accusation that Salinas, the man who had picked Zedillo for the presidency, would surely take as a personal attack on him. As opposed to the Ruiz Massieu brothers, who had been distant from one another, Raúl and Carlos Salinas were as close as brothers could be. They were the oldest of five children by former Commerce and Industry minister Raúl Salinas Lozano, and they were inseparable.

Raúl, who as firstborn was honored with carrying his father's first name, was only one year and seven months older than Carlos. As children, they shared the same room, went to the same elementary and high schools, took piano lessons together, and even shared the burden of a childhood tragedy: When Raúl had just turned five and Carlos was three years old, they had — together with an eight-year-old friend — killed the family maid with a .22-caliber rifle.

According to December 18, 1951, Mexico City newspapers, the children had "executed" the twelve-year-old maid, named Manuela, with the rifle, which their father had left loaded in a closet. The published reports, which had mysteriously disappeared from Mexican libraries by the time Salinas had become a public figure, said that it was not entirely clear which of the youngsters had pulled the trigger. The children had been playing war games, and Manuela was condemned to death. They had asked her to get down on her knees, and one of them had shot her.

"Carlos, when asked what had happened, said, 'I killed her with one shot. I'm a hero,' the daily *El Universal* said at the time. *La Prensa* lashed out against "the irresponsibility of a father who, having children under age, allowed them to get near to a 22 caliber rifle." It said the children's crushed mother, Margarita Salinas Lozano, was spending the day and night at the police station next to the children, "who, totally ignorant of the intense drama they had caused, were running around last afternoon along the corridors of the Eighth Delegation police station."

In the end, however, the incident was ruled an accident. Nobody was ever charged, and the later destruction or forced removal of the old newspaper copies from libraries throughout Mexico would raise questions as to whether the shooting had ever taken place. During Salinas's presidency, a flattering Salinas biography written by Nicaragua's former Sandinista Interior minister, Tomás Borge, a frequent recipient of the Mexican president's generosity, told the story — but pinned the blame on the eight-year-old friend of the Salinas brothers, who was presented as "the author of the accident." That had been the new official story until, once Salinas stepped down, the old Mexico City newspaper clippings materialized as mysteriously as they had disappeared and were reprinted by Mexican newspapers.

As teenagers, Raúl and Carlos had taken horseback riding lessons together, as well as karate and guitar classes. They vacationed together every year at their uncle Alfredo's ranch in the northern state of Nuevo León, where they would hunt and prepare for international horseback riding competitions. When Raúl had finished high school at age seventeen, their father — a cabinet minister by then — had sent the two children and their sixteen-year-old cousin Guillermo on a trip to the United States and Europe.

The three had visited Washington, Chicago, Boston, and New York, and from there had traveled by ship to London to continue their travels through Germany, Denmark, Finland, France, and the Soviet Union. With Raúl driving a Volvo they had rented in Spain, they shared the kind of youthful adventures that mark one for life. Back in Mexico, they went to college — Raúl to study engineering, Carlos economics — and were accepted together into Mexico's national steeplechase team, which took them to represent their country at a competition at New York's Madison Square Garden and at the 1971 Pan-American Games in Cali, Colombia. When Carlos graduated from Mexico's National Autonomous University (UNAM) he did not dedicate his thesis to his parents, but to his older brother. His dedication read, "To Raúl, companion of a hundred battles."

Raúl did not seem to resent Carlos's phenomenal career in government: In fact, he supported him all along. He performed sensitive business and political missions for him — sometimes under an assumed identity, as when he traveled abroad using a passport he had obtained with his picture and the phony name of Juan Guillermo Gomez Gutiérrez — and took care of family affairs.

When Adriana complained to her brothers that she was being mistreated by Pepe Ruiz Massieu and wanted to divorce him, it was Raúl who had taken up her cause and offered legal advice and protection. As far as the family was concerned, the older brother, who had driven the young men's rented Volvo during their trip though Europe in the sixties, was still at the helm thirty years later.

"They were much more than brothers," said a former Salinas cabinet minister who was among his closest friends. "They were best friends."

When the attorney general entered Zedillo's office at the presidential palace and laid on a desk a folder containing the charges against Raúl Salinas de Gortari, the president was shocked, Lozano Gracia told me later. But Zedillo could not step back: He had promised in his inaugural speech to turn Mexico into a country of laws and end the impunity that corrupt members of his party had enjoyed for decades. Even if he had been tempted to look the other way, he was being prompted to act by an opposition-party attorney general who could turn against him in the future and accuse him of covering up for the former president, just as every previous PRI president had done for his predecessor. Besides, the Zedillo government was beset by economic problems and badly needed a galvanizing political issue to restore its popularity.

After listening stone-faced to the attorney general's report, Zedillo kept silent for a few seconds. Then, according to Lozano Gracia, he looked him straight in the eye and said, *"Conforme a derecho. Proceda!"* — "Whatever the law dictates. Go ahead!"

▼

Zedillo faced an even more difficult task: telling former president Salinas, his longtime boss and the man to whom he owed his career, that he was about to arrest his brother. Zedillo's dealings with Raúl had been distant, but he still kept a friendly relationship with the president. The day of his inauguration, after receiving the sash of office from Salinas, he had exchanged a few friendly words with him on their way out of the Congress building, from where Salinas had gone to his mother's grave at a Mexico City cemetery and had been seen standing silent — tears streaming down his cheeks — in front of it. Since then, they had only talked once on the phone, on December 24, when Salinas had called Zedillo to wish him and his family a merry Christmas. Moving against Raúl would not only break what was left of his ties with the former president, it would shatter Mexico's oldest political tradition: that incoming presidents always covered the backs of outgoing ones. He was about to enter terra incognita.

Zedillo chose not to call Salinas — there was not much he could tell him by way of support without compromising his own position. He sent a representative instead. At about eleven A.M. on February 28, 1995, a government envoy — former security chief and Labor minister Arsenio Farell, a mutual friend of Zedillo and Salinas — visited former president Salinas at his home in Mexico City and presented him with the bad news: A thick folder with alleged evidence of his brother Raúl's involvement in the murder. By that time, dozens of government agents had discreetly taken positions around Adriana Salinas's home, where Raúl was staying.

Upon hearing the news, the former president — back just hours earlier from a world tour to promote his candidacy for the World Trade Organization — exploded in anger. This was a hoax! It was totally outrageous! The government could not do this! he protested.

About three hours later, Salinas struck back with a vengeance. If Zedillo was prepared to break the rules of the game, so was he. At exactly 2:45 P.M., Salinas called Televisa's around-the-clock ECO newscast, asked for anchorman Abraham Zabludovsky, and said, "Please, put me on the air." Within minutes, Salinas was broadcasting his outrage to the nation in an unprecedented break with the time-honored tradition of Mexican presidents' disappearance from public life after stepping down. This vow of silence had been a key to the ruling party's success over the years: In reaction to former strongman Porfirio Díaz's thirty-year stay in power, the victorious revolutionary forces had constitutionally banned reelection of former heads of state. When the first postrevolutionary presidents tried to rule from behind the scenes after they had stepped down, the ruling party reacted by condemning them and their successors to political ostracism. At best, they were sent abroad on a cushy ambassadorship.

Former president López Portillo, who was remembered for once vowing to defend the Mexican peso "like a dog" and later ordering a massive devaluation, had spent the rest of his life at home and endured silently the humiliation of being greeted with scornful barks by patrons at Mexico City restaurants. President Luis Echeverría had stoically swallowed his outrage when he was appointed to a post the official announcement described as ambassador to Australia "and the Fiji islands," in case he did not get the idea that he was wanted as far away from Mexico as possible. But Mexico's code of conduct had been suddenly pulverized. Salinas went public with his complaints, hinting that he had enough information — and contacts — to discredit the new administration.

"I cannot allow these assertions to remain unchallenged, not even as innuendo," Salinas said, referring to newspaper reports that quoted government officials as saying the former president had intentionally derailed the investigations into the recent political killings. "I firmly reject them and I demand a satisfactory retraction from the proper authorities."

Then he struck at Zedillo where it hurt the new president the most — the economic debacle of a few weeks earlier. "Because of the terrible devaluation of December, thousands of people have lost their jobs, many companies are on the brink of bankruptcy, and . . . Mexico's image in the world has been tarnished." He denied that he was to blame for the devaluation, laying all the burden on "the mistakes that were made in December" after Zedillo had taken office.

By that time, the more than seventy elite troops from the Federal Judicial Police and the Presidential Guard, clad in their black uniforms and bullet-proof vests, were taking up positions around Adriana Salinas's house. Salinas could only hope that the arrest warrant against Raúl they were carrying was an initiative of the new attorney general, and that a crisis triggered by a possible clash between the two armed convoys would force Zedillo to strike a middle-ground solution. The battle was averted at the last minute by General Miranda's order over the Presidential Guard's radio system.

▼

Two days later, a housewife in a working-class section of the northern industrial city of Monterrey would get the surprise of her life. At about one A.M., shortly after being told on the telephone that former president Salinas might seek refuge at her modest house, a concrete-floored building on a street traveled mostly by donkey carts and bicycles, she heard a knock on the door. A haggard-looking Salinas, unshaven and clad in a black leather jacket, was standing in front of her, asking for sanctuary.

The woman, Rosa Coronado, was — like most of her neighbors — a longtime Salinas supporter and a local organizer of the former president's Solidarity public works program. This was Salinas territory: The street behind Coronado's home was named Solidarity Avenue, and most residents had in recent times benefited from the government's social program. Hours earlier, they had heard the news that Salinas would go on a hunger strike to reclaim his honor and that of his family.

Shortly after Raúl's arrest, the former president had told Tim Golden of the *New York Times* in a telephone interview that he was "completely convinced of [Raúl's] innocence." To dramatize his protest, Salinas would fly in a friend's private jet to Monterrey and stage his hunger strike surrounded by supporters at Coronado's humble house at 8716 Tritón Street. On March 3, 1995, saying he had not eaten anything solid in more than a day, he began to receive groups of reporters in the small bedroom of Mrs. Coronado's four children. There was only a twin-sized bed, a metallic chair, a night table, a Mexican flag, and pictures on the wall of Mrs. Coronado with Salinas when he was president.

It was an extraordinary scene: Until a few weeks earlier, he had been the hero of Latin America's economic opening, the darling of Wall Street, and the U.S.-backed front-runner to head the World Trade Organization. Now he was an exhausted protester sitting on a bed, telling reporters that he had just filed a complaint with Mexico's Human Rights Commission. He had turned into the main character of a melodrama not unlike the soap operas that kept millions of Mexicans glued to their television sets night after night.

But Salinas's fast didn't last long: A mutual friend of Salinas and Zedillo, Agrarian Reform Secretary Arturo Warman, was sent urgently to Monterrey to try to persuade the former president to fly back to the capital. His demands for a government statement clearing him of any responsibility in the Colosio case and the December 20 devaluation would be considered, he was told. There was panic in the presidential palace of Los Pinos: At least two former Salinas ministers had told two top Zedillo aides, Chief of Staff Luis Tellez and Private Secretary Liébano Sáenz, that the former president was so distraught that he might "do something crazy" — like commit suicide. It was a new scandal Mexico could not afford. Warman and Salinas returned to the capital early in the afternoon, aboard the same private plane that had taken Salinas to Monterrey.

▼

Mexico's presidential press office said Zedillo and Salinas never spoke on that occasion. A spokesman for the president, who asked me not to mention his name — perhaps because he knew he was telling me a blatant lie — told me months later that Zedillo had last talked with the former president December 24, when he had taken a Christmas call from him.

In fact, Salinas and Warman had gone straight from the airport to the house of former security chief Farell on Fuente de Diana Street in the northern Mexico City neighborhood of Tecamechalco, where a secret meeting — never revealed by the time of this writing — took place shortly after eight P.M. Zedillo arrived minutes after his predecessor, accompanied by his chief of staff, Luis Tellez, and his military escort. While Tellez, Farell, and two other top officials waited in a nearby room, the president and Salinas held a long private meeting. According to Zedillo aides, Salinas reiterated the demands he had made in previous days: that the government put out a statement clearing him of any wrongdoing in the Colosio case and the December devaluation. Strangely, he didn't mention his brother Raúl's situation, perhaps because no government official had yet linked the former president to his brother's alleged crime. After a long conversation, Zedillo and the former president emerged from the room in a tense but not hostile mood. They wished one another well, shook hands, and parted in different directions.

Whether Zedillo and Salinas struck a deal whereby the former president would be protected from any government charges in exchange for his exile — and silence — was not revealed even to the two men's closest aides.

"No agreement to that effect was made in the presence of others, but what the two presidents said when they were talking among themselves, I have no way of knowing," said one of the senior officials who were waiting outside the room. When I submitted a question to Zedillo about what was said in the private conversation, he responded through his private secretary, Sáenz: "I have never struck any agreement with the former president. I limited myself to telling him that there was a specific criminal action against his brother Raúl, and that the proper authorities would act with strict adherence to the law."

But what happened after Zedillo and Salinas walked out of the house on Fuente de Diana Street raises questions as to whether nothing else was said. Three things are known for a fact. One: The Zedillo government put out a statement hours later clearing Salinas of any responsibility in the Colosio case and watering down previous criticism of his role in the December devaluation. Two: That very Sunday, the former president was silently flying to the United States. Three: The government's press office continued to claim that Zedillo had never spoken to Salinas following their Christmas salute a month earlier.

▼

Attorney General Lozano Gracia, the young, ambitious opposition politician serving on Zedillo's cabinet, received me at his office a few days after Salinas had left the country. He was — like Mario Ruiz Massieu had been only a few months earlier — Mexico's man of the hour. He had just been profiled in various Mexican newspapers and even the *New York Times* as the man who was untangling the country's recent political killings at record speed. As the first member of his party to occupy such a high-profile government job, he seemed determined to to set an example of integrity in a notably corrupt environment. He was the object of unanimous praise — except for subtle off-the-record comments by ruling party government officials, who noted privately to reporters with a touch of cynicism that he had changed the attorney general's office logo for a new one with the white-and-blue PAN colors in the backdrop.

I asked him to clear up some of the many things that remained unclear to me. Granted, fugitive congressman Muñoz Rocha was said by the government to have placed a phone call to Raúl Salinas the night of the murder, and to have visited with him on the following day. Couldn't he have just been seeking protection from his old friend, who may have had nothing to do with the murder? As for Raúl Salinas's lying about not having seen the missing congressman in twenty years, that amounted to a crime of perjury, but would it hold up in court as evidence of murder? And the prisoners' testimony singling out Raúl Salinas de Gortari, wasn't it hearsay — things they had heard the missing congressman say the president's brother had allegedly told him?

The attorney general nodded, accepting all those possibilities. What I didn't know, he said, was that there were several other pieces of evidence pointing to Raúl's role in the murder that the government was keeping under wraps. There was a security guard at Raúl's residence who had taken calls from Muñoz Rocha, and other witnesses who had seen the two men together days before the murder. And Fernando Rodriguez, the congressman's aide, had proved to have highly reliable information about Raúl's involvement in the murder.* "We are talking about a person who was Muñoz Rocha's right-hand man, who was being kept up to date constantly by his boss about how things were going," the attorney general told me. "His information is accurate as far as we have been able to verify."

But the Zedillo government had only chosen to accept part of Fernando Rodriguez's "accurate" testimony. The prisoner had made other — more explosive — statements that Lozano's office declined to show me despite initial promises to do so and that the government

---

* Months after the author's interviews with Lozano Gracia and Chapa Bezanilla, government prosecutors found a key witness against Raúl Salinas: Maria Bernal, a Spaniard with whom Raúl was having an extramarital relationship, and who said she had heard him say that he was planning to kill Pepe Ruiz Massieu. She became the prosecution's star witness — until it was reported that she had tried to extort money from the Salinas family to remain silent.

would keep secret. Just as his predecessor had steered the investigation away from Raúl Salinas, the new attorney general seemed to be avoiding a full investigation of former president Salinas. That might have been too much to absorb for a country that was already in shock.

Among Fernando Rodriguez's statements that were not made public at the time:

• The decision to kill Pepe Ruiz Massieu was made in March 1993 at a Salinas family meeting in the presence of President Carlos Salinas, Raúl Salinas, Adriana Salinas, and their father, Raúl Salinas Lozano. Muñoz Rocha had later told Fernando Rodriguez that the family had decided to "eliminate" Pepe Ruiz Massieu "because, while he shared the goal of modernizing the country, he represented an obstacle to the ultimate goal of the Salinas family: to continue wielding power even after Carlos's term was over," according to court records of Fernando Rodriguez's testimony. Pepe had become a Zedillo loyalist and he was not likely to admit competition from the Salinas group in his new capacity as a top political strategist for the new president.

• The funds for the assassination of Pepe Ruiz Massieu had "originated directly from the office of the president through his private secretary," Justo Ceja, Rodriguez said. "I saw Mr. Justo Ceja, private secretary of then-president Carlos Salinas, arrive at Raúl Salinas's home from the presidential office with two bags of money, which were handed over to Muñoz Rocha," Rodriguez had testified. At least $300,000 had been given to Muñoz Rocha that way, he said.

• The man who had tipped Muñoz Rocha about Pepe Ruiz Massieu's daily movements and advance schedule — including his breakfast meeting with the ruling party congressmen, which had not been publicized — was Ignacio Ovalle, a senior official of the PRI's National Political Council, Rodriguez said.

Lozano Gracia later confirmed to me that the prisoner had testified that a partial payment of $75,000 for the killing had been made from Salinas's office to Raúl, but immediately played down the story. "It may or may not be true," the attorney general said. "If Raúl got the money from the president's office, it would have been improper, but it could have been earmarked for a number of purposes given the close links between Raúl and the president." He added that his investigators had interrogated Salinas's former private secretary, and he had denied the prisoner's allegations.

Sensing that Lozano Gracia was trying to steer me away from the prisoner's claims that funding for the killing had come from Salinas's office, I persisted: Let's say you are right and Raúl Salinas is guilty of masterminding Pepe Ruiz Massieu's murder, I said. How could the former president not have known about his brother's involvement, when Raúl Salinas was his soul mate and closest partner? And assuming that he was unaware of it at the time of the murder, how could he have not known it afterward, when he was being briefed almost daily by his appointed prosecutor, Mario Ruiz Massieu? Furthermore, Mario had later admitted under questioning by the new government prosecutors that he had indeed informed Salinas at a meeting around October 18, less than a month after the killing, that some of the prisoners were mentioning Raúl's name. Was Mario lying on that count too?

Lozano Gracia laughed and raised his eyebrows, as if to say I had hit on the obvious question everybody around him was asking. "Well, it may have happened that way, who knows?" he said, eager to move on to the next issue. "Was there an agreement [between the president and the prosecutor] to protect Raúl? To guarantee immunity for Mario? There could have been. The only thing I know for sure is that a crime was committed, and that Mario Ruiz Massieu deleted Raúl's name from the statements."

▼

Could Raúl Salinas have acted alone, without his brother's knowledge? Was that possible, given the two brothers' closeness?

It could have been the case. Raúl Salinas was so used to the impunity that he and other members of the ruling camarilla had long enjoyed that he could indeed have masterminded the murder without ever contemplating that he could one day be taken to task for it. Power and wealth may have clouded his vision. It wasn't until several months after

Raúl's arrest that Mexicans got a clue as to the extent of his fortune: In November 1995 his wife, Paulina Castañon, was arrested by Swiss authorities in Geneva as she was trying to withdraw funds from an $83.9 million account held by Raúl under his fake identity of Juan Guillermo Gomez Gutiérrez. But that fabulous sum — found by Swiss investigators during an investigation into suspected drug-money laundering activities — was only part of Raúl Salinas's fortune. It was soon revealed that the presidential brother also kept dozens of millions stashed in U.S., British, German, and Caribbean banks, as well as at least twelve real estate and construction companies and more than forty-five properties — including several mansions and ranches — throughout Mexico. Much of his fortune had been amassed in the late eighties and nineties, while he was working as manager of the government's food distribution program and later as a top adviser to the president's Solidarity program, when he was declaring a maximum income of $190,000 a year, the attorney general's office said.

It was conceivable that Raúl Salinas, at the height of his power, may have subconsciously sabotaged the younger brother who had taken his role as depository of the family's political hopes. Sure, the two had always been very close, but it was just as important to remember that Raúl was the firstborn who bore their father's name and who had been the family's chosen to make a political career. By conspiring to kill Ruiz Massieu, Raúl may have thought he was helping his brother while actually destroying him.

"Deep down, Raúl felt a big resentment toward Carlos," I was told by Dr. Sergio Sanchez Pintado, a retired army lieutenant colonel and well-known psychiatrist and psychoanalyst who was among those espousing this theory. "He may have subconsciously tried to get even with him."

Most of those who believed that Carlos Salinas couldn't have been ignorant of his brother's alleged conspiracy argued that the Ruiz Massieu murder — just like Colosio's — was part of the president's effort to prolong his rule beyond his six-year term. Carlos had consented to both killings in order to create a climate of chaos that would allow him to declare a state of emergency and remain in power for another few years, or because Colosio had not agreed to pave the way for his return to power in the year 2000, they said.

Their main argument was that Salinas had sought to change the Mexican Constitution to allow the president's reelection, much as his counterparts Carlos Menem of Argentina and Alberto Fujimori of Peru had done recently. One former Salinas cabinet minister told me that Salinas, in private conversations with his aides, had consistently delayed a strong denial of his reelection intentions in 1992. A barrage of criticism in the press had ultimately forced him to give up the idea of reelection a year later. Later, Salinas — who had become increasingly Machiavellian toward the end of his term — had given an extraordinary political push to Chiapas peace negotiator Camacho at the expense of his presidential nominee, Colosio, and had subsequently helped build up the candidacy of PAN candidate Fernandez de Cevallos in his race against Zedillo: Salinas obviously wanted the PRI candidates to win by a very narrow margin so his successor would be a weak president and he could remain as the government's ultimate power broker.

Carlos Salinas dismissed such accusations as ludicrous. What was really going on in Mexico, he argued, was a fierce battle in which opponents of his free-market reforms — led by former president Echeverría — had tried to destabilize the country. "Nothing of what has happened in Mexico this year is alien to the tremendous struggle for power. What has been at stake here is what sort of national project will prevail," Salinas wrote from exile, reacting to the mounting accusations against him in the media. "During my term, I had to affect many interests to be able to carry out key aspects of the political and economic opening. . . . The reaction of the affected groups was tremendous. . . . In September 1995, Mr. Echeverría declared publicly that he opposed [the Salinas administration's free-market policy of] Social Liberalism, and what he described as the possibility that it would be carried on for another six-year term. It would seem that, to him and others, the candidacy of Luis Donaldo Colosio represented precisely the possibility that the model of Social Liberalism would endure."

Salinas's explanation was self-serving and aimed at shifting the focus of the dispute to the ideological arena, where he — at least in the eyes of the rest of the world — represented the forces of modernization. But on the other hand, the theory that he had ordered the murders as part of a plan to remain in power had many flaws. Salinas had not used the opportunity of Colosio's assassination to postpone the elections, nor

had he taken advantage of Ruiz Massieu's killing to put off Zedillo's inauguration. And several people who had seen him in the days following
the murders told me that the president was in a shambles — a man personally destroyed by his sudden loss of international prestige and, possibly, his place in history. Carlos Salinas most likely was no stranger to
his brother's shady business deals, to which he had been alerted by several aides. But why would he have ordered the killings that shattered his
presidency? It didn't look plausible.

▼

Weeks later, as Raúl Salinas was going into what promised to be a long
trial claiming he was a victim of political persecution, I sat down with
all my notebooks and tapes and tried to make sense of the whole Ruiz
Massieu scandal. I had ended up with half a dozen notebooks filled with
interviews, and mixed feelings about the trial's outcome.

Perhaps the Ruiz Massieu case marked the first time in the country's
recent history that the truth had finally come through. The Zedillo
government was under unprecedented social pressure to turn Mexico
into a nation of laws and could possibly have taken a dramatic step to
stress its resolve to put an end to Mexican politicians' long-enjoyed impunity.

But Mexico was also a country of smoke and mirrors, where yesterday's heroes are today's villains and today's champions of justice may be
tomorrow's crooks. Perhaps the new prosecutors were protecting another powerful person, just as the old ones had protected Raúl Salinas.
Only one thing was clear: If Raúl had indeed ordered the killing, as the
latest official story went, Carlos Salinas had most likely helped prevent
his arrest once he was informed about his brother's involvement.

Zedillo had boldly broken new ground by allowing a presidential
brother's arrest. But after his secret meeting with Salinas, he had ab-
stained from immediately taking the logical next step and ordering an
investigation into whether the former president had covered up his
brother's crime. The ultimate lesson of the Ruiz Massieu affair was that
Mexico was still a country of men — not of institutions.

CHAPTER 11

The Christmas Nightmare

Finance Minister Jaime Serra Puche had arrived at his office early in the morning that Monday, December 19, 1994. As he did every day, he turned on his computer to monitor Infosel — a Mexican news service with several windows that simultaneously showed the latest stock market quotes in New York, London, Tokyo, and Mexico City, as well as the top national and international news. A tall, self-assured former commerce secretary under Salinas who was one of President Zedillo's closest friends since their days as classmates at Yale, Serra was sitting on top of the world. He was internationally recognized as the chief Mexican official who had negotiated the NAFTA deal — the very prototype of the Salinas generation of U.S.-educated technocrats who moved as easily in Mexican political circles as in the corridors of power in Washington, D.C. At home, he was not only the most influential voice in Zedillo's cabinet, but one of the leading ruling party candidates for the next presidential election in the year 2000.

That morning it was the domestic news window at the center of his computer screen that caught the Finance minister's eye: It said, "Renewed fighting in Chiapas." The Zapatista rebels had broken the nearly one-year-old de facto truce with the army, sneaking out of their bases under the cover of night, and were claiming to have conquered "new rebel territories," including thirty-eight Mayan towns outside the Zapatista-controlled region. Alarmed, Serra turned around, grabbed the red phone behind his desk that connected him to the president and fellow cabinet members through the government's communications system, referred to as *"la red,"* or "the network," and called Central Bank president Miguel Mancera.

"Have you seen the news?" Serra asked.

"Yes," was the short answer from the central banker, a man about twenty years Serra's senior.

A few hours later, after the markets had closed, the two men were again on the phone. The central banker's one-word diagnosis was "Devastating."

▼

Mexico's foreign reserves had dropped dangerously low. What had started as periodic withdrawals of foreign deposits in the aftermath of the Colosio assassination and the Ruiz Massieu scandal had become a stampede that was about to deplete Mexico's foreign reserves and force the country to default on its foreign debts. Mexico's reserves had plummeted from $17 billion in October to $6 billion — about one month's imports bill — by the second week of December. What was worse, the government was facing more than $30 billion in short-term payments to foreign creditors in coming months. And that morning, with the news of new tensions in Chiapas, nervous investors were selling their Mexican pesos and buying U.S. dollars at record speed.

Serra felt a helpless victim of the information age. Marcos's claims to be "in control" of dozens of Chiapas towns was grossly exaggerated — in fact, rebel sympathizers had briefly occupied a handful of municipal palaces and blocked a few highways with fallen trees, rocks, and trash — but the rebels had scored another propaganda coup, and government denials would end up as last paragraphs in wire agency stories that would not stop the panic in the markets. By the afternoon of Monday, December 19, Mexico's foreign reserves were about to hit rock bottom. Two more days of continued capital flight, and Mexico would have to declare a moratorium on its foreign payments. Serra called the president, who was in the state of Sonora — the home state of slain candidate Colosio — on his first presidential tour out of the capital.

"Mr. President, it's been a terrible day," Serra said. "We must do something."

Despite two decades of close friendship — Zedillo was a man of few friends, and Serra was one of the chosen few — the Finance minister had ceased calling the president in the Spanish familiar *tu* from the very day of his inauguration. As awkward as it sounded, it was part of Mexico's political culture: Presidents were near-kings, and even their closest friends felt compelled to treat them as such. Even in private, Serra and other former Zedillo friends now addressed him as "Mr. President" and in the more respectful *usted*. It was no coincidence that many of Zedillo's predecessors, after several years of receiving this quasi-royal treatment, had ended up with a bloated image of their own place in world affairs.

When Zedillo asked what was his recommendation, Serra told him Mexico had to float the peso — allow the market to fix its price. A meeting was arranged with ninety-five-year-old Mexican Confederation of Workers leader Fidel Velazquez to obtain his agreement for a six-month freeze in wage increases, which they hoped would help stop an inflationary spiral once the peso began to lose ground against the dollar. Velazquez was the dream of any president in need of labor concessions: In his feeble voice — one had to put one's ear in front of his mouth to hear him — the aging labor leader muttered his consent.

As soon as he got Velazquez's green light, Serra called for a meeting of the Pacto — the task force of government, labor, and business representatives that recommended wage and price policies — for later that evening to obtain everybody's seal of approval for the new measures. That's when the new Zedillo government began to make a string of blunders that — mixed with a dose of bad luck — turned a critical situation inherited from Salinas into a financial debacle for Mexico, and a severe blow for Americans who had invested in the crown jewel of the emerging markets. Overnight, American investors would lose 15 percent of their savings, and more than twice that much over the next few months. Even more troubling, Mexico's financial debacle threatened to cause a chain reaction that could tumble the stock markets of major Latin American, Eastern European, and Southeast Asian countries.

▼

Lawrence H. Summers, U.S. undersecretary of the Treasury for International Affairs, received a phone call from Mexico at home at about midnight that night. Washington was already taken over by the holiday spirit on December 19, with most government offices celebrating year-end parties and crowds of tourists gathering in front of the White House to see the giant Christmas tree. Summers, a forty-year-old former Harvard professor and chief economist of the World Bank, was looking forward to a much-deserved holiday. With his wife, Victoria, their son, and twin daughters, he was planning to spend four days in Daytona Beach, December 24 through 27, and the New Year weekend skiing in Park City, Utah.

At first, that night's phone call from a senior Mexican official did not amount to devastating news. The U.S. Treasury had been warning Mexico for months that its peso was overvalued and that a devaluation of some sort was necessary. Summers told his Mexican colleague that he understood the situation and recommended measures to obtain foreign capital and help offset a possible rush of panic bank withdrawals. If it was handled prudently, the devaluation could actually help correct Mexico's huge current-account deficit. But it wouldn't happen that way: A chain of Mexican Government blunders would soon turn a manageable foreign reserves crisis into a financial catastrophe.

In the days that followed, Summers ended up spending most of his time at his in-laws' home in Florida on the phone — seven hours straight on one occasion — trying to muster international support to prevent Mexico's escalating financial troubles from spilling over to world markets, and had to cancel his year-end skiing vacation altogether. Over the weeks that followed, the Mexican crisis would degenerate from a tolerable 15 percent devaluation of the peso into a devastating 50 percent slide of the Mexican peso against the U.S. dollar.

▼

On a chilly Sunday morning nearly a month later, Mexico's ambassador to the United States, Jorge Montaño, walked into the White House offices of Clinton's National Security Council deputy director, Sandy Berger. The Mexican, a tall, dapper man in his forties, was looking anxious. He was carrying a folder filled with clips from Mexican newspapers, which he spread over the desk of Clinton's National Security aide shortly after they began their conversation.

"You see, this is what the Mexican press is saying," Montaño told

Berger with an air of urgency. "Let me translate some of these articles for you."

They were clips from the op-ed pages of *Reforma* and *La Jornada* in which leading Mexican columnists were forecasting the imminent fall of the Zedillo government. The U.S. Congress, after initial shows of support from House Speaker Newt Gingrich and Senate Majority Leader Bob Dole, had not come up with the votes to support a Mexico bailout package. The Mexican reserves were continuing to fall. The Zedillo government had lost credibility with foreign and domestic investors. Mexicans were outraged, and Zedillo lacked a solid political base from which to govern. There was a serious possibility that he would be forced to resign, the analysts had written.

"I'm told that we do not have enough foreign reserves to make it past Tuesday," the ambassador told Berger. "Either we have a clear sign [of U.S. support], or we have to declare a moratorium."

On Monday, January 30, 1995, Gingrich and Dole informed the Clinton administration that there were not enough votes in Congress to approve the Mexican bailout package. Hours later, the president announced his unprecedented $50 billion bailout program for Mexico, of which the United States would contribute about $20 billion.

▼

The disastrous December 19, 1994, government-labor-business talks that led to the devaluation of the peso — and ultimately forced Clinton to put together his international bailout package — had started late that night, long after the markets had closed. Perhaps the Mexican government's first mistake was holding the talks with business and labor leaders at all: It tipped off Mexico's businesspeople that a devaluation was in the air and drove many of them to rush to exchange pesos for U.S. dollars as fast as they could.

"There is no question that the whole thing was mishandled," Mexico's ambassador to the United States, Jesús Silva Herzog, who had lived through more than one devaluation of the peso himself as Finance minister in the eighties, would concede to me later. "It's the first time in history that a devaluation was consulted on [with business and labor representatives]. You don't discuss a devaluation with anybody . . . not even with your wife."

Even before the meeting started, Mexican business leaders had withdrawn large amounts of pesos from Mexican banks, either because they had inside information or because they sensed that something extraordinary was about to happen. The Mexican stock market fell by more than 4 percent before the evening meeting. News of the impending meeting had spread explosively hours earlier within the small world of government and business insiders: Amid the banner headlines about a resurgence of the Chiapas conflict, there was growing speculation that the government would be unable to keep buying U.S. currency to defend Mexico's weakening peso. At the very least, insiders knew that there would be a top-level meeting to discuss Mexico's price and wage policy that night.

Labor Minister Santiago Oñate, who presided over the meeting, says he received a call from Serra at about lunchtime that day informing him that there would be a meeting of the Pacto that evening, and that his office may have made some calls to invite labor and business leaders to it. But Oñate stressed that neither he nor anybody at his office knew what exactly the meeting would be about, and that he didn't find out until later that evening, after the markets had closed. Yet he conceded that any astute businessperson could have seen the writing on the wall.

"It wasn't an invitation for an ordinary meeting," Oñate told me in an interview at his office a few months after the devaluation. "The very fact that people were invited to an unscheduled meeting that was to start at eight P.M. marked a clear sense of urgency. . . . Business representatives could sense it. You could see their great preoccupation in their faces as they began to arrive at this building."

By the time the meeting began, a small army of reporters was already camping out at the lobby of the Labor ministry's building in southern Mexico City. The grave-looking business leaders and labor representatives rushed past the reporters toward the top floors of the building. Once there, they locked themselves in separate rooms: Business leaders with Finance Minister Serra, and labor representatives with Labor Minister Oñate.

As soon as the closed-door meetings started, the government representatives would make their second fatal mistake: announcing a proposal, subject to discussion, to allow the peso to float freely, letting the market set its value. Many of those who hadn't been alarmed enough to buy dollars that afternoon would do it when they heard Serra and Central Bank president Miguel Mancera make their presentations. The two government officials confirmed at the meeting that Mexico was running out of foreign reserves and argued that the currency exchange rate should be set free. Business leaders protested: They said the measure would provoke an even worse rush to purchase U.S. dollars that would cripple economic activity. Instead, they proposed a compromise solution: a moderate expansion of the range within which the Mexican peso was allowed to fluctuate against the dollar. After five hours of discussions, Serra and Mancera gave in. Past midnight, Serra walked down to the lobby and announced that "in order to confront the uncertainties that have been generated by the conflict in Chiapas," the currency fluctuation range would be widened by 15 percent.

But during the talks, business representatives had heard the Finance minister and the head of the Central Bank acknowledge that Mexico's foreign reserves were hitting rock bottom — critical information that differed from the government's upbeat public statements — and that their first choice had been to devalue. Mexican business leaders had in effect been put on alert of the government's plans. Some of them were reported to have discreetly left the room with their cellular phones to call their brokers in London and Tokyo and order them to sell their positions in Mexican pesos as fast as they could. Others would rush to buy dollars as soon as the Mexican markets opened the following morning. They made a killing — by the end of the week, their newly acquired greenbacks had increased their purchasing power in Mexico by more than a third.*

▼

Much of Wall Street, meantime, was caught off guard. Some money managers who were not following Latin America or Mexico with spe-

---

* In an interview with the author, former Finance minister Serra described as "grotesque" the claims that some participants at the meeting immediately phoned their brokers in London and converted their Mexican peso holdings into dollars, adding that the London and Tokyo markets did not handle Mexican-peso denominated transactions. Other government officials, however, say that it could have been done through sophisticated currency exchange transactions.

cial attention were relying on Serra's categorical statements to the *Wall Street Journal* and the *Financial Times* a week earlier that there would be no devaluation, and on Zedillo's promise in a December 9 address to Congress that the currency exchange rate would be maintained. In the eyes of these U.S. investors, there was no cause for alarm: These were Salinas's heirs, Harvard- and Yale-educated technocrats who would do anything but stab the U.S. business community in the back. But even given that, how could sophisticated money managers for some of New York's leading brokerage houses and investment banks not have foreseen the Mexican devaluation?

It was a combination of deficient information, assumptions that Mexico's sophisticated financial officials would not make gross mistakes, and the New York securities firms' own eagerness to keep the lucrative emerging markets success story alive. Wall Street firms would explain later that they were working on the basis of deficient information about Mexico's foreign reserves: Mexico only disclosed its foreign reserves figures three times a year and had last reported them to stand at $17 billion in October. Economists knew the reserves had dropped significantly since, but could not estimate exactly by how much. In addition, most Wall Street analysts assumed that Mexico would do what every country does before devaluing its currency: seek international financial assistance to protect itself against panic deposit withdrawals. Since there were no indications that Mexico was knocking on anybody's door asking for money, it seemed Zedillo would stick by his word and maintain the existing exchange rate — at least for a few months.

By Wednesday, December 21, a day after the Mexican government had announced the expansion of the currency fluctuation range, an additional $4 billion had left Mexico. The Mexican stock market fell to a new record low. By the end of the day, Zedillo was forced to do what he had wanted to do from the start: A government announcement on national television said the trading band had been jettisoned in favor of a free-floating peso. Within days, as panicked investors rushed to get rid of their Mexican currency, the peso fell further, hurting everybody who owned Mexican stocks, and U.S. exporters who had begun to ship a growing number of goods to Mexico under the new free-trade agreement. The Wisconsin Investment Board lost $95 million on peso trades it later said were unauthorized. Chemical Bank lost $70 million on a similar transaction. Wall Street firms ended 1994 reporting sizable losses for their previously booming Latin American funds. Among the most hurt: Fidelity's Emerging Markets fund reported a 1994 loss of 17.9 percent, and Scudder's Latin America fund ended the year with a drop of 9.4 percent.

One of the few U.S. fund managers who could brag about riding out the Mexican devaluation relatively unhurt was Josephine Jimenez, the intrepid San Francisco–based manager of the Montgomery Emerging Markets fund who had visited Chiapas in the early days of the Zapatista rebellion and decided afterward to cut down her fund's exposure in Mexico.

In a recorded message to its clients on its special 800 number hours after the devaluation was announced, Montgomery reminded its clients about Jimenez's bearish reports following her visit to Chiapas early in the year and discreetly congratulated itself for having pulled out of Mexico ahead of time. Thanks to its timely decision, Montgomery had reduced its exposure in Mexico from an already small 7 percent at the beginning of the year to barely 4 percent by the time of the December 20 devaluation, the recording stated.

What Montgomery didn't go out of its way to emphasize was that it had shifted much of its Mexican funds to Brazil — an emerging market whose stocks had also plummeted as the ripple effects of the Mexican devaluation hit stock markets throughout Latin America. In an oblique — and unintended — way, Mexico had gotten even with the "smart" money managers who had deserted it.

▼

Not everybody in Mexico had lost that much that fast, either. Television tycoon Emilio "El Tigre" Azcarraga, the self-declared soldier of the president of the republic, had quietly been converting his huge debts from dollars to pesos over the previous months. In August that year, at about election time, Televisa had obtained a $1.1 billion loan in pesos, which the company had partly used to restructure its debt from dollars to pesos. The giant network's debt in U.S. currency was cut from 58 percent to 36 percent of the company's total debt. It was more likely a caution-inspired business decision by Azcarraga than the product of an inside tip — few anticipated a massive devaluation at the time

Televisa restructured its debt — but, given the television baron's cozy ties with the presidency, Televisa's move raised many eyebrows when it came to light after the devaluation.

"Fortunate provision? Inside information? Whatever it was, Televisa chose to restructure its dollar-denominated debt right on time," the daily *El Financiero* said on November 23. "Meantime, other companies are finding themselves in a situation plagued by uncertainty."

▼

The biggest mystery of all was why the Zedillo government had failed to cover its back by obtaining a U.S. emergency loan before devaluing the peso. After all, an international loan of as little as $6 billion — just over one-tenth of the $50 billion that would be required later — could have helped calm investors' fears that Mexico's reserves were about to run dry. In fact, Mexico had tried repeatedly to get such financial backing, but a combination of unfortunate circumstances — and bad U.S. judgment, according to some — had kept the Clinton administration from helping out.

At first, when Mexico realized the seriousness of its foreign reserves problem in late November 1994, both Salinas's outgoing government and Zedillo's transition team had asked the U.S. Treasury to activate the $6 billion in loan guarantees that U.S. Treasury Secretary Lloyd Bentsen had privately offered more than a year earlier. Bentsen had offered the funds in case the NAFTA deal was not approved and had later made the offer public in the aftermath of Colosio's assassination. But now the U.S. Treasury turned down Mexico's request for the funds on grounds that Mexico was not ready to follow its recommendation that it devalue its currency. The $6 billion loan guarantee, Summers explained months later, was "not to be used to bolster exchange rate or macroeconomic policies which were fundamentally unsustainable."

Failing that, the incoming Zedillo administration had contacted Bentsen in the early days of December in search of a new source of loan guarantees to defend the peso. Shortly after Zedillo's December 1 inauguration, Finance Minister Serra called Bentsen, an old friend from the days of the NAFTA negotiations. He said he wanted to get together with him to propose creation of a "North American Currency Stabilization Fund" to provide emergency loans to countries that — as was

Mexico's case now — suffered sudden and massive waves of capital flight. According to Serra, he had drafted the plan in a November 21 memo to Zedillo, with a recommendation to raise it with Clinton during a preinauguration trip to Washington, D.C., in late November. But the Zedillo-Clinton meeting turned out to be largely introductory small talk, and there had not been another opportunity for Mexico to make its proposal until after Zedillo's inauguration.

"Lloyd, I have to talk to you on instructions of the president," Serra told his old friend Bentsen. But the Mexican Finance minister never got to raise the issue of his proposed stabilization fund. Bentsen told him he would call him on the following day because he had to tell him "something personal." A day later, Bentsen told Serra that he would announce his resignation in the next few hours.

"What do you suggest I do?" Serra asked. Bentsen told him to call Robert Rubin, the former head of the New York investment bank Goldman Sachs, whom the Mexican official knew well from meetings with U.S. investors. Rubin would be appointed shortly to replace him, Bentsen said.

Serra called Rubin right away. "Congratulations," he said. Rubin responded in kind, saying he was excited about his new responsibilities and looked forward to doing wonderful things together with his Mexican colleague. After exchanging pleasantries for a few moments, Serra went to the point. He asked to see Rubin as soon as possible.

Sure, Rubin responded. But a few days later, Rubin informed the Mexican Finance minister that his lawyers had advised him to wait for his ratification by the Senate before conducting any official business. That would not happen until January 11, he added. Mexico's hopes to create an emergency fund to weather a potential financial storm had to be put on hold. Meanwhile, the Clinton administration was refusing to disburse the $6 billion loan guarantees, and the drain on Mexico's foreign reserves continued to worsen.

Serra flew to New York to an icy reception Thursday, December 22, from more than a hundred U.S. fund managers and analysts. He explained his actions and tried to rebuild investors' confidence in Mexico's new economic measures, but failed to win them over.

"Why didn't you tell us about the devaluation?" one angry investor asked, echoing the question in everybody's mind.

"Devaluations are not announced in advance," Serra responded with a nervous smile.

Among the many former Mexico fans in the audience who were not smiling was John Purcell, the head of Salomon Brothers' emerging markets research division who had been among the first to spot Mexico as an investment opportunity in the late eighties.

"I did not find it convincing," Purcell told a reporter shortly after the meeting. "I think it's going to take them a very long time, probably the whole of this administration, to regain the confidence of investors."

Serra got the message: "Nobody threw any tomatoes at me, but it was obvious that there was a bad feeling in the air," he would recall later.

A few days later, Serra was off to Washington, D.C., for a meeting with Federal Reserve Board Chairman Alan Greenspan. In Mexico, the floating peso was plummeting. But there was little Greenspan could do: It was Christmastime, and he would not be able to summon European central bankers and international financial institutions to put together a package bailout for Mexico until after the year-end holidays. "They worked and tried very hard, but the key people were not around," Serra recalled.

Serra returned to Mexico December 26. On the plane and over the next day, he gave the finishing touches to a new economic program with drastic austerity measures aimed at restoring investors' confidence and beginning what was likely to be a long road to resurrecting the Mexican economy.

At two A.M. on December 28, Serra had to rush to the hospital: His English-born wife was about to deliver a baby boy. They waited for several hours. At 6:30 A.M., Serra got a call from the president's office telling him that Zedillo would meet with his cabinet's economic team at eight A.M. Serra took his cellular phone with him to the presidential palace of Los Pinos, asking the doctor to call him as soon as the baby was about to be born: He would sneak out of the meeting, if necessary, to be there on time. He had already contemplated stepping down.

"Mr. President, we need a new person to announce this economic package," he told Zedillo once the two were alone after the meeting. "If I announce it, it will not have any credibility in the eyes of investors."

Was he sure? the president asked. It was a semirhetorical question:

Zedillo badly needed a change of course — or faces — to put the crisis behind him and to appease furious international investors and angry Mexicans.

Yes, Serra said. His staying in the job would be an additional burden on the government's economic program. If there was any other way in which he could be helpful, he would always be there, he said. He stood up, and the two friends embraced. Serra went from there to the hospital to witness his son's birth, and would soon leave the country for a teaching assignment at Princeton University.

▼

Months later, in a conversation aboard the presidential plane as he was returning from a visit to Veracruz, Zedillo eluded my question as to whether he had ever pressed Salinas to devalue the currency. He waved his hand as if saying that such rumors were inaccurate, and ducked going into further details by stressing, "I started to rule on December first."

In fact, Zedillo had been so conscious of the financial time bomb he was inheriting that he had repeatedly asked outgoing president Salinas to either devalue the currency or at least begin drawing from the $6 billion emergency fund offered by the Clinton administration. Several cabinet members who participated at the meetings told me in separate interviews that Zedillo had been discussing a devaluation of the currency with the Salinas government as early as March 1994, following Colosio's murder. Why not take advantage of the political crisis to solve Mexico's structural economic problem at once? he had asked. Then, in September 1994, shortly after he had won the election, he had suggested to Salinas that he devalue before the change of government. He had repeated that request, in more urgent terms, at a key meeting in late November.

On Sunday morning, November 20, Zedillo had convened an urgent meeting of his economic kitchen cabinet at his transition offices. The situation was serious, he said. More than $1.6 billion had left the country Friday, and the financial bleeding was likely to intensify in the coming week. The president-elect asked key participants — Serra, central banker Mancera, and Finance Minister Pedro Aspe — to come up with suggestions. As they were drafting various currency exchange scenarios, word came in that President Salinas was back at his home from a military parade he had attended that morning and would receive them there.

Protocol and political sensibilities barred the president-elect from setting foot in the presidential palace before his inauguration. Zedillo and his top economic aides went to the president's house in the southern Mexico City suburb of Tlalpan and waited in Salinas's library. Half an hour later, when the president arrived, Zedillo's team stressed the need to move to a more realistic exchange rate before his inauguration, and Mexico's top economic policy makers began to go over the pluses and minuses of the various scenarios drafted earlier that morning. A consensus was reached to meet the next day and, barring a swift recovery in the markets prompted by a meeting the president-elect would have that night with labor and business leaders, devalue the currency by between 10 and 15 percent.

"Salinas said, 'If you think that there's no alternative but to devalue, I'm prepared to devalue,' " one cabinet minister who participated at the meeting recalls.

But if Salinas truly meant what he said, he backed off hours later. After a second meeting between the two economic teams at six P.M. that same day in his library, during which the president had reiterated his disposition to announce a devaluation if that was best for Mexico, Salinas had changed his mind. His Finance minister, Aspe, had told him in a private conversation after the meeting that he would resign if they went ahead with the devaluation plan. During the day's meetings, Aspe had argued that the currency devaluation should take place gradually, with proper foreign reserves backing and within the framework of a new economic plan that could only be announced by the Zedillo administration after the new president took office.

"I mentioned in front of the group that . . . modifying only the exchange rate would generate more financial turbulence than the one we were trying to abate," Aspe recalled later. "Ten days before leaving office, it was not possible for an administration to abruptly change the exchange rate regime and implement an economic policy package."

Salinas was in a bind: Aspe was Mexico's most trusted official in the eyes of the Wall Street community. His resignation would set off panic in the markets — the very thing the planned devaluation was meant to avoid. And Salinas, at the height of his campaign for the leadership of the World Trade Organization, had a natural interest in concluding his term without headlines about a devaluation or a scandal over Aspe's resignation.

Hours later, he called Zedillo at his home. He had concluded that it would be best for the country not to devalue at the time, Salinas said. A gradual devaluation carried out by the new administration and camouflaged within a new economic program would be far less traumatic. Things would work out all right, Salinas said. For a few days, it seemed they would: The next day, the markets reacted favorably to Zedillo's agreement with labor and business leaders to continue anti-inflationary policies, and capital flight diminished. Over the next few days, Salinas became increasingly confident that he had done the right thing.

On his last day in office, during a farewell visit to a hospital built during his administration in the Mexico state town of Chalco (a final effort to grab headlines that the publicity-needy incoming Zedillo team badly resented), Salinas boasted before his closest aides about the rosy economic figures with which he would hand over the government. Aboard the presidential bus, flanked by two of his children, Press Secretary José Carreño, Mexico's ambassador to Washington, D.C., Jorge Montaño, and several other top aides, Salinas received a call from Finance Minister Aspe. As soon as he hung up the cellular phone, he told his aides with a big smile that the markets had closed down virtually unchanged.

"First president in twenty-five years who doesn't devalue the currency!" he said proudly.

Everybody applauded. There was a victorious climate on the bus. But Mexico's financial stability was largely an illusion. Most experts agreed that a well-planned devaluation before Zedillo's inauguration would have allowed the new administration to start with a new — more realistic — economic program that would have spared the country its financial collapse four weeks later.

▼

In the aftermath of the devaluation and President Clinton's emergency $20 billion loan guarantee package to Mexico, U.S. officials were just as coy about admitting that they had been pressing Salinas to devalue.

They had a public relations problem: Clinton stood to look pretty bad in his expected 1996 reelection bid if it became evident that his administration had been fully aware of Mexico's financial troubles while it was publicly saying that the country was doing great.

For several months before the devaluation, the Clinton administration had been increasingly alarmed over Mexico's financial situation, yet it had continued to publicly praise Mexico as an economic success story, according to documents released months later by the Senate Banking Committee. As late as December 9, less than two weeks before the devaluation, President Clinton had praised Mexico's economic management as a model for other world economies.

Internal administration memorandums disclosed by the Senate committee show that top U.S. officials had begun worrying about Mexico's finances as early as in February 1994. In an internal memo dated April 26, Summers had told his boss, Treasury Secretary Bentsen, that the Mexican Central Bank had been forced to intervene in support of the peso and that Mexico's dependency on largely volatile foreign investments remained "a serious problem." That same day, Summers had said publicly, "Mexico's institutions are fundamentally strong . . . they have a great future and we do not expect any long-term damage."

Critics of Clinton's $20 billion bailout of Mexico brandished these and other memos — neglecting to mention that many of them were couched in ambiguous language — as evidence that the Clinton administration had deceived the American people and caused U.S. investors to lose billions. There was indeed a fuzzy line between sound confidentiality and deception.

"I started getting worried I would say in August and September [of 1994]" Bentsen told the *Wall Street Journal* after he had stepped down. "I was telling them . . . that their current account deficit was such and such and that they had to do a devaluation. Obviously, the decision was theirs. They are a sovereign nation, very sensitive about the colossus of the North."

Why weren't U.S. officials more critical in public?

"God sakes," Bentsen responded. "You don't trigger some run on another country's currency."

Clinton had bet heavily on Mexico by circumventing a skeptical

Congress and using his executive powers to commit $20 billion from the Treasury's Exchange Stabilization Fund — a mechanism normally intended to stabilize the dollar — and win commitments of an additional $30 billion from international financial institutions and friendly nations to save Mexico from bankruptcy. The U.S. bailout program for Mexico amounted to a phenomenal sum: It was far larger than any economic help Washington, D.C., had ever given the Chrysler Corporation, the City of New York, Israel, or Russia. Boris Yeltsin's American economic adviser, Jeffrey Sachs, lamented that "Russia's tragedy is that no investment banker's Christmas bonus has ever depended on Russia's financial stability."

A broad coalition of conservative Republicans, prolabor Democrats, Ross Perot supporters, and other activists of the anti-NAFTA forces was even more caustic in its criticism. Many, including Britain, Germany, and several other European countries, saw Rubin's push for the bailout program as a move to help his old pals on Wall Street. European countries, which ended up contributing reluctantly to the bailout plan, argued that the rescue program would be counterproductive in the long run: It would encourage Mexico to act irresponsibly in the future. What would be the incentive for Mexico to live by its means if Washington, D.C., came to its rescue every time it went bankrupt? Others showered the media with a long list of I-told-you-so's aimed at hurting Clinton's 1996 reelection bid. Republican hopeful Patrick Buchanan went to the extreme of claiming, "This country [Mexico] is not a worthy trade partner."

What had moved Clinton to act so boldly? It wasn't merely Mexico. According to participants at the late-night meetings in the White House during which the decision was taken, Clinton's decision to switch to "Plan B" — forgetting about Congress and launching the support package by executive order — was primarily based on the possible international repercussions of a Mexican default.

"The first point made at the meeting was that if we allowed Mexico to default, the repercussions would be felt throughout Latin America, Eastern Europe, Southeast Asia, and even in some weak Western European economies such as Spain, Portugal, and Greece," said a senior U.S. official. "It was also argued that Mexico would be a major issue during the 1996 presidential campaign, and that the president had placed his bet on the success of NAFTA and a free-trade zone in Latin America."

Clinton was also persuaded that the Mexico rescue package would not cost the United States a penny. "At that point, we saw the Mexico problem as a crisis of confidence, in which a massive show of support would calm down the markets," the official said. "We thought no money would ever have to be disbursed to Mexico."

But, perhaps reluctantly, there was also a growing realization at the White House that the new trade partnership with Mexico entailed new responsibilities for America. Mexico would not go away, either as a problem or as an opportunity: It was already one of the top three U.S. trading partners and one of America's most promising foreign markets, as well as its largest source of illegal immigrants and the main entry point of drugs into U.S. territory. The United States could not afford to ignore Mexico, or to turn its back on it in times of need.

As Eurocentric as U.S. foreign policy continued to be — by 1995, the State Department still had only nine officers assigned to its Mexican desk, compared with more than ninety at its former Soviet Union desk — Clinton had little choice but to bail out Mexico. By 1995 the United States was hitched to Mexico, for better or for worse.

▼

There was one claim that Clinton administration officials were particularly worried about: that Mexico had kept its currency artificially high during the NAFTA negotiations to appease U.S. opponents of the treaty with assurances that the U.S. market would not be flooded with inexpensive Mexican products. Now, a small minority of well-placed Mexican analysts was joining Mexico bashers in the U.S. Congress in speculating that Zedillo had planned to devalue the currency not just as an emergency measure to stop capital flight, but as a calculated policy to boost Mexican exports.

Luis Enrique Mercado, publisher of the influential financial daily *El Economista* and a rabid supporter of Salinas's economic policies, says he first became suspicious of Zedillo's economic plans on August 25, 1994, four days after the elections, when the Spanish daily *ABC* published an interview quoting the president-elect as saying that a 10 percent depreciation of the Mexican peso against the dollar in 1993 "has allowed us to gain competitiveness, which has been reflected in a 25 percent increase in exports." Furthermore, Zedillo was quoted as saying that "I don't see the economic need for an abrupt devaluation." But he did find it convenient to "slide within a [currency exchange] band to gradually recover our lost competitiveness."

Mercado reacted by writing a biting front-page column September 6, in which he assailed the president-elect's comments as potentially devastating for Mexico's economy. His argument: Zedillo's recipe of "competitiveness as a result of a devaluation" would trigger inflation — and would amount to a return to the bad old times when Mexican presidents were under the illusion that they could have economic growth with inflation. Zedillo called him that same evening, alarmed over the negative impact the column had had in the financial markets, and saying his quotes had been misinterpreted by the Spanish publication. He then granted a long interview to *El Economista*, in which he stressed that there would be no change in the country's economic policy and that he was convinced there could be no growth without stability — and that included stability in prices.

Months later, when I visited Mercado at his newspaper offices following the devastating December 20 devaluation, he was convinced that the president-elect had been more truthful in his remarks to the Spanish daily than in his subsequent denials to his newspaper. After all, wasn't Zedillo pressing Salinas behind closed doors to devalue the currency? Hadn't he stepped up his demands at a November 10 meeting with the outgoing president and their respective economic teams?

"When I put everything together, I can't help concluding that Zedillo had long wanted to devalue the peso as a way to stimulate foreign investments in the manufacturing sector and promote Mexican exports," Mercado said. "Chiapas, the current account deficit, and collapse of foreign reserves were most likely nothing but excuses."

▼

In exchange for the U.S.-sponsored rescue package, Zedillo was forced to launch an unusually tough economic program. There would be steep government spending cuts and other austerity measures that would cause massive layoffs — independent economists estimated there would be a million pink slips in 1995 — and wage and prize freezes, as well as a new round of privatizations that would seek to raise more than $12 billion. In addition, the February 20, 1994, agreement with the U.S. government stipulated that Mexico had to provide collateral with money from its oil exports — a politically sensitive issue in Mexico, where the state-owned oil sector was still seen as a symbol of national sovereignty — and demanded that the Mexican government provide "timely and accurate data" on its foreign reserves.

"It's a tragedy," Zedillo confided to one of his closest aides as they were struggling to come up with a new economic program at the height of the financial crisis. "It will be a long time before we Mexicans will once again have options."

It was indeed a tragedy for a country that had convinced itself it was about to join the First World. As in the Greek story of Sisyphus, the legendary king of Corinth who was condemned by the gods to roll a heavy rock up a hill only to see it come down again every time it neared the top, Mexico seemed to be the victim of a cruel jinx that periodically raised it to the top of the developing world's economies and then allowed it to collapse thunderously amid generalized shock.

Mexico had already suffered dramatic devaluations in 1954, 1976, 1982, and 1987. In every case, they had followed several years of quasi-imperial rule by Mexican presidents whose economic policies were automatically approved by a rubber-stamp Congress, applauded by government-controlled media, and celebrated by international bankers. And almost always, Mexico's autocratic system, its lack of transparency, and the gullibility of international money managers had ended up deceiving everybody — except for the small group of Mexican insiders who made millions from being in the right government office at the right time.

CHAPTER 12

Unmasking Marcos

The mysterious writer who only identified himself as "Javier" had been sending letters for several months, some to Mexico's Interior ministry, some to the Defense ministry, and others to the attorney general's office. His first letter, dated in May 1994, had simply stated, "I have information about the Zapatista army that may be of interest to you," and gave a P.O. box in Mexico City. When he obtained no response, he had sent a second and a third one, claiming to have important information about Subcommander Marcos and the Zapatista National Liberation Army. It was hot stuff, he said, the kind of inside information the government would be eager to get.

At first, nobody in the government paid any attention to the letters — they got lost among the hundreds that arrived daily in government offices from pranksters, prisoners, or other people with lots of time to waste. By the time the letters were brought to President Zedillo's attention in January 1995, the aspiring informant had been unsuccessfully trying to share his knowledge of the Zapatista leaders' real identities for nine months.

But in late December 1994, as everybody was consumed by Mexico's financial crisis, government investigators began to notice that Javier was salting his correspondence with small bits of interesting detail, as if to prove that he had real information. One letter provided a full description of the rebel camp of Las Calabazas in a remote corner of Chiapas; another gave details of Zapatista officer David's past as a peasant organizer. In all cases, the data seemed to coincide with the sketchy intelligence the government had gathered on the rebels. Whoever was hiding under the pen name Javier knew something. The Mexican Army's intelligence branch, known among the military as the Second Section, immediately combed through its files for all the previous letters the mysterious Javier had sent.

The army's enthusiasm was understandable — not just because of its eagerness to crack down on the Zapatistas. For decades, Mexico's military had been almost totally banned from the government's intelligence-gathering business as a result of Mexican political leaders' traditional fear of giving the military too much power. Chiapas had provided the Mexican military with a golden opportunity to expand its intelligence apparatus, and the army's Second Section was determined to make the most of it. Within days, the Second Section had launched a full-fledged search for the mysterious letter writer.

The lead turned out to be an intelligence gold mine: The man who was volunteering the information through a third party was Subcommander Daniel, the former rebel officer in charge of the Altamirano region. He had been — alongside Subcommanders Marcos and Pedro — one of the three top NLF military commanders in Chiapas throughout the eighties and early nineties. Subcommander Daniel, it turned out, had broken with Marcos shortly before the January 1, 1994, uprising. He now seemed determined to get back at his former comrade.

His real name was Salvador Morales Garibay, and he was a thirty-four-year-old former roommate and fellow professor of Marcos at Mexico City's Autonomous Metropolitan University who had been one of the first members of the group to move to Chiapas in the early eighties. Second Section agents had sent him several messages promising clemency in exchange for his cooperation and — after intense bargaining — had located him in Los Angeles, California, where he was hiding. Soon, Morales would tell them his full story — and that of his former comrades.

▼

Morales, one of four children of a middle-class family from the central state of Michoacán, had met Marcos in the early eighties, when the two were philosophy and graphic design professors at the Autonomous

Metropolitan University's Xochimilco campus. It was a time of high hopes for Latin America's left: By 1979 Cuba's Fidel Castro had reached the peak of his political influence in the region by chairing the Sixth Summit of the Movement of Non-Aligned Countries in Havana; the Sandinista guerrillas had just taken power in Nicaragua; nationalist strongman General Omar Torrijos was in power in Panama; Jamaica and Grenada seemed to be heralding a string of socialist governments in the Caribbean; and Cuban-supported insurgencies had a good chance of taking power in El Salvador and Guatemala.

As in many other countries in the region, a relatively small but determined group of Mexican leftists felt they had a chance to ignite a revolutionary movement in their own country. And, according to those who taught or studied there at the time, the graphic design school where Morales and Marcos were teaching was a hotbed of political activism — a place where the young professors could simultaneously earn a living and hone their revolutionary skills.

"The graphic design school encouraged its faculty to embark on very concrete projects," recalls Alberto Hijar Serrano, a former guerrilla of the National Liberation Forces who had been Marcos's philosophy professor and mentor during his college years. "Professors taught their students how to design a book cover, produce a pamphlet, prepare banners for a strike, or mural newspapers for popular organizations. These were very valuable agitation and propaganda tools."

Like many other Marxist professors eager to turn their words into action, Morales had begun his revolutionary career with a relatively innocuous mission — doing the layout for the in-house leftist magazine *Proletarian Conscience*. Its circulation was only three hundred copies, but amid the revolutionary fever that swept Latin American colleges in the late seventies, it was considered an honor to be part of the magazine's editorial board. For the Marxist militants behind it, people like Commander in Chief Germán and other members of the National Liberation Forces, it was an important tool for promoting political consciousness and recruiting new militants.

Morales's transition from magazine layout editor to guerrilla officer started in 1980, when he was invited by a fellow *Proletarian Conscience* editor to participate with a handful of professors and students in a "first aid" training course in the Chiapas jungle. It was a thinly disguised guerrilla training course run by the National Liberation Forces, which he was told would be run by a young man who used the nom de guerre "Zacarías."

Once in Chiapas, Morales was amused to discover that Zacarías had a familiar face: He was his buddy at the Xochimilco college, the same man who a decade later would become known throughout the world as Subcommander Marcos. By then, the National Liberation Forces had largely abandoned the Cuban-inspired "focal point" strategy, under which a single guerrilla column was expected to send out revolutionary waves throughout the country, and had adopted the Maoist path of a "prolonged people's war." The latter — influenced by the revolutionary wars in Nicaragua and El Salvador — called for simultaneous rebellions that would "liberate" rural areas and wear down the government little by little.

Morales had soon become a member of the Zapatista army, and had taken increasingly longer and more rigorous military training courses in the Lacandon jungle under the direction of the future Subcommander Marcos and Commander in Chief Germán. The next ten years would be a period of intense preparation. Many members of the clandestine movement — including Yolanda, Josué, Iván, and Pedro — had been sent to cities around the country to train as nurses, radio technicians, and mechanical engineers. Non-Indian officers such as Germán, Elisa, Marcos, and Daniel shuttled between Mexico City and Chiapas in preparation for the military offensive. Several of them, including Marcos and Elisa, had spent time in Sandinista-ruled Nicaragua, taking insurgency and special operation courses, according to Mexican military intelligence reports, and may have received additional support from Salvadoran and Guatemalan splinter groups of those countries' largest guerrilla movements.

As the date for the Zapatistas' military offensive approached, Subcommander Daniel had become increasingly disenchanted with both Marcos and Germán. Morales's story evoked the power struggles that had led to the collapse of Marxist guerrilla movements in El Salvador and Guatemala, and that now seemed to be destroying the Zapatista movement from within. From his statements to government agents, it was clear that Morales was bitter at having been sidelined — perhaps even demoted — shortly before the Zapatista uprising: Marcos, he said, had not wanted to share the limelight with any other white face within the movement.

Subcommander Daniel's troubles with Marcos had begun — or at least became known within the Zapatista army — in May 1993, on the occasion of the shoot-out that had followed the army patrol's discovery of the rebel camp of Las Calabazas on Mount Corralchén. A few weeks after the battle, which despite government denials had alerted the media for the first time to the existence of rebel camps in Chiapas, Subcommander Marcos had convened a meeting of top Zapatista officers to review the incident.

At the meeting, Subcommander Marcos had blamed Daniel, who was in charge of the Las Calabazas camp, for much of what had happened. Long before the clash with the army, Marcos had recommended that the Las Calabazas camp be dismantled: It was located in an area where the Mayan communities were split over their support for the Zapatistas and thus presented a high security risk. Subcommander Daniel had disagreed, asserting that the camp needed to remain in its place precisely to secure the surrounding Mayan villages' support for the revolution. Daniel was stripped of his command of the camp and sent to a Zapatista hideout in San Cristóbal de las Casas to carry out routine fund-raising and logistics support operations.

He felt humiliated. His resentment against Marcos would increase after the January 1, 1994, rebel uprising. Bolstered by the spectacular impact of the Zapatista rebellion on public opinion, Marcos had begun to distance himself from his longtime comrades in Mexico City and Chiapas, and was building up the all-Indian Clandestine Committee as his main source of support. Much like Commander in Chief Germán in his Mexico City hideout, Subcommander Daniel had soon found himself as an officer without a role in a rebel army whose self-promoting field commander was eager to assert his movement's Indian credentials.

When asked why he was volunteering to turn in his former comrades, Morales told government investigators that he was outraged at the rampant corruption within the Zapatista leadership. The Zapatistas' arms purchasing practices had become a major point of contention between Marcos and Daniel. For many years, the defector said,

Subcommander Marcos had asked the destitute Mayans to contribute whatever they could — a pig, a goat, or, if they had them, a few pesos — to purchase weapons for the rebel movement. The idea had been to commit the Mayans to the rebellion by making them sacrifice some of their most precious possessions. Many of the desperately poor Indians had turned over their life savings to buy weapons.

Yet Marcos, according to one published account, had consistently overcharged them: He sold the Mayans an AK-47 rifle, which the NLF bought on the U.S. black market for about $800, for more than $2,000. This was what Mexican meat processing plants paid Indians for two cows — a real fortune. It was fair for the Zapatista army to add freight costs and an additional extra for the risk of transporting the weapons across Mexican Army territory, but the margins Marcos was charging amounted to exploitation, the defector said. Morales had firsthand knowledge of weapons market prices: He had purchased some shipments himself, from a Los Angeles–based arms supplier to Central American guerrillas whom the Zapatistas knew as "Johnson."

Morales, who in his capacity as a Chiapas-based liaison with Commander in Chief Germán kept track of the Zapatistas' financial affairs, had grown increasingly upset over Marcos's use of the Indians' money. Marcos had used part of the funds to buy electronic gadgets and to promote causes that had more to do with his self-aggrandizement than with the revolutionary cause. And Germán was having a good time in Mexico City, he said: The commander in chief took advantage of his authority within the movement to sleep with as many female militants as he could, and even traveled to the United States with the excuse of gathering funds for the movement — usually to return with empty pockets.

As months went by, Morales had become increasingly determined to quit the Zapatista army. Trouble was, he couldn't. The rebel statutes called for a drastic punishment for defectors: death. It was a threat that couldn't be dismissed: The history of Latin American rebel movements was full of examples of militants who had been executed by their own comrades following revolutionary trials for their real or imagined transgressions. And Mexico's short history of guerrilla movements was no exception: Some accused the National Liberation Forces of having executed its former officers Napoleón Glockner and Nora Rivera in 1976 as traitors to the movement.*

At least one Mayan, a Chol Indian known as Benjamin, had been summarily executed in the eighties after a Zapatista martial court had found him guilty of stealing rebel funds and talking too much while drinking with townspeople.

Desperate and afraid that his increasingly open criticism of Subcommander Marcos would lead him to a guerrilla martial court, Morales had fled his guerrilla camp and soon crossed the border to hide in Los Angeles. Unhappy and unable to make a living there, he had returned to Mexico City and, fearing for his life, had left a few internal documents of the Zapatista army at the house of a friend he had asked for help. Shortly thereafter, his friend had sent his first letter to the Mexican government.

"Nobody paid any attention to him: We receive hundreds of letters a day and it's impossible to check them all out," Attorney General Lozano Gracia told me later. "But the mysterious writer's insistence in saying, 'I have information, I have information,' led somebody in the government to say, 'Hey, this guy has written so many times that it may be worth it to check him out.' "

In January 1995, after several debriefing sessions with Morales, officials concluded that the defector was indeed a high-ranked Zapatista officer. His information was crucial to confirming the identities of top Zapatista leaders, which the military had by then established tentatively but had not been able to confirm.

Morales had also corroborated that several suspected guerrilla safe houses throughout the country were indeed part of the Zapatista movement. The government's intelligence services had been discreetly watching for more than two months a suspected guerrilla weapons repair shop in Yanga, Veracruz, and another one in Mexico City, photographing people coming in and out of them. The latter was the two-

---

* An NLF internal document released by military authorities after the two rebels' deaths asserts that they were executed by the guerrillas after they tipped police about a guerrilla hiding place. Glockner's son Fritz, however, says his father disclosed the hiding place under torture, and that he was killed by the police.

story house in Mexico City's middle-class neighborhood of Colonia Letrán Valle from where Subcommander Elisa was directing the Zapatistas' propaganda network and nursing her newborn baby.

With Morales's testimony in hand, the army's intelligence wing and those within the government who were urging a crackdown on the Zapatistas had found what they needed: an insider who could identify top Zapatista leaders and justify a warrant for their arrest. If nothing else, the revelation of the Zapatista leaders' identities would help undo Subcommander Marcos's larger-than-life image and reduce him to an ordinary terrorist. It was a potentially precious chance for Mexico's beleaguered president to regain the upper hand in what had increasingly become a propaganda war the rebels seemed to be winning. The army's Second Section began to draft a plan for a full-scale military offensive against the Zapatistas.

Once he had been located by the army, Morales didn't have much of a choice: He was told that he could either collaborate with the government and go on a witness protection plan, or end up being killed by his former comrades. By early February, Morales had signed a written testimony about his guerrilla past, and about his former comrades.

▼

Zedillo was under growing pressure to act in Chiapas. On February 9, 1995, he was to attend an important army ceremony and face his generals, who were growing increasingly restive over the president's apparent acceptance of the Zapatistas' control over much of Chiapas territory. In a confidential report that landed on Zedillo's desk about a week earlier, Defense minister General Enrique Cervantes assured the president that the army was able to make a massive deployment of troops in Zapatista territory within six hours, and that — if there was any fighting — it could wipe out the Zapatista guerrillas within five days. The proposed army offensive was informally known as Operation Rainbow, after the Chiapas-assigned Rainbow military command force that was to carry it out.

The generals had long been furious over what they saw as Salinas and Zedillo's wavering policy on Chiapas. Their main complaint was that Mexico's armed services were failing in their constitutional duty to guarantee national sovereignty because the government was allowing an extraneous force to control part of the country's territory. It was only the latest of several recent crises in government-military relations that had brought Mexico's traditionally low-key army to an unusual state of anxiety. In 1992 the army had felt unfairly attacked by the new high school history books put out by Zedillo when he was minister of Education, in which the military was blamed for the 1968 massacre of leftist students at Tlatelolco Square. Two years later, the generals were incensed by the government's failure to come out in their defense following human rights groups' reports critical of the military's handling of the 1994 war in Chiapas.

During his last year in office, Salinas had tried to placate the military's discontent by substantially increasing its new weapons purchases — and the juicy commissions the generals made from them. Salinas had also allowed the army's Second Section intelligence wing to expand and effectively compete with the Interior ministry's intelligence branch on the Chiapas conflict. His measures had only helped prevent the generals from going public with their complaints. In an effort to improve his rickety ties with the military, Zedillo had allowed the armed services an even greater say in intelligence affairs. But none of these tokens had succeeded in appeasing the increasingly anxious generals.

"The military saw all these attacks on the army as part of a huge civilian plot against them," a senior Interior ministry official with close ties to the army explained. "In their minds, if the government failed to stop stories in the media about army human rights violations in Chiapas, it was because it didn't want to."

As days went by, the arguments for a military raid on the Zapatista headquarters in Chiapas were piling up on Zedillo's desk. In addition to placating the army, Zedillo needed to appease PRI hard-liners in anticipation of the February 12 elections in Jalisco — Mexico's second-largest state. The vote was almost sure to be won by the PAN — and to be contested by the ruling party's dinosaurs. It would be easier for Zedillo to assert his democratic credentials and allow a PAN victory if he simultaneously made a show of force in Chiapas.

The planned military offensive was also likely to please Wall Street bankers, many of whom were pressing for a decisive action against the Zapatistas as a way to help reverse Mexico's new image of instability. A memo by Chase Manhattan Bank's emerging markets group, which had made its way to the *Washington Post*, had argued that "the [Mexican] government will need to eliminate the Zapatistas to demonstrate their effective control of the national territory and of security policy." Chase Manhattan fired the author in an effort to distance itself from the memo once it was made public and drew fire from international human rights groups, but Zedillo knew it represented the view of many in the banking community.

If he had harbored any doubts that investors' confidence in his government was sagging, they were dispelled by the financial markets that Wednesday morning, February 8: The Mexican peso had hit an all-time low against the dollar, and Mexico's stock market index had lost 6.4 percent of its value to close at its lowest level in seventeen months. Investors were panicking. Zedillo needed to act fast.

▼

On paper, the plan looked perfect. Days before the army's foray into Zapatista-controlled territory, the president would escalate his offers of peace to the rebels. Then, hours before the crackdown, a top-level Zapatista defector — Morales, the former Subcommander Daniel — would be brought to testify before a judge and would disclose the existence of the Zapatista safe houses in Mexico City and Veracruz. The army would raid the rebel safe houses and would announce the discovery of a fabulous arsenal of weapons and matériel, together with compromising documents indicating a Zapatista plan to launch terrorist acts throughout the nation. The military offensive in Chiapas would be explained to the world as a defensive action to prevent the death of innocent civilians in Chiapas and across Mexico.

Within hours, Zedillo gave the green light, and the plan was set in motion. At eight P.M. on Wednesday, February 8, 1995, as news reports were talking about the collapse of the stock market, a nervous Morales was escorted into a Mexico City district attorney's office under heavy protection from government troops. Within minutes, he revealed in front of a federal judge what he had been telling government investigators for several weeks: Marcos's real name was Rafael Sebastián Guillén.

"He was a former professor of graphic design at the Autonomous

Metropolitan University, at the campus of Xochimilco," he added, his hands shaking. He went on to testify about the two guerrilla safe houses he knew about, and gave their exact addresses.

The plan was in motion. Within hours, the army would have in its hands the arsenals found in the Zapatista safe house in Yanga, Veracruz, and Subcommander Elisa's house in Mexico City. The Rainbow military command force in Chiapas would move in on Zapatista-controlled areas of Chiapas at six A.M. the next morning. If everything went well, the president would be able to make an announcement to the nation about Marcos's arrest at about noon the next day, after the military ceremony.

The next morning came and went without any dramatic news, however. By lunchtime, the president had not taken to the airwaves to announce Subcommander Marcos's apprehension or the takeover of Zapatista-controlled territory by the army. Mexican television did not interrupt its regular programming to broadcast Zedillo's address to the nation until six P.M. that Thursday, February 9. Looking aggravated, standing in front of a microphone and reading from a prepared text, the president announced to the nation the discovery government troops had just made in raids of Zapatista safe houses in Veracruz and Mexico City.

"I must inform the nation that while the government was stressing its commitment to dialogue and negotiations, the EZLN was preparing new and bigger acts of violence, not only in Chiapas but throughout the country," an angry-looking Zedillo told the nation. He said the army raids of Zapatista safe houses had uncovered "an arsenal of high-caliber weapons," including mortars and explosives, that indicated that the Zapatistas "were about to start new actions of violence" outside Chiapas.

At that point, Zedillo dropped the bombshell: The Army raids and the subsequent arrests had allowed government investigators to establish the Zapatista leaders' real identities and political backgrounds. Subcommander Marcos's real name was Rafael Sebastián Guillén, and his movement's commander in chief, Germán, was a veteran guerrilla leader named Fernando Yañez. They had both been found to be part of the National Liberation Forces, an offspring of a guerrilla group founded in 1969 whose nature was "neither popular, nor Indian, nor from Chiapas," the president said. He ended his speech by announcing that he had issued warrants for the Zapatista leaders' arrest and had issued orders to the army to move into rebel territory and capture the Zapatista leaders.

As all of Mexico was glued to the television to watch the apparent revelation of Subcommander Marcos's identity — the mystery that had been at the center of Mexicans' political conversations for more than a year — the cameras shifted to a government prosecutor holding a picture of Guillén in his days as a university professor printed on a transparency. Taking a newspaper photograph of the same size showing Subcommander Marcos with his black ski mask, the official superimposed the transparency over it in an effort to prove that the two men's eyebrows matched. Whether they did was a much-debated issue in Mexico over the following days. The prosecutor then read from Guillén's dossier: It said among other things that Mexico's most-wanted man was thirty-seven years old, five feet seven inches tall, and a graduate in philosophy and sociology.

▼

"They got him!" I heard myself saying as I watched Zedillo's speech to the nation and the subsequent description of Marcos by government prosecutors. As opposed to other suspects whose names the government had leaked to the media in previous months, this one matched the features of the person I had interviewed in the Lacandon jungle a few months earlier.

Until Subcommander Daniel's defection, Mexico's Interior ministry's intelligence service believed that Marcos's real name was Samuel Orozco, another leftist activist who had disappeared from public view after going to Chiapas in the early eighties, and who had recently missed his father's funeral in the northern state of Sonora. Before interviewing Marcos in Chiapas, I had seen an Interior ministry sketch of Orozco: He was six-foot-three and about forty-two years old. When I returned to Mexico City from Chiapas and reread the description of Orozco, it became clear to me that Marcos was shorter and younger than the government's main suspect. Orozco, it turned out, was a former leftist militant who had indeed disappeared about a decade ago, but was now living happily in Fresno, California, working on a morning Mexican *ranchera*-music radio show.

Besides Guillén's height and age, his background matched my first hunch after meeting him in the Lacandon jungle: I had come out of our interview convinced that he was more likely to be a product of Mexico's state-run university's sociology school — still stuck in the theories of the sixties — than a former Roman Catholic priest that many others believed him to be. A word Marcos had used during our interview immediately came to my mind: As he was stressing that the Zapatista uprising had finally brought the long-ignored Indians of Chiapas to the attention of Mexico, he had stated — quite naturally — that his rebel movement had opened the doors for this "disymmetrical" sector to have a say in society.

"Excuse my ignorance, but what does *disymmetrical* mean?" I asked.

"In the social sciences, it's those who don't have a political participation," and have fallen out of view, he had responded.

When I talked to Zedillo's top aides a few days after the president's speech, and after Subcommander Marcos had issued a statement denying he was Rafael Sebastián Guillén, they offered further assurances that they had identified the right person. Hours before the president's announcement, Zedillo's office aides had invited two of Guillén's former university professors to the presidential palace for an informal chat about their former student. The professors corroborated most of the data supplied by Subcommander Daniel. They had long suspected that Subcommander Marcos was their former student, but had kept the secret to themselves. Now it was hard for them to deny it.

One of Guillén's former faculty advisers had opened his hands in a gesture of resignation as soon as he had entered the offices of a top Zedillo aide in the presidential palace and — before anybody had asked him anything — muttered, "I already know why you've called me." Yes, he would say seconds later, Marcos had a strong resemblance to his former student. At the same time, government officials had interviewed Guillén's parents and former classmates, who had slipped a crucial detail: Guillén happened to be a pipe smoker, just like Subcommander Marcos, in a country where pipe smoking was a rarity. The circle had been closed.

"If we hadn't been one hundred percent sure of Marcos's identity, we wouldn't have allowed the president to make the announcement: We would have had the Interior minister or a lower-level official make it," said one of Zedillo's top advisers, who personally checked the last details of Marcos's identity before the president went on the air. "A mistake like that could cost us the presidency."

▼

Yet, from a military standpoint, Operation Rainbow was a miserable failure: Marcos had managed to flee his headquarters shortly before the army attack. The official explanation was that a local judge in Chiapas had delayed for several hours the paperwork to carry out the president's order to arrest Marcos. "The attorney general's office kept telling us, 'It's coming, it's coming,' but we spent the whole morning waiting and the arrest warrant in Chiapas was not coming," one of the president's closest aides told me. "The operation started about twelve hours late because of that."

Most likely, Marcos had been tipped off a day earlier, when government troops had raided the rebel safe houses in Veracruz and Mexico City. The Zapatistas had a sophisticated radio communications system in the jungle: Because Chiapas was so poor and had so few telephone lines, the government and the Roman Catholic Church had long ago set up elaborate radio systems throughout the state to help bring Indian communities in the jungle closer to civilization. The Zapatistas were now in control of many of these hamlets and operated their radios. So it didn't take much to warn Marcos of the impending army attack: Zapatista sympathizers who had heard about the capture of their comrades in Veracruz and Mexico City had telephoned their contacts in San Cristóbal de las Casas, who in turn had radioed Marcos in the jungle.

Marcos fled his headquarters in Guadalupe Tepeyac hours before a cloud of heavily armed military helicopters had descended on the place and a column of two thousand army men in military vehicles arrived at his jungle headquarters. In his rush to flee, Marcos had left behind virtually all his belongings: When reporters arrived at his abandoned headquarters a few days later, they found — in addition to his books and computer terminal — one of the rebel leader's black skimasks, several packages of pipe tobacco, and his backpack full of medicines.

Military intelligence officers would later comment with some amazement about another discovery: The medication proved that — like his revolutionary predecessor Che Guevara — Marcos suffered from asthma.

Adding to the embarrassment of its failure to grab Marcos, the government's story that Morales's testimony in court had led investigators to the rebel safe houses in Veracruz and Mexico City, and that the subsequent raids had unearthed huge arsenals of weapons for an imminent attack, proved to be full of holes. It soon became clear from neighbors and relatives that government forces had occupied both rebel hideouts at least three hours before Morales had testified in court. And the arms caches found at both places, while not minimal, did not amount to arsenals — or at least did not give the sense of a massive terrorist plot about to unfold.

At the Zapatista hideout in Yanga, Veracruz, government troops had found, among other weapons, one Uzi machine gun, six grenade launchers, more than a dozen grenades, various chemicals used to make bombs, and eight pistols. At Subcommander Elisa's house in Mexico City, government troops had arrested the woman — whose real name was Maria Gloria Benavides — and found two 9 mm pistols, several army weapons, and various old documents from the National Liberation Forces and the EZLN.

Marcos had been unmasked and exposed to public opinion as a hard-line Marxist guerrilla, yet the government had failed in its plan to arrest him and offer a gracious release in exchange for a political agreement that would solve the Chiapas crisis. Marcos was still at large — if weakened by revelations that he was hardly the postmodern social democrat depicted by *La Jornada* and many leftist intellectuals.

▼

So who was the charismatic rebel leader who was hiding under the name of Subcommander Marcos? Rafael Guillén turned out to be one of eight children of a middle-class furniture store owner in the Gulf Coast city of Tampico. He had grown up with his six brothers and one sister in a pink stucco house in one of the city's upper-middle-class neighborhoods.

Rafael's father, Don Alfonso Guillén, was a self-described "Quixotic" small businessman whose passion was writing and reciting poetry. A high school dropout, he had worked his way out of poverty, first selling newspapers and lottery tickets on the streets, then opening a small clothing store, a shoe store, and finally the first of what would become a small chain of furniture stores. Along the way, he had become a director of the city's Marketing Executives Association and had reared his children to become high achievers: Paloma, his only daughter, was a lawyer, economist, and a local congresswoman for the ruling party, while the boys had earned university degrees in business administration, sociology, engineering, agronomy, philosophy, public accounting, and economics. Rafael, the fourth of Don Alfonso's children, was the philosopher. During his high school days at the Jesuit-run Tampico Cultural Institute, he had been a writer for the school's newspaper and an actor in and director of the school's theater plays. He and his brother Simón Carlos, the sociologist, were the socially conscious part of the family: As teenagers they had volunteered for humanitarian work in the poverty-stricken Tarahumara region, and on visits home as adults they had together shot a home movie about Paloma's three-year-old son's escape from preschool one day, which they had interpreted as a child's spontaneous rebellion against the constraints of formal education.

Rafael had left his family at seventeen, after his high school graduation, to pursue his studies in Mexico City. During college years he was a leftist student activist who was infatuated with the works of Marxist French philosopher Louis Althusser. He was not a bookworm type, according to his professors and classmates. Hijar, the professor and former guerrilla who introduced him to Althusser's work, remembers him as "an outgoing young man who was always making jokes and who, unlike most philosophy students, was also into sports: He was a pretty good basketball player."

Rafael was known, among other things, for his clever plays on words during political discussions. Inverting a statement by Fidel Castro in which the Cuban strongman had stated that "Yesterday, we were a handful of men; today, we are an entire people conquering the future," Rafael had quipped that, in the case of Mexico's revolutionaries, "Yesterday, we were an entire people conquering the future; today, we are a handful of men." It was typical of the irreverent style that would make him popular under his new identity as Subcommander Marcos a decade later.

For his 1980 graduation thesis at the National Autonomous University of Mexico, Rafael had picked the same issue he had explored in the home movie he had shot with his brother a few years earlier: the trappings of formal education. The 121-page thesis, entitled "Philosophy and Education," was a mixture of radical arguments for class struggle and somewhat adolescent calls for rebellion against what he saw as the primary source of capitalist oppression — the family. In it, the future guerrilla leader — at the time twenty-five — would call for "a new philosophical praxis: philosophy as a revolutionary weapon." The text, peppered with quotes from Althusser and Karl Marx, claimed that philosophy, understood as a discipline to help understand the world, was a tool of capitalist society to divert philosophers from their real mission: to fight for a new social order. Coffee-table philosophers — whom he mockingly described as long-haired intellectuals crowding Mexico City's smoke-filled cafés — were one of the main targets of the aspiring revolutionary's scorn.

"He is sitting in the lotus position," he wrote:

No, it's not Kung-Fu, nor Siddhartha, much less a crab with transcendental aspiration. It is, even if neither you nor I may believe it, a philosopher. . . . A philosopher is a strange character who lives at night and resides in an obscure location (a cave or something like that); starts his forays at 7 P.M. or 8 P.M.; who can be found in cafés, parks or the most solitary places. . . . [He] is presented to us as somebody who doesn't worry about material possessions, and yes, instead, about spiritual possessions. . . . Suspected of being homosexual, or in the best case asexual, like the angels, the philosopher is also a stereotype in the way he dresses, in his personal appearance: uncombed hair, messy beard, his look of permanent ecstasy, as if in a never-consummated orgasm, cigarette and coffee are already part of his persona, [his] guttural sounds pretending to be the most disconcerting and obscure words, [his] blue jeans faded by many moons. . . . With ample knowledge of all issues, the philosopher can offer his opinions just as much about the general decline in profits as about the defeat of the national soccer team in [the World Cup tournament in] Argentina.

Because of this skewed definition of their discipline, philosophers shunned political activism, the graduate student explained:

Coffee-table Marxists . . . look at political activism with Olympic disdain. They shake their head with disapproval when presented with a pamphlet talking about the struggle in a given factory, farm workers here or peasants there. Political activism, rallies, assemblies and street protests are petty things for them. . . . Radical defenders of their individuality and of "humanity," they criticize the Soviet Union, China, and Cuba, for having failed to respect individual rights. . . . Philosophy is thus articulated in such a way as to justify the repressive politics and education of the capitalist state regime.

In a fascinating chapter of his dissertation entitled "The Family," Rafael seemed to be trying to justify his decision to virtually break ties with his parents following his graduation and his increased involvement in the National Liberation Forces. As if confirming psychologists' family constellation theories, according to which middle children are the most psychologically troubled ones, Rafael — the fourth of Don Alfonso's eight children — seemed eager to find a political justification for breaking with his parents.

"As a unity of consumption and reproduction of the labor force, the family in the capitalist system is also the basic unit of reproduction and transformation of the dominant ideology," he wrote. The next unit of oppression, obviously, is school. Rafael's thesis concluded that a child's entire education is geared toward securing his submissiveness to the ruling class. "Ideology thus conforms to practices that support forms of domination, which in turn support forms of capitalist production, which amount to forms of exploitation," he wrote. Rafael's thesis ended with a call for breaking the state's subtle mechanisms of ideological domination. "The only thing that makes this possible is the practice of proletarian politics," he concluded.

Rafael's thesis fit right in with the state-run university's Marxist fervor: It got a top grade and allowed the future rebel leader to graduate with honors. Three years later, after spending some time in Paris, Rafael got a job as a professor at the Autonomous Metropolitan University and, according to his father, worked briefly as a bus driver and labor organizer at what would be later known as the Route 100 union. In both places, Rafael met many of his future guerrilla comrades and financial supporters. Shortly thereafter, he would put his dissertation's words into action and disappear into the Chiapas jungle.

▼

And who was the even more mysterious Commander in Chief Germán, of whom Mexicans had not heard a word until the president had announced his existence in his televised speech? He was Mexico's most secretive guerrilla leader: In nearly three decades of revolutionary activity, he had never issued a communiqué or given an interview. He was as fanatical about secrecy as Marcos was about self-promotion and political propaganda.

It was Fernando Yañez's obsession with anonymity that had allowed him to survive decades in hiding while most of his comrades had been killed or captured by government forces, government officials said. The fifty-year-old rebel leader had good reason to be obsessive about his personal security: His own brother Cesar Germán Yañez — better known as "El Hermano Pedro" and one of Mexico's best-known guerrilla heroes — had died in a 1974 clash with security forces in Chiapas after a rebel defector had tipped the government as to his whereabouts. Fernando had taken over the command of the National Liberation Forces after his brother's death and — in his memory — had adopted Germán as his new military name. Since then, not even his closest aides knew where he lived or had a telephone number to reach him: It was he who called them or visited their hideouts at the most unexpected times. He was determined to carry out his brother's revolutionary mission without getting caught.

The two brothers were among the six children of Dr. Margil Yañez, a prominent surgeon from the northern city of Monterrey who was active in Mexico's Communist Party. The boys grew up in a middle-class neighborhood and went to private schools, but their father and grandfather — a rural teacher and social activist who prided himself on having a bullet lodged in his arm from one of his many clashes with the police — made sure that the family remained loyal to leftist causes. One of the Yañez boys' proudest childhood memories was of their father's little victory over the U.S. Government, when he had obtained a special visa for a one-day trip to Texas to give a lecture at a medical conference despite being banned from entering the country because of his Communist affiliation. After weeks of negotiations with U.S. Immigration offices, the conference organizers had obtained a waiver to allow Dr. Yañez to make the trip — and to be escorted by U.S. marshals to the border immediately after finishing his lecture.

"We were very influenced by our father and grandfather, who in addition to leftist activists were Freemasons," remembers Margil Yañez Jr., the eldest brother of Cesar and Fernando, who became a medical doctor like his father. "Each of us, when we turned fourteen, joined the Hope and Fraternity Youth Association, a Masonic lodge where we learned to speak in public and get involved in community affairs. Soon we all became student leaders in our respective classes."

Cesar, who would later become "El Hermano Pedro," was the pride of his father: he was shorter and skinnier than his brothers — he had been born two months ahead of time — but was by far the brightest. He had become a lawyer and defender of striking workers, and an ideologue of the Marxist cause. In his room, he kept a framed sign: Vietnam is the tomb of Yankee imperialism. Fernando had graduated from architecture school and was planning to pursue graduate studies in Florence. "He was less of an ideologue and more action-oriented than Cesar," their older brother recalled.

In the sixties, the two brothers devoted their entire political energies to supporting the Cuban revolution. They made several trips to Havana as part of international worker and student brigades and in 1967 founded the Mexican-Cuban Friendship Institute in Monterrey, one of the many Cuban embassy–supported groups aimed at spreading the gospel of the Cuban Revolution. By the early seventies, the two brothers felt they needed to take their activism a step further and ignite the revolutionary flame in their own country. They soon founded the National Liberation Forces.

In an emotional farewell scene in 1972, Fernando broke with his parents and his own family — he had already married and had three young children — to fade into total anonymity. Fernando showed up at his parents' home one morning and told them he had decided to join his brother Cesar and devote his life to the revolution. He told them they would never see him again, nor hear from him. He would never get in touch with them, for their own security. Before leaving the room, he asked them not to get worried if they read in the newspapers that he or his brother had been killed: The government often printed false stories about rebels' deaths as a way to break the guerrillas' morale and dissuade students and workers from joining rebel groups. He kissed his mother and left.

"My parents used to approve of his actions, until he decided to vanish forever," Margil told me with more admiration than sadness for his two brothers. "When he decided to go clandestine, he did it all the way. Neither my parents nor I ever heard from him again."

The Yañez brothers' new rebel group was largely an urban guerrilla organization with cells scattered throughout the country and rural arms in Chiapas, Oaxaca, and Tabasco. In late 1973, President Luis Echeverría had ordered a massive manhunt for the rebels. It ended in the February 1974 military raid in Ocosingo, Chiapas, where government troops killed Cesar on the tip of a defector and arrested a young woman with him. Her name was Maria Gloria Benavides — the same woman who would reappear two decades later as Subcommander Elisa.

"The Yañez brothers were fundamentalists: They wouldn't even talk with other revolutionary groups because they considered the rest of us to be too bland," says Gustavo Hirales, a former member of the 23 of September Communist League's politburo in the early seventies. "They were also staunchly pro-Cuban, and although Cuba was not known to help any rebel movements in Mexico, they were widely believed by the rest of us to be receiving some kind of discreet support from the Cubans."

In line with Fernando's idea of doing the revolution rather than discussing endlessly how it should be, his guerrilla group produced virtually no statements over the next few years. Its first major internal document was drafted in 1980 under the name of "National Liberation

Forces Statutes" and remained languishing in the Interior ministry's archives until it was rediscovered at Subcommander Elisa's house after the government raid. The document was as hard-line as one could find among Latin America's Marxist rebel groups.

"The National Liberation Forces fight against Imperialist ideology by challenging it with the science of history and society: Marxism-Leninism, which has demonstrated its validity in all triumphant revolutions of this century," the document stated in its first pages. "That's why, in addition to fighting against the ideological domain of capitalism, we also fight against those who, infiltrated in the labor and peasant movement and within the leftist movement, renege on the revolutionary essence of Marxism and promote reformist ideas and collaboration among the classes, instead of fighting to death for the exploited against the oppressors."*

▼

And who was really providing financial support for the Zapatista rebel army?

According to Mexican military intelligence reports, much of the money had been sent by European — mostly German — and Canadian humanitarian groups for social projects, and had been diverted to the Zapatista movement. One of the main groups that channeled foreign donations to the rebel movement was a nongovernmental organization called Economic and Social Development for the Mexican Indians,

---

* Yañez was arrested in Mexico City on October 21, 1995, on charges of illegal possession of an AK-47 rifle, a 9 mm pistol, and sixty-four cartridges of ammunition, but was released six days later after an avalanche of accusations from leftist groups and congressional peace-negotiators that the government had violated a temporary amnesty for rebel leaders. In a series of interviews after his release, Yañez confirmed that he had been a founder of the NLF in the late sixties, but denied any participation in the Zapatista rebellion of 1994. He refused, however, to give details about his whereabouts in the eighties and nineties, except to assert that he was "a poor architect" working in hiding because of fears of government repression and that he had spent some years in Chiapas looking for his disappeared brother. (*La Jornada*, October 24, October 28, 1995; and *Proceso*, November 6, 1995.) But, as in Subcommander Elisa's case, sources close to the Zapatista leadership told the author that Yañez's denial may have been aimed at discrediting Zedillo's assertion that the Zapatistas were "neither popular, nor Indian, nor from Chiapas."

known by its Spanish acronym, DESMI, which had close ties to the San Cristóbal Archdiocese. DESMI's leader, Jorge Santiago, was a man in his late thirties who, according to army sources, was known by the Zapatista rebels by the nom de guerre Jacobo. He had studied theology in Rome and, upon his return to Mexico, had joined church groups working in Chiapas's Mayan communities. In the early eighties, he had fallen in love with a young woman from Monterrey who soon began to work as his main liaison with the Zapatista rebel leadership. She was Subcommander Elisa.

In addition to DESMI's funds, the rebels were also getting funds from friendly leftist labor unions in Mexico City, especially the Route 100 Bus Drivers' Union, some of whose leaders Marcos knew from his days as a union worker in Mexico City. It was no coincidence that the Zapatista guerrillas were wearing the same dark brown shirts worn by the eight thousand bus drivers of Mexico City's Route 100 corporation. The government-subsidized company's labor union was awash in money: Its declared assets surpassed $46 million — some press accounts put them as high as $600 million — and included twenty-four properties in the capital and several more in the countryside.

Other sources of cash were government loans to farmers that were diverted to the Zapatistas by sympathetic Mayans, and sales of cattle by the Zapatista troops.

There are credible reports that the Zapatistas also sought assistance from sympathetic rebel movements in Central America and Cuba, but did not get it. But if Cuba had ever provided any moral support or logistic help to the Yañez brothers in the seventies, an increasingly isolated Castro was unwilling to risk antagonizing the Mexican government, one of its last remaining allies, in the eighties. If Marcos was later able to claim that the Zapatistas were not receiving outside support, it wasn't because they hadn't sought it.

In early 1986, a group of Mexicans who identified themselves as members of a new Zapatista rebel movement in southern Mexico had approached El Salvador's Farabundo Martí National Liberation Forces in search of military training and logistic support. A meeting with two top officers of the Salvadoran guerrilla group was arranged to take place in Managua, Nicaragua.

"We told them it was crazy, that there was nothing we could do for them," recalls former Salvadoran guerrilla leader Ana Guadalupe Martinez, who was in daily contact with her movement's representatives at the meeting. "We would not help a rebel movement in the only country with which we had good relations.

"From there, they went on to Cuba," Martinez said. "A few weeks later, [Communist Party Americas' department head Manuel] Piñeiro told us at a meeting in Havana that the Mexicans had gone to them, and that he had turned them down as well. For Cuba, messing up with Mexico would amount to committing a political hara-kiri, Piñeiro told us."

Conceding that the bulk of the Zapatistas' funding came from inside Mexico, military intelligence officials say the biggest mystery is how much they received from the leftist Route 100 Bus Drivers' Union, and whether any government agency was endorsing such financial aid. The labor group not only provided the Zapatistas with money and uniforms, but had also printed most of the guerrillas' pamphlets in its Mexico City printing shops. Were disgruntled sectors of the ruling party funding the rebels through the union? Or were the leftist union leaders taking money from city authorities and using it at their whim?

One of the few people who could have answered that question died in a bizarre April 1995 incident at a Mexico City government office that government prosecutors ended up ruling a suicide. The murky episode took place at 6:30 A.M. on Monday, April 10, 1995, after Mexico City transportation chief Luis Miguel Moreno had asked his security guard to lend him his 38-caliber Taurus pistol for a few minutes. The fifty-three-year-old career bureaucrat had been working throughout the night and over the entire weekend on an explanation for $8 million in nonaccounted expenditures that an independent audit had just found in the Route 100 bus service, whose union was suspected of having helped fund the Zapatista rebellion in Chiapas. Moreno had spent all night at the office and was going to the corner to buy some cigarettes and breathe some fresh air. He took the gun and went for his walk.

A few minutes later, the guards heard two shots from Moreno's office. His body was found lying next to his desk with two bullet holes in the chest. A government investigation ruled the killing a suicide. It was a curious suicide, however. Can a man fire two shots at himself? To his heart? In Mexico, apparently, yes: The attorney general's office said it was scientifically possible, and was indeed what had happened in Moreno's case.

Moreno's death had taken place only a day after the weekend arrest at a Mexico City restaurant of Route 100 union legal counsel Ricardo Barco, who had also been a legal representative for the Zapatista National Liberation Front in Mexico City. Although Barco denied having funneled funds to the Zapatistas — he asserted that the move against him was a government effort to behead one of the few large unions outside the ruling party's control — there was little question that the Mexico City bus drivers had contributed clothing, food, and large sums of money to the rebels. The question was, had there been a government link to the Zapatistas? Somebody made sure the truth would never come out: Moreno's body was reported cremated on the following day, preventing an autopsy that would have helped clarify the circumstances of his death.

▼

Three weeks after Zedillo's disclosure about Subcommander Marcos's identity, the rebel leader would once again try to turn a military setback into a propaganda victory by poking fun at the government's inability to catch him, and by turning his escape into a military feat of epic proportions. A poet-novelist at heart, he even managed to turn his personal suffering into a comic adventure. In a long letter to several Mexican newspapers dated March 5, Marcos chronicled his retreating army's fight against dehydration on the day he would inscribe in history as "the sixth day of the withdrawal."

"At dawn on Feb. 15, we were going to drink urine," he wrote:

> I say "we were going to," because we did not do it. We all started vomiting after the first mouthful. Prior to this, there was a discussion. Although all of us agreed that each of us would drink his own urine, Camilo said we would have to wait overnight for the urine to cool down in the canteen, and then drink it thinking it was a cold drink.
>
> In defense of his position, Camilo argued that he had heard on the radio that the imagination is capable of anything. I opposed, alleging that time would only make the odor of the urine stronger.

I also warned that lately the radio stations had not been conspic-
uous for their objectivity. . . . We finally decided to take one
mouthful, all of us at the same time, to see what would happen. I
don't know who began the "concert," but almost immediately we
all vomited what we had eaten and other things as well. Our dehydration increased and we threw ourselves on the ground, like
ninepins, stinking of urine. I do not believe we looked very military.

A few hours later, before the sun came up, a sudden rain
drenched us, quenched our thirst, and raised our spirits.

In that same letter, the poet-prankster-revolutionary tried to deny
Zedillo's assertion that he was a Marxist zealot named Rafael Guillén.
Emulating the pompous language of the attorney general's office's warrant for his arrest, he wrote a fictitious police interrogation of him — a
text that denoted both his ever-growing knack for sarcasm and his
colossal ego:

Urged to tell the truth and nothing but the truth, this individual
said his name is Marcos Montes de la Selva [Marcos Mounts of
the Jungle]. . . . This man, in full exercise of his mental and physical capabilities and under no pressure (other than being sought
dead or alive by 60,000 federal soldiers) gave the following testimony:

He was born in a guerrilla camp called Agua Fria, Lacandona
Jungle, Chiapas, on an August, 1984 morning. The man with the
voice said he was born again on Jan. 1, 1994, and then again on
June 10, 1994, Aug. 8, 1994, December 19, 1994, February 10,
1995, and every second since then until the moment he made this
declaration.

In addition to his name, he has the following assumed names:
"Sub," "Subco," "Marquitos," "Damned Sup," "Sup son of a . . ."
and others we do not list because of consideration for the virtues
of this prosecutor's office. . . .

The man with the voice admitted that, before he was born, and
being able to possess everything only to have nothing, decided to
own nothing to have everything. . . .

The man with the voice admitted that he has been irreverent toward the truths that are called supreme, except toward those that emanate from human beings. These truths, according to the deponent, are: dignity, democracy liberty and justice. A murmur expressing apprehension spread throughout the Holy Inquisition, excuse me, the Office of the Special Prosecutor.

The man with the voice admitted that efforts have been made to threaten him, to buy, to corrupt, to jail and to murder him, and that he has not become scared, has not sold out, and has been neither jailed nor murdered ("so far," the special prosecutor quipped ominously). . . .

The man with the voice admitted that he firmly believes that bad government should be overthrown by any means everywhere. He admitted he believes a new political, economic, and social relationship among all Mexicans and among all human beings must be built. It should be pointed out that these irreverent intentions made people at the prosecutor's office shudder. . . .

Following all the admitting, the man with the voice was urged to spontaneously declare himself either innocent or guilty of the following charges. He pleaded to all the charges as follows:

White people accuse him of being black. Guilty.

Blacks accuse him of being white. Guilty.

The people of Chiapas (auténticos) accuse him of being Indian. Guilty.

Traitor Indians accuse him of being mestizo. Guilty.

Male chauvinists accuse him of being a feminist. Guilty.

Feminists accuse him of being a male chauvinist. Guilty.

Communists accuse him of being an anarchist. Guilty.

Anarchists accuse him of being orthodox. Guilty.

Anglo-Saxons accuse him of being chicano. Guilty.

Anti-Semites accuse him of being pro-Jewish. Guilty.

The Jews accuse him of being pro-Arab. Guilty.

Europeans accuse him of being Asian. Guilty.

Government people accuse him of being in the opposition. Guilty.

Reformists accuse him of being a radical. Guilty.

Radicals accuse him of being a reformist. Guilty.

The "historic vanguard [of the proletariat]" accuses him of appealing to civil society and not to the proletariat. Guilty.

Civil society accuses him of disturbing peace. Guilty.

The stock market accuses him of ruining lunch. Guilty. . . .

Serious people accuse him of being a comedian. Guilty.

Comedians accuse him of being serious. Guilty.

Adults accuse him of being childish. Guilty.

Children accuse him of being an adult. Guilty. . . .

Everybody accuses him of whatever goes wrong with them.

But Marcos's literary extravaganza, spiced up by the adrenaline of having a whole army running behind his heels, could not overcome the fact that his real identity was no longer a mystery, and that his hard-line Marxist past was much less romantic than many of his admirers had thought. His cover had been blown.*

---

* As this book was going to press, Subcommander Marcos was still in Chiapas, surrounded by the Mexican Army, while government and Zapatista negotiators held monthly meetings in search of a peace agreement. It was not immediately clear whether Marcos and his Indian supporters would accept laying down their weapons and becoming an open political movement.

CHAPTER 13

Unmasking Mexico

I almost choked over my coffee as I was having breakfast and reading the newspaper on a Wednesday morning more than two years after the private banquet at Don Antonio Ortiz Mena's residence at which Mexico's top billionaires had pledged $25 million each for the ruling party's electoral campaign chest. The newspaper was reporting that Senator Miguel Alemán, the aristocratic-looking son of a former president who was the PRI financial secretary at the time, had just written a book claiming that the famous pledges had been "a joke."

"A joke!?" I couldn't believe my eyes. The newspaper report said the new book, entitled *Finances in Politics*, claimed that some of the thirty guests at the fund-raiser had "misunderstood" part of the conversation at the table: They had taken at face value a joke somebody had made to a guest who had arrived late, and who was told mockingly that everybody at the table was being asked to fork out $25 million. Nobody had ever given anything like that, the author claimed.

Unbelievable!! I had done extensive interviews with three well-known guests at the meeting who had separately confirmed to me that the PRI had requested $25 million from each participant. What was even more amazing was that the source who had given me the most thorough description of what had gone on at the banquet had been Senator Alemán himself, the very man who had now written a book claiming that there had never been such a solicitation of funds. Topping it all, the senator had talked to me on the record in a formal interview at his office, with my tape recorder rolling, giving me a detailed account of the banquet in the name of what he said was a new openness in Mexican politics and the need to achieve the ruling party's financial independence from the government.

Amazed, I rushed to see the editor of a major newspaper, carrying the tape of my interview with Senator Alemán in my pocket. Could he believe it? I asked him, brandishing the newspaper clip in the air. The man had told me on the record exactly the opposite of what he was saying now!

The veteran journalist looked at me with the eyes of a cow, puzzled by my outburst of journalistic excitement. A PRI senator had told a blatant lie. . . . So what else was new? He shrugged. The big news would have been if he had told the truth. The fact that I had him on tape didn't make much of a difference. In Mexico, words were the cheapest commodity. You could change them around at a moment's notice, and nobody would be terribly surprised by it. "If you publish that you have him on tape contradicting what he wrote in his book, he would probably say that you had misinterpreted his words, or that the voice on your tape is somebody else's, and the whole issue would fade away under a cloud of questions," the editor continued. "Chances are he may not even bother to answer — he may not care."

▼

It was far from an isolated incident. Mexican newspapers jolted you almost daily with a seemingly endless stream of bizarre revelations that — unless you learned to take them with a heavy dose of skepticism — kept you in a permanent state of agitation. Trouble was, you could not ignore them: Some of them occasionally turned out to be accurate. Being a foreign correspondent trying to sort out reality from fantasy in Mexico could easily become an exasperating task.

One morning, splashed across the front pages of virtually all Mexican newspapers was a headline reading, "Aburto is not Aburto!" It wasn't a joke: The story was datelined in New Jersey, where former government prosecutor Mario Ruiz Massieu was fighting an extradition request from the Mexican government, and quoted the former top government investigator as charging that the man who had been arrested in Tijuana following Colosio's killing was not the same man as the one who was serving a forty-five-year prison sentence in a Mexico state prison. Somebody had replaced Aburto shortly after the murder, on his way to prison!

The story resurrected a debate that had surfaced shortly after Colosio's killing, when the government had first presented Aburto to the media with a freshly shaven face and a new haircut, prompting questions in the media as to whether he bore any resemblance to the gunman who appeared in a televised videotape of the killing. Several months later, the new headlines seemed to give new credence to the theory. Was there an "Aburto of Tijuana" and an "Aburto of Mexico state"? Did the eyebrows of the Aburto arrested in Tijuana match those of the Aburto imprisoned in Mexico state? Were their eyes the same color? Did their hands look the same? The question became the hottest issue in radio talk shows, office conversations, and supermarket lines.

I was totally enmeshed in trying to establish whether Aburto was Aburto when Mexico's public opinion was suddenly diverted to a new case of clouded identities: The Zapatistas were not Zapatistas, or at least some of them weren't! Subcommander Marcos, who was still wearing his ski mask and refusing to confirm his identity, was maintaining that "fake Zapatistas" had made their appearance throughout the country, soliciting funds and offering military training. The Mexican people should be alert, because the fake Zapatistas could be government agents, the rebel leader had warned in a statement.

I was throwing my hands up in the air in despair when a childhood friend of President Zedillo I had long wanted to interview returned my call. He too believed — contrary to what was stated in Zedillo's biography and what I had been assured by his aides — that the president was not the biological son of electrician Rodolfo Zedillo. Rather, he was the son of a bureaucrat who worked at the Finance ministry and who had abandoned the president's mother shortly after Ernesto's birth, he claimed.

I was, as most journalists in Mexico often are, at a total loss. Was Aburto the real Aburto? Were the Zapatistas real Zapatistas? Was Zedillo a true Zedillo? How could one write about a country where one could not only not trust what people said, but wasn't even sure whether people were who they were supposed to be? Studying Mexico, as one U.S. academic had once told me, was like working in Plato's cave: You only saw shadows and never knew which shadow belonged to whom.

Senator Alemán's flip-flop had long been typical of government officials' public behavior and fit right in to Mexico's tradition of no accountability. With a single party in power for more than six decades, a rubber-stamp Congress, and an obedient Supreme Court, government officials had long had only one constituency to please: "El Señor Presidente." The Mexican people counted very little in a strong-party system in which the government party held no primary elections and where political promotions and demotions had long been decided single-handedly by the head of state. Within this context, it was no wonder that government critics routinely insisted that one of Mexico's main problems was *"la impunidad,"* the impunity from legal punishment or social condemnation that progovernment politicians had historically enjoyed.

Mexicans on the street were so used to being lied to by government officials that most considered it a given. Polls showed that Mexicans' trust in government officials was only a notch ahead of their faith in car salesmen, who were at the bottom of the list: 87 percent of the Mexican people said they had "little" or "no" trust in their government. Another study comparing Mexican and U.S. attitudes found that only 18 percent of Mexicans had "a lot" of confidence in government institutions, while the figure in the United States was 32 percent.

You couldn't blame them for being so skeptical. A quick recollection of what Mexicans had been told during the wave of violence that shook the country in the mid-nineties was enough to turn the most gullible characters into total cynics. Hadn't the Salinas government claimed that the PRI's presidential candidates had been elected by the party, when everybody in the country knew they had been handpicked by Salinas? Hadn't the government sworn it had known nothing about the unrest in Chiapas before the uprising had taken place, when in fact it had detailed information about it? Hadn't the government announced after Colosio's killing that the murderer was a lone gunman named Mario Aburto, then announced the spectacular discovery of a "concerted action" by half a dozen people to kill the candidate, then switched back to the lone killer theory, and then changed once again to say that there had been two killers? Hadn't government prosecutors in the Ruiz Massieu assassination first accused the two legislators from Tamaulipas, only to later switch the blame to Raúl Salinas, while exempting former president Salinas of any cover-up responsibility all along?

The succession of contradictory government announcements and Mexicans' historic skepticism about their leaders had helped cement a feeling of political numbness in the population. Mexicans had become so used to being lied to that they were taking each new government announcement as corroboration that the previous one had been a fabrication, and as a warning that the latest one should not be taken too seriously. The country was coming dangerously close to losing its capacity for surprise, shock, and outrage over the political scandals that were rocking it simply because there was widespread belief that the truth would never be known.

▼

The word *evidence* had lost much of its meaning in Mexico. Even boxes full of original documents proving massive government fraud in a mid-1995 state election in Tabasco were easily dismissed by government officials as fake, turning what in most other countries would be a national scandal into total confusion. Just about the time when Alemán had changed his story about the 1993 PRI fund-raiser, a new — and perhaps even more scandalous — electoral financial scandal in the southeastern state of Tabasco had revealed the colossal size of the government's secret funding for the ruling party.

As was customary, the evidence appeared mysteriously. Leftist militants were staging a rally at Mexico City's Zócalo Square on June 5, 1995, to protest the result of a recent gubernatorial election in their home state of Tabasco that they charged had been stolen by the PRI, when a stranger pulled up his car on a side of the square and began to unload fourteen boxes containing folders of documents. The stranger said he wanted defeated center-left Tabasco gubernatorial candidate Andrés López Obrador to take a look at the documents: He would certainly find them interesting. As the stranger vanished, opposition militants began to browse through the papers and found a real political treasure: They contained thousands of original PRI campaign-spending receipts from the recent election, including payments to journalists, labor leaders, a Roman Catholic priest, "*acarreados*," or people who attended progovernment campaign rallies, and even opposition politicians.

A closer look at the documents in the days that followed by a group of PRD campaign-finance workers turned up evidence of massive fraud: The PRI had spent the equivalent of $65 million, nearly fifty-nine times its legal campaign-spending ceiling for that election! What was more, this amounted to 73 percent of what the ruling party had declared as its total national expenditures for the 1994 elections, including the presidential, congressional, and municipal races. It was a discovery that allowed skeptics for the first time to question, documents in hand, government claims that it was no longer providing secret financing for the PRI. The sham was obvious: If the ruling party had spent in a minuscule state such as Tabasco — which housed less than 2 percent of the nation's registered voters — more than two thirds of its declared national expenditures, it was obvious that the PRI's official financial statements for the 1994 presidential elections were a mockery.

"It was the kind of massive documentation that had never before been available to those who are not part of the inner circle, of the Mexican *cosa nostra*," political scientist Lorenzo Meyer said, referring to the Tabasco documents. "Never before had anybody outside the PRI had access to documents that allow a reconstruction of the key element of the ruling party's electoral mechanics: Its payments to people to attend rallies, its ties with an unending number of [political] actors."

Yet the scandal lasted little more than a week. The victorious hard-line PRI governor of Tabasco staged allegedly spontaneous demonstrations of supporters in his home state to discourage any thoughts by Zedillo or his advisers of calling a new election. As the pro-PRI sit-ins and work stoppages in Tabasco escalated and dinosaurs within the PRI began to rally around beleaguered governor Roberto Madrazo, government officials began to play down the scandal, saying the documents had been faked by the opposition. Within days, it was the government's word against the opposition's — and no authoritative body to decide on the matter.

As usual, the issue was quickly buried under an avalanche of mutual accusations that turned it into an incomprehensible mess and ended up boring even the most interested observers. Only several months later, when the issue had disappeared from the headlines, would a senior Interior ministry official concede to me privately that while a few of the documents were not linked to campaign expenditures, more than 70 percent of them were legitimate evidence of campaign-financing abuses. Oh, well.*

▼

There was nothing new about Mexico's tradition of lying, of course. Since as far as historians could remember, double-talk and deceit had been part of Mexico's national character. Historians said deceit was the way in which Spanish viceroys defended themselves against kings who demanded ever-growing levies from the New World, and the Indians' way of protecting themselves against the exploitation of their Spanish rulers. Mexicans in the colonial days would say yes to everything while doing as little as possible. Centuries later, Mexicans would sum up this national tradition with the saying *"Obedezco, pero no cumplo"* ("I obey, but I don't comply").

Mexicans had such an inborn skepticism that they regarded the very concept of "truth" with great suspicion, as the Coca-Cola Company and other U.S. corporations found in their various marketing studies in Mexico. The Coca-Cola Company, for instance, had discovered with puzzlement that advertising campaigns emphasizing the concepts of re- liability and trustworthiness did not work in Mexico.

Coke had conducted extensive marketing studies in Mexico as it was introducing the company's worldwide slogan "It's the real thing," which had worked wonders throughout the world, advertising industry sources recall. In line with Coca-Cola's international advertising cam- paign, it had translated the slogan in Mexico almost literally to *"Esta es la verdad,"* or "This is the truth." But it didn't work. Several focus groups assembled in Mexico City to test the slogan's acceptance reacted coldly to it.

---

* The attorney general's office announced weeks later that the documents were legiti- mate and that it would open an investigation into the Tabasco state PRI finances. The investigation was said to be in progress at the time of this writing.

"We found that the word *truth* had a negative connotation in Mexico," I was told by Jorge Matte Langlois, the Chilean-born psychologist, sociologist, and theologian who had conducted confidential polls for the Zedillo campaign, and who had conducted the focus groups for Coca-Cola years earlier. "People's reaction was, if it's the truth, it must be bad."

Coca-Cola's Mexico division soon changed its slogan to *"La chispa de la vida"* — "The spark of life."

▼

Writers had often described Mexicans' characteristic kindness as a mask for distrust. There were indeed a surprising number of everyday customs that reflected a kindness bordering on submissiveness. When Mexicans answered the phone, they didn't say *"hola"* — the Spanish translation of hello, as in other Spanish-speaking countries — but *"bueno,"* as in "OK," or *"mande,"* which literally means "at your orders." When they introduced themselves to strangers, they presented themselves as *"su servidor,"* literally "your servant." When they talked about their homes, they referred to *"su casa,"* meaning "your home" — a figurative way of speaking that confounded virtually every first-time visitor to Mexico.

There was an ingratiating trait that seemed to permeate the Mexican character. One of my favorite stories reflecting this feature was told to me one day over lunch by historian Héctor Aguilar Camin. He recalled driving around a Mexico City neighborhood in search of a street he could not find. He had stopped at a corner and asked a man standing there if he could please tell him where Magdalena Street was.

"Magdalena Street? Magdalena Street? I couldn't possibly tell you," the man replied apologetically. *"Se le ofrece otra?"* ("Can I offer you another one?")

Yet there was a generalized acceptance that — even though Mexicans often sounded as if they meant it — such efforts to please and expressions such as *"mande"* or *"su servidor"* were largely mechanical formulas of good social behavior, much as when Americans told strangers, "Have a nice day." In Mexicans' stereotypes about themselves, the definition of good behavior was adulation and courtesy, which were often not too far from deceit.

Even the Mexican *abrazo* — the warm greeting whereby males smiled from ear to ear, embraced one another, and patted one another repeatedly on the back — was said to be a by-product of Mexico's culture of deceit. According to some, far from a gesture of warmth, the *abrazo* custom had started during the Mexican Revolution as a shrewd way to find out whether the person you were greeting was carrying concealed weapons. Of course, a good number of *abrazos* — at least nowadays — were legitimate shows of affection, but it was often hard to tell the hearty ones from the fake ones. This was a culture in which kids had long been taught to fake affection and where they were expected to act submissively once they joined the work force — especially if, as was the case with millions, their boss was the government.

Form, not substance, had long been the rule of the game. If you wanted to get respect, you needed to wear a tie and call yourself a *"licenciado,"* regardless of whether you had obtained a legitimate college degree, bought your title in a diploma-mill university, or simply made up your title. I never ceased to be amazed at how Mexican secretaries, when I asked for their bosses and left my name, would instinctively inquire under which title I should be introduced: *"Licenciado?" "Doctor?" "Ingeniero?"* It was clear from the tone of their voices that a plain "Señor Oppenheimer" could delay indefinitely my chances of getting a response from their superiors.

Sometimes even the lowest academic degrees could be turned into major status symbols: Hank Gonzalez, the former Mexico state governor and Agriculture minister under Salinas, had been reverentially referred to for decades as "the Professor." In fact, he had only completed high school, but he had turned his short career as an elementary-school teacher into a portly professional degree. "The Professor" Hank was living proof that a title — no matter what title — was essential to becoming a respectable member of society.

▼

Nobody had described Mexico's culture of deceit as thoroughly as Nobel prize–winning poet-essayist Octavio Paz, one of the most brilliant minds in the Americas. In his 1950 classic *The Labyrinth of Solitude*, Mexico's premier psychological profile, Paz said Mexicans wore masks — smiles, courtesy, respect — as a way to defend themselves against a world they perceived as hostile and threatening. "We lie out of pleasure and fantasy, just like all imaginative people, but also to hide and protect ourselves from strangers," Paz wrote. "Lying has a decisive importance in our daily lives, in politics, in love, in friendship. By lying, we not only pretend to deceive others, but also ourselves. . . . That's why denouncing it is futile."

Much of it had to do with Mexico's original conflict. Mexicans were — or at least saw themselves as — descendants of conquistador Hernán Cortés and his Indian common-law wife, "La Malinche," a woman who quickly became his translator, guide, and most trusted adviser. But, far from a love story, theirs was a relationship that had begun with rape and ended with treason, and had left Mexicans with conflicting loyalties and searching for their true identities for centuries to come. As soon as Cortés had conquered the Aztecs with the help of the Toltecs and other native tribes, he had abandoned Malinche and reduced the Indians to slavery.

It was no coincidence that the worst curse in Mexico until nowadays was *"hijo de la chingada,"* or "son of the raped one," rather than the Spanish equivalent of "son of a bitch" that was prevalent elsewhere in the Spanish-speaking world. In other countries, the maximum offense was being the son of a woman who voluntarily gave herself for money; in Mexico, it was being the product of a rape. In Mexico, the world was perceived as a place divided between rapists and raped, where the first were perceived as winners and the latter as losers. In this context, the maximum values were machismo and the capacity to impose one's will over others, and political chieftains, feudal landholders, and unscrupulous business tycoons were perceived as winners in one part of Mexico's collective mind, Paz noted.

"The strange permanence of Cortés and Malinche in the Mexicans' imagination and sensibility reveals that they are more than historic figures: they are symbols of a secret conflict that we still have not resolved," Paz wrote. The Mexican people lived with a permanent feeling of orphanage, always looking for a strong identity to make up for their insecurities, always putting on masks to shield themselves from the world.

▼

Had anything changed in Mexico since Paz had written his book more than three decades earlier? I went to see the celebrated poet at his amazingly unpretentious apartment on Mexico City's Reforma Avenue on a sunny winter morning, eager to ask him whether Mexico's recent opening to the world and its new trade partnership with the United States had begun to change its culture of deceit.

Paz was already in his eighties, but exceptionally sharp for a man his age. Although one of the oldest living intellectuals in his country, he was still the enfant terrible of Mexico's intelligentsia: He constantly defied the politically correct stands of his leftist-leaning colleagues with provocative articles in the left-of-center *La Jornada*, in the pages of his own literary magazine, *Vuelta*, and in fiery letters to the editor in other publications. He was incensed by the Marxist nostalgia that permeated the writings of many of his colleagues — he was credited with having coined the phrase "Mexico has no intellectual class, it has a sentimental class" — and felt a passionate need to rebuke conventional wisdoms in the media with which he disagreed.

In early 1994, when Mexico's intellectuals — with very few exceptions — were mesmerized by Subcommander Marcos and almost unanimously embraced the idea that his Indian uprising was a novel phenomenon of the postcommunist world rather than a late incarnation of the Marxist guerrillas of the sixties, Paz threw a cold shower on them by writing an article entitled "The Relapse of the Intellectuals." He didn't mince words: "History has not cured our intellectuals. The years of atonement they have gone through since the end of totalitarian socialism, far from dissipating their deliriums and softening their rancors, have exacerbated them," he had written. What was more, he had predicted at the peak of Subcommander Marcos's popularity that the rebel leader's theatrical ways could be best described as show business — and that, as in the case of hot movie stars, society would receive his manifestos with a "big yawn" once his time in the limelight expired.

Not surprisingly, while widely respected as Mexico's national poet, Paz was not well liked in Mexico's left-of-center media and academic circles. Many members of the leftist intelligentsia criticized Paz for what they asserted were his excessively progovernment stands and — to a larger extent — for his close ties with Televisa, the mighty progovernment television network of billionaire Emilio Azcarraga. The first charge was unfair: Paz had been denouncing Mexico's authoritarian democracy and calling for a political opening since the sixties, long before most of his leftist critics had come to terms with "bourgeois democracy." The second allegation was based on the fact that Paz had long been promoted by Televisa, and his literary magazine had the network among its main advertisers. Paz knew that his closeness to Televisa was giving extra ammunition to his critics, but explained to fellow writers that he had a soft spot for Azcarraga: The two had been close personal friends for many decades.

I found Paz working in his studio, a glass-built winter house squeezed into what had once been the patio of his apartment. Meandering around the sofas in the book-filled room were at least three cats, some of the fourteen that the poet and his dynamic French-born wife, Marie José, kept at their home. As I entered the room, Paz was bent under a sofa trying to extract a kitten. He was determined to banish the cats out of the room so we could chat without being disturbed, the octogenarian author said with a smile as he invited me in.

Mexico was changing, although slowly, away from its culture of hypocrisy, Paz told me. For the first time, politicians were openly admitting that they aspired to higher offices — a small but significant step in a country where the custom had been to deny any political ambitions and claim that one was only accepting a nomination at the request of the people. You could also perceive some changes in Mexico's everyday political language, Paz said. Increasingly, politicians were talking about themselves using the previously taboo word "I." President Cárdenas had referred to himself as "the Executive Power." Since then, most presidents had referred to themselves in the third person or using euphemisms. The masks that had long marked Mexico's national character were a product of oppression. The trend toward greater openness was beginning to tear them down.

"I think we are moving in that direction, although I wonder to what extent," Paz said. "It's partly because of American influence, partly because the country has become more complex, partly because the PRI system has run out of steam. But when we talk about the culture of simulation, the most decisive influence is that of the northern part of the country. In northern Mexico, there is less hypocrisy than in the rest of the nation."

Shortly after our conversation, a surprising political scandal drew my attention to what the poet had said. There was indeed a geographic dimension to Mexico's social conflict.

CHAPTER 14

The Northern Offensive

An extraordinary event happened in early 1995 while Mexico was absorbed by the repercussions of its financial crash and, to a lesser extent, the revelations about Subcommander Marcos's identity. For the first time in memory, a Mexican newspaper's investigative reporting led to the toppling of a cabinet minister for doing what government officials had been brought up to do — lying.

Reforma, the new Mexico City daily founded by the owners of Monterrey's independent newspaper *El Norte*, had caused the unusual political scandal in January by reporting that Education Minister Fausto Alzati had lied about his academic credentials. Alzati, a respected member of the new generation of U.S.-educated technocrats, had not earned a Ph.D. in political economy from Harvard University, as his official biography stated, the newspaper had revealed. Nor had he completed a master's degree in public administration at Harvard, as his résumé claimed. And there was even a big question over whether he had completed his college degree at Mexico's national university's law school.

At first, government officials shrugged off the report, painting it as a case of journalistic hype by the new daily to establish itself as a courageous government watchdog. But *Reforma* persevered, charging ahead a few days later with a second story stating that at least half a dozen other prominent members of Zedillo's cabinet had lied about their U.S. academic titles. The stories revealed that earning a U.S. postgraduate degree had become such an unwritten prerequisite for senior Mexican officials of the Salinas-Zedillo generation that those who didn't have it simply made it up.

While studying in the United States had been a rarity — if not a source of mistrust — in the sixties and seventies, it had become such a fad in recent times that 82 percent of the members of the Zedillo cabinet had included on their résumés real or imagined foreign academic titles, the vast majority of them from Ivy League U.S. universities.*

Labor Secretary Oñate's résumé in the presidential office–published *Biographic Dictionary of Mexican Government Officials* included a Ph.D. from the University of Wisconsin that he had never earned, and Tourism Secretary Silvia Hernandez's biography listed a master's degree from the London School of Economics that she had not completed. The newspaper's quick investigation had only scratched the surface of a widespread title-fabrication phenomenon. It wasn't the first time that top officials were exposed for not holding degrees they claimed, but it was the most comprehensive reporting on such abuses.

As soon as the stories were published, *Reforma* publisher Alejandro Junco de la Vega was swamped with telephone calls from other senior government officials whose résumés also listed U.S. doctorate degrees they had never earned, and who were now claiming the presidential office had somehow made a mistake when typing their biographies. Like Education Minister Alzati, who had interrupted his studies short of graduation several times to accept government jobs, most had done graduate work at U.S. universities but had not obtained their diplomas.

Alzati and his aides were flabbergasted when the newspaper story forced the young minister's resignation a few days later. "Who in this country has not stretched out his résumé a bit?" an outraged senior ad-

---

* In his insightful studies on Mexico's camarillas, including *The Zedillo Cabinet: Continuity, Change or Revolution?* Center for Strategic International Studies (CSIS), Washington, D.C., January 5, 1995, Tulane University professor Roderic Ai Camp states that "most Mexicans born prior to 1950 who studied abroad attended school in Europe, primarily at elite French and English institutions. The Zedillo/Salinas generation marks a decided shift to North American universities, particularly those with strong programs in economics."

viser to the Education ministry asked me then. Alzati was a victim of a rapidly changing system's need to set new guidelines for ethical behavior, he said. "They pulled the rug from under his feet," the minister's aide added. "Until now, it wouldn't have crossed any newspaper editor's mind to investigate whether anybody's academic credentials were true, much less to publish it. If a reporter had somehow found out, it would most likely have been considered irrelevant and would at best end up as a caustic paragraph in an editorial column."

Lying about one's credentials — or about anything else, for that matter — had never been a crime in Mexico. Rather, it was a socially tolerated transgression such as cheating on taxes or on one's wife. And while the scandal was quickly forgotten after Alzati's resignation — the other ministers managed to cling to their jobs, perhaps because their academic degrees were not considered as critical to their positions — the incident was symptomatic of Mexico's embryonic uneasiness with its culture of deceit.

▼

Reforma's investigative journalism was a symptom of the growing clout of northern Mexico and its often U.S.-emulated ways over the rest of the country — the cultural and political phenomenon that Paz had brought to my attention when I asked him about his country's future.

Mexico had always been three countries, as Mexicans would constantly remind visitors. There was Mexico's industrialized north, centered in Monterrey, which was a rapidly modernizing region energized by U.S.-style private sector entrepreneurs. Then there was central Mexico, dominated by the capital in its geographic center, the hub of the country's almighty government. Finally, there was Mexico's southern belt of poverty-stricken states, including Chiapas, Oaxaca, and Guerrero, which had more in common with their Central American neighbors than with the rest of Mexico.

In recent memory, especially since the PRI had begun to run the country after the chaotic years of the Mexican Revolution, virtually all major political and economic decisions had come from the capital. Only recently had some northern Mexican institutions — including *Reforma* and a handful of private universities — extended their operations to the capital and begun to have a significant impact on national affairs.

▼

The new Mexico City daily made its debut with a big splash in November 1993. Even before the newspaper had come out, it had raised eyebrows in Mexico's political circles: Monterrey's Junco family had bowed out at the last minute from a planned joint venture with the *Wall Street Journal* after the U.S. publishing firm had demanded editorial control over the new daily, and had decided to go it alone with a $50 million investment in the project. It was a fabulous sum in a country with one of the lowest newspaper readership levels in Latin America, but the Junco family had decided to conquer the capital in a big way. They soon built a monumental $9 million headquarters — a neo-Roman building complete with classical columns, dome-crowned ceilings, and marble floors — and hired away Mexico's best-known columnists from rival newspapers by paying them twice their previous salaries.

It was a new corporate culture descending on the low-paid, hard-drinking, and semibohemian world of Mexico City journalism. *Reforma*'s top editors walked around their glass-walled offices in expensive dark suits, starched shirts, and cuff links as if they wanted to make sure nobody would mistake them for the financially strapped — and often easily corruptible — editors of some of the other newspapers in town. Their offices were decorated with Mexican oil paintings and fine wood British- and French-style furniture, resembling bankers' executive offices, and the subtle light brown and olive green color scheme gave the distinct impression that it had been chosen by interior decorators.

They also made it clear that they wouldn't play by Mexico City's traditional rules of newspapering. The *Reforma* publishers decided to launch the paper on November 20, a national holiday marking the Mexican Revolution when no other paper was published. The northern publishers' nerve irked local labor-union bosses, not to mention the established newspapers. Who did these people think they were? The powerful PRI-backed Newspaper Distributors' Union refused to deliver *Reforma* on the holiday and offered instead to distribute its first issue either November 19 or November 21.

Alejandro Junco, the boyish-looking publisher of *El Norte* and *Reforma*, decided to go ahead with his own publication date, circumventing the union if necessary. When he failed to reach an agreement with the labor leaders, he took to the streets with his staff on November 20 to sell *Reforma*'s first issue themselves. If part of his intention was to draw attention to the new daily, he succeeded: Within hours, international news agencies were spreading pictures of Junco and his well-paid columnists selling copies of *Reforma* to intrigued motorists at key city intersections.

"It was our first test of independence: We wanted to make it clear that we wanted to work with the union, but on our own terms," Junco recalled later. From then on, *Reforma* broke several other rules that had long governed the capital's media community: It prohibited reporters from selling ads, warned journalists that they would be fired immediately if they accepted bribes, refused to sign agreements with the government to publish propaganda disguised as news, and banned all Christmas presents to staffers.

In sharp contrast with some of his colleagues at other papers, Junco prided himself on refusing to attend presidential receptions for newspaper publishers unless they promised to be of news value. He also turned down an offer from Salinas to be part of a citizens' committee on human rights, which he saw as a subtle attempt to co-opt him. It wasn't the first time that a Mexican newspaper tried to do independent journalism, but — unlike the left-of-center *La Jornada* and others before it — the new daily had a key advantage over its predecessors: tons of money.

▼

Sitting behind his desk in his baronial-looking office a few months after the Education minister's resignation over the fake academic degrees story, Junco described the incident as a clash of cultures.

"The scandal is somewhat illustrative of Mexico City's culture: It's a culture of make-believe where appearances are what count the most," the Monterrey publishing tycoon said. "Northern Mexico, on the other hand, is more result-oriented. There is a tradition of hard work."

While top members of *Reforma*'s editorial staff had university degrees, they were not listed in the newspaper's masthead. While extremely formal, the *Reforma* publisher was in regular touch with his reporters and contributors, in sharp contrast to publishers of other Mexico City dailies who were off-limits to their employees. And in line with northern Mexico's style, Junco rarely stayed at business lunches past four P.M. and moved around without a coterie of assistants and bodyguards.

"When we were preparing to come to Mexico City, a politician close to Colosio called me aside and gave me some advice after he saw me arriving in a taxi," Junco recalled. "Look, Alejandro, he told me, Mexico City is different: You can't be a newspaper publisher and arrive in a taxi. Nobody will take you seriously unless you have guards, assistants, and somebody to announce by telephone that you are about to arrive."

Junco did not change his ways. "The trouble with Mexico City is that people take themselves too seriously," he told me, shaking his head. Like other businesspeople from Monterrey who had recently moved to the capital, Junco was convinced it was time for Mexico City to catch up with Monterrey, and the rest of the world.

"There is a growing influence of northern Mexico over the center and the south," the publisher said. "The culture of Monterrey is much more attuned to the culture of an economically and politically open Mexico. We are more used to the new buzzwords of competitiveness, productivity, hard work. In Mexico City, it's who you know, who is about to get what government job, how you can make a contact with whom. It's two different cultures."

▼

The first thing that struck me about Monterrey — after its gray, monotonous high-rise buildings and its proliferation of McDonald's, Wendy's, and 7-Eleven outlets — was its street names. Unlike Mexico City's, Monterrey's streets did not carry the names of revolutionary heroes, but of businessmen. Its main avenues bore names such as Avenida Eugenio Garza Sada, or Felix López — big industrialists who had helped turn Monterrey into Mexico's industrial mecca.

Monterrey, only one hundred fifty miles south of the U.S. border, was an all-business town. Its concentration of high-rise buildings in a small downtown area, with several-story-high parking garages, was no accident: Its planners had obviously wanted to make the city look like Houston. Although it was Mexico's third largest city, there was virtually no nightlife in Monterrey. Its working hours were not in tune with those of Mexico City — with its two-hour business breakfasts and three-hour lunches — but with Texas. Often there were more flights per day from Monterrey to Dallas or Houston than to Mexico City.

In the early eighties, Monterrey had bulldozed its charming three-century-old central plaza and replaced it with a twenty-two-story-high concrete column that was named the Guiding Light of Commerce. At night, the monument beamed laser lights into the sky in all directions, as if proclaiming Monterrey's existence to the four winds. Once a government-subsidized steel town, the city had also recently shut down its ninety-year-old steel mill — once the biggest in Latin America — and converted it into a giant showroom of Mexican exports surrounded by a 250-acre ecological park. What had once been the aging Fundidora de Fierro steel mill was now proudly promoted as Monterrey's International Business Center.

Monterrey was the epicenter — and symbol — of Mexico's booming north. Although it had always benefited from its closeness to the U.S. border, Mexico's north was poised to benefit the most from the country's economic opening. First with the *maquilas*, or foreign-owned assembly plants, set up on duty-free territory along the U.S.-Mexican border, and later with the NAFTA deal, the north had been the biggest beneficiary of the free-trade era: Given the choice of investing in Mexico's industrialized north or in the rural south, where much of the population was made up of Mayans who didn't even speak Spanish, virtually all foreign investors were setting up their Mexican operations in northern cities such as Monterrey or Hermosillo. It was a natural choice: Productivity rates were much higher and freight costs to the United States much lower.

By the mid-nineties, investors based in the north controlled 60 percent of all stock in Mexican banks and were at the helm of Mexico's largest industries. Monterrey was the home of most of the new billionaires who were listed by *Forbes* magazine in the early nineties as the products of Mexico's economic miracle. The biggest Mexican conglomerates — including Cemex, the western hemisphere's biggest cement maker, the Vitro glass manufacturing giant, and the Visa soft drink and banking empire — were based in Monterrey.

There were dozens of allegedly historical explanations for Monterrey's success. Many Mexican historians said Monterrey was founded in the sixteenth century by Jewish families who were searching for precious metals in the Mexican desert and — not finding any — began to trade first with Indian slaves and later with merchandise bound for America. Others say Monterrey was a sleepy desert town until the American Civil War in 1860, when scores of Italian, German, and British traders arrived to set up shops that became an important source of provisions for the southern army. But virtually everybody agrees that, unlike in southern Mexico, capitalism had always worked in Monterrey.

Some historians, making parallels with northern European industrialized countries, said Monterrey developed faster than other parts of Mexico because its first settlers had found few natural resources and a hostile climate, which had forced them to work harder than other Mexicans living in a more generous environment. Others stressed that Monterrey people were more efficient because they were not used to relying on the government to solve their problems. Their geographic distance from the capital — a major problem in the days of the highly centralized Spanish colonial bureaucracy — had generated skills that were suddenly becoming a blessing in the new era of private entrepreneurship. "In Monterrey, there is a century-old capitalist tradition whereby if you wake up at five A.M. and work all day, you will earn decent money," Victor Zuñiga, a professor with the College of the Northern Frontier in Monterrey, explained to me over coffee in one of the city's brand-new five-star hotels. "In southern Mexico, there is less productivity because they have a precapitalist system: People work but make almost nothing."

▼

It was the beer industry that had spearheaded Monterrey's economic boom and had helped found another major institution that would expand northern Mexico's influence over the rest of the country: the Monterrey Technological Institute.

It had all started when Eugenio Garza Sada, the son of real estate and beer magnate Isaac Garza, was sent by his father to study engineering at the Massachusetts Institute of Technology (MIT) in the mid-1910s — partly to get him a U.S. education, partly to keep him away from the violence of the Mexican Revolution. Shortly after his return to Mexico, Garza Sada had joined his father's Cervecería Cuauhtémoc brewery and would over the next several decades turn it into a giant industrial complex. But as Cervecería Cuauhtémoc and other big Monterrey firms grew, their owners began to face a serious problem: They couldn't find skilled administrators among the graduates of Mexico's state-run universities.

Distressed by the increasingly socialist bent of Mexico's public schools, they sent their most promising employees to MIT. Soon they found themselves sending so many students to MIT that they decided it would be cheaper for them to bring MIT to Monterrey. They founded the Monterrey Technological Institute, a Mexican version of the U.S. university, in 1943.

By the mid-nineties, "El Tec," as the university is still commonly referred to, had become Mexico's most coveted school for students wanting to make a career in engineering or business administration. As *Reforma* would do later in the newspaper business, El Tec lured away the best professors from other Mexican universities by paying them top dollar. Now young people from all over the country were coming to El Tec, and one of the first things they learned there was that their future would depend on their skills rather than on their political or family connections. El Tec became such a key passport to success in the private sector that it began to set up campuses throughout the nation to accommodate its ever-growing number of students.

By 1995 El Tec had more than fifty-seven thousand students enrolled in thirty-two majors on twenty-six campuses across the nation. After its U.S.-style campus in Monterrey ran out of space to accommodate so many students, El Tec set up a big campus in Mexico City and smaller ones in states as remote as Chiapas. It was a twenty-first-century school: Many classes were dictated from El Tec's Monterrey campus and transmitted live through television and computer link to its other campuses around the nation. Individual students sent their questions to the professor via e-mail and received instantaneous answers that were read by the whole cyber-classroom. Over the years, El Tec had become a major agent of northern Mexico's cultural penetration into central and southern Mexico.

▼

But the most politically influential northern Mexico institution was the center-right PAN — the half-century-old opposition party that had finished a strong second in the 1994 elections. By history and way of thinking, the PAN was a northern Mexico phenomenon: It stressed individual rights over intrusive state policies and championed the cause of federalism over Mexico City's authoritarian centralism.

The PAN was born in 1939, partly in reaction to the government of General Lázaro Cárdenas, the populist leader who — claiming to follow the basic principles of the Mexican Revolution — had among other things launched a drastic land reform program and nationalized the oil industry. According to the PAN's official "History of the National Action Party, 1939–1989," the 1934–1940 Cárdenas administration had snubbed basic values such as "work, sacrifice and perseverance" and taken Mexico "back to the illusion of [easy] solutions coming from the top."

PAN founding father Manuel Gomez Morin, an academic born in the northern border state of Chihuahua, had worked with the postrevolutionary regime and become quickly disillusioned with it. He stated that he had founded the new party "to openly oppose the total collectivization of the economy, and . . . the inept and corrupt intervention of the Mexican state as owner and administrator of Mexico's shattered economy." Gomez Morin and his fellow PAN founders, most of whom were born in the countryside but lived in Mexico City, elected the new party's national leadership in December 1939 and immediately set off on a tour of northern states. There they found a small but loyal following among businesspeople and young professionals who would lay the base for the party's first show of force in local elections in the mid-forties.

Rather than a party with a defined ideology — many of its leaders would later embrace Catholicism as they searched for a doctrine with which to challenge the growing popularity of socialism — the PAN grew as a federation of regional parties made up mostly of city people in Mexico's interior who shared an aversion to the central government and its authoritarian ways. Despite government repression and stolen elections, the PAN slowly but systematically succeeded over the next few decades in forcing the government to recognize its victories in growing numbers of municipal and legislative elections. Its first major breakthrough had come in 1989, when PAN candidate Ernesto Ruffo Appel won the gubernatorial elections in Baja California and — for the first time in history — an opposition politician was allowed to take office. Since then the PAN had conquered, among others, the central state of Guanajuato, the northern border state of Chihuahua, and the key state of Jalisco, one of Mexico's biggest election prizes. With the postdevaluation economic crisis, the PAN seemed poised to sweep even more central Mexican states — the country's electoral belt, where the bulk of the country's votes were concentrated.*

▼

If you had any doubts that northern Mexico was a different country, you just needed to mention the word *Chiapas* there — most often it prompted reactions ranging from total indifference to bitter criticism of the Zapatista guerrillas.

Ernesto Coppel Kelly, the president of a hotel firm that was planning to build a $25 million hotel in the northern Pacific state of Sinaloa, shrugged when I asked him shortly after the Zapatista rebellion whether he was afraid that it would scare off American tourists. Didn't he fear that a climate of political turbulence would hurt his project?

"Not at all: *Aquí no pasa nada*" ("there's nothing wrong here"), he said, echoing a phrase I would hear repeatedly in northern Mexico at

---

* Even within the PRI, northerners were taking over the top government positions. Salinas had close family ties in Monterrey; Zedillo was raised in the northern border state of Baja California, while his immediate predecessor as PRI presidential candidate, Colosio, was born and raised in the northern border state of Sonora.

the time. "When the Zapatista uprising took place, I had to go to the map to find out where San Cristóbal de las Casas was. To us, Chiapas is Central America. We feel very far from it."

▼

In the nearby state of Sonora, ruling party governor Beltrones told me with a mischievous smile that on some issues his state did indeed act as a separate country. It had, for instance, erected customs barriers at its southern border to inspect food imports from central and southern Mexico. He could not afford to allow such cargoes to contaminate Sonora's production and make it ineligible for export to the United States. Sonora, he explained, was one of the few Mexican states whose food production met U.S. Food and Drug Administration standards. "We inspect everything that comes in through our southern border and when we see contaminated fruit, we turn it back to the state where it came from," he said.

Sonora politicians often saw themselves siding with their counterparts in southern U.S. states over key binational issues. Brushing aside Mexico's traditional nationalism, they often talked about an "inevitable cultural symbiosis" among Mexican and U.S. border states. Arizona needed Sonora as a gateway to the sea, just as Sonora needed Arizona as a bridge to the United States, they stressed.

The two border states even shared some of the same concerns about Mexicans' illegal immigration to the United States. When Arizona governor Fife Symington complained to Beltrones that illegal crossings along the Sonora-Arizona border had risen by 50 percent in 1994, Beltrones challenged him to check how many of the immigrants were coming from Sonora. "I'll bet you that all of them come from southern Mexico," Beltrones said.

Indeed, the number of northern Mexicans who moved to the United States was relatively small: Most preferred to work in the *maquiladora* assembly plants along the border, closer to home. So many northern Mexicans were abandoning agricultural work for the factories that workers from central and southern states were arriving in growing numbers to take their places doing the hard work in orange and grape fields. Many of these migrants would spend a few months in northern Mexico — nearly 1.8 million people from central and southern Mexico migrated to northern border towns in 1994 alone, according to the Northern Frontier College figures — and then move on to the United States in search of even higher wages.*

▼

A northern revolt was brewing. PAN local officials — and many of their PRI colleagues — were increasingly angry over what they said was their states' disproportionate contributions to Mexico's central government. Northern Mexican taxes were paying for Mexico City's subsidies for tortillas and buses, and dozens of costly new social programs for the south that had been launched since the Chiapas rebellion. On top of this, they were taking growing numbers of southern Mexican migrants, who were straining their states' already overstretched public services, they said. Of every tax dollar collected in Sonora, only nineteen cents returned to the state, Beltrones complained. The people of Sonora felt they were getting a raw deal.

"There is a growing isolationist sentiment among the northern states," Beltrones admitted, reflecting what had long been an opposition battle cry in his state. "We are getting more and more people from Oaxaca, Chiapas, and other southern states who don't pay taxes and need social services. How are we going to pay for these services when we are getting less money from the central government than last year?"

A few weeks after that conversation, Ciudad Juárez's PAN mayor, Francisco Villarreal, decided to take action: Supported by a dozen northern Mexico border-town mayors who were complaining about the little their cities were getting back from the millions of dollars in tolls that the central government was collecting at border crossings, he ordered tollbooths built in front of those operated by the central government on the bridge between Ciudad Juárez and El Paso, Texas. As Mexican federal officials watched openmouthed, Villarreal collected a dollar thirty-five from each motorist crossing the bridge. "We're fight-

---

* According to Northern Frontier College researcher Maria Eugenia Anguiano, 1.8 million Mexicans — mostly from the states of Michoacán, Jalisco, Guanajuato, Zacatecas, and Oaxaca — moved to northern Mexico in 1994, of whom 797,000 moved on to the United States.

ing for our freedom," Villarreal, a sixty-five-year-old man who looked full of energy despite a long battle with cancer, told a *Houston Chronicle* reporter. "We are rebelling in peace, without masks and without guns."

When the federal government recovered from the initial shock, it issued a warrant for Villarreal's arrest. The mayor turned himself in and spent four days in jail. But by then, civic groups and business associations throughout northern Mexico were rallying to his support and demanding that a sizable portion of the duties collected at the U.S. border be allowed to remain in northern Mexico.

"Mexico may have more trouble handling the threat of violence in Chiapas," said Tulane University Mexico expert Roderic Ai Camp, "but what we're seeing in the north poses a more significant, potentially longer-lasting threat."

▼

Laredo, Nogales, Tijuana, and other towns along the U.S. border had become international cities that — much like the city-states of medieval Italy — often had more in common with their counterparts across the border than with their respective capitals. Newspapers throughout northern Mexico states carried full-page English-language ads for department stores in San Diego or Laredo, not bothering to make the slightest editing changes to target a foreign audience. It wasn't really a foreign audience: Tens of thousands of northern Mexico residents were regular shoppers on the U.S. side of the border.

Already before NAFTA, sister cities across the border were celebrating the two countries' respective national holidays: Flags went up on both sides on Mexico's September 16 national holiday and on the Fourth of July. It wasn't an official imposition, but a cultural phenomenon boosted by the escalating cross-border family and business links over the years. Growing numbers of families were split on the two sides of the border. On Thanksgiving Day it was not unusual for those on the Mexican side to prepare a turkey dinner for their relatives on the other side.

In Tijuana, 9 percent of the economically active population — or about two hundred thousand people — worked on a regular basis on both sides of the border. Most of them were Mexicans who crossed to *"el otro lado"* — or "the other side," as Mexicans usually referred to the United States — to work in San Diego as maids, gardeners, or handymen. More amazingly, a large number of Tijuana families sent their children to U.S. schools: They usually got San Diego addresses with the help of Mexican friends who lived on "the other side" and crossed the border daily to take them to school there.

"We do car pooling," a Tijuana mother of two children enrolled in a San Ysidro public school explained to me. "We are five women, and each of us takes the kids one day of the week. When it's my turn, I drop the children at school in the morning, spend my day shopping for the whole week in San Ysidro, and pick up the kids from school in the afternoon."

All along the border, the national lines were getting fuzzier all the time. In Nogales, Sonora, I found a four-man band named Digital that played American rock music Monday through Thursday on the Mexican side of the border, and Mexican music over the weekends in Tucson, Arizona. The lead guitar was played by an American, and the bass, drums, and keyboard players were Mexicans.

"Last Saturday, we played at a wedding in Tucson, Arizona," Pablo Jesús Martinez, Digital's twenty-five-year-old keyboard player told me matter-of-factly, somewhat surprised by my astonishment at his cross-border routine. "We played *rancheras, cumbias,* and *quebraditas*: That's what the people on the other side want to hear."

▼

One of the most peculiar characters I found along the U.S.-Mexican border was Joel Bojorquez, the forty-eight-year-old host of an XENY 7.60 AM radio talk-show in Nogales, Sonora. Was he Mexican? Was he American? It largely depended on what time of the day you caught up with him.

White-haired, bearded Bojorquez, who was the station's leading talk-show host, lived with his Mexican American wife and their children on "the other side" in Nogales, Arizona. He woke up every morning at 7:15 A.M. and crossed the border to his job at the Nogales, Mexico, radio station in time to start his morning show at eight A.M. It took him an average of eight minutes to cross. The car line at that time of the morning was short, he explained: Most motorists were headed in the opposite direction, to take their children to school on the U.S. side of the border.

At 1:30 P.M., after concluding his show in Mexico — "I like to emphasize Mexican issues such as the Mexican Revolution and Independence Day, because I want to encourage Mexicans to maintain their traditions" — Bojorquez went home to America for lunch. At 3:30 P.M., he headed back to Mexico for another three hours of work at the radio station.

At seven P.M., he headed for home in America once again. This time, the car line at the crossing was a bit longer, but it seldom took him more than a fifteen-minute wait. Because he had a U.S. green card — he had obtained it after marrying an American citizen — U.S. immigration guards rarely asked any questions.

Bojorquez's children went to school on the U.S. side of the border, and his wife worked there, but the family often had dinner with relatives and friends on the Mexican side. When the family went to the movies, they had to go either to the Mexican side or to Tucson, because there was no decent movie theater in Nogales, Arizona. Bojorquez's dentist was in Mexico, but his children's dentist was on the U.S. side. Some of his friends' dentists took care of families like his by working mornings on the Mexican side and afternoons on the U.S. side.

Why did he prefer to live on the U.S. side of the border?

"Because in *el otro lado*, there is always water and there is much less crime than here," Bojorquez told me during a break in his show. "Here there are always problems of one kind or another."

What did he foresee in the future? Would northern Mexico become even more enmeshed with the United States, or would there be a nationalist revival?

"In five or ten years, it will be much more American," Bojorquez responded with conviction. "The [Mexican] center has consistently ignored us. That's why border people increasingly identify themselves with the United States."

Bojorquez cited recent examples of listeners' calls to his radio show. Once, after he had criticized U.S. border guards for the harsh way in which they turned back Mexicans trying to make it illegally to "the other side," many people had called in to defend the U.S. guards. To Bojorquez's amazement, listeners said that the American border agents were just doing their job and that they were usually much more respectful than the Mexican police. It was a reaction that would be hard to find in Mexico City or in Mexico's southern states.

"People along the border think that everything in the United States is better," Bojorquez said. "They think there is no corruption in America, that there is more democracy, that everything works there."

▼

Francisco J. García Encinas, a psychiatrist I met in Nogales, Sonora, was one of the many professionals who — like the dentists Bojorquez had mentioned — worked on both sides of the border. García Encinas, who was also living on the U.S. side of the border and had become a U.S. citizen, worked from nine A.M. to four P.M. as a family counselor in U.S. territory, and from 4:40 P.M. to eight P.M. as a psychiatrist in Mexico.

On the Mexican side of Nogales, there was a tendency to idealize everything that is American and to diminish everything Mexican, he told me. So much so that Mexicans seemed to go through a miraculous transfiguration when they crossed the border. "As soon as we cross the line, we Mexicans change our behavior: We immediately secure our seat belts and stop throwing papers out the window," García Encinas said. "There is a generalized assumption that you obey the law in America."

▼

The love affair was largely restricted to border towns, but Mexico's trade opening of the early nineties had dramatically spread the U.S. presence from northern Mexico to the rest of the country. With the massive arrival of McDonald's and hundreds of other U.S. franchises, and the avalanche of U.S. goods that soon filled the shelves of Mexican supermarkets and electronics stores, America's consumer society — or, rather, the illusion of it — was brought closer to millions of residents of central Mexico and to a lesser extent to those living in southern states. Millions who lived far from the border and had never crossed to *el otro lado* began to get a taste of it right at home. Consumption of U.S. goods skyrocketed, moving critics to warn that the "Americanization" process that had swept Mexico's northern states a long time ago was now taking over the entire country.

Life in virtually every Mexico City neighborhood had been touched by the arrival of big U.S.-owned supermarkets. By combining a vast supply of glitzy American products and lower prices they could afford thanks to lower customs duties and bulk buying, retailers such as Price Club, Wal-Mart, Kmart, and Homemart were driving tens of thousands of mom-and-pop stores out of business and changing the pace of life in Mexican cities. By the mid-1990s, American-style supermarkets were already accounting for about 40 percent of all grocery shopping in big Mexican cities, according to industry estimates.

The new supermarkets became the center of U.S.-fashioned shopping malls: They were soon flanked by pharmacies, twenty-four-hour dry cleaners, and Kodak photo labs. In growing numbers of towns, you could now do all your shopping in one place. The tradition of leisurely shopping, where you met with friends and exchanged the latest neighborhood gossip, was on the way out.

Entire suburbs of Mexico City had been built around giant malls such as Perisur, on the southern outskirts of the city, just as old Mexican towns had been built around the local church or municipal palace. On an average weekend, Perisur was teeming with families strolling along the impeccably clean promenades in Adidas jumpsuits and Reebok sneakers, looking at windows displaying the latest U.S. imports. Young couples walked sipping Cokes from McDonald's paper cups, while their children munched on Chee-tos potato chips. Loudspeakers coming from a video arcade blared Willie Nelson songs.

"Mexico is losing some of its dearest traditions, such as close family ties," Guadalupe Loaeza, one of Mexico's best-selling writers, complained to me one day. "In the past, Mexican families used to get together at their homes for lunch on Sundays, with grandparents, uncles, and cousins present. Where do you find them now on Sundays? They are at the mall!"

▼

When I walked into the Blockbuster Video store in Mexico City's Coyoacán section, I couldn't help wondering whether the American home-entertainment giant had not taken the new spirit of North American integration a little bit too far: Blockbuster's classification of movies seemed to suggest that the United States had already swallowed Mexico into its territory.

The store looked exactly like the chain's U.S. prototypes. Its white outside walls were crossed by a wide blue-and-yellow stripe that carried the company's logo. Inside, the walls were lined with videos, and rows of white racks crossed the room diagonally. At each corner, synchronized television sets hanging from the ceiling were beaming an Arnold Schwarzenegger film. Much as in the United States, the store had several sections marked by labels that classified each aisle under categories such as "drama," "action," "comedies," and "foreign movies." It was the latter that immediately caught my attention: When I looked at its contents, I found that it only contained Latin American and European movies. In the Mexican Blockbuster's view of the world, U.S. films were not considered "foreign": They were lumped together with Mexican movies all over the store, in what in effect was a huge domestic section.

"I know, I know, there is something wrong about it," admitted Edgar Leal, Blockbuster of Mexico's movie purchasing manager, when I noted to him that his store may have taken an overenthusiastic view of North American integration. "The problem is that we have so many American movies that if we placed them in the foreign movie category, we would have to put the whole store under that label."

Of course, Mexico's "Americanization" was not a spontaneous phenomenon: The buy-American spree resulted largely from the novelty of free trade and was made possible by Mexico's overvalued currency. But Mexico's previous protectionist policies had been just as artificial in that they had tried to stop a cultural influence that was a natural by-product of geographic proximity and growing trade ties. Just as the Mexican presence in California and Texas was spreading to the rest of America, and millions of Yankees were beginning to eat and sing Mexican, the U.S. presence that had long been visible in northern Mexican states was inching its way down to the rest of Mexico.

▼

But was the gap between northern and southern Mexico likely to narrow anytime soon? At the Tijuana-based Northern Frontier College, a modern U.S.-style campus on a hillside overlooking the Pacific Coast, most experts were pessimistic. The gap was abysmal to begin with. Looking at northern and southern Mexico's respective levels of income, health, and education — categories that they had lumped together in an "index of human development" — researchers had concluded that southern Mexican states were an average of twenty years behind northern states.

Pointing at figures from his charts, the school's academic director, Eduardo Zepeda, said that some states were even further behind. In Nuevo León, life expectancy was 73 years, and the average schooling was 7.4 years, whereas in Chiapas and Oaxaca, life expectancy was barely 67 years, and the average schooling was 3.9 years.

Another comparative study by Northern Frontier College researcher Diana Alarcon Gonzalez revealed that the per capita income in the six northern Mexico border states was about twice that of Mexico's poverty-ridden southern states. No matter what statistics you looked at, the disparities were enormous: While 12 percent of the residents of northern states lacked running water, the percentage in southern states was 38. And the economic differences between northern and southern states were growing, she said, because an agricultural crisis brought about by free trade was hitting southern states especially hard. Northern states relied on agriculture for only 27 percent of their income, whereas southern states' economies depended on it for 55 percent. "Free trade has brought about a huge increase in U.S. shipments of wheat, corn, and fruits that has badly hurt Mexican growers, especially in the south," Alarcon said. "Meanwhile, the few industries that are growing are in the export manufacturing sector, and virtually all of them are based in the north."

▼

So how did northern Mexicans think the country could solve its lopsided growth problem and lift southern states from what Subcommander Marcos had described as "Mexico's basement"? I posed the question to Lorenzo H. Zambrano, the fifty-year-old chief executive officer of the Monterrey-based Cemex S.A. giant, which owned plants in Texas, Spain, and Venezuela and was considered the world's fourth largest cement manufacturer.

Zambrano, a white-haired, youthful-looking single man whose family fortune had been estimated by *Forbes* at $3.1 billion, received me at the seventh-floor penthouse offices of Cemex headquarters in Monterrey. I didn't mind waiting a few minutes for him: His office walls were decorated with some of the best Latin American contemporary paintings you could find anywhere — most of them recent purchases from Sotheby's and Christie's Latin American art auctions in New York.

Zambrano, one of the business tycoons who had participated in the $25 million-a-plate 1993 fund-raiser for the ruling party, suggested it would be only a matter of time until more Mexican and foreign companies moved farther down into the Mexican heartland. "There is a major decentralization under way," the Stanford-educated cement baron said. "There are areas such as Aguascalientes, in the center of the country, which has become a very important auto manufacturing center since Nissan set up a plant there and attracted many auto supply industries. The same thing is happening in San Luis Potosí."

Mexico's rapid industrialization would bring about a geographic trickle-down effect, according to Zambrano. Some Monterrey industrialists were even beginning to invest in Chiapas: Alfonso Romo of La Moderna enterprises, Mexico's biggest cigarette manufacturer, had just set up a plant in Chiapas and was doing great. It was only a matter of time until others followed suit, he said.

Would he consider setting up new cement plants in southern Mexico? I asked. He already had some, it turned out.

"It's a fact that in the industrialized parts of northern Mexico, there is a greater work discipline, and people show up for work every day at a given hour. In rural parts of the country, on the other hand, many people are used to working until they have enough money to eat for the rest of the week and then stop showing up for work," he said. "But my experience in southern Mexican states is that after two years of high worker rotation, you end up with a stable work force. And once you reach that point, you have the same productivity as in the north."

▼

There were two problems with the geographic trickle-down theory, however.

First, the northern Mexican development engine wasn't pulling the poorer southern states along with it, at least not fast enough: While free trade had worked wonders for a few giant Mexican corporations, it had led many smaller manufacturers to bankruptcy, slowing down Mexico's overall economic growth.

Second, and most important, the trouble with the northern economic expansion model was that — despite occupying a huge geographic area — Mexico's northern states accounted for only 16 percent of the country's population.

This was not just a problem for Mexico's future, but also for America's: As long as Mexico failed to find a way to develop its central and southern states, there would be no end in sight to the steady migration to the north. As things stood, Mexico's free trade–based economic model was benefiting its least populated states.

CHAPTER 15

The Police Connection

The spectacular circumstances of the June 1995 capture of Sinaloa drug cartel baron Héctor "El Guero" Palma confirmed what most Mexicans had long known — in Mexico, the police are for sale, and the criminals are buying. When the army detained the thirty-three-year-old cocaine baron after his executive jet crashed near the airport of Tepic, Nayarit, it discovered that most members of his heavily armed entourage were agents of the Federal Judicial Police. What was more, Palma was staying at the home of the local police commander and had been eluding capture by wearing the black uniform of the judicial police, ID included. The incident was outrageous by any standards, but even more outrageous was the fact that it wasn't all that unusual. The corruption in Mexican law enforcement was deep and growing, raising serious questions that it could be linked to the series of political assassinations that had rattled Mexico and that it posed as much a threat to Mexican ambitions of becoming a country of laws and a modern democracy as the rebels in Chiapas, drug traffickers, or crooked politicians.

Palma was one of Mexico's bloodiest gangsters. A former car thief who had started his career in the cocaine business as a gunman for Sinaloa cartel chief Miguel Angel Felix Gallardo, he had broken with his boss in the late seventies to start his own drug smuggling business with a Venezuelan partner, Rafael Enrique Clavel. He was arrested in 1978 on drug trafficking charges in Arizona and spent eight years in a

U.S. jail, then went back into business as soon as he was returned to Mexico in 1986. By then, things had changed at home: His Venezuelan partner had not only teamed up with his former boss, but had also seduced Palma's wife, Guadalupe, lured her to San Francisco, and killed her there.

As a souvenir from his former business partner, Palma received a priority mail package from America — with Guadalupe's head in it. The Venezuelan hadn't stopped there: He had kidnapped Palma's two young children, Jesús and Nataly, and taken them to Venezuela, where he killed them by dropping them from a bridge.* Palma returned the favor, going on a killing spree to avenge the murder of his family and killing dozens of people, including Felix Gallardo's lawyer and three of Clavel's friends.

He had escaped arrest through scores of daylight shoot-outs, only to be captured by sheer chance on June 23, 1995, a day after his plane crashed. He had left Ciudad Obregón, Sonora, at 8:10 P.M. the night before in a twelve-seat Lear jet bound for Guadalajara, Jalisco, where he was planning to attend a wedding party for which he had booked one hundred fifty rooms for his friends and relatives at the five-star Fiesta Americana Hotel. But Palma's jet could not land in Guadalajara: As the pilot approached the city, he was informed that the airport's runway was being repaired.

The pilot began to call nearby airports in search of a place to land and headed for the airport of Tepic, which had been closed since sunset. Palma asked the federal police to open up that airport for him — which they immediately did — and his plane began to circle while waiting to be assigned a runway. But the jet ran out of fuel and crashed on a field about four miles from the airport. Meanwhile, the local army unit — noticing that the airport's lights had come back on hours after closing — had alerted nearby garrisons that something funny was going on.

Yet the situation did not look critical for Palma at that point: While the plane had been wrecked attempting an emergency landing and the pilot and copilot had been seriously injured, he got off the plane rela-

---

* Venezuelan mafia boss Rafael Enrique Clavel was later sentenced to thirty years in prison in Venezuela for the murder of the two children, according to Mexican press reports.

tively unhurt and, fortunately for him, the police were near. A Federal Judicial Police contingent appeared at the scene minutes later aboard Suburban vans and, at Palma's request, drove him and his men back to Guadalajara. Once there, Palma was taken to a private house, where he got immediate medical attention and extra police protection. It was a safe place: The house belonged to Apolinar Pintor, the Federal Judicial Police's number two commander in Jalisco.

The next day, neighbors of the house called the local army unit to report that they had seen men carrying a suspicious-looking bundle emerging from the house early that morning. When an army patrol stopped the vehicle shortly thereafter, it found a dead body in a sleeping bag: It belonged to Palma's pilot, who had died hours earlier. A massive army raid of Palma's safe house hours later resulted in the arrest of the cocaine lord, eight private bodyguards, and thirty-two judicial police agents.

Later investigations showed that Palma had made several payments of $40 million to the top Federal Judicial Police commanders of Guadalajara — each of which amounted to the whole country's monthly federal police budget. Palma, who headed Mexico's fourth largest cocaine cartel, had also paid millions to the Federal Judicial Police commanders of Sonora, Sinaloa, Chihuahua, and Nayarit, who in turn shared part of the pay with their personnel. Only a few weeks earlier, Palma had been staying at one of Nayarit's luxury hotels and had leisurely ridden down its main street on a thoroughbred with a silver saddle, with his custom-made Colt .38 emerging from his belt displaying a palm tree engraved with precious stones — a total of 208 white diamonds, officials would say later — on its handle. He was guarded by "several dozen" armed men carrying police IDs, a local newspaper reported at the time. Palma had Federal Judicial Police commanders in five western Mexican states literally working for him.

▼

It wasn't the first time that Mexican law enforcement officials were caught providing protection to drug barons. On several occasions in recent years, most notably in the 1985 murder of U.S. DEA agent Enrique "Kiki" Camarena, Mexican police and army commanders had been on the criminals' side.

One of the most grotesque episodes of teamwork between law enforcement agents and cocaine traffickers had taken place on November 7, 1991, when seven government antidrug agents were gunned down by a local army unit as they were trying to capture a group of cocaine traffickers who had just landed a cocaine-laden plane at an airstrip in Tlatlixcoyan, Veracruz. This time, the good cops were members of the Federal Judicial Police, and the men who had killed them were members of a local army detachment that had long been protecting cocaine traffickers who refueled their planes in Veracruz on their way to the United States. As usual, the government first portrayed the incident as a tragic mistake, then flooded public opinion with an array of contradictory evidence that left everybody equally mixed up. In the end, the government imprisoned the Veracruz army commander in charge of the unit, and at the same time fired a deputy attorney general in order to make it seem that both sides — not just the army — had been at fault.

By 1995, according to an internal Interior ministry report, there were an estimated nine hundred armed criminal bands in Mexico, of which more than 50 percent were made up of current or retired members of law enforcement agencies. And some of the bloodiest gun battles in Mexico's war on drugs pitted these law enforcement–related gangs against each other. On March 3, 1994, a team of antinarcotics agents of the Federal Judicial Police was attacked by the Baja California Judicial Police as it was trying to arrest a local drug cartel chief. The drug trafficker escaped during the shoot-out, in which the head of the Federal Judicial Police unit was killed, and two of his men were badly wounded. The case turned into a political scandal, but a very brief one: Several of the State Judicial Police agents arrested in the shoot-out were released a few days later, while others — including the chief of the homicides division of the State Judicial Police — fled from their prisons and remained at large.

▼

Was corruption running rampant in most of Mexico's law enforcement agencies? Pretty much. According to the Interior ministry's conservative estimates, more than 60 percent of the members of all police forces in the country had received bribes or had criminal records themselves.

An official report from the attorney general's office stated that, even with Mexico's strong job protection laws, more than four hundred members of its Federal Judicial Police — or more than 10 percent of the force's personnel — had been fired or suspended from their jobs over the three years ending in mid-1995 because of suspected ties to the drug cartels.

Some officials estimated that more than 50 percent of Federal Judicial Police agents were making money from drug traffickers in some form or another, either through direct bribes or by keeping parts of confiscated cocaine shipments and selling them on the side. And corruption in State Judicial Police forces was even worse: More poorly paid than federal agents and more likely to succumb to pressures from local drug tycoons, many of Mexico's state police forces were little more than uniformed crime syndicates.

"Every day, it becomes harder to do this job," a regional Mexican investigator told the *Los Angeles Times* as he listed his professional frustrations in a most peculiar order of importance. "There are powerful obstacles within the state police forces, people allied with the narcos. The federal police are another obstacle. And the third enemy is the bad guys themselves."

▼

Police mafias were, like the ruling party's camarillas, a symptom of the fragmentation of power that had turned Mexico into a country divided in thousands of fiefdoms that could only be distinguished from one another according to the racket in which they were engaged. Each of Mexico's police forces was a family protecting its own business interests — if anything in a cruder and more violent way than the dozens of political tribes that dominated the ruling party.

The various clans within the police were more visible than those in politics because Mexico had a bizarre variety of police forces: There were 2,400 conventional police forces operating in the country, including the Federal Judicial Police, the states' judicial police forces, riot police, customs police, bank police, rural police, forestry police, traffic police, subway police, and hundreds of varieties of municipal police forces. And that didn't count the private police forces: Mexico City alone had 627 private companies — many of them run by former police officers with criminal records — with a total of 27,500 men working as guards for businesses and their executives, more than the 24,500 policemen that the city had to patrol the streets.

While national, state, local, and private police units engaged in a variety of crimes, most were known to have their own — distinctive — specialization. The state police in Tijuana, for instance, were famous for running car-theft rackets in San Diego, California: Tijuana police officers had repeatedly been arrested red-handed by California police while stealing vehicles on the U.S. side of the border. The Mexico City police force, on the other hand, was known to make its millions from taxi inspections, bribes to motorists, and — when times were hard — kidnappings for ransom.

To make things worse, each of these police forces had scores of secret agents who were known as *"madrinas,"* or godmothers, who were kept off the books but whose responsibilities went far beyond those of informers. They were often allowed to carry guns and were used by federal and state police chiefs to do the dirty work that couldn't be done by those on the government's payroll — from stealing cars across the border to killing opposition activists.

Human rights activists said the fact that the *madrinas* were not kept on a regular payroll gave them a virtual license to commit crimes and fostered additional corruption within the regular forces: The freelance police agents were often paid out of the proceeds of drug busts, car thefts, protection money supplied by drug traffickers, ransom money from police-executed kidnappings of businessmen, or the revenues from bribes paid by restaurant owners and motorists.

There was no civil service career concept in most of Mexico's police forces: You were hired off the street by a police chief, became his protégé, and most often lost your job when your protector was fired, transferred, or retired. For many this was an incentive to steal as much — and as fast — as possible: The minute a new police chief was appointed, he was likely to bring his own friends to replace you and other members of the old family. Your best hope was to buy your job — by paying your superiors the going rate for your position.

Juan Carlos Valerio Roldan, a Mexico City cop who was demoted by his superiors when he spoke up against corruption in his department, complained that corruption in Mexico's police forces came from the top and not from the ground up. Recruits had to pay their superiors extra for a good pistol, a promotion, or for night duty, when it is easier to stop allegedly suspicious cars on the street and demand bribes. Most cherished was a patrol car, which required a sizable extra payment: "As a patrolman, if there's nothing going on here, you can go somewhere else to rob or extort," he told a U.S. reporter.

"The idea of the chiefs is to enrich themselves," Valerio Roldan said. "They can't live on their salaries. They live on corruption. They're not in business to serve the public. They're there to make money."

And there wasn't too much time to waste in that pursuit. For most police agents there were no career opportunities if they were laid off by a new chief or couldn't afford to buy their position: More than 65 percent of the country's police had only completed elementary school. So Mexican police routinely extorted bribes from crime victims, store owners, or motorists as part of institutionalized corruption schemes that were administered by their top commanders and — as the times got tougher in the aftermath of the December 1994 devaluation — increasingly resorted to kidnapping, extortion, and robbery.

▼

Although most of these crimes went unreported, a hilarious attempted mugging by police officers in March 1995 drew national attention to police corruption. According to official accounts, it happened when Mexico state police agents, led by their commander, stopped a Jeep Cherokee in the Mexico City suburb of Tecamachalco and tried to force its driver at gunpoint to turn over his money and valuables. They were quite unlucky, however: The driver happened to be Ernesto Zedillo, the president's nineteen-year-old son.

The young man's bodyguards immediately showed up from a car driving about a block behind Ernesto's Jeep and arrested the police commander and his men after a tense shouting match. Days later, government officials conceded that the squad commander had served a jail sentence for murder in the state of Guerrero before joining the Mexico state police force, and a stern-looking President Zedillo told the Mexican people in a televised speech that "nothing and no one will weaken my resolve to lead the construction of the true rule of law that the Mexican people deserve."

But for millions of Mexicans the story brought to the surface the drama of the average citizen who was routinely harassed by corrupt law enforcement officials and who — unlike the young Zedillo — didn't have bodyguards to rescue them from the criminal cops. As the president's son's attempted robbery became the talk of the day, it seemed that the whole country had been a victim of police abuses. Everybody had his or her own tale of police corruption. It was no coincidence that one of the most popular jokes making the rounds in Mexico City at the time was "If you get mugged on the street, don't yell: You may attract the police!"

▼

The drug trafficking boom and the unprecedented police corruption it had brought about raised speculation that Mexico — like Colombia before it — had become a "narco-democracy": a country where drug traffickers had bought themselves significant political clout and periodically resorted to violence as a way to maintain it. Many Mexican and U.S. political analysts seemed truly convinced that Mexico's drug barons were behind the assassinations that had shaken the country in 1994.

I had my doubts. Why would Mexico's drug barons want to draw world attention — and the eyes of U.S. law enforcement agencies — by carrying out high-profile political killings? Unlike their Colombian counterparts, who had launched a campaign of terror in the late eighties to press their demands for revocation of an extradition treaty with the United States, the Mexican drug lords were not known to have made political demands. Why would they want to kill prominent politicians and risk becoming prime suspects in their deaths when they were comfortably doing their business with the protection of friendly police and army commanders?

One of the many counterarguments I heard from well-placed Mexicans was that the narcos had launched a campaign of political killings after the Salinas government had reneged on an alleged nonaggression pact between the government and the cocaine cartels in the early nineties. According to this theory, championed by political scientist Jorge G. Castañeda, the Salinas administration had made a secret agreement with Mexico's drug lords at a time when it desperately needed good headlines in the American press to achieve its top priority: signing the NAFTA deal with the United States.

In the early nineties the government — allegedly through presidential brother Raúl Salinas — had made an explicit or tacit agreement with Mexico's drug lords that they would be allowed to operate certain air corridors to ship drugs to America in exchange for keeping a low profile, not exceeding "tolerable" levels of cocaine smuggling, and depositing most of their profits in Mexico, the theory went. But as the NAFTA proposal began to be seriously debated in the U.S. Congress, the Salinas administration saw itself under growing international pressure to crack down on the traffickers — not the least because drug shipments were soaring — and captured notorious Mexican drug cartel leaders Rafael Caro Quintero and Joaquin "El Chapo" Guzmán. All of a sudden the deal was off, and the drug cartels — feeling betrayed by the government — began a campaign of political assassinations to warn authorities that they could easily destabilize Mexico if they wanted, according to this school of thought.

Was it a coincidence that Cardinal Posadas and Colosio were respectively murdered in Guadalajara and Tijuana — the capitals of Mexico's drug business? supporters of this hypothesis asked. Was it just by chance that Ruiz Massieu's assassins were hired guns from Tamaulipas, another top drug-smuggling region? Not so, they argued: Mexico's drug barons had ordered high-level killings as a warning message to the government. They had not made explicit demands because that was not the way things were done in Mexico: This was a country of hidden signals, where oblique warnings were taken seriously and direct messages were quickly dismissed as too obvious to be true.

There was another drug-related explanation for the series of political killings that had shaken Mexico: The Posadas, Colosio, and Ruiz Massieu killings had been part of a turf war among the rival drug cartels, a senior Mexican official with good access to intelligence agencies speculated. During the Salinas administration there had been a much harsher repression of Pacific Coast cartel leaders than those of the Gulf cartel: The two captured cartel leaders Caro Quintero and El Chapo Guzmán had led Pacific cartel drug rings, and most of the government's antidrug efforts had been aimed at those organizations.

Toward the end of the Salinas administration, the official asserted, the Pacific cartel — now run by Sinaloa drug kingpin Amado Carrillo — had grown increasingly concerned that its rival Gulf cartel would be even better positioned in the Colosio administration. Pacific cartel leaders had reason to be fearful: The brother of Gulf cartel leader Juan García Abrego had been invited to an exclusive Colosio campaign fund-raiser, and several Colosio aides — including a close relative — were known to have ties to the Gulf cartel. "The Pacific cartel people feared a repeat of what had happened in Colombia, where the Cali cartel had helped the government destroy the rival Medellin cartel," the Mexican official told me. "They killed Colosio, among other things, to prevent that from happening."

This explanation seemed to be in line with a 1993 U.S. intelligence report alleging that Colosio had briefly befriended drug traffickers in his home state of Sonora when he was starting his political career. According to the report, Colosio had knowingly or unknowingly acted as a carrier of funds from a local drug mafia to a powerful Sonora politician who was his protector. In a separate report leaked later to the *Washington Post*, U.S. Customs agents had stated that a Colosio relative owned an airstrip that was used as a transit point for drugs. True or false, these reports pointed at connections between the Salinas and Colosio inner circles and the Gulf cartel.

Both theories made sense but left many questions unanswered, including why the drug traffickers would risk drawing international attention to themselves. In addition, these theories failed to provide a convincing explanation for the murder of Pepe Ruiz Massieu: His sloppy execution — the Uzi that got stuck after the first shot, the gunman who stumbled while fleeing the scene, and the congressional aide who hosted the killers at his home for several days before the hit — seemed more the product of an amateurish group than the work of a professional drug mafia hit squad. It just didn't look like a drug mafia execution.

The wave of killings that was shaking Mexico was more complicated than a war launched by the drug barons or between the cocaine cartels, or the clash between free-market reformers and old-guard nationalists that Carlos Salinas had talked about. Mexico's violence was most likely coming from several sides, including political camarillas and police mafia families that were fighting for turf in an increasingly tight economy and that operated some of the nine hundred armed bands active in the country.

▼

In Washington, D.C., Clinton administration officials were reluctant to talk about a Mexican narco-democracy or to compare the Mexican drug cartels with their Colombian counterparts. Mexican criminals were nowhere near the levels of power — and violence — of the South Americans, officials asserted. "We haven't seen any group in Mexico reach the level of influence that the Cali cartel has reached in Colombia," a senior federal law enforcement official dealing with narcotics issues told me. "In Mexico the drug cartels have not been able to create a legal environment that favors them, nor have they made any major contributions to political campaigns that we know of, nor have they launched public relations campaigns to create doubts in the public mind over whether they are good or bad for the country."

That was true. But it was also true that the Clinton administration — like its most immediate predecessors — was reluctant to speak out loudly against Mexico's cocaine cartels or its drug money–infested law enforcement agencies. Most immediately it feared that any unpleasant disclosure about Mexico would give ammunition to Senator Jesse Helms and other conservative Republicans that could be used against Clinton's $20 billion Mexico bailout package in the 1996 presidential campaign. From a more historical perspective, there was also a built-in culture of caution — some would say of denial — among U.S. foreign policy makers regarding criticism of Mexico.

U.S. officials argued that the Mexican government's dramatic shift from regarding the United States as its enemy to seeing it as an economic opportunity was too recent — the marriage had only been consummated with NAFTA's approval late in 1993 — and too incipient to risk a U.S.-provoked nationalist backlash in Mexico.

▼

"Mexico is treated like an untouchable," complained U.S. Deputy Assistant Secretary of State Cresencio "Chris" Arcos, raising his hands in a sign of helplessness. "No U.S. administration wants to hear the bad things about Mexico: It would be put in a domestic political position to have to do something about them. If it had to act it would risk disrupting the established bilateral mechanisms of the last decade, such as NAFTA."

Examples of the administration's reluctance to make public demands on Mexico abounded. During the NAFTA negotiations in 1993, the administration had hidden from the American public its serious concerns about high-level drug corruption in Mexico, even as it was privately warning the Mexican government that a prosecutor named Mario Ruiz Massieu, among others, was suspected of having links to the drug cartels. Likewise, U.S. Treasury officials in 1994 had concealed from the public their fears of a financial collapse in Mexico and had even voiced public praise for Mexico's economic performance while they were writing internal memos warning of the urgent need for a devaluation.

The conflicting pressures on U.S. policy with Mexico became apparent when the Clinton administration was discussing whether to grant the $20 billion bailout to Mexico in the aftermath of the December 1994 devaluation of the Mexican currency. Clinton's Council of Economic Advisers and other top government officials who were not particularly familiar with Mexican history had argued for demanding that Mexico privatize the Pemex oil monopoly and cool its ties to Cuba in exchange for the U.S. economic salvation package. Why should American taxpayers save Mexico when its own government could do it by privatizing its oil industry? pragmatic government economists asked.

The Mexico experts at the State Department and the National Security Council counterargued that any such demand at this early stage of the U.S.-Mexico marriage would have spoiled the two nations' increasingly close relationship. The Pemex oil monopoly and Cuba were two symbols that the Mexican government considered it needed to pay tribute to in order to maintain a semblance of nationalism at home, even if Mexican officials privately agreed they were relics of the past. Pemex's privatization and a more prodemocracy Mexican policy toward Cuba could come more easily and less traumatically when Mexico revamped its economy, and at the initiative of the Mexican government rather than as a U.S. imposition, the Mexican experts argued.

The U.S. Government's Mexico experts' prognosis was that if Mexico was helped to overcome its present financial collapse, it was bound to continue opening its political and economic systems. The NAFTA agreement had radically changed the nature of U.S.-Mexican ties, they argued, among other things by making the U.S. Congress a major player in a relationship that had previously been led by the two countries' executive powers. With the U.S. Congress as part of the game, there would be a growing number of congressional hearings on issues such as corruption, drug trafficking, and economic policy in Mexico, and civic groups and independent government critics would have unprecedented platform to influence Mexican policies. Mexico would be under growing internal and outside pressure to try to adapt to the moral standards of its trading partners.

The Mexico hands prevailed in the January 1995 White House discussions on the Mexican bailout plan: The Clinton administration made no explicit reference to Pemex or Cuba when granting its bailout package to Mexico. But the Clinton administration's internal debate over the bailout package reflected the growing pressure within the U.S. Government to engage in more open discussions with Mexico over key issues affecting the two countries. Increasingly, the pragmatists' demands were being worked into the U.S. Mexican policy.

"Ten years ago, the top U.S. priority regarding Mexico was stability," a well-placed U.S. official who participated in those meetings told me afterward. "Following the collapse of the Soviet bloc, the definition was expanded to stability and prosperity, because only a prosperous Mexico could help stop the flow of Mexican immigrants to America. Today, the objectives of U.S. policy toward Mexico have been further expanded: We want a stable, prosperous, and democratic Mexico that also acts strongly to combat drug trafficking."

▼

Arcos was among the many U.S. narcotics officials who were frustrated by what they saw as a U.S. double standard: It was much easier for American antidrug officials to lash out against drug trafficking in Colombia than against similar scandals in Mexico. U.S. antidrug policy with Colombia was one of confrontation; that with Mexico was one of persuasion. The explanation was that Colombia, unlike Mexico, was not a U.S. national security concern. Too much was at stake with America's giant neighbor and new big-time trade partner, as well as with the powerful domestic constituencies in California and Texas that had a big stake in smooth relations with Mexico.

The day I visited Arcos at his State Department office, he was cleaning up his desk: He was quitting the U.S. Government to take a high-paying corporate job in Miami. In his most recent job he had often argued — most often unsuccessfully — for a more aggressive U.S. antidrug policy with Mexico. The longer Washington, D.C., kept quiet about drug-related corruption in Mexico, the more inroads the drug traffickers would make in that country and the more difficult it would be for Mexico itself to root out the drug cartels, he had argued.

So what should the United States do? I asked him. Wasn't it the conventional wisdom in Washington, D.C., that it would serve little to engage in a shouting match with the Mexican government given Mexico's reservoir of anti-American opinion makers?

There were several avenues that the United States could pursue without infringing on Mexico's national sovereignty, he said. Among them, it could increase the level of U.S. Government — and not just congressional — contacts with opposition leaders in order to give them a higher profile within Mexican society and thus help accelerate the country's transition to a system in which government officials would be accountable for their crimes.

Traditionally, U.S. diplomats had only held discreet meetings with Mexican opposition leaders and heads of civic groups opposed to the government for fear of being accused of interfering in the country's internal affairs. But with the end of Cold War–era fears that Mexico could turn toward a hostile power, and with the new partnership brought about by NAFTA, there was little rational basis for maintaining the U.S. reluctance to confront Mexico's ruling elite on issues affecting both sides.

"We should empower the legitimate critics of the system by talking to them on a more equal basis," Arcos proposed. "They, and not the U.S. Government, should be the ones to challenge the system on issues such as greater accountability, corruption, and drug trafficking."

Other experts suggested a more outspoken U.S. role in the context of an increasingly candid dialogue between the two countries. Hadn't the U.S. Treasury contributed to the December 1994 crisis by putting out upbeat public statements about the Mexican economy while its own internal memos warned of a dangerous drop in Mexico's foreign reserves? they asked.

There was something to be said for the argument that times had changed from the old days when any statement by Mexico or the United States about one another could be construed as a blatant intervention in domestic affairs. The Mexican Government, after all, was openly condemning California's Proposition 187, as well as U.S. policy on Cuba. The NAFTA partnership had opened the door to a more open relationship between the two partners, much like that among members of the European union. As the two countries prepared to enter a new millennium, the old see-nothing, hear-nothing diplomacy was becoming increasingly obsolete.

▼

Members of Zedillo's inner circle, especially the U.S.-educated technocrats, seemed resigned to the idea that drug trafficking and official corruption were bound to become a source of growing disputes between Washington, D.C., and Mexico, even if they characterized the new tensions as the sign of a more mature relationship.

And Mexico had its own gripes against the United States regarding drug trafficking, which it would put on the table whenever it felt unfairly blamed for the problem. America would have to do more to reduce drug consumption if it wanted to slow down drug trafficking, Mexican officials argued. It would also have to do more about something that was rarely talked about in the U.S. media: cracking down on the U.S. drug cartel bosses.

"You keep talking about the Mexican drug cartels, but what about the U.S. drug cartels?" a member of Zedillo's inner circle asked me. "Are you going to tell me that there is a thirty-billion-dollar drug smuggling business into the United States and that there aren't any Mafia bosses handling that business on your side of the border?"

He had a point. Virtually every major U.S. newspaper had written long exposés on Mexico's increasingly powerful drug cartels in recent times, but there were few — if any — references to their U.S. counterparts. It was an issue that was bound to arise as the two countries divided their responsibilities in the war on drugs.

CHAPTER 16

Fall and Resurrection

*"It is useless to maintain that social progress takes place
by itself, bit by bit. . . . It is really a leap forward which
is only taken when society has made up its mind to try
an experiment. This means that society must have allowed itself to be convinced, or at any rate allowed itself to
be shaken, and the shake is always given by somebody."*

— Henri-Louis Bergson, French
philosopher (1859–1941)

As I was winding up my reporting for this book in late 1995, Mexico
was going through its worst economic crisis in recent history. The impact of the December 1994 devaluation on Mexicans' lives was devastating: The gross domestic product was expected to fall by 7 percent in
1995 — its biggest drop since the 1930s — and was not projected to
rise in real terms in 1996; interest rates in recent months had reached
100 percent; car sales had plummeted by 70 percent; more than ten
thousand businesses had closed down, and many more were threatened
by a vicious circle of slumping sales and unpayable debts; more than
one million people had been laid off, and the unofficial unemployment
rate had reached a record 13 percent. Mexico was, to put it mildly, in a
near depression.

You did not have to look hard to realize how serious the crisis was: Every day you saw more women selling crafts on the sidewalks and boys washing windshields on the streets; reports of muggings and armed robberies were skyrocketing, and For Rent signs were springing up everywhere.

In the residential Mexico City neighborhood where I was staying at the time, I could measure the crisis by the rising number of people ringing the doorbell: A seemingly endless stream of peddlers dropped by to offer everything from fresh lemons to freelance work as gardeners. In the past, most door-to-door vendors had been middle-aged women, many of them clad in Indian robes, who were selling fresh fruits or vegetables. Now many were young men who had just arrived from states such as Chiapas, Hidalgo, and Michoacán, victims of the devaluation that had pushed debt-ridden ranches and town stores to lay off much of their work force.

"Is there any work I can do for you?" a young man named Pedro asked me, his hands clenched to the bars of the front yard fence. He said there was no work in the Michoacán village where he lived, and he had not been able to find employment in the capital. "Can't you give me *una ayudita* ["a little help"] for my family? Don't be bad! We have to eat."

▼

"After the bad things that have been happening to us, we are beginning to think that within Mexico there is a small group, very small, of bad guys . . . who would like things to remain as they were before," President Zedillo told his fellow Mexicans on a Friday morning long after the Colosio and Ruiz Massieu killings, when the country was once again in a state of shock over the murder of a prominent Mexico City judge and the mysterious two-shot suicide of the Mexico City official overseeing the Route 100 bus company finances.

Was there indeed a conspiracy of "bad guys" behind all the evils that had befallen Mexico since the January 1, 1994, Zapatista uprising? As months went by, the Mexican president had begun to talk about a "destabilization" plan by the small group of culprits whose real identity he conceded remained a mystery even to him.

Mexicans reacted with characteristic skepticism — and were right in doing so. By now, after the two Aburtos story and dozens of government flip-flops on the political assassinations that had rocked the country, it really didn't matter who officials would name next as the bad guys: The government had singled out — and later discarded — so many suspects that its findings had become almost meaningless. The ruling elite faced a credibility crisis that was even greater than its traditional legitimacy crisis.

An eventual move to charge Salinas, as much of the independent press was demanding, could appease Mexican critics for a while but — within the pandemonium of conflicting charges and in the absence of institutions whose judgments would be taken seriously — was not likely to provide a convincing explanation for the country's ills, nor to put the crisis to rest. The country's fresh wounds were not likely to heal with one or two dramatic headlines.

Mexico's political system was not facing a classic people's revolution, but a gradual meltdown. The political assassinations that had shaken the country in the mid-nineties were not coming from down below nor from the fringes, but from its core. The business bonds and complicity ties that had kept the ruling party's political tribes united for so long were breaking up. The ruling party no longer had a strong — unanimously feared and revered — president to settle its internal disputes, nor a "revolutionary" ideology to keep it together, nor the economic resources to patch up its differences with tons of money. The wave of privatizations had significantly reduced the ruling elite's financial clout — a dramatic phenomenon in a country where, as writer Alan Riding had noted in his 1984 book *Distant Neighbors*, corruption provided the oil that made the government machine turn and the glue that sealed political alliances. Now each camarilla was fighting for its life, competing for a shrinking economic pie.

In all likelihood, there wasn't one group of bad guys behind the killings of Posadas, Colosio, Ruiz Massieu, and those who came after them, but many. The hundreds of criminal bands within Mexico's 2,400 law enforcement agencies, the various regional PRI political bosses, the leaders of ruling party camarillas that had been left aside in the distribution of power in recent years, the former Salinas government officials who wanted to extend their political clout beyond their president's term — all sides had wanted to make a show of force in an effort to survive in a system of political alliances that was cracking. This was not Mexico in the 1910s, but Chicago in the 1930s.

▼

The decay of Mexico's ruling elite — best illustrated by the stories of brutal internal fighting that emerged in the aftermath of Raúl Salinas's arrest — was not just a by-product of the economic opening of the eighties. Its decline had begun much earlier and resulted from what political scientist Lorenzo Meyer described as an inevitable process akin to biological decay. Just as scientific experiments with mice proved that repeated crosses of members of the same families over several generations produced monsters, Mexico's ruling elite was suffering from a similar phenomenon of gradual degeneration. The first generations of politicians handpicked by Mexican presidents because of family or business ties in the aftermath of the Mexican Revolution had shown minor defects, which had worsened over the years. After decades of rulers drawn from a closely knit circle of political families, ruling class politicians were showing serious psychological deformities that had turned some of them into murderers.

The violence at the highest levels of Mexican politics may not have been the product of a sound confrontation of ideas over the country's economic or political future, but of disputes over mundane issues such as ownership of a cornmeal plant in Guerrero or the European vacation of Pepe Ruiz Massieu and Adriana Salinas's fifteen-year-old daughter. As in many old monarchies, the ruling class was consuming its energies in palace struggles amid an atmosphere of progressive decadence.

The cross fire within Mexico's political class was not the result of a clear-cut struggle between dinosaurs and political reformers, as it was so often represented in the press. Politics was only one of its elements — and probably among the least important ones. To understand Mexico's crisis you had to look at the tribal and personal nature of its conflicts — who had broken what deal with whom over what, and who stood to lose the most. The bonds that tied Mexico's ruling elite were largely based on mutual assistance and reciprocal blackmail. Members of the ruling class had such a long history of mutual grievances over promotions, demotions, and decisions over who got what business — or whose father or grandfather had been ruined by somebody else's ancestor — that they often had more hate for one another than for their political adversaries.

▼

The weakening of the Mexican president's once almighty powers in the turbulent months that followed the Colosio and Ruiz Massieu assassinations had prevented a peaceful resolution of the ruling party's internal conflicts. In the past, disputes among the various tribes had been rapidly resolved through the intervention of the president, who settled them according to his own judgment and avoided any rumors of internal conflicts from becoming public knowledge. Under the old rules of the game, the president's decision was sacred: There was a general understanding within the ruling elite that winners and losers would abide by it.

But times had changed: The perception — no matter how unfounded — that Salinas had masterminded the killings of Colosio and Ruiz Massieu, or had at least covered up for his brother, had left the leaders of the hundreds of PRI tribes with deep suspicions about their maximum leader. If the president or his aides had resorted to violence to get rid of internal adversaries, how could they know if they would not be the next targets? they thought.

As political scientist Castañeda said at the height of public suspicions that Carlos Salinas had engineered the Colosio and Ruiz Massieu assassinations, "Rather than being a source of stability, continuity and peace, the Mexican presidency had become an institution of instability, discontinuity and violence."

Adding to that, Zedillo had stated shortly before his inauguration that he would no longer be the maximum leader of the party and become instead a "passive member" of it — a recognition of the excesses of presidential powers during the Salinas years. Although his claim was largely rhetorical, there was a growing feeling among party leaders that everybody was on his own and had to fight for his own share of power.

▼

Octavio Paz, who in his eighty years had seen much of Mexico's contemporary history, was among the many who feared that the infighting within the PRI, coupled with an escalation of strikes, street protests, and perhaps even guerrilla attacks, could bring about a chaotic future.

The weakening of the presidency posed a threat that Mexico would not be able to control the various forces that were chipping away at the country's law and order from inside and outside power, he said. Sitting on the couch in his apartment's library, Paz saw some analogies between what was happening in the country now and the situation in 1911, following the collapse of the Porfirio Díaz dictatorship and the takeover of President Francisco I. Madero. The country had been split into dozens of factions, none of which had been strong enough to prevail over the others. What followed was an armed conflict that lasted more than a decade. If a similar situation was allowed to escalate in Mexico nowadays, the danger would be a period of instability that could be followed by a dictatorship, he said. Like many moderates from across the political spectrum, he felt that only a political agreement among the various factions could get the country back on track.

"We are witnessing the end of the PRI system, which could pave the way to a multiparty system," Paz said. "But if we don't achieve that, if the different forces don't succeed in agreeing on a peaceful transition toward a new political situation, we will have demonstrations, possible violence in the countryside and in the cities, internal fighting, and subsequently a period of a regime of force, a dictatorship or something like that. . . .

"In the long run, the forces of openness, modernization, and democracy will prevail," he concluded. "But it will be a very painful, very difficult road."

▼

How could Mexico find a new — more democratic and long-lasting — source of stability? From what I could conclude after witnessing the dramatic events of the mid-nineties, by recognizing that its problem was largely political and by doing something about it. The incidents that had triggered Mexico's latest economic crisis — Chiapas, Colosio's assassination, and the Ruiz Massieu murder — were of a political nature and would not go away just with economic corrections. The country would hardly emerge from its cyclical economic tragedies unless it completed its conversion to a working democracy, among other things by striking a deal with opposition parties to launch far-reaching electoral, media, labor, education, and anticorruption reforms.

The PRI, which had already undergone hundreds of cosmetic internal reforms, was highly unlikely to implement such sweeping changes. By the time of this writing, Zedillo was still relying heavily on the PRI and stating that the party's internal reforms would help propel Mexico into a full democracy, but even some of his top aides were skeptical that the party would renounce the privileges that helped keep it in power.

"Under the current circumstances, I don't think that the PRI can regenerate itself," Genaro Borrego, the former PRI president who was now head of the government's twenty-three-thousand-employee Social Security Institute, told me at his office under the official portrait of President Zedillo. "The traditional party has run its cycle. Now there should be a new political option."

One was hearing increasingly more comments like these in government offices — statements that would have been unthinkable only two years earlier. In this case the skepticism was coming from the same official who, as PRI president, had organized the billionaires' fundraising banquet to collect funds for the 1994 presidential election. Like other senior officials, Borrego had arrived at the conclusion that Mexico needed dramatic changes to find a new source of political balance. A ruling party that had just won a presidential election with 17 million votes was not likely to preside over its own undoing.

Most independent analysts agreed that the best scenario for Mexico would be for Zedillo to break with the past, quit the party altogether, expand the number of opposition politicians in his cabinet, and create a coalition government that could get all political parties to agree on an agenda for a transition to a full democracy. By doing that, Zedillo was likely to assure himself a place in history as the founder of a fully democratic Mexico.

The Mexican government, as growing numbers of officials were beginning to discover, needed to come to grips with the idea of political, economic, and geographic diversity, and to see it as a source of creativity rather than as a threat. For too long the government had used national sovereignty as an excuse to quash Mexicans' individual sovereignty. Mexico City's ruling elite had too long dismissed full democracy and political pluralism as dangerous ideas that could divide and weaken the country. Far from it, diversity held the key to Mexico's political and economic future.

Just as political diversity demanded that Zedillo accept opposition proposals for far-reaching political reforms, economic and geographic diversity called for him to recognize that what was good for Mexico's north was not necessarily good for Mexico's south. Without returning to the calamitous populism of the seventies, or withdrawing from its opening to the world, Mexico needed to allow pockets of economic paternalism for its most backward areas of the south until they were ready to begin to compete in the global economy. Absolute ideas and rigid domestic policies made little sense in the new world environment.

▼

There were many reasons to hope for a better future for Mexico. Despite the absence of evidence by the time of this writing that the government was ready to enforce radical democratic reforms, the country was stumbling toward a modern democracy.

There was a positive side to the explosion of mutual accusations within the ruling elite and among the various political parties. The state of confusion and constant agitation that had taken over the country was not marking the end of a solid political system that could have given Mexico many more years of stability, but was signaling the demise of a corrupt order whose foundations had begun to crack a long time ago.

Most likely, efforts to shore up the old system or delay creation of a new one would only worsen the country's internal tensions and bring about even greater violence in the future. In that sense, the crisis of the mid-nineties was as much a symptom of the meltdown of the old order as a hint of the impending birth of a new — and better — one.

There was undeniable progress on various fronts — little spurts of a moral-political renewal that were moving the country, though often erratically, toward a more dynamic society. Mexico was a significantly more open country than that I had visited in the seventies and eighties. In the past, interviewing government officials was like talking to Soviet bloc apparatchiks: They were very polite, smiled all the time, and gave you nothing but the party line. Now everybody said everything — perhaps because nobody knew what the party line was — and while some were expert practitioners of the art of disinformation, others made honest efforts to open up what had been a secret-shrouded society.

Zedillo had even begun the practice of offering monthly press conferences, in sharp contrast with past presidents, who used to make their public statements largely through one-on-one interviews with their favorite reporters. Publications such as *Reforma, La Jornada*, and the weekly *Proceso* were slowly pushing the rest of the press to more independent reporting.

Growing public demands for more evenhanded reporting in electronic media and the creation of the new Television Azteca network — which among other things had begun broadcasting Tom Brokaw's *NBC Nightly News* to Mexicans — were putting pressure on Azcarraga's Televisa to open up its news programs to nongovernment opinions. Growing numbers of U.S. news programs, many of them in Spanish, were reaching small but influential audiences through cable television, making it increasingly difficult for the government to ignore important news.

The culture of deception within Mexico's political class was alive and well but was no longer fully tolerated by the media, as the scandal over the academic degrees of Zedillo's cabinet members had shown. Barring a dramatic turn of events, the Mexican Government seemed condemned to allowing an increasingly open flow of information. NAFTA had brought the U.S. Congress into the equation of Mexican-American relations, opening a new court of last resort for Mexican Government critics if all other doors were shut at home and the White House decided — as it usually did — not to rock the boat.

On the political front, the government had been forced to allow foreign-funded domestic observers and "international visitors" to monitor the 1994 elections, dropping its dubious claims that such observations violated its national sovereignty. Citizens' groups such as the Civic Alliance, the umbrella group that had led the 1994 elections monitoring effort, were springing up everywhere and becoming important independent observers of government practices whose opinions carried growing domestic and international weight. The ruling party candidate had set another precedent by participating in the first nationally televised pre-election debate — the first time that millions of Mexicans had watched a PRI candidate being trounced by his rivals on live television.

Members of opposition parties were serving in growing numbers of high-profile jobs, such as the attorney general's office, and were running nearly half a dozen state governorships and more than ten major cities. By governing key states such as Jalisco and Baja California, the center-right PAN was tearing down the ruling party's traditional claims that only its members had enough experience to run public offices.

Moderate opposition leaders such as PAN leaders Carlos Castillo Peraza and Vicente Fox, PRD leader Porfirio Muñoz Ledo, and former foreign minister Camacho, who quit the ruling party in late 1995, were helping dispel fears that an opposition victory would throw the country into chaos. Both the PAN and the center-left opposition were expecting important victories in the 1997 congressional elections, which they hoped would change the Mexican Congress from a rubber-stamp institution into a real legislative power. A new Mexico was fighting its way to modernity, inch by inch.

And there were some reasons to hope that Zedillo would break with the past and lead his country to a modern democracy. Zedillo had sent an unprecedented warning to the ruling elite by placing a presidential brother behind bars, had appointed an opposition politician as his attorney general, and had begun his term by offering a political agreement to opposition parties to write a new — more evenhanded — electoral code.

In late 1995 Zedillo had taken another potentially far-reaching step by proposing creation of a Congress-run auditor's office to oversee the government's accounting and spending practices. In a country where nobody but the president used to monitor government expenditures and where much of the ruling elite's power stemmed from its ability to spend at its will, the new plan paved the way for a real system of checks and balances if opposition parties gained a significant number of seats in Congress.

Zedillo had some valuable cards to play: He was an accidental president with an image of honesty who had won the least objectionable elections in Mexico's history by a comfortable margin. He was a smart, no-nonsense administrator. These were no small political assets in his favor. They provided him with a reservoir of credibility that could help him — if he so chose — to become the Mexican president to lead his country out of its morass.

▼

The danger was that the perhaps unavoidable $50 billion bailout of Mexico and the ensuing Clinton administration buoyancy over Mexico's economic recovery would give Zedillo an ill-founded sense of security, and that he would once again postpone the sweeping political reforms Mexico needed to find a more solid source of stability.

It had happened on every occasion after Mexico's 1954, 1976, 1982, and 1987 economic crises, and it could happen once again. A continuation of the old system, no matter how thinly disguised, was bound to fail: Mexico's economy depended heavily on foreign and domestic investors, who demanded the kind of stability that the country's aging political system could no longer provide.

To continue opening up and expanding its economy, Mexico badly needed a system that would channel social tensions — including the escalating battles within the ruling elite — in a constructive way. Without it, the country would continue within the vicious cycle that led to its periodic economic crises — a system in which a government without accountability spent at its will, paid for its excesses with foreign investment, periodically went bankrupt, and then imposed draconian sacrifices on the poor to pay its debts.

As this book was going to press, there were some signs that key players in Mexico's drama of the mid-nineties had not learned the lessons of the past and that — once again — meaningful political reforms would be put off for better times. Not even a year had passed since the Clinton administration had bailed out the Mexican economy, and the Zedillo government was making sounds of triumphalism despite the lack of any progress in curing Mexico's chronic ills.

"After seven months of discipline and hard work, the most important indicators of our national economy are already showing signs of improvement," Zedillo said, as he predicted better times for 1996. "In the exchange markets, in interest rates, in the inflation index, we are already seeing some clear signs that we will soon overcome this crisis." Furthermore, Zedillo said, this was no time for "audacious actions" or "changes in the flight plan." Like his predecessors, Zedillo was citing selected macroeconomic indicators to project a promising future. Hadn't the Mexican people just watched that same movie recently? skeptics asked themselves.

Not two years had passed since the Zapatista uprising, and top Mexican officials were vehemently rejecting press reports that there were half a dozen guerrilla groups training in the state of Guerrero, just as they had once rejected the existence of rebels in Chiapas. Guerrero governor Rubén Figueroa stated following June 1995 clashes between leftist peasants and the military that had left thirty-four peasants dead that "nothing is going on in Guerrero."

Clinton administration officials, eager not to allow Mexico to become a campaign issue for anti-NAFTA populists or anti-immigration Republicans, continued to treat Mexico's ruling elite as its best source of tranquility. "Today, the signs of success are substantial," Treasury Secretary Rubin told Congress in a mid-1995 progress report on the Mexican bailout. U.S. officials were going out of their way to stress that Mexico was recovering sooner than expected, and that it had many things going for it — including a young, Yale-educated economist for a president with a true commitment to free-market reforms. The words sounded awfully familiar to those who had witnessed Salinas's rise to international stardom six years earlier.

Bolstered by the U.S. rescue package, the Mexican stock market had made a spectacular turnaround: Barely eight months after the December 1994 devaluation, its peso-denominated index was back to its pre-crisis levels. What's more, investors who had purchased Mexican stock two months after the December crash had made a killing: Mexico's stock market index had risen by more than 50 percent over the next six months.

"The Mexican economy has turned the corner," proclaimed President Clinton as he gave a red-carpet welcome to Zedillo in Washington, D.C., in September 1995. "Mexico's success is a tribute first to President Zedillo's leadership, his courage, and his government's steadfast commitment to carry through tough economic reforms."

Was the White House helping build a new house of cards on shaky political ground? Were we entering a new cycle of Wall Street infatuation with Mexico, big profits, overstated praise from Washington, D.C., and the U.S. media, and sudden financial collapse (followed, as usual, by giant U.S. rescue packages)? Maybe Mexico's recent steps toward greater openness would help prevent it, but the fact that it had happened so often in the recent past — and that so many reforms remained to be carried out — made such a scenario difficult to rule out.

As this book was being completed, it was Morgan Stanley & Company that was taking the lead on Wall Street, putting the gloomy postdevaluation predictions aside and upping its Mexican position from a market-neutral 24 percent to a "slight overweighing" 26 percent of its Latin American portfolio. "Mexico has the best near-term upside of any of the major Latin American markets," Morgan Stanley announced. Other major New York money funds, not wanting to stay behind, followed suit.

Pretty soon, the herd was on the move. The atmosphere on Wall Street was jubilant — just as it had been on that long-forgotten Tuesday morning, four days before Christmas, 1994.

Sources

CHAPTER 1. *The Party Is Over*

December 20 scene at Salomon Brothers, John Purcell's reaction to Mexican devaluation, from author's telephone interview with Purcell, May 26, 1995, and interviews with three other Wall Street money managers. Background on Salomon's emerging markets division from "On the Campaign Trail with a Mexico Analyst," by Jonathan Kandell, *Institutional Investor*, October, 1994.

Time magazine naming Salinas International Newsmaker of the Year, "Man of the Year" section, "The World's Other Newsmakers," from *Time* (U.S. edition), January 4, 1993, p. 44.

Figures for Mexico's inflation, down to single-digit figures from 160 percent a year, from "Balance de la Transformación Económica Durante la Administración del Presidente Carlos Salinas de Gortari," by Finance Minister Pedro Aspe, July 12, 1994.

Forbes magazine's ranking of the world's wealthiest people, "You can't any longer think of Mexico as the Third World," from "Meet the World's Newest Billionaires," *Forbes*, July 5, 1993, p. 76.

President Clinton's quote, "Enormous admiration for President Salinas . . . ," from White House press conference, March 23, 1993.

Clinton's quote, "One of the world's leading economic reformers," from remarks to U.S.-Mexico Binational Commission, June 21, 1993.

"This new image wasn't just good public relations, for which the Salinas government was doling out about $11 million a year just in the United States," figure of $11 million a year, from *La Jornada*, November 29, 1994.

"He had privatized 252 state companies . . . netting about $23 billion," from Mexico's Ministry of Finance "White Book" on privatizations, as quoted in *Reforma*, July 13, 1994, p. 26.

Mexico changing from a 78 percent oil dependency in the early eighties to relying on manufactured goods for 81 percent of its foreign income in 1993, from "Balance de la Transformación Económica Durante la Administración del Presidente Carlos Salinas de Gortari."

Account of Salinas's New Year's party, from author's separate interviews with three governors who attended the party, including Nuevo León governor Sócrates Rizzo; a private guest at the party; and a presidential aide.

CHAPTER 2. *The Scepter of the Seven Forces*

Account of transfer of staff of command ceremony in Chiapas jungle, Zapatista anthem, Indian ritual, from *La Jornada*, report by Hermann Bellinghausen, November 19, 1994, pp. 1 and 20.

Account of Zapatista takeover of San Cristóbal de las Casas, from author's interviews with Zapatista leader Subcommander Marcos, Chiapas jungle, July 23, 1994; Rancho Nuevo military barracks commander General José Rubén Rivas Peña, San Cristóbal de las Casas, July 19, 1994; San Cristóbal de las Casas anthropologist Arturo Lomelí, one of the first to witness the Zapatista rebellion in the early hours of January 1, 1994, who taped it on his home video recorder; as well as Mexican and U.S. press reports.

Comandante Felipe's quote, "We have come to San Cristóbal de las Casas to do a revolution against capitalism," and his seven A.M. salute, "Long live the Mexican Revolution," etc., from Lomelí's video recording.

Felipe's original role as Zapatista spokesman and his first press conference, from the Chiapas daily *La República*, whose reporters were among the first to arrive at the San Cristóbal public square shortly after the uprising, January 2, 1994, p. 3.

Marcos's quote, "One of our main priorities will be to make sure . . . ," from "No nos dejaron otro camino," special section Perfil de *La Jornada*, *La Jornada*, January 19, 1994, p. 2.

Marcos's quote, "Well, those of us who are the most handsome . . . ," from "No nos dejaron otro camino," p. 2.

Anecdote about tourists' fears, their chat with Subcommander Marcos, and Marcos's quotes beginning, "I wasn't even supposed to show up . . . ," from author's interview with Marcos, Chiapas jungle, July 23, 1994.

President Salinas's past support for state controls, criticism of Pazos, from *El*

Prinosaurio: La Bestia Politica Mexicana, by Manú Dornbierer, Editorial Grijalbo, Mexico City, 1994, pp. 58–59, quoting Salinas's stories in *Excelsior,* September 23–26, 1981.

Zapatistas better armed than originally reported, from author's interviews with Marcos, Chiapas jungle, July 23, 1994; Rivas Peña, San Cristóbal de las Casas, July 19, 1994; and Lomelí's video recording.

Commander in Chief Germán's anger over Marcos's showmanship, visit to Subcommander Elisa's house, Elisa's background, cracks within the guerrilla organization, from signed testimonies by Salvador Morales Garibay (Subcommander Daniel), February 8, 1995, and Maria Gloria Benavides Guevara (Subcommander Elisa), February 9, 1995. Benavides later said her confession had been signed under torture, but well-placed sources close to the Zapatistas confirmed the thrust of it in an interview with the author in Mexico City.

Salazar's brother's quote, "He was outside, and he was hit by a bullet . . . ," *La Jornada,* January 3, 1994, cited in "Chiapas: La Línea de Fuego," by Carlos Tello Diaz, *Nexos,* January 1995, p. 46.

Robert Felder's quote, "At first I thought it was a joke . . . ," from author's interview with Felder, Washington, D.C., June 8, 1994.

Salinas's claim that the uprising resulted from "a total failure of the state's intelligence systems," from author's interview with Salinas, Cartagena, Colombia, June 15, 1994.

Account of Mount Corralchén battle, from *La Rebelión de las Cañadas,* by Carlos Tello Díaz, Editorial Cal y Arena, Mexico City, 1995, pp. 168–169.

Army statement asserting that the fighting in Mount Corralchén had been "against a group of individuals, whose number has not yet been determined . . . ," from *Proceso,* June 7, 1993, quoted in *La Rebelión de las Cañadas.*

Patrocinio Gonzalez's quote, "There is definitely no guerrilla activity in Chiapas . . . ," from author's interview with Gonzalez, Mexico City, June 25, 1993.

Marcos's quote, "The army proceeded the way armies proceed . . . ," from author's interview with Marcos, Chiapas jungle, July 23, 1994.

Luis Donaldo Colosio's quote, "Looking back and considering the levels of suffering and the demands of the people . . . ," from author's interview with Colosio, Mazatlán, Sinaloa, March 22, 1994.

CHAPTER 3. *Chiapas: Opera and Revolution*

Patrocinio Gonzalez's sale of Aviacsa for $5 million, *Proceso,* February 14, 1994, p. 29.

Murders of transvestites in Chiapas, Patrocinio Gonzalez's quote on scandal being caused by gay groups "who over the past few months have not been able to carry out in liberty their sexual deviations along Central Avenue," from *El Dia*, August 12, 1992, by Cesar Espinosa, quoted in *La Muerte Viste de Rosa: El Asesinato de los Travestis en Chiapas*, by Victor Ronquillo, Ediciónes Roca, Mexico City, 1994, p. 18.

Chiapas police chief branding the transvestite killings as "passional crimes," from *La Muerte Color de Rosa: El Asesinato de los Travestis en Chiapas*, p. 18.

"In Mexico City, Salinas was facing a rebellion within his own cabinet," Manuel Camacho quotes beginning, "My point is simple . . . ," from *Yo Manuel: Memorias — Apócrifas? — de un Comisionado*, Rayuela Editores, Mexico, 1995, pp. 91–92. Also, author's interview with a top Camacho aide, Mexico City, January 30, 1995.

Ernesto Zedillo's March 19, 1994, memorandum to Colosio, content and quote, from complete text of memo as published by *Reforma*, October 3, 1995. The letter's authenticity was later confirmed by Zedillo.

CBS's *60 Minutes* quote, "What Robin Hood was to the people of Sherwood Forest, Subcomandante Marcos has become . . . ," from *60 Minutes*, CBS News, August 21, 1994. Transcript from Burrelle's Information Services.

National Liberation Forces' program, plans to "create a single political party based on the principles of Marxism-Leninism," from "Statutes of the Fuerzas de Liberación Nacional," Article Six, 1980.

NLF's main enemies were "north-American imperialism, and its local partners, the Mexican bourgeoisie," from "Statutes of the Fuerzas de Liberación Nacional."

The Zapatista uprising carried out by "the poor, the exploited and the miserable of Mexico," etc., from *El Despertador Mexicano*, official organ of the Zapatista army, December 1, 1993.

"Declaration of the Lacandon Jungle" declaring war on the "Salinas dictatorship," listing eleven basic demands: "work, land, roof . . . ," vowing to "advance to the capital of the country, overpowering the Mexican federal army," etc., from *El Despertador Mexicano*, December 1, 1993.

Subcommander Marcos's quote, "The change resulted from a decision by the [Zapatista] Committee to respond to government charges that we were foreigners . . . ," from author's interview with Marcos, Chiapas jungle, July 23, 1994.

NLF's 1993 document setting as its goal to "establish the dictatorship of the proletariat, understood as a government of the workers that will stave off counter-revolution . . . ," From NLF's "Declaration of Principles," quoted in *La Rebelión de las Cañadas*, by Carlos Tello Díaz, Editorial Cal y Arena, Mexico, 1995, p. 157.

Marcos's library, from "Sin Dejar Rastros . . . ," *El Universal*, February 17, 1995.

Marcos's quote to *La Jornada* about threat of government takeover by "fascist right" embodied by the PAN, from "No Sería un Golpe Militar," by Carmen Lira, *La Jornada*, August 25, 1995, p. 1.

"Land reform . . . had never been fully implemented in Chiapas," etc., from *Democracy and Human Rights in Mexico*, by Andrew Reding, World Policy Papers, World Policy Institute, New York, 1995, p. 18.

"Article 225 of Chiapas's Criminal Code called for sentences of up to four years in prison for those seizing land, buildings, public squares, 'or obstructing communication arteries . . . ,' " cited in *La Rebelión de las Cañadas*, p. 147

Chiapas's population explosion figures, from "Latin Rates of Growth Explosive," by Andres Oppenheimer, *Miami Herald*, January 31, 1994, p. 8.

"Most Indian communities in the jungle had illiteracy rates of more than 50 percent. In the city of Altamirano, 75 percent of the households lacked electricity . . . ," etc., from Mexico's National Statistics and Geography Institute (INEGI), XI Censo General de Poblacion y Vivienda, 1990.

Josephine Jimenez's quote, "We had already seen the guerrillas blowing up oil pipes in Colombia . . . ," from author's telephone interview with Jimenez, June 27, 1995.

"With 3,700 basketball courts across the state and 12,000 basketball teams . . . Chiapas had been turned into Mexico's most basketball-intensive state," from *Proceso*, January 17, 1994, p. 70.

Gonzalo Ituarte's quote, "They made these beautiful courts so that our undernourished Indians could play basketball after working fourteen hours a day . . . ," from author's interview with Ituarte, San Cristóbal de las Casas, on or about January 10, 1994.

Chiapas election results, La Trinitaria, etc., from "Chiapas, se acabo la madre de todos los carros completos," *El Financiero*, August 20, 1994, p. 16.

Marcos's quote about Chiapas, "There is a law in guerrilla warfare according to which a guerrilla column . . . ," from *Proceso*, February 23, 1994, p. 15.

CHAPTER 4. *Marcos*

Subcommander Marcos's quote, "What do we have to ask pardon for? . . . ," from January 20, 1994, letter from Marcos to *Proceso*, *La Jornada*, *El Financiero*, and *Tiempo*, as printed in *La Jornada*, January 21, 1994, p. 13.

Marcos's quote, "I propose the following . . . ," from January 20, 1994, letter to

Proceso, *La Jornada*, *El Financiero*, and *Tiempo*, as printed in *La Jornada*, January 21, 1994, p. 13.

Marcos's quote, "What? Me president of Mexico? . . . ," from author's interview with Marcos, Chiapas jungle, July 23, 1994.

Marcos's quotes, "*Hola, soy Marcos,*" and "Chocolate, that's the only thing . . . ," from author's interview with Marcos, Chiapas jungle, July 23, 1994.

Marcos's letter to Carlos Fuentes, "I must do everything possible . . . ," from *La Jornada*, July 4, 1994, p. 13.

Marcos's quote, "Because they are public opinion leaders . . . ," from "Si sólo fuera Marcos . . . ," by Elena Poniatowska, *La Jornada*, July 31, 1994, p. 1.

Marcos's quote, "It's the kind of life I'm leading now that makes me want to write . . . ," from "Mexico's Poet Rebel," by Ann Louise Bardach, *Vanity Fair*, July 1994, p. 135.

Marcos's quote, "I listen to the Voice of America . . . ," from author's interview with Marcos, Chiapas jungle, July 23, 1994.

Marcos's quote, "When we started, we did so . . . ," from author's interview with Marcos, Chiapas jungle, July 23, 1994.

Marcos's quote, "I have the honor of having as my superiors . . . ," from January 20, 1994, letter to *Proceso*, *La Jornada*, *El Financiero*, and *Tiempo*, as printed in *El Financiero*, January 24, 1994, p. 54.

Marcos's quote, "I was always the military chief . . . ," from author's interview with Marcos, Chiapas jungle, July 23, 1994.

Marcos's quotes, "In January, when the government . . . ," and "They see me like they always have . . . ," from author's interview with Marcos, Chiapas jungle, July 23, 1994.

Sections on Marcos's past, reaction to peace talks, quotes on taking off his ski mask, and Zedillo's "toughness and intolerance," from author's interview with Marcos, Chiapas jungle, July 23, 1994.

Ruling party not a fundamental element of the political elite, etc., from *La Segunda Muerte de la Revolución Mexicana*, by Lorenzo Meyer, Editorial Cal y Arena, Mexico City, 1992, p. 142.

"Between 1928 and 1971, only 14 percent of the Mexican government's successive cabinet ministers had held top positions within the party," Peter H. Smith, *The Labyrinths of Power*, cited in *La Segunda Muerte de la Revolución Mexicana*, p. 141.

The PRI's favorite sons, nepotism cases within the inner circle, are best described in *Después del Milagro*, by Héctor Aguilar Camin, Editorial Cal y Arena, Mexico City, 1993, pp. 134–135.

Zapatista Major Rolando's quotes beginning, "If there's fraud . . . ," from author's interview with Rolando, La Garrucha, Chiapas, July 20, 1994.

CHAPTER 5. *The Banquet*

Account of PRI fund-raiser, from author's separate interviews with half a dozen participants, including PRI president Genaro Borrego, Mexico City, September 9, 1993; ICA president Gilberto Borja, Acapulco, May 17, 1994; and Senator Miguel Alemán, Mexico City, March 2, 1993.

President Salinas in Davos, small audience shocked Salinas, from *Continental Shift: Free Trade and the New North America*, by William A. Orme Jr., The Washington Post Company, Washington, D.C., 1993; Salinas's quote, "It's becoming clear that our future lies . . . ," from author's interview with a Mexican official who accompanied Salinas to the Davos meeting, August 10, 1995.

Telmex rate increases, from *El Financiero*, January 7, 1991, and January 9, 1991.

Lorenzo Meyer's quote, "With wage increases . . . ," from *La Segunda Muerte de la Revolución Mexicana*, by Lorenzo Meyer, Editorial Cal y Arena, Mexico City, 1992, p. 189.

Lorenzo Meyer's quote, "They discovered how convenient it was for them to use the government's power . . . ," from *La Segunda Muerte de la Revolución Mexicana*, p. 188.

Founding of Council of Mexican Businessmen, from *El Financiero*, January 19, 1993.

Gilberto Borja's quotes beginning, "I think I'm putting about thirty hours a week . . . ," from author's interview with Borja, Acapulco, May 17, 1994.

Octavio Paz's quote about the Mexican Revolution being "a compromise between opposing forces . . . ," from *El Laberinto de la Soledad*, by Octavio Paz, Fondo de Cultura Economica, Mexico City, 1950, p. 195.

Results of poll asking Mexicans whether they considered themselves "very proud" of being Mexicans, from *Convergencia en Norteamerica: Comercio, Politica y Cultura*, by Ronald Inglehart, Miguel Basañez, and Neil Nevitte, Siglo XXI Editores, Mexico City, 1994, p. 119. Similar poll had originally appeared in *Este Pais*, April 1991, p. 7.

Results of MORI's poll on December 20, 1994, devaluation, given to the author by MORI directors Enrique Alduncin and Miguel Basañez, Mexico City, January 24, 1995. Poll consisted of 1,450 interviews and was conducted December 26–28, 1994.

Banamex-sponsored poll on Mexicans' sympathies toward the United States, from *Los Valores de los Mexicanos*, volume 2, by Enrique Alduncin, Fomento Cultural Banamex, Mexico City, 1991, p. 69.

Miguel Basañez quotes, "I used to think that only upper class Mexicans . . . ," and "It's a myth . . . ," from author's interview with Basañez, Mexico City, January 24, 1994.

Carlos Fuentes's assertion that there hadn't been one Mexican Revolution, but at least two, from *El Espejo Enterrado*, by Carlos Fuentes, Fondo de Cultura Economica, Mexico City, 1992, p. 321.

Alfonso Zárate's quote, "It's a cohesive myth . . . ," from author's interview with Zarate, Mexico City, May 2, 1995.

Coca-Cola marketing study, from author's interview with NutraSweet's marketing manager in Mexico, Alexandra Freeland Magin, Mexico City, January 27, 1995.

Alexandra Freeland's quote, "In the United States, you are either a Coke consumer . . . ," from author's interview with Freeland, Mexico City, January 27, 1995.

Jesús Silva Herzog's quote about politics as the most profitable profession in Mexico, from *La Revolución Mexicana en Crisis*, by Jesús Silva Herzog, Cuadernos Americanos, 1944, pp. 33–34, quoted in *The Politics of Mexican Development*, by Roger D. Hansen, Johns Hopkins University Press, Baltimore, 1971, p. 125.

Anecdote about Porfirio Díaz's dialogue with old friend Gonzalez, from "Giro del Gobierno Zedillista," by Elias Chavez, *Proceso*, May 8, 1995, p. 25.

Section on how the story about the fund-raiser became public, from author's interview with *El Economista* publisher Luis Enrique Mercado, Mexico City, September 13, 1993, and with *El Economista* reporter Francisco Barradas, Mexico City, September 12, 1993.

Luis Enrique Mercado's quote "I heard them talking . . . ," from author's interview with Mercado, Mexico City, September 13, 1993.

Gilberto Borja's quote, "The whole thing had been well planned . . . ," from author's interview with Borja, Acapulco, May 17, 1994.

Senator Miguel Alemán's quotes beginning, "Some people got scared the other day . . . ," from author's interview with Alemán, Mexico City, March 2, 1993.

Salinas's quote, "On many occasions . . . ," from Salinas's "Comments to the speech by PRI president Genaro Borrego," faxed to the author by Mexico's presidential office, March 9, 1993.

CHAPTER 6. *The Accidental Candidate*

Scene at Qualli television studios, Ernesto Zedillo's unsuccessful attempts at taping a campaign commercial, fighting back tears, from author's separate interviews with two top campaign aides who witnessed the scene, Mexico City, July 6 and September 13, 1994.

Ernesto Zedillo's quote, *"Pinche Donaldo, donde estás . . . ,"* from a Zedillo campaign worker who witnessed the scene, as quoted to the author, Mexico City, August 1994.

Zedillo's official biography data, from *Ernesto Zedillo, Architect of a Modern Mexico: Profile and Policies of a Candidate for President,* Institutional Revolutionary Party, Mexico City, 1994. Also, from "Siete en Punto," by Javier Lozada, September 1993, p. 326.

Quote starting, "In elementary school, Ernesto and Luis Eduardo had another last name . . . ," from author's interview with a former Zedillo classmate, Mexico City, June 1995.

Quote starting, "He was a little bit skinny . . . ," from author's telephone interview with Zedillo's family friend Rosalba Castro in Mexicali, May 5, 1995.

Fernando Prince's quote, "In elementary school, we made fun of him . . . ," from "Hace más de 30 años quiso ser Presidente," *Reforma,* special edition, March 30, 1994, p. 26.

Quotes about Zedillo's personality from CIA's Leadership Analysis Section were read to the author by a U.S. diplomat with access to U.S. intelligence reports, and confirmed by another U.S. official familiar with the reports, Washington, D.C.

Zedillo's quote, "I led quite a monastic life . . . ," and anecdotes from the president's days at Yale, from author's interview with Zedillo, Acapulco, May 17, 1994.

Zedillo's quote, "The first year was very tough . . . ," from author's interview with Zedillo, Acapulco, May 17, 1994.

Zedillo's career in government, from official biography and "Hace más de 30 años quiso ser Presidente," p. 26.

Zedillo's claim that he made his own bed and that his wardrobe consisted of half a dozen suits, "one for each day of the week," from author's interviews with Zedillo, Acapulco, May 17, 1994, and Mexico City, December 6, 1994.

Quote beginning, "The joke among us was if Zedillo invites you to lunch . . . ," from author's interview with well-placed Mexican official, Mexico City, September 4, 1994.

Carlos Salinas's quote, "Only a few hours had passed . . . ," from Salinas's eight-page statement to the media dated December 3, 1995, which Mexican officials said was sent by the former president from Cuba. From "Salinas acusa a Echeverría," *Reforma,* December 4, 1995, and "Texto integro de la declaración de Carlos Salinas de Gortari," *La Jornada,* December 4, 1995.

Salinas's quote recalling that Echeverría "showed up unannounced . . . ," from "Texto integro de la declaración de Carlos Salinas de Gortari," *La Jornada,* December 4, 1995.

Governor Manlio Fabio Beltrones quotes beginning, "Don't you see? It's you! . . . ," and "It's crystal clear . . . ," from author's interview with Beltrones, Sonora, February 4, 1995.

Account of Beltrones's discovery of the Colosio tape, conversation with Zedillo, from author's interview with Beltrones, Sonora, February 4, 1995.

Account of March 29, 1994, meeting where Zedillo was nominated as PRI candidate, from author's interview with Beltrones, Sonora, February 4, 1994. Also, from "Ante la Incipiente Rebelión Priista, Salinas Aplacó a Ortiz Arana," by Elias Chavez, *Proceso*, April 4, 1994, pp. 6–11, and *La Jornada* articles the week of March 28, 1994.

Zedillo's quote, "This is not the beginning of a campaign, but the continuation of a campaign . . . ," from transcript of Zedillo's acceptance speech, *Reforma*, special supplement, March 30, 1994, p. 31A.

Zedillo's quote, "At that moment, I was going through a very strange mixture of feelings . . . ," from author's interview with Zedillo, Acapulco, May 17, 1994.

CHAPTER 7. The Cleanest Election

Quote starting, "After the Zapatista rebellion, Televisa bombarded viewers . . . ," from author's interview with a well-placed PRI official, Mexico City, September 12, 1994.

Study of television campaign coverage by the Federal Electoral Institute, from "Al PRI, 44 por ciento de la cubertura . . . ," by Mireya Cuellar, *La Jornada*, July 3, 1994, p. 1.

Account of transvestites incident, from "El Gobierno Veracruzano pagó a los Travestis," by Ricardo Ravelo and Rodrigo Vera, *Proceso*, October 4, 1993, pp. 6–7, and "Otra provocación . . . ," by Alejandro Caballero, *La Jornada*, September 24, 1993, p. 5.

Cuauhtémoc Cárdenas's quote, "We won't have accurate, balanced and diverse information . . . ," from *Proceso*, July 4, 1994, p. 16.

"In the final week of the campaign, Cárdenas got 6.1 minutes of air time on *24 Horas* . . . ," from "Las Elecciónes Federales en Mexico, Segun Seis Noticiarios de Television," by the Mexican Academy of Human Rights and Civic Alliance, August 1994.

Emilio Azcarraga's quote, "We are soldiers of the president of the republic . . . ," from "Soldados: Azcarraga," *Reforma*, March 28, 1995. Same quote was carried that day by Mexico's official news agency, Notimex.

Radio announcement by Mexico City broadcasters starting, "Hi . . . ," from "Voto Razonado o Miedo," by Jessica Kreimerman, *Reforma*, August 27, 1994.

Scene from *Galio's War*, from *La Guerra de Galio*, by Héctor Aguilar Camin, Editorial Cal y Arena, Mexico City, 1991, p. 113.

Excelsior publisher Regino Díaz Redondo's quotes, starting with "There aren't any . . . ," from author's interview with Diaz Redondo, Mexico City, February 1, 1995.

La Jornada editor's quote, "I wish one day we will be able . . . ," from author's 1992 interview quoted in "Mexican Media Remain in the Ruling Party's Pocket," by Andres Oppenheimer, *Miami Herald*, July 31, 1992.

Labor Party founder Teodoro Palomino's quote, "Anaya made a long presentation . . . ," from author's interview with Palomino, Mexico City, August 25, 1994.

Labor Party leader Alberto Anaya's quote, "In this country, all political parties . . . ," from author's interview with Anaya, Mexico City, September 27, 1994.

Chiapas governor Javier López Moreno's quote, "I decided to provide support . . . ," from author's interview with Lopez Moreno, Mexico City, January 27, 1995.

President Salinas's quote, "The level of our [foreign] reserves . . . ," from Salinas's Sixth State of the Nation Address, November 1, 1994.

Pedro Mendoza's story, quotes, from author's interview with Mendoza, Mexico City, April 15, 1994.

Shoe shiners' Union leader David Betancourt quotes, from author's interview with Betancourt, Mexico City, April 20, 1994.

Jorge Matte Langlois's polls, submitted to the author by Matte Langlois after clearance from President Zedillo's office, April 1995.

Matte Langlois's quotes beginning, "If you look at U.S. newspaper and television networks' coverage . . . ," from author's interview with Matte Langlois, Mexico City, January 31, 1995.

UNAM's economics school dean Juan Pablo Arroyo quotes, beginning, "We were facing . . . ," from author's interview with Arroyo, Mexico City, February 1, 1995.

Account of Chilean pollster Juan Forch's visit to Mexico, from *Vamos a Ganar*, by Adolfo Aguilar Zinser, Editorial Océano, Mexico, 1995, p. 175.

Adolfo Aguilar Zinser's quote, "He saw the [U.S.] electoral process as a circus . . . ," from *Vamos a Ganar*, p. 193.

CHAPTER 8. *A Bittersweet Victory*

Finance Minister Jaime Serra Puche's quote, "The government reacted to each political event . . . ," from author's interview with Serra Puche, Mexico City, April 27, 1995.

Seventy-five percent of drug smuggling to U.S. coming from Mexico, from U.S. Drug Enforcement Administration head Thomas A. Constantine, quoted in *Proceso*, May 8, 1995, p. 15.

Mexican drug mafias' annual earnings between $10 billion and $30 billion, from Mexico's attorney general's office report on drugs, *La Jornada*, May 16, 1994, p. 60, and "Rise of Drug Cartels Is Feared in Mexico," by Steve Fainaru, *Boston Globe*, March 18, 1995.

August 4 drug shipment on French-made Aeroespatiale Caravelle jet, from "Trail of Cocaine Shipment in Mexico Points to Official Corruption," by Tim Golden, *New York Times*, April 18, 1995.

PRI's historic vote decline, from Mexico's Federal Electoral Institute figures, cited in Center for Strategic and International Studies (CSIS)'s *The 1994 Mexican Election, Post-Election Report*, by John Bailey, CSIS Americas Program, October 8, 1994.

Breakdown of voters by age, PAN winning among younger voters, from "1994: Quién votó por cual partido y por que?" by Julio Madrazo and Diana Owen, *Nexos*, October 1994, p. 20.

José Luis Salas's quote, "The young people of 1968 . . . ," from author's interview with Salas, Monterrey, October 3, 1994.

Figures of declining PRI voting among urban Mexicans, well-educated Mexicans, from "1994: Quién votó por cual partido y por que?" p. 20.

Literacy projections for the year 2000, cited in *Después del Milagro*, by Héctor Aguilar Camin, Editorial Cal y Arena, Mexico City, 1993, p. 253, quoting *Estadísticas Históricas de Mexico*, tomo 1, Educación, and Antonio Alonso, "Foro Mexico 2010. Escenario Base Común."

General Alvaro Obregón winning election by 1,660,453 votes in favor and 0 against, cited in *La Segunda Muerte de la Revolución Mexicana*, by Lorenzo Meyer, Editorial Cal y Arena, Mexico City, 1993, p. 52.

The number of nongovernmental organizations had soared to 1,300 in the mid-nineties, from Interior ministry's Directory of Civic Organizations, cited in "ONG: Los Nuevos Protagonistas," by Daniel Moreno, *Enfoque*, Sunday magazine of *Reforma*, June 25, 1995.

Superbarrio's quote, "Social struggle shouldn't be formal . . . ," from author's interview with Superbarrio, Mexico City, January 28, 1995.

Excelsior story saying the program was aimed at "manipulating public emotions," etc., from "Corruption Cure: Adopt a Politician," *Miami Herald,* October 31, 1994, p. 8.

Manuel "El Meme" Garza's story, quotes, from author's interview with Garza, Mexico City, October 6, 1994.

Don Fernando Gutiérrez Barrios's story, quotes, from author's interview with Gutiérrez Barrios, Mexico City, April 25, 1995.

Carlos Hank Gonzalez's quotes, beginning "Noo, Don Andres . . . ," from author's interview with Hank Gonzalez, Mexico City, May 13, 1994.

Hank Gonzalez's $1.3 billion fortune, from "Evolution of a Dinosaur," by Joel Millman, *Forbes,* December 5, 1994.

President Zedillo's quote, "You are wrong . . . ," from author's conversation with Zedillo at the end of briefing to a small group of foreign correspondents, August 21, 1994.

CHAPTER 9. *Murder in the Family*

Account of near-clash between Carlos Salinas's personal guard and government agents, from *Epoca,* March 6, 1995, pp. 10–22, and author's interviews with government officials familiar with the case, March 1995.

General Miranda's quote, "Stop that action . . . ," from *Epoca,* March 26, 1995, and author's interview with General Miranda aboard the presidential plane, April 21, 1995.

President Zedillo's quote, "The government is not a place for amassing wealth . . . ," from Zedillo's inaugural address, December 1, 1994.

Carlos Salinas's quote, "I wish you good luck, Ernesto . . . ," from "Zedillo y Salinas, del Amor al Odio," by César Romero Jacobo, *Epoca,* March 6, 1995, p. 11, and author's interview with top Zedillo aide, March 15, 1995.

José Francisco Ruiz Massieu's quote, "I may have to intercede . . . ," from *La Jornada,* September 29, 1994, p. 3.

Account of Ruiz Massieu's assassination, from "Vuelve la Pesadilla," *La Jornada,* September 29, 1994; and *La Jornada, Reforma, El Financiero,* September 30, 1994.

Rodriguez Gonzalez's testimony that he had acted "on direct orders" of Congressman Muñoz Rocha, etc., from Attorney General's Office Communiqué No. 665/94.

Mario Ruiz Massieu's quote, "There were no conditions . . . ," from Ruiz Massieu's resignation letter, November 23, 1994, reprinted in *Caso Ruiz Massieu,* a booklet written by Ruiz Massieu, p. 21.

Mario Ruiz Massieu's story, quotes, from author's interview with Ruiz Massieu, Mexico City, January 24, 1995.

José Francisco Ruiz Massieu's background, quote beginning "In most state governments . . . ," from author's interview with Ruiz Massieu, Mexico City, July 16, 1994.

CHAPTER 10. *The Secret Meeting*

Manuel "El Meme" Garza's quote, "They mixed water with oil . . . ," from author's interview with Garza, Mexico City, March 13, 1995.

Prosecutor Pablo Chapa Bezanilla's story of how investigation led to Raúl Salinas de Gortari, from author's interview with Chapa Bezanilla, Mexico City, March 10, 1995, also, from author's interview with Chapa's aide José Cortés Osorio, March 10, 1995.

Manuel Muñoz Rocha's telephone call to Raúl Salinas, and latter's later claim that he hadn't seen the congressman "in more than twenty years," from Attorney General's Office Communiqué No. 213, Febuary 28, 1995.

Chapa Bezanilla's quotes beginning, "We asked him . . . ," from author's interview with Chapa Bezanilla, Mexico City, March 10, 1995.

José Cortés Osorio's quote, "We think Mario Ruiz Massieu may have taken advantage . . . ," from author's interview with Cortés Osorio, Mexico City, March 10, 1995.

Salinas brothers' story, from "Juntos Crecieron," by Francisco Ortiz Pinchetti, *Proceso*, March 6, 1995, p. 21.

El Universal's quote, "Carlos, when asked what had happened . . . ," from *El Universal*, December 18, 1951; *La Prensa*'s quote about irresponsibility of Salinas's parents, from *La Prensa*, December 18, 1951.

Tomas Borge claiming family friend was "author of the accident," from *Salinas: Los Dilemas de la Modernidad*, by Tomas Borge, Siglo XXI Editores, Mexico City, 1993, p. 62.

Carlos Salinas's dedication, "To Raúl, companion of a hundred battles," from *Proceso*, November 27, 1995, p. 13, and *El Financiero*, November 27, 1995, p. 42.

Raúl Salinas's use of fake passport under the name of Juan Guillermo Gomez Gutiérrez, from "Se descubrió que Raúl tenía un pasaporte oficial con otro nombre," *La Jornada*, October 28, 1995. Story was later confirmed by the attorney general's office.

President Zedillo's quote, "Whatever the law dictates . . . ," from author's interview with Attorney General Antonio Lozano Gracia, Mexico City, March 14, 1995.

Account of Salinas's call to television station, Salinas's quotes beginning, "I cannot allow these assertions to remain . . . ," from "La llamada que desató la guerra," *Epoca*, March 6, 1995, pp. 12–13.

Carlos Salinas's quote, "I am completely convinced . . . ," from "Former President's Brother Is Held in Mexican Assassination," by Tim Golden, *New York Times*, March 1, 1995.

Account of Salinas-Zedillo secret meeting, from author's separate interviews with two top government officials, including one who was present at the meeting, Mexico City, June 1995.

Senior official's quote, "No agreement to that effect was made in the presence of others . . . ," from author's interview with top official who was present at the meeting, Mexico City, June 1995.

Zedillo's statement through his private secretary, Liébano Sáenz, "I have never struck any agreement with the former president . . . ," from author's interview with Sáenz, Los Pinos presidential palace, Mexico City, November 29, 1995.

Attorney General Antonio Lozano Gracia's story, quotes, from author's interview with Lozano Gracia, Mexico City, March 14, 1995.

Fernando Rodriguez's statements that were not made public at the time, from author's interview with Lozano Gracia, Mexico City, March 14, 1995.

Mario Ruiz Massieu's assertion that he told Salinas around October 18 that some of the prisoners arrested in the case were mentioning Raúl's name, from *Reforma*, May 8, 1995.

Dr. Sergio Sanchez Pintado's quote, "Deep down . . . ," from author's interview with Sanchez Pintado, Mexico City, June 18, 1995.

Raúl Salinas's $83.9 million Swiss bank account, corporations, and real estate holdings, from attorney general's office press communiqué, November 23, 1995; "La esposa de Raúl Salinas, detenida," *La Jornada*, November 24, 1995, p. 1; and "Cecilia Occelli, socia de Raúl Salinas," *El Financiero*, November 30, 1995, p. 31.

Carlos Salinas's quote, "Nothing of what has happened in Mexico this year has been alien . . . ," from "Texto íntegro de la declaración de Carlos Salinas de Gortari," *La Jornada*, December 4, 1995.

CHAPTER 11. *The Christmas Nightmare*

Finance Minister Jaime Serra Puche's arrival at his office, dialogue with Central Bank president Miguel Mancera, quote beginning, "Have you seen . . . ," from author's interview with Serra, Mexico City, April 27, 1995.

Serra felt a victim of the information age, quote beginning, "Mr. President . . . ," from author's interview with Serra, Mexico City, April 27, 1995.

Account of Ambassador Jorge Montaño's meeting with Sandy Berger, Montaño's quote, "You see, this is what . . . ," from author's interview with Montaño, Mexico City, August 2, 1995.

Ambassador Jesús Silva Herzog's quote, "There is no question that the whole thing was mishandled . . . ," from author's interview with Silva Herzog, Washington, D.C., June 2, 1995.

Labor Minister Santiago Oñate's quote, "It wasn't an invitation for an ordinary meeting . . . ," from author's interview with Oñate, Mexico City, March 14, 1995.

Montgomery Fund pulling out of Mexico, into Brazil, etc., from author's telephone interview with fund manager Josephine Jimenez, June 27, 1995, and "Innocents Abroad," by John Anderson, *Smart Money*, March 1995, p. 107.

Television tycoon Emilio Azcarraga converting pesos into dollars before devaluation, *El Financiero*'s quote, "Fortunate provision? . . . ," from *El Financiero*, January 5, 1995, p. 21.

U.S. Treasury Undersecretary Lawrence H. Summers's explanation that the United States's $6 billion was "not to be used to bolster exchange rate . . . ," from Summers's prepared testimony before the Senate Committee on Banking, Housing and Urban Affairs, March 10, 1995.

Serra's call to U.S. Treasury Secretary Lloyd Bentsen, quotes beginning, "Lloyd, I have to talk to you . . . ," from author's interviews with Serra, Mexico City, April 27 and June 14, 1995.

Serra's call to U.S. Treasury Secretary Robert Rubin, Serra's quote, "Congratulations . . . ," from author's interview with Serra, Mexico City, April 27, 1995.

Serra's trip to New York, dialogue with angry investors, from author's interviews with Serra, Mexico City, April 27 and June 14, 1995.

Salomon Brothers analyst John Purcell's quote, "I did not find it convincing . . . ," from "Crisis in Mexico," by Anthony De Palma, *New York Times*, December 22, 1994.

Serra's trip to Washington, D.C., quotes beginning, "They worked and tried very hard . . . ," and "Mr. President, we need . . . ," from author's interview with Serra, Mexico City, April 27, 1995.

Account of November 20 meeting at Salinas's house, from author's separate interviews with three participants at the meeting, including Serra, and former Finance minister Pedro Aspe's account, "Razones de la Politica Cambiaria," by Pedro Aspe, *Reforma*, July 14, 1995, and "Mexico's ex-finance minister sets the record straight," by Pedro Aspe, *Wall Street Journal*, July 14, 1995.

President Salinas's quote, "First president in twenty-five years who doesn't de-value the currency!" from author's interview with a senior Mexican official who was present at the scene, Mexico City, August 2, 1995.

Disparity between Clinton administration's public and private statements on Mexico's economy, Summers's memorandum, from "Mexico Crisis Report and Chronology," floor statement by U.S. senator Alphonse D'Amato, June 19, 1995.

Lloyd Bentsen's quotes, "I started getting worried . . . ," and "God sakes . . . ," from "How Mexico's Crisis Ambushed Top Minds in Officialdom, Finance," *Wall Street Journal*, July 6, 1995, p. 1.

Jeffrey Sachs's quote, "Russia's tragedy is that no investment banker's . . . ," from "Mexico, Si. Russia, Nyet," by Jeffrey Sachs, *The New Republic*, February 6, 1995.

Patrick Buchanan's quote, "This country . . . ," from "Clinton's peso rescue is politically risky," by Marcia Stepanek, Hearst Newspapers, February 22, 1995.

U.S. official's quotes beginning, "The first point made at the meeting . . . ," from author's interview with a senior U.S. official who was directly involved in the White House discussions over the Mexican bailout, June 1995.

President Zedillo's statements to *ABC*, from "Economia Zedillista," by Luis E. Mercado, *El Economista*, September 6, 1994.

Luis Enrique Mercado's story, quotes, from author's interview with Mercado, Mexico City, April 26, 1995.

U.S.-Mexico agreement's provision calling for "timely and accurate" Mexican foreign reserves data, from "U.S. Agrees to Give Mexico $20 Billion to Rescue Its Economy," by Robert A. Rosenblatt and Juanita Darling, *Los Angeles Times*, February 21, 1995.

Zedillo's quote, "It's a tragedy," from author's interview with top Mexican official, Los Pinos presidential palace, Mexico City, June 14, 1995.

CHAPTER 12. *Unmasking Marcos*

Account of Salvador Morales Garibay's letter, defection, from author's interview with Attorney General Antonio Lozano Gracia, Mexico City, March 14, 1995, and top Mexican Army officer familiar with intelligence matters, March 1995.

Morales background, from transcript of Morales's confession, February 8, 1994, given to the author by a senior government official, and author's interviews with Lozano Gracia and four Mexican intelligence officials, January 1994–September 1995.

Alberto Hijar Serrano's quote, "The graphic design school encouraged its faculty . . . ," from author's interview with Hijar, Mexico City, June 17, 1995.

Account of Marcos-Daniel differences over the Las Calabazas clash with the army and over weapons charges to the Mayans, from *La Rebelión de las Cañadas*, by Carlos Tello Diaz, Editorial Cal y Arena, Mexico City, 1995, pp. 168–174.

Attorney General Lozano Gracia's quote, "Nobody paid any attention to him . . . ," from author's interview with Lozano Gracia, Mexico City, March 14, 1995.

Confidential report by Defense minister General Enrique Cervantes, Operation Rainbow, from "Templo Mayor," by F. Bartolome, *Reforma*, February 9, 1995.

Chase Manhattan Bank's emerging markets group memo about need to "eliminate" the Zapatistas, from "Recall Mexican Army, Chiapas Rebels Warn," by Tod Robberson, *Washington Post*, February 17, 1995.

Morales's quote, "He was a former professor of graphic design at the Autonomous Metropolitan University . . . ," from transcript of Morales's testimony, February 8, 1995.

President Zedillo's quotes beginning, "I must inform the nation that while the government was stressing . . . ," from Zedillo's televised address to the nation, February 9, 1995.

Subcommander Marcos's quote about "disymmetrical" sector, dialogue, from author's interview with Marcos, Chiapas jungle, July 23, 1994.

Account of Marcos's youth, work as bus driver at Route 100, from German journalist Rita Neubauer's taped interview with Rafael Guillén's parents, Alfonso Guillén and Maria del Socorro Vocente, in Tampico, July 27, 1995. Also, from author's interviews with former professors Hijar, Mexico City, June 17, 1994, and Cesáreo Morales, Mexico City, August 4, 1995.

Marcos's quote, "Yesterday, we were a handful of men . . . ," from author's interview with Hijar, Mexico City, June 17, 1995.

Quotes from Rafael Guillén's thesis beginning, "He is sitting in the lotus position . . . ," from "Filosofia y Educación: Prácticas Discursivas y Prácticas Ideológicas," by Rafael Sebastián Guillén Vicente, Universidad Nacional Autónoma de Mexico, Faculty of Philosophy, October 1980.

Fernando Yañez (Commander in Chief Germán) background, from author's interviews with half a dozen Mexican Army and civilian intelligence officers, January 1994–September 1995; author's interview with Yañez's brother

Margil Yañez, Mexico City, June 16, 1995; and interview with former 23 of September League guerrilla leader Gustavo Hirales, Mexico City, March 15, 1995.

Yañez farewell anecdote, Margil Yañez's quote, "My parents used to approve of his actions . . . ," from author's interview with Margil Yañez, Mexico City, June 16, 1995.

Gustavo Hirales's quote, "The Yañez brothers were fundamentalists . . . ," from author's interview with Hirales, Mexico City, March 15, 1995.

National Liberation Forces Statutes' quote, "The National Liberation Forces fight against Imperialist ideology . . . ," from 1980 document given to the author and other foreign correspondents by top Mexican officials in 1994, and recognized as authentic by sources close to the NLF.

Financial aid to the Zapatista army, from Mexican intelligence sources and *La Rebelión de las Cañadas*, by Carlos Tello Díaz, Editorial Cal y Arena, Mexico City, 1995, p. 144.

Route 100 assets, $46 million figure, from *Epoca*, April 24, 1995, p. 12; $600 million figure from *Proceso*, March 20, 1995, p. 43.

Former Salvadoran guerrilla leader Ana Guadalupe Martinez quotes beginning, "We told them it was crazy . . . ," from author's interview with Martinez, Cartagena, Colombia, May 5, 1995.

Marcos's letter to Mexican newspapers, beginning, "At dawn on Feb. 15 . . . ," from March 5 letter from Marcos to *Proceso, La Jornada, El Financiero*, and *Tiempo*.

CHAPTER 13. *Unmasking Mexico*

Newspaper headline about Senator Miguel Alemán's book, from "Fue Broma lo del Pase de la Charola," *Reforma*, June 14, 1995.

U.S. academic's reference to Plato's cave, from author's interview with Delal Baer, of the Center for Strategic and International Studies (CSIS), Washington, D.C., June 2, 1995.

Polls showing 87 percent of the Mexican people have "little" or "no" trust in their government, only 18 percent of Mexicans have "a lot" of confidence, etc., from *Convergencia en Norteamerica: Comercio, Politica y Cultura*, by Ronald Inglehart, Miguel Basañez, and Neil Nevitte, Siglo XXI Editores, Mexico, 1994.

Lorenzo Meyer's quote, "It was the kind of massive documentation . . . ," from "Tabasco o la Profundidad de la Crisis," by Lorenzo Meyer, *Reforma*, June 15, 1995.

Coca-Cola marketing study, from industry sources and author's interview with Jorge Matte Langlois, Mexico City, January 31, 1995.

Jorge Matte Langlois's quote, "We found that the word 'truth' had a negative connotation in Mexico . . . ," from author's interview with Matte Langlois, Mexico City, January 31, 1995.

Octavio Paz's quote, "We lie out of pleasure and fantasy, just like all imaginative people . . . ," from *El Laberinto de la Soledad*, by Octavio Paz, Fondo de Cultura Economica, Mexico City, 1950, p. 44.

Paz's quote, "The strange permanence of Cortés and Malinche . . . ," from *El Laberinto de la Soledad*, p. 95.

Paz's quote, "History has not cured our intellectuals . . . ," from "Chiapas, Nudo ciego o Tabla de Salvación?" "The Relapse of the Intellectual" section, *Vuelta*, special supplement, February 1994, p. C.

Paz's quote, "I think we are moving in that direction . . . ," from author's interview with Paz, Mexico City, January 27, 1995.

CHAPTER 14. *The Northern Offensive*

Education minister's aide's quotes beginning, "Who in this country . . . ," from author's interview with one of Fausto Alzati's top advisers, Mexico City, June 15, 1995.

Reforma publisher Alejandro Junco's quote, "It was our first test of independence . . . ," from author's interview with Junco, Mexico City, January 26, 1995.

Junco's quotes beginning, "The scandal is somewhat illustrative of Mexico City's . . . ," from author's interview with Junco, Mexico City, January 26, 1995.

More flights to Dallas than to Mexico City, northern Mexican investors' owning 60 percent stake in Mexican bank stocks, from "Northern Pioneers Drive Mexico's Industrialization," by Esther Schrader, Knight-Ridder Newspapers, August 10, 1994.

Victor Zuñiga's quote, "In Monterrey, there is a century-old capitalist tradition . . . ," from author's interview with Zuñiga, Monterrey, September 27, 1994.

PAN's position that Cárdenas administration had snubbed basic values such as "work, sacrifice and perseverance" and taken Mexico "back to the illusion of [easy] solutions coming from the top," from *History of the National Action Party 1939–1989*, National Action Party, p. 6.

PAN founding father Manuel Gomez Morin's quote saying he had founded the party "to openly oppose the total collectivization of the economy ...," from "Definida desde su fundación por Gomez Morin ...," by Enrique Maza, *Proceso*, June 5, 1995, p. 23.

Ernesto Coppel Kelly's quote, "Not at all: *Aquí no pasa nada ...*," from author's interview with Coppel Kelly, Mazatlán, Sinaloa, March 22, 1994.

Sonora governor Manlio Fabio Beltrones's quotes about food inspections, beginning, "We inspect everything ...," from author's interview with Beltrones, Hermosillo, Sonora, February 4, 1995.

Nearly 1.8 million Mexicans migrated to northern border towns in 1994, from author's interview with Maria Eugenia Anguiano, researcher in the Social Studies Department of the College of the Northern Frontier, Tijuana, February 6, 1995.

Beltrones's quote, "There is a growing isolationist sentiment ...," from author's interview with Beltrones, Hermosillo, Sonora, February 4, 1995.

Ciudad Juárez mayor Francisco Villarreal's quote, "We're fighting for our freedom ...," from "Northern Revolt Over Bridge Tolls Targets Mexico's Old Political Ways," by Thaddeus Herrick, *Houston Chronicle*, July 16, 1995.

Roderic Ai Camp's quote, "Mexico may have more trouble handling the threat of violence in Chiapas ...," from "Northern Revolt Over Bridge Tolls."

Nine percent of Tijuana's active population working on both sides of the border, etc., from author's interview with College of the Northern Frontier academic director Eduardo Zepeda, Tijuana, February 6, 1995.

Musician Pablo Jesús Martinez quote, "Last Saturday, we played at a wedding in Tucson, Arizona ...," from author's interview with Martinez, Nogales, Sonora, February 3, 1995.

Radio talk-show host Joel Bojorquez's story, quotes beginning, "I like to emphasize ...," from author's interview with Bojorquez, Nogales, Sonora, February 3, 1995.

Psychiatrist Francisco J. García Encinas's story, quote beginning, "As soon as we cross the line ...," from author's interview with García Encinas, Nogales, Sonora, February 3, 1995.

Writer Guadalupe Loaeza's quote, "Mexico is losing some of its dearest traditions ...," from author's interview with Loaeza, Mexico City, March 6, 1993.

Northern and southern Mexico's level of income, from "Liberación Comercial, Equidad y Desarrollo Economico," by Diana Alarcon Gonzalez, Eduardo Zepeda Moramontes, and Friedrich Ebert Stiftung, 1992; "The Welfare Effect of Structural Adjustment in Mexico and Its Differential Impact by Gender," by Diana Alarcon, Human Development Office, United

Nations Development Program, January 1995; and author's interview with Alarcon, Tijuana, February 7, 1995.

Researcher Diana Alarcon Gonzalez's quote beginning, "Free trade has brought about a huge increase in U.S. shipments of wheat . . . ," from author's interview with Alarcon, Tijuana, February 7, 1995.

Cemex chief executive officer Lorenzo Zambrano's quotes beginning, "There is a major decentralization under way . . . ," from author's interview with Zambrano, Monterrey, October 3, 1994.

Mexico's northern states accounting for only 16 percent of the population, from "The United States of Mexico: General Summary of the XI General Census of Population and Housing," National Institute of Statistics and Geography (INEGI), Chart II, 1990, pp. 2–24.

CHAPTER 15. *The Police Connection*

Héctor "El Guero" Palma's background, Rafael Enrique Clavel's story, from "Corruptor, Criminal y Vengativo, Palma Cayo," *Epoca*, July 3, 1995, p. 22.

Palma riding along Nayarit streets, Colt .38 with diamonds, from "No me cabe la menor duda: El Guero Palma era protegido por judiciales," by Felipe Cobian, *Proceso*, July 10, 1995.

Local newspaper report of Palma's silver saddle, *Realidades*, Tepic, April 19, 1995, cited in *Proceso*, July 10, 1995.

Account of November 7, 1991, clash between government agents, from *Democracy and Human Rights in Mexico*, by Andrew Reding, World Policy Papers, World Policy Institute, New York, May 1995, p. 26.

More than nine hundred gangs in Mexico, from author's interview with senior Mexican Interior ministry official, July 7, 1995.

More than four hundred members of Federal Judicial Police were fired or suspended over the three years ending in mid-1995, from "Incluídos, delegados de la Procuraduría hasta agentes del Ministerio Público," by David Aponte and Juan Manuel Vegas, *La Jornada*, June 30, 1995.

Mexican investigator's quote, "Every day, it becomes harder to do this job . . . ," from "Mexico's Cartels Sow Seeds of Corruption, Destruction," second part of series "The Rise of Narco Politics," by Sebastian Rotella, *Los Angeles Times*, June 16, 1995.

Mexico's 2,400 police forces, from "Inseguridad y Violencia en el Pais," by Ernesto Zavaleta Gongora, *Epoca*, March 17, 1995, and *Democracy and Human Rights in Mexico*, p. 26.

Mexico City alone had 627 private companies — many of them run by former police officers with criminal records — with a total of 27,500 men, from "Mas policias privados que preventivos en el distrito federal," by Ricardo Olayo, *La Jornada*, July 19, 1995.

Account of *"madrinas,"* or godmothers, who were kept off the books, from *Democracy and Human Rights in Mexico*, p. 25.

Juan Carlos Valerio Roldan's story, quote, from "The Greedy Get Silver and the Honest Get Lead," by Peter Slevin, *Miami Herald*, June 5, 1995, p. 1.

President Zedillo's quote, "Nothing and no one will weaken my resolve . . . ," from "Zedillo's Challenge: Mexico Lives by Virtual Law," by Anthony De Palma, *New York Times*, March 27, 1995.

Report leaked later to the *Washington Post* saying U.S. Customs agents had briefed Treasury Department law enforcement officials that a Colosio relative was involved in drug trafficking, from *Washington Post* story by Pierre Thomas and Daniel Williams, March 17, 1995.

U.S. Deputy Assistant Secretary of State Cresencio Arcos's story, quotes beginning, "Mexico is treated like an untouchable . . . ," from author's interview with Arcos, Washington, D.C., May 31, 1995.

CHAPTER 16. *Fall and Resurrection*

Henri-Louis Bergson's quote, "It is useless to maintain that social progress . . . ," cited by Arnold Toynbee in *A Study of History*, Portland House, New York, 1988, p. 140.

President Zedillo's quote, "After the bad things that have been happening to us . . . ," from "Malosos detrás de las cosas que ocurren: Zedillo," *La Jornada*, June 24, 1995, p. 1.

Lorenzo Meyer's references to ruling class's "biological decay," from "Una Clase Politica en Descomposición," by Lorenzo Meyer, *Reforma*, April 27, 1995.

Jorge G. Castañeda's quote, "Rather than being a source of stability, continuity and peace . . . ," from author's interview with Castañeda, Mexico City, June 22, 1995.

Octavio Paz's quotes beginning, "We are witnessing the end of the PRI system . . . ," from author's interview with Paz, Mexico City, January 27, 1995.

Genaro Borrego's quote, "Under the current circumstances, I don't think that the PRI . . . ," from author's interview with Borrego, Mexico City, June 23, 1995.

Zedillo's quote, "After seven months of discipline and hard work . . . ," from Zedillo's speech in Altamira, Tamaulipas, July 27, 1995. Transcript from Presidential Press Office.

Zedillo's quote about "audacious actions," and "changes in the flight plan," from Zedillo's speech to Mexican Association of Pilots, Mexico City, August 4, 1995. Transcript from Presidential Press Office.

Guerrero governor Rubén Figueroa's quote, "Nothing is going on in Guerrero," from "Crece la efervescencia política en el país," *Epoca*, July 17, 1995, p. 29.

Robert Rubin's quote, "Today, the signs of success are substantial," from "Statement of the honorable Robert E. Rubin," Secretary of the Treasury, before the Senate Committee on Banking, Housing and Urban Affairs," July 14, 1995.

President Clinton's quotes beginning, "The Mexican economy...," from "Zedillo, Clinton See Mexican Economic Rebound," by Gene Gibbons, Reuters, October 10, 1995, and transcripts of remarks by President Clinton, White House Press Office, October 10, 1995.

Morgan Stanley & Company press release, "Morgan Stanley increases recommended weighting of Mexican stocks," by Morgan Stanley Corporate Communications division, New York, August 2, 1995.

Selected Bibliography

Aguilar Camin, Héctor. *Después del Milagro*. Mexico City: Editorial Cal y Arena, 1993.

———. *La Guerra de Galio*. Mexico City: Editorial Cal y Arena, 1991.

Aguilar Camin, Héctor, and Lorenzo Meyer. *In the Shadow of the Mexican Revolution*. Austin: University of Texas Press, 1993.

Ai Camp, Roderic. *Who's Who in Mexico Today*. Boulder, Colorado: Westview Press, 1993.

———. *The Zedillo Cabinet: Continuity, Change or Revolution?* Washington, D.C.: Center for Strategic and International Studies (CSIS), 1995.

Alemán Velasco, Miguel. *Las Finanzas de la Política*. Mexico: Editorial Diana, 1995.

Basañez, Miguel. *El Pulso de los Sexenios*. Mexico City: Siglo XXI Editores, 1990.

Borge, Tomas. *Salinas: Los dilemas de la Modernidad*. Mexico City: Siglo XXI Editores, 1993.

Burbach, Roger, and Peter Rosset. *Chiapas and the Crisis of Mexican Agriculture*. San Francisco: Institute for Food and Development Policy, 1994.

Castañeda, Jorge G. *The Mexican Shock: Its Meaning for the U.S.* New York: The New Press, 1995.

Cornelius, Wayne A., and Ann L. Craig. *Politics in Mexico: An Introduction and Overview*. San Diego: Center for U.S.-Mexican Studies, University of California, 1988.

Dornbierer, Manú. *El Prinosaurio: La Bestia Política Mexicana*. Mexico City: Editorial Grijalbo, 1994.

Fuentes, Carlos. *El Espejo Enterrado*. Mexico City: Fondo de Cultura Economica, 1992.

———. *Nuevo Tiempo Mexicano*. Mexico City: Aguilar, 1994.

Grayson, George W., and Delal Baer. *A Guide to the 1994 Mexican Presidential Election*. Washington, D.C.: Center for Strategic and International Studies (CSIS), 1994.

Hansen, Roger. *The Politics of Mexican Development*. Baltimore: Johns Hopkins University Press, 1971.

Huchim, Eduardo. *Mexico 1994: La Rebelión y el Magnicidio*. Mexico City: Nueva Imagen, 1994.

Inglehart, Ronald; Miguel Basañez; and Neil Nevitte. *Convergencia en Norteamerica: Comercio, Politica y Cultura*. Mexico City: Siglo XXI Editores, 1994.

Kandell, Jonathan. *La Capital: The Biography of Mexico City*. New York: Henry Holt and Co., 1988.

Krauze, Enrique. *Por una Democracia sin Adjetivos*. Mexico City: Joaquin Mortiz-Planeta, 1986.

———. *Textos Heréticos*. Mexico City: Editorial Grijalbo, 1992.

Marquez, Enrique. *Por Qué Perdió Camacho: Revelaciones del Asesor de Manual Camacho Solis*. Mexico City: Editorial Océano, 1995.

Meyer, Lorenzo. *La Segunda Muerte de la Revolución Mexicana*. Mexico City: Editorial Cal y Arena, 1992.

Orme, William A. Jr. *Continental Shift: Free Trade and the New North America*. Washington, D.C.: The Washington Post Co., 1993.

Pastor, Robert, and Jorge Castañeda. *Limits to Friendship: The United States and Mexico*. New York: Alfred A. Knopf, 1989.

Paz, Octavio. *El Laberinto de la Soledad: Postdata y Vuelta al Laberinto de la Soledad*. Mexico City: Fondo de Cultura Economica, 1993.

———. *Los Signos en Rotación y Otros Ensayos*. Madrid: Alianza Editorial, 1971.

Perot, Ross, and Pat Choate. *Save Your Job, Save Our Country*. New York: Hyperion, 1993.

Puga, Cristina, and Ricardo Tirado. *Los Empresarios Mexicanos, Ayer y Hoy*. Mexico City: Ediciones El Caballito, 1992.

Ramirez, Carlos. *Cuando Pudimos no Quisimos*. Mexico City: Editorial Océano, 1995.

Reding, Andrew. *Democracy and Human Rights in Mexico*. New York: World Policy Papers, World Policy Institute, 1995.

Reyes Heroles, Federico. *Sondear a Mexico*. Mexico City: Editorial Océano, 1995.

Riding, Alan. *Distant Neighbors*. New York: Random House, 1984.

Rodriguez Castañeda, Rafael. *Prensa Vendida*. Mexico City: Editorial Grijalbo, 1993.

Romero Jacobo, César. *Los Altos de Chiapas*. Mexico City: Planeta, 1994.

Ronquillo, Victor. *La Muerte Viste de Rosa: El Asesinato de los Travestis en Chiapas*. Mexico City: Ediciónes Roca, 1994.

Sáenz, Liébano. *Colosio: "Un Año Ayer . . . "*. Liébano Sáenz Ortiz, private edition, 1995.

Samaniego, Fidel. *En las Entrañas del Poder*. Mexico City: Rayuela Editores, 1995.

Scherer García, Julio. *Estos Años*. Mexico City: Editorial Océano, 1995.

Schulz, Donald E. *Mexico in Crisis*. Strategic Studies Institute, U.S. Army War College, 1995.

Schwarz, Mauricio José. *Todos Somos Superbarrio*. Mexico City: Planeta, 1995.

Smith, Peter H. *Labyrinths of Power: Political Recruitment in Twentieth-Century Mexico*. Princeton, N.J.: Princeton University Press, 1979.

Tello Díaz, Carlos. *La Rebelión de las Cañadas*. Mexico City: Editorial Cal y Arena, 1995.

Trejo Delabre, Raúl. *Las Redes de Televisa*. Mexico City: Claves Latinoamericanas, 1988.

Wager, Stephen J., and Donald Schulz. *The Awakening: The Zapatista Revolt and Its Implications for Civil-Military Relations and the Future of Mexico*. U.S. Army War College, Strategic Studies Institute, 1994.

Zaid, Gabriel. *Adios al PRI*. Mexico City: Editorial Océano, 1995.

———. *Como Leer en Bicicleta*. Secretaria de Educación Publica, 1986.

———. *El Progreso Improductivo*. Mexico City: Editorial Contenido, 1991.

Zoraida Vazquez, Josefina, and Lorenzo Meyer. *The United States and Mexico*. Chicago: University of Chicago Press, 1985.

Index